✳ *Highlights* ✳
of this
Study Guide

 Each Chapter of this **Study Guide** includes—

 ✳ Chapter **Introduction**

 ✳ Easy to Read & Understand, Comprehensive **Outline**

 ✳ **True-False** Questions

 ✳ **Fill-In** Questions

 ✳ **Multiple-Choice** Questions

 ✳ **Short Essay** Questions

 ✳ **Issue Spotters**—hypothetical fact problems & black letter law questions on key issues

 Each Unit of this **Study Guide** ends with—

 ✳ **Cumulative Hypothetical** & corresponding **Multiple-Choice** Questions

 ✳ **Multiple-Choice** Questions covering *Focus on Legal Reasoning* section

 ✳ **Multiple-Choice** Questions covering *Focus on Ethics* section

 This **Study Guide** also contains an **Answer Appendix** with answers to all of the Questions & explanations of the Answers

Study Guide

to Accompany

West's Legal Environment of Business
Text & Cases—Ethical, Regulatory, International and E-Commerce Issues
Fifth Edition

FRANK B. CROSS
Associate Director,
Center for Legal and Regulatory Studies
University of Texas at Austin

ROGER LeROY MILLER
Institute for University Studies
Arlington, Texas

Prepared by

William Eric Hollowell
Member of
  U.S. Supreme Court Bar
  Minnesota State Bar
  Florida State Bar

Roger LeRoy Miller
Institute for University Studies
Arlington, Texas

THOMSON

———★———™

SOUTH-WESTERN

WEST

Australia · Canada · Mexico · Singapore · Spain · United Kingdom · United States

THOMSON

SOUTH-WESTERN

WEST

Study Guide to Accompany *West's Legal Environment of Business*, Fifth Edition

By Frank B. Cross and Roger LeRoy Miller

Editorial Director:
Jack Calhoun

Vice President/Editor-in-Chief:
George Werthman

Senior Acquisitions Editor:
Rob Dewey

Senior Developmental Editor:
Jan Lamar

Marketing Manager:
Steve Silverstein

Production Editors:
Bill Stryker and Anne Sheroff

Manufacturing Coordinator:
Rhonda Utley

Printer:
Edwards Brothers

COPYRIGHT © 2004
by West Legal Studies in Business, a division of Thomson Learning. Thomson Learning™ is a trademark used herein under license.

Printed in the United States of America
1 2 3 4 5 05 04 03

For more information
contact South-Western,
5191 Natorp Boulevard,
Mason, Ohio 45040.
Or you can visit our Internet site at:
http://www.westbuslaw.com

ALL RIGHTS RESERVED.
No part of this work covered by the copyright hereon may be reproduced or used in any form or by any means—graphic, electronic, or mechanical, including photocopying, recording, taping, Web distribution or information storage and retrieval systems—without the written permission of the publisher.

For permission to use material from this text or product, contact us by
Tel (800) 730-2214
Fax (800) 730-2215
http://www.thomsonrights.com

ISBN: 0-324-15460-7

Table of Contents

To the Student

This ***Study Guide*** is designed to help you read and understand ***West's Legal Environment of Business,*** **Fifth Edition.**

How the *Study Guide* Can Help You

This *Study Guide* can help you maximize your learning, subject to the constraints and the amount of time you can allot to this course. There are at least six specific ways in which you can benefit from using this guide.

1. The *Study Guide* can help you decide which topics are the most important. Because there are so many topics analyzed in each chapter, many students become confused about what is essential and what is not. You cannot, of course, learn everything; this *Study Guide* can help you concentrate on the crucial topics in each chapter.

2. If you are forced to miss a class, you can use this *Study Guide* to help you learn the material discussed in your absence.

3. There is a possibility that the questions that you are required to answer in this *Study Guide* are representative of the types of questions that you will be asked during examinations.

4. You can use this *Study Guide* to help you review for examinations.

5. This *Study Guide* can help you decide whether you really understand the material. Don't wait until examination time to find out!

6. Finally, the questions in this *Study Guide* will help you develop critical thinking skills that you can use in other classes and throughout your career.

The Contents of the *Study Guide*

The legal environment sometimes is considered a difficult subject because it uses a specialized vocabulary and also takes most people much time and effort to learn. Those who work with and teach the legal environment believe that the subject matter is exciting and definitely worthy of your efforts. Your text, ***West's Legal Environment of Business,*** **Fifth Edition,** and this student learning guide have been written for the precise purpose of helping you learn the most important aspects of the legal environment. We always try to keep you, the student, in mind.

Every chapter includes the following sections:

1. What This Chapter Is About: You are introduced to the main subject matter of each chapter in this section.

2. Chapter Outline: Using an outline format, the salient points in each chapter are presented.

3. True-False Questions: Ten true-false questions are included for each chapter. Generally, these questions test knowledge of terminology and principles. The answers are given at the back of the book. Whenever an answer is false, the reasons why it is false are presented at the back of the book also.

4. Fill-in Questions: Here you are asked to choose between two alternatives for each space that needs to be filled in. Answers are included at the back of the book.

5. Multiple-Choice Questions: Ten multiple-choice questions are given for each chapter. The answers, along with an explanation, are included at the back of this book.

6. Short Essay Questions: Two essay questions are presented for each chapter.

7. Issue Spotters: These questions alert you to certain principles within the chapter. Brief answers to these questions are included at the end of this text.

8. Special Information for CPA Candidates: This section alerts CPA candidates to principles within the chapter that are of special importance for the CPA exam and includes study tips of particular utility to these students.

How to Use this Study Guide

What follows is a recommended strategy for improving your grade in your legal environment class. It may seem like a lot of work, but the payoffs will be high. Try the entire program for the first three or four chapters. If you then feel you can skip some steps safely, try doing so and see what happens.

For each chapter we recommend you follow the sequence of steps below:

1. Read the What This Chapter Is About and Chapter Outline.

2. Read any of the Concept Summaries that may be included in the chapter you are studying in *West's Legal Environment of Business,* **Fifth Edition**.

3. Read about half the textbook chapter (unless it is very long), being sure to underline only the most important topics (which you should be able to recognize after having read no more than two chapter outlines in this *Study Guide*). Put a check mark by the material that you do not understand.

4. If you find the textbook's chapter easy to understand, you might want to finish reading it. Otherwise, rest for a sufficient period before you read the second half of the chapter. Again, be sure to underline only the most important points and to put a check mark by the material you find difficult to understand.

5. After you have completed the entire textbook chapter, take a break. Then read only what you have underlined throughout the entire chapter.

6. Now concentrate on the difficult material, for which you have left check marks. Reread this material and *think about it*; you will find that it is very exciting to figure out difficult material on your own.

7. Now do the True-False Questions, Fill-In Questions, and Multiple-Choice Questions. Compare your answers with those at the back of this book. Make a note of the questions you have missed and find the pages in your textbook upon which these questions are based. If you still don't understand, ask your instructor.

8. If you still have time, do one or both of the essay questions.

9. Before your examination, study your class notes. Then review the chapter outline in the text. Reread the Chapter Outline in this *Study Guide*, then redo all of the questions within each chapter. Compare your answers with the answers at the back of this *Study Guide*. Identify your problem areas and reread the relevant pages in ***West's Legal Environment of Business,* Fifth Edition**. Think through the answers on your own.

If you have followed the strategy outlined above, you should feel sufficiently confident and be relaxed enough to do well on your exam.

Study Skills for *West's Legal Environment of Business*, Fifth Edition

Every student has a different way to study. We give several study hints below that we think will help any student to master the textbook ***West's Legal Environment of Business,* Fifth Edition**. These skills involve outlining, marking, taking notes, and summarizing. You may not need to use all these skills. Nonetheless, if you do improve your ability to use them, you will be able to understand more easily the information in ***West's Legal Environment of Business,* Fifth Edition**.

MAKING AN OUTLINE

An outline is simply a method for organizing information. The reason an outline can be helpful is that it shows how concepts relate to each other. Outlining can be done as part of your reading or at the end of your reading, or as a rereading of each section within a chapter before you go on to the next section. Even if you do not believe that you need to outline, our experience has been that the act of *physically* writing an outline for a chapter helps most students to improve greatly their ability to retain the material in ***West's Legal Environment of Business,* Fifth Edition** and master it, thereby obtaining a higher grade in the class, with less effort.

To make an effective outline you have to be selective. Outlines that contain all the information in the text are not very useful. Your objective in outlining is to identify main concepts and to subordinate details to those main concepts. Therefore, your first goal is to *identify the main concepts in each section*. Often the large, first-level headings within your textbook are sufficient as identifiers of the major concepts within each section. You may decide, however, that you want to phrase an identifier in a way that is more meaningful to you. In any event, your outline should consist of several levels written in a standard outline format. The most important concepts are assigned a roman numeral; the second most important a capital letter; the third most important, numbers; and the fourth most important, lower-case letters. Even if you make an outline that is no more than the headings in the text, you will be studying more efficiently than you would be otherwise. As we stated above, the process of physically writing the words will help you master the material.

MARKING A TEXT

From kindergarten through high school you typically did not own your own textbooks. They were made available by the school system. You were told not to mark in them. Now that you own your own text for a course, your learning can be greatly improved by marking your text. There is a trade-off here. The more you mark up your textbook, the less you will receive from your bookstore when you sell it back at the end of the semester. The benefit is a better understanding of the subject matter, and the cost is the reduction in the price you receive for the resale of the text. Additionally, if you want a text that you can mark with your own notations, you necessarily have to buy a new one or a used one that has no markings. Both carry a higher price tag than a used textbook with markings. Again there is a trade-off.

Different Ways of Marking   The most commonly used form of marking is to underline important points. The second most commonly used method is to use a felt-tipped highlighter, or marker, in yellow or some other transparent color. Marking also includes circling, numbering, using arrows, brief notes, or any other method that allows you to remember things when you go back to skim the pages in your textbook prior to an exam.

Why Marking Is Important   Marking is important for the same reason that outlining is—it helps you to organize the information in the text. It allows you to become an *active* participant in the mastery of the material. Researchers have shown that the physical act of marking, just like the physical act of outlining, helps you better retain the material. The better the material is organized in your mind, the more you will remember. There are two types of readers—passive and active. The active reader outlines or marks. Active readers typically do better on exams. Perhaps one of the reasons that active readers retain more is because the physical act of outlining and/or marking requires greater concentration. It is through greater concentration that more is remembered.

Points to Remember When Marking

1. Read one section at a time before you do any extensive marking. You can't mark a section until you know what is important and you can't know what is important until you read the whole section.

2. Don't over mark. Just as an outline cannot contain everything that is in a text (or in a lecture), marking can't be of the whole book. Don't fool yourself into thinking you've done a good job just because each page is filled up with arrows, asterisks, circles, and underlines. When you go back to review the material you won't remember what was important. The key is *selective* activity. Mark each page in a way that allows you to see the most important points at a glance. You can follow up your marking by writing out more in your subject outline.

SUMMARIZING THE MATERIAL

Even if a certain chapter has a concept summary, it is still worthwhile for you to make your own summary points. The reason is that the more active you are as a reader, the better you will understand the material.

Summarization helps you in your reading comprehension. It is the final step in reviewing the book. There is probably nothing else you can do that works as well to help you remember what your textbook has to say.

The importance of summarization is that the notes you make are in your own words, not in the words of the author. Writing down a summary in your own words is the most effective use of your time. This allows you to process the information into your own memory by being required to think about it. You also have to make it part of your vocabulary. Whenever you cannot state important legal concepts in your own words, you probably haven't understood the concepts necessary to master the material. Indeed, summary notes are a good way to determine whether you have actually understood something. Don't simply make a mechanical listing of quotes taken right out of the textbook. Rather, you should make summary notes using complete sentences with correct grammar. This forces you to develop your ideas logically and clearly. Also, summary notes written in this matter can be more easily remembered.

Be Brief. Your notes should condense the information in the text into statements that summarize the concepts. It is when you force yourself to make the statements brief that you best learn the material. By making only brief summary notes, you have to think about the essence of each concept and present it in a form that is compact enough to remember. You should typically have no more than a one-paragraph summary for each important topic in the chapter.

What Format to Use? The authors find that using 5" x 8" cards is the best way to take summary notes. Don't fill up each note card. You need to leave room to make additional notes later on when you are reviewing for the final exam. That is to say, leave margins for further notes and study markings. Additionally, if you leave enough room, you can integrate the notes that you take during lectures onto these summary note cards.

Another reason to place your summary notes on 5" x 8" cards is because in so doing you have a set of flash cards that you can use in studying for a final exam.

HOW TO STUDY AND TAKE EXAMS

There is basically one reason why you have purchased the *Study Guide*—to improve your exam grade. By using this *Study Guide* assiduously, you will have the confidence to take your mid-terms and final examinations and to do well. The *Study Guide*, however, should not just be used a day before each exam. Rather, the guide is most helpful if you use it at the time that you read the chapter. That is to say, after you read a chapter in **West's Legal Environment of Business, Fifth Edition** you should directly go to the appropriate chapter in the *Study Guide*. This systematic review technique is the most effective study technique you can use.

Besides learning the concepts in each chapter as well as possible, there are additional strategies for taking exams. You need to know in advance what type of exam you are going to take—essay or objective or both. You need to know which reading materials and lectures will be covered. For both objective and essay exams (but more importantly for the former) you need to know if there is a penalty for guessing incorrectly. If there is, your strategy will be different: you will usually only mark what you are certain of. Finally, you need to know how much time will be allowed for the exam.

FOLLOWING DIRECTIONS

Students are often in a hurry to start an exam so they take little time to read the instructions. The instructions can be critical, however. In a multiple-choice exam, for example, if there is no indication that there is a penalty for guessing, then you should never leave a question unanswered. Even if there only remains a few minutes at the end of the exam, you should guess for those questions about which you are uncertain.

Additionally, you need to know the weight given to each section of an exam. In a typical multiple-choice exam, all questions have equal weight. In some exams, particularly those involving essay questions, different parts of the exam carry different weights. You should use these weights to apportion your time accordingly. If an essay part of an exam accounts for only 20 percent of the total points on the exam, you should not spend 60 percent of your time on the essay.

You need to make sure you are answering the question correctly. Some exams require a No. 2 lead pencil to fill in the dots on a machine-graded answer sheet. Other exams require underlining or circling. In short, you have to look at the instructions carefully.

Lastly, check to make sure that you have all the pages of the examination. If you are uncertain, ask the instructor or the exam proctor. It is hard to justify not having done your exam correctly because you failed to answer all the questions. Simply stating that you did not have them will pose a problem for both you and your instructor. Don't take a chance. Double check to make sure.

TAKING OBJECTIVE EXAMINATIONS

The most important point to discover initially with any objective test is if there is a penalty for guessing. If there is none, you have nothing to lose by guessing. In contrast, if a half-point is subtracted for each incorrect answer, then you probably should not answer any question for which you are purely guessing.

Students usually commit one of two errors when they read objective-exam questions: (1) they read things into the questions that don't exist, or (2) they skip over words or phrases.

Most test questions include key words such as:

- all
- always
- never
- only

If you miss these key words you will be missing the "trick" part of the question. Also, you must look for questions that are only *partly* correct, particularly if you are answering true/false questions.

Never answer a question without reading all of the alternatives. More than one of them may be correct. If more than one of them seems correct, make sure you select the answer that seems the most correct.

Whenever the answer to an objective question is not obvious, start with the process of elimination. Throw out the answers that are clearly incorrect. Even with objective exams in which there is a penalty for guessing, if you can throw out several obviously incorrect answers, then you may wish to guess among the remaining ones because your probability of choosing the correct answer is high.

Typically, the easiest way to eliminate incorrect answers is to look for those that are meaningless, illogical, or inconsistent. Often test authors put in choices that make perfect sense and are indeed true, but they are not the answer to the question under study.

WRITING ESSAY EXAMS

To write an essay exam, you should be prepared. One way of being prepared is to practice writing timed essays. In other words, find out in advance how much time you will have for each essay question, say fifteen minutes, and then practice writing an answer to a sample essay question during a fifteen-minute time period. This is the only way you will develop the skills needed to pace yourself for an essay exam. Do your timed essay practice without using the book, because most essay exams are closed book.

Usually you can anticipate certain essay exam questions. You do this by going over the major concept headings, either in your lecture notes or in your text; search for the themes that tie the materials together and then think about questions that your instructor might ask you. You might even list possible essay questions as a review device; then write a short outline for each of those most likely questions.

As with objective exams, you need to read the directions to the essay questions carefully. It's best to write out a brief outline *before* you start writing. The outline should present your conclusion in one or two sentences, then your supporting argument. It is important to stay on the subject. We can tell you from first hand experience that no instructor likes to read answers to unasked questions.

Finally, make a strong attempt to write legibly. Again speaking from experience, we can tell you that it's easier to be favorably inclined to a student's essay if we don't have to reread it five times to decipher the handwriting.

Acknowledgments

We wish to thank Suzanne Jasin of K & M Consulting for her expert design and composition of this guide.

We welcome comments and criticisms to help us make this guide even more useful. All errors are our sole responsibility.

Roger LeRoy Miller
Eric Hollowell

Chapter 1
Business and Its Legal Environment

WHAT THIS CHAPTER IS ABOUT

The first chapters in Unit 1 provide the background for the entire course. Chapter 1 sets the stage. From this chapter, you must understand that (1) the law is a set of general rules, (2) in applying these general rules, a judge cannot fit a case to suit a rule, but must fit (or find) a rule to suit the case, and (3) in fitting (or finding) a rule, a judge must also supply reasons for the decision.

CHAPTER OUTLINE

I. WHAT IS LAW?

Law consists of enforceable rules governing relationships among individuals and between individuals and their society.

II. SCHOOLS OF JURISPRUDENTIAL THOUGHT

Judges interpret and apply the law. When the law is expressed in general terms, there is some flexibility in interpreting it. This interpretation can be influenced by a judge's personal philosophy. Legal philosophies include the following.

A. THE NATURAL LAW SCHOOL

Natural law is a system of moral and ethical principles that are believed to be inherent in human nature and discoverable by humans through the use of their natural intelligence.

B. THE POSITIVIST SCHOOL

Legal positivists believe that there is no higher law than a nation's positive law (the law created by a particular society at a particular point in time). The law is the law and must be obeyed.

C. THE HISTORICAL SCHOOL

Followers of this school focus on legal principles that have been applied in past cases, emphasizing that those principles should be applied strictly in present cases.

D. LEGAL REALISM

Legal realists believe that in making decisions, judges are influenced by their own beliefs, the application of principles should be tempered by each case's circumstances, and extra-legal sources should be consulted.

III. BUSINESS ACTIVITIES AND THE LEGAL ENVIRONMENT

The law is split into different topics to make it easier to study, but more than one of those areas of the law can affect individual business decisions. Whether an activity is ethical is an important part of deciding whether to engage in it, but simply complying with the law may not meet all ethical obligations.

IV. SOURCES OF AMERICAN LAW

A. CONSTITUTIONAL LAW

The U.S. Constitution distributes power among the branches of government. It is the supreme law of the land. Any law that conflicts with it is invalid. The states also have constitutions, but the federal constitution prevails.

B. STATUTORY LAW

Statutes and ordinances are enacted by Congress and by state and local legislative bodies. Uniform laws (such as the Uniform Commercial Code) and model codes are created by panels of experts and scholars and adopted at the option of each state's legislature.

C. ADMINISTRATIVE LAW

Administrative law consists of the rules and regulations issued by administrative agencies, which derive their authority from the legislative and executive branches of government.

D. CASE LAW

Case law includes courts' interpretations of constitutional provisions, statutes, and administrative rules. Because statutes often codify common law rules, courts often rely on the common law as a guide to the intent and purpose of a statute. Case law governs all areas not covered by statutes.

V.   THE COMMON LAW TRADITION

The American legal system, based on the decisions judges make in cases, is a common law system, which involves the application of principles applied in earlier cases with similar facts. This system comes from early English courts, which made a distinction between remedies at law and remedies in equity.

A. REMEDIES AT LAW AND REMEDIES IN EQUITY

As a rule, courts grant an equitable remedy only if the remedy at law is inadequate.

1. Remedies at Law

Remedies at law include awards of land, money, and items of value. A jury trial is available only in an action at law.

2. Remedies in Equity

Remedies in equity include decrees of specific performance, injunctions, and rescission. Decisions to award equitable remedies are guided by equitable maxims.

B. THE DOCTRINE OF *STARE DECISIS*

The use of precedent as binding authority in a common law system is the doctrine of *stare decisis*. *Stare decisis* makes the legal system more efficient, just, uniform, stable, and predictable.

1. When There Is No Precedent

When there is no precedent, a court may look at other legal principles and policies, social values, or scientific data.

2. When a Precedent Is Incorrect

A judge may decide that a precedent is incorrect if there have been changes in technology, business practices, or society's attitudes.

C. LEGAL REASONING

1. Issue-Rule-Application-Conclusion (IRAC)

Legal reasoning requires learning the facts of a case, identifying the issues and the relevant legal rules, applying the rules to the facts, and coming to a conclusion.

2. Forms of Legal Reasoning

In applying an old precedent or establishing a new one, judges use many forms of reasoning—deductive reasoning, linear reasoning, reasoning by analogy, and others—to harmonize theirs decisions with earlier cases.

VI.   CLASSIFICATIONS OF LAW

A. SUBSTANTIVE AND PROCEDURAL LAW

Substantive law includes laws that define, describe, regulate, and create rights and duties. *Procedural law* includes rules for enforcing those rights.

B. **CRIMINAL AND CIVIL LAW**

Criminal law regulates relationships between individuals and society. *Civil law* regulates relationships between individuals.

C. **PRIVATE AND PUBLIC LAW**

Private law concerns relationships between private entities. *Public law* addresses the relationship between persons and their government.

D. **CYBERLAW**

Cyberlaw is the emerging body of law (court decisions, new and amended statutes, etc.) that governs cyberspace transactions.

VII. FINDING AND ANALYZING THE LAW

A. **FINDING STATUTORY LAW**

1. **Publication of Statutes**

Federal statutes are arranged by date of enactment in *United States Statutes at Large*. State statutes are collected in similar state publications. Statutes are also published in codified form (the form in which they appear in the federal and state codes) in other publications.

2. **Finding a Statute in a Publication**

Statutes are usually referred to in their codified form. In the codes, laws are compiled by subject. For example, the *United States Code* (U.S.C.) arranges by subject most federal laws. Each subject is assigned a title number and each statute a section number within a title.

B. **FINDING ADMINISTRATIVE LAW**

1. **Publication of Rules and Regulations**

Rules and regulations adopted by federal administrative agencies are published initially in the *Federal Register*. They are also compiled by subject in the *Code of Federal Regulations* (C.F.R.).

2. **Finding a Rule or Regulation in a Publication**

In the C.F.R., rules and regulations are arranged by subject. Each subject is assigned a title number and each rule or regulation a section number within a title.

C. **FINDING CASE LAW**

1. **Publication of Court Opinions**

State appellate court opinions are often published by the state in consecutively numbered volumes. They may also be published in units of the *National Reporter System*, by West Publishing Company. Federal court opinions appear in other West publications.

2. **Finding a Court Opinion in a Publication**

After a decision is published, it is usually referred to by the name of the case and the volume, name, and page number of one or more reporters (which are often, but not always, West reporters). This information is called the citation.

D. **HOW TO READ AND UNDERSTAND CASE LAW**

1. **The Parties**

a. **Plaintiff v. Defendant**

In the title of a case (*Alpha v. Beta*), the *v.* means versus (against). Alpha is the plaintiff (the party who filed the suit) and Beta the defendant. Some appellate courts place the name of the party appealing a decision first, so this case on appeal may be called *Beta v. Alpha*.

      b. Appellant v. Appellee
      The appellant (or petitioner) is the party who appeals a case to another court or jurisdiction from the one in which the case was originally brought. The appellee (or respondent) is the party against whom an appeal is taken.

    2. The Court's Opinion
    An opinion contains a court's reasons for its decision, the rules of law that apply, and the judgment.

      a. Unanimous Opinion
      When more than one judge (or justice) decides a case, and they all agree, a unanimous opinion is written for the whole court.

      b. Majority Opinion
      If a decision is not unanimous, a majority opinion outlines the views of the majority.

      c. Concurring Opinion
      A concurring opinion is one in which a judge emphasizes a point that was not emphasized in the unanimous or majority opinion.

      d. Dissenting Opinion
      A dissenting opinion may be written by a judge who does not agree with the majority. A dissent may form the basis of arguments used years later in overruling the majority opinion.

TRUE-FALSE QUESTIONS

(Answers at the Back of the Book)

____ **1.** Law is a body of enforceable rules governing relationships among individuals and between individuals and their society.

____ **2.** Legal positivists believe that law should reflect universal moral and ethical principles that are part of human nature.

____ **3.** The doctrine of *stare decisis* obligates judges to follow precedents established within their jurisdictions.

____ **4.** Common law develops from rules of law announced in court decisions.

____ **5.** Statutory law is legislation.

____ **6.** The U.S. Constitution takes precedence over a conflicting provision in a state constitution.

____ **7.** Congress enacted the Uniform Commercial Code for adoption by the states.

____ **8.** Criminal law covers disputes between persons, and between persons and their governments.

____ **9.** In most states, the same courts can grant legal or equitable remedies.

____ **10.** A citation includes the name of the judge who decided the case.

FILL-IN QUESTIONS

(Answers at the Back of the Book)

    The common law system, on which the American legal system is based, involves the application of principles applied in earlier cases _____(with similar facts/whether or not the facts are similar). This use of previous case law, or _____ (prece-dent/preeminent), is known as the doctrine of *stare decisis*, and _____ _____ (emphasizes a flexible/permits a predictable) resolution of cases.

MULTIPLE-CHOICE QUESTIONS

(Answers at the Back of the Book)

____ **1.** Adam is a legal positivist. Adam believes that

a. the law should be applied the same in all cases in all circumstances.
b. the law should reflect universal principles that are part of human nature.
c. the law should strictly follow decisions made in past cases.
d. the written law of a society at a particular time is most significant.

____ **2.** In a suit between Best Products, Inc., and Central Sales Corporation, the court applies the doctrine of *stare decisis*. This means that the court follows rules of law established by

a. all courts.
b. courts of higher rank only.
c. courts of lower rank only.
d. no courts.

____ **3.** In a suit between Delta Data Company and Eagle Information, Inc., the court applies the doctrine of *stare decisis*. This requires the court to find cases that, compared to the case before it, has

a. entirely different facts.
b. no facts, only conclusions of law.
c. precisely identical facts.
d. similar facts.

____ **4.** In a suit between Fine Manufacturing Company and Great Goods, Inc., the court orders a rescission. This is

a. an action to cancel a contract and return the parties to the positions they held before the contract's formation.
b. an award of damages.
c. an order to do or refrain from doing a particular act.
d. an order to perform what was promised.

____ **5.** In a given case, most courts may grant

a. equitable remedies only.
b. legal remedies only.
c. equitable or legal remedies, but not both.
d. equitable remedies, legal remedies, or both.

____ **6.** The U.S. Constitution takes precedence over

a. a provision in a state constitution or statute only.
b. a state supreme court decision only.
c. a state constitution, statute, and court decision.
d. none of the above.

____ **7.** Case law includes interpretations of federal and state

a. administrative rules and statutes only.
b. constitutions only.
c. administrative rules, statutes, and constitutions.
d. none of the above.

____   8.   Civil law concerns

   a.   disputes between persons, and between persons and their governments.
   b.   only laws that define, describe, regulate, and create rights and duties.
   c.   only laws that establish methods for enforcing rights.
   d.   wrongs committed against society for which society demands redress.

____   9.   Matt is a judge. To reason by analogy, Matt compares the facts in one case to

   a.   the facts in another case.
   b.   the defendant's arguments.
   c.   the plaintiff's hypothetical.
   d.   none of the above.

____   10.   A concurring opinion, written by one of the judges who decides a case before a multi-judge panel, is

   a.   an opinion that is written for the entire court.
   b.   an opinion that outlines only the views of the majority.
   c.   a separate opinion that agrees with the court's ruling but for different reasons.
   d.   a separate opinion that does not agree with court's ruling.

SHORT ESSAY QUESTIONS

1.   What is the primary function of law?

2.   What is *stare decisis*? Why is it important?

ISSUE SPOTTERS

(Answers at the Back of the Book)

1.   Under what circumstance might a judge rely on case law to determine the intent and purpose of a statute?

2.   The First Amendment provides protection for the free exercise of religion. A state legislature enacts a law that outlaws all religions that do not derive from the Judeo-Christian tradition. Is this law valid within that state? Why or why not?

3.   What is included in the citation of a case?

Chapter 2
The Court System

WHAT THIS CHAPTER IS ABOUT

This chapter explains which courts have power to hear what disputes and when. The chapter also covers the judicial process—the application of procedural rules and what happens before, during, and after a civil trial.

CHAPTER OUTLINE

I. THE JUDICIARY'S ROLE IN AMERICAN GOVERNMENT

Under the power of judicial review, the courts can decide whether the laws or actions of the executive branch and the legislative branch are constitutional.

II. BASIC JUDICIAL REQUIREMENTS

A. JURISDICTION

To hear a case, a court must have jurisdiction over (1) the defendant or the property involved and (2) the subject matter.

1. Jurisdiction over Persons or Property

A court has *in personam* (personal) jurisdiction over persons within the court's geographic area. Long arm statutes permit courts to exercise jurisdiction over persons outside that area who have *minimum contacts* within it (e.g., do business there). A court has *in rem* jurisdiction over property within its area.

2. Jurisdiction over Subject Matter

A court of general jurisdiction can decide virtually any type of case. A court's jurisdiction may be limited by the subject of a suit, the amount of money in controversy, or whether a proceeding is a trial or appeal.

3. Jurisdiction of the Federal Courts

a. Federal Questions

Any suit based on the Constitution, a treaty, or a federal law can originate in a federal court.

b. Diversity of Citizenship

Federal jurisdiction covers cases involving (1) citizens of different states, (2) a foreign government and citizens of a state or of different states, or (3) citizens of a state and citizens or subjects of a foreign government. The amount in controversy must be more than $75,000.

4. Exclusive v. Concurrent Jurisdiction

Exclusive: when cases can be tried only in federal courts or only in state courts. Concurrent: When both federal and state courts can hear a case.

B. JURISDICTION IN CYBERSPACE

Whether a court can compel the appearance of a party outside the geographic area of the court's jurisdiction depends on the amount of business the party transacts over the Internet with parties within the court's area ("sliding scale" test). Internationally, the minimum contacts test mentioned above generally applies.

C. **VENUE**
Venue is concerned with the most appropriate location for a trial.

D. **STANDING TO SUE**
Standing is the interest (injury or threat) that a plaintiff has in a case. A plaintiff must have standing to bring a suit, and the controversy must be justiciable (real, as opposed to hypothetical or purely academic).

III.   THE STATE AND FEDERAL COURT SYSTEMS

A. **STATE COURT SYSTEMS**

1. **Trial Courts**
Trial courts are courts in which trials are held and testimony is taken.

2. **Appellate Courts**
Courts that hear appeals from trial courts look at *questions of law* (what law governs a dispute) but not *questions of fact* (what occurred in the dispute), unless a trial court's finding of fact is clearly contrary to the evidence. Decision of a state's highest court on state law is final.

B. **THE FEDERAL COURT SYSTEM**

1. **U.S. District Courts**
The federal equivalent of a state trial court of general jurisdiction. There is at least one federal district court in every state. Other federal trial courts include the U.S. Tax Court and the U.S. Bankruptcy Court.

2. **U.S. Courts of Appeals**
The U.S. (circuit) courts of appeals for twelve of the circuits hear appeals from the federal district courts located within their respective circuits. The court of appeals for the thirteenth circuit (the federal circuit) has national jurisdiction over certain cases.

3. **United States Supreme Court**
This is the highest level of the federal court system. The Supreme Court can review any case decided by any of the federal courts of appeals, and it has authority over some cases decided in state courts.

4. **How Cases Reach the Supreme Court**
To appeal a case to the Supreme Court, a party asks for a writ of *certiorari*. Whether the Court issues the writ is within its discretion.

IV.   JUDICIAL PROCEDURES: A CASE IN THE COURTS

A. **PROCEDURAL RULES**
The Federal Rules of Civil Procedure govern trials in federal district court. Each state has its own rules of procedure that apply in its courts, as well as to the federal courts within the state.

B. **CONSULTING WITH AN ATTORNEY**
The time and expense of litigation are important considerations when deciding what legal course to pursue. Attorney fees can be fixed, may accrue on an hourly or a contingency basis, or may be set by a judge.

V.   PRETRIAL PROCEDURES

A. **THE PLEADINGS**
The pleadings inform each party of the claims of the other and specify the issues in the case. They include the complaint and answer (and counterclaim and reply).

1. **The Plaintiff's Complaint**
   Filed by the plaintiff with the clerk of the trial court (with the proper venue). The complaint contains (1) a statement alleging the facts necessary for the court to take jurisdiction, (2) a short statement of the facts necessary to show that the plaintiff is entitled to a remedy, and (3) a statement of the remedy the plaintiff is seeking.

2. **Service of Process**
   The complaint is delivered to the defendant, with a summons. The summons tells the defendant to answer the complaint and file a copy of the answer with the court and the plaintiff within a specified time (usually twenty to thirty days). Corporations receive service through their officers or registered agents.

3. **The Defendant's Response to the Complaint**

   a. **Answer**
      An answer admits the allegations in the complaint or denies them and sets out any defenses.

      1) **Affirmative Defense**
         Exists when the defendant admits the truth of the complaint but raises new facts to dismiss the action (for example, the time period for raising the claim has passed).

      2) **Counterclaim**
         The defendant's claim against the plaintiff, who will have to answer it with a reply, which has the same characteristics as an answer.

   b. **Motion to Dismiss**
      This motion alleges that even if the facts in the complaint are true, their legal consequences are such that there is no reason to go on with the suit and no need for the defendant to present an answer.

      1) **Denial of the Motion**
         If the court denies the motion, and the defendant does not file a further pleading, a judgment will be entered for the plaintiff.

      2) **Grant of the Motion**
         If the court grants the motion, the defendant is not required to answer the complaint. If the plaintiff does not file an amended complaint, a judgment will be entered for the defendant.

   c. **No Response**
      Results in a default judgment for the plaintiff (who is awarded the relief sought in the complaint).

B. **DISMISSALS AND JUDGMENTS BEFORE TRIAL**

   1. **Motion to Dismiss**
      (See above.) Either party may file a motion to dismiss if they have agreed to settle the case. A court may file such a motion on its own.

   2. **Motion for Judgment on the Pleadings**
      Any party can file this motion (after the complaint, answer, and any counterclaim and reply have been filed), when no facts are disputed and only questions of law are at issue. A court may consider only those facts stated in the pleadings.

   3. **Motion for Summary Judgment**
      Any party can file this motion, if there is no disagreement about the facts and the only question is which laws apply to those facts. A court can consider evidence outside the pleadings (for example, sworn statements by witnesses).

C. DISCOVERY

1. What Discovery Is

This is the process of obtaining information from the opposing party or from witnesses. Privileged material is safeguarded and only relevant matters are discoverable.

a. Depositions

Sworn testimony, recorded by a court official. Can be used as testimony, if a witness is unavailable, or to impeach (challenge the credibility of) a party or witness who testifies differently at trial.

b. Interrogatories

A series of written questions for which written answers are prepared and signed under oath. Interrogatories are directed to the plaintiff or the defendant.

c. Request for Admissions

A written request to a party for an admission of the truth of matters relating to the trial. Any matter admitted is considered to be true.

d. Request for Documents, Objects, and Entry on Land

A written request to examine documents and other items not in the party's possession.

e. Request for Examinations

Granted when a party's physical or mental condition is in question.

2. What Discovery Does

This allows both parties to learn as much as they can about what to expect at a trial and helps to narrow the issues so that trial time is spent on the main questions.

D. PRETRIAL CONFERENCE

After discovery, the attorneys may meet with the judge to discuss resolving the case or at least to clarify the issues and agree on such things as the number of expert witnesses or the admissibility of certain types of evidence.

E. JURIES

1. The Right to a Jury Trial

The Seventh Amendment to the U.S. Constitution guarantees the right to a jury trial for cases at law in federal courts when the amount in controversy exceeds $20. Most states have similar guarantees in their own constitutions (with a higher dollar-amount). The right to a trial by jury does not have to be exercised.

2. Jury Selection

Most civil matters can be heard by six-person juries. Some trials must be heard by twelve persons.

a. *Voir Dire*

The process by which a jury is selected. The parties' attorneys ask prospective jurors questions to determine whether any are biased or have a connection with a party or a witness.

b. Challenges

1) Peremptory Challenge

Without providing a reason, asking that an individual not be sworn in as a juror.

2) Challenge for Cause

For a specific reason, asking that an individual not be sworn in as a juror.

VI.   THE TRIAL

A. OPENING STATEMENTS

Each side sets out briefly his or her version of the facts and outlines the evidence that will be presented. The plaintiff goes first.

B. PRESENTATION OF EVIDENCE

1. Burden of Proof

In a civil case, a plaintiff must prove his or her case by a *preponderance of the evidence* (the claim is more likely to be true than the defendant's). Some claims (such as fraud) must be proved by *clear and convincing evidence* (the truth of the claim is highly probable). Evidence includes the testimony of witnesses.

2. Admissible Evidence

Evidence that is relevant to the matter in question (tends to prove or disprove a fact in question or to establish that a fact or action is more probable or less probable than it would be without the evidence).

3. Inadmissible Evidence

Relevant evidence whose probative value is substantially outweighed by other considerations (the issue has been proved or disproved, or the evidence would mislead the jury, or cause the jury to decide the issue on an emotional basis). Hearsay is not admissible.

4. Examination of Witnesses

a. Plaintiff's Side of the Case

After the opening statements, the plaintiff calls and questions the first witness (direct examination); the defendant questions the witness (cross-examination); the plaintiff questions the witness again (redirect examination); the defendant follows (recross-examination). The plaintiff's other witnesses are then called.

b. Defendant's Side of the Case

1) Motion for a Directed Verdict

At the conclusion of the plaintiff's case, the defendant can ask the judge to direct a verdict for the defendant on the ground that the plaintiff presented no evidence that would justify granting the plaintiff relief. The judge grants the motion if there is insufficient evidence to raise an issue of fact.

2) Defendant's Witnesses

If the motion is denied, the defendant calls the witnesses for his or her side of the case (and there is direct, cross-, redirect, and recross-examination). At the end of the defendant's case, either side can move for a directed verdict.

c. Rebuttal

At the conclusion of the defendant's case, the plaintiff can present a rebuttal (additional evidence to refute the defendant's case).

d. Rejoinder

The defendant can refute the plaintiff's rebuttal in a rejoinder.

C. CLOSING ARGUMENTS

Each side summarizes briefly his or her version of the facts, outlines the evidence that supports his or her case, and reveals the shortcomings of the points made by the other party. The plaintiff goes first.

D. JURY TRIALS

1. Jury Instructions

In a jury trial, the judge instructs (charges) the jury in the law that applies to the case. The jurors may disregard the facts as stated in the charge, but they are not free to ignore the statements of law. (A reviewing court ordinarily remands a case for a new trial if a judge misstates the law in the jury instructions.)

2. **Jury Verdict**
   In a jury trial, the jury specifies the factual findings and the amount of damages to be paid by the losing party. This is the verdict. After it is announced, the trial is ended, and the jurors are discharged.

VII. POSTTRIAL MOTIONS

A. **MOTION FOR A JUDGMENT IN ACCORDANCE WITH THE VERDICT**
   The prevailing party usually files this motion.

B. **MOTION FOR A NEW TRIAL**
   This motion is granted if the judge believes that the jury erred but that it is not appropriate to grant a judgment for the other side (for example, the jury verdict resulted from a misapplication of the law or misunderstanding of the evidence, or there is newly discovered evidence, misconduct by the parties, or error by the judge).

C. **MOTION FOR JUDGMENT N.O.V.**
   The defendant can file this motion, if he or she previously moved for a directed verdict (n.o.v. is from the Latin *non obstante veredicto*, "notwithstanding the verdict;" federal courts use "motion for judgment as a matter of law"). The standards for granting this motion are the same as those for granting a motion to dismiss or a motion for a directed verdict.

VIII. THE APPEAL

A. **FILING THE APPEAL**
   The papers to be filed include—

1. **Notice of Appeal**
   The appellant (the losing party—or the winning party, if that party is dissatisfied with the relief obtained) must file a notice of appeal with the clerk of the trial court within a certain period of time.

2. **Record on Appeal**
   The appellant files in the reviewing court: (1) the pleadings, (2) a transcript of the trial and copies of the exhibits, (3) the judge's rulings on the parties' motions, (4) the arguments of counsel, (5) the jury instructions, (6) the verdict, (7) the posttrial motions, and (8) the judgment order from which the appeal is taken.

3. **Brief**
   The appellant files with the abstract a brief, which contains (1) a short statement of the facts; (2) a statement of the issues; (3) the rulings by the trial court that the appellant contends are erroneous and prejudicial; (4) the grounds for reversal of the judgment; (5) a statement of the applicable law; and (6) arguments on the appellant's behalf, citing applicable statutes and relevant cases.

4. **Reply**
   The appellee (respondent) may file an answering brief.

B. **APPELLATE REVIEW**
   Appellate courts do not usually reverse findings of fact unless they are contradicted by evidence at the trial. An appellate court can affirm, reverse, or modify a trial court's decision, or remand the case to the trial court for further proceedings consistent with the appellate court's opinion.

C. **FURTHER APPEALS**

If the reviewing court is an intermediate appellate court, the case may be appealed to the state supreme court. The state supreme court can affirm, reverse, or remand. If a federal question is involved, the case may be appealed to the United States Supreme Court, which may agree to hear it. Otherwise, the case is ended.

IX. **ENFORCING THE JUDGMENT**

The court can order a sheriff to seize property owned by the defendant and hold it until the defendant pays the judgment owed to the plaintiff. If the defendant fails to pay, the property can be sold at an auction and the proceeds given to the plaintiff, or the property can be transferred to the plaintiff in lieu of payment.

TRUE-FALSE QUESTIONS

(Answers at the Back of the Book)

____ 1. Under a long arm statute, a state court can compel someone outside the state to appear in the court.

____ 2. Doing substantial business in a jurisdiction over the Internet can be enough to support a court's jurisdiction over a nonresident defendant.

____ 3. The United States Supreme Court is the final authority for any case decided by a state court.

____ 4. Suits involving federal questions originate in federal district courts.

____ 5. Before a trial, if there are no issues of fact, and only questions of law, a court may grant a summary judgment.

____ 6. Pleadings consist of a complaint, an answer, and a motion to dismiss.

____ 7. In ruling on a motion for summary judgment, a court cannot consider evidence outside the pleadings.

____ 8. An answer may admit or deny the statements or allegations in a complaint.

____ 9. Only a losing party may appeal to a higher court.

____ 10. A motion for a new trial will be granted if a jury verdict is the obvious result of a misapplication of the law.

FILL-IN QUESTIONS

(Answers at the Back of the Book)

Courts of original jurisdiction are _____ (trial/reviewing) courts. Courts of appellate jurisdiction are _____ (trial/reviewing) courts. Trial courts resolve disputes through determining _____ (factual issues/the law) and applying _____ (the facts to the law/ the law to the facts). Reviewing courts most commonly reverse cases on the basis of errors _____ (of law but not of fact/of fact and of law) committed by lower courts within the same system.

MULTIPLE-CHOICE QUESTIONS

(Answers at the Back of the Book)

____ 1. Bob, who lives in Texas, advertises his business on the Web. Bob's page receives hundreds of "hits" by residents of Ohio. If a resident of Ohio files a suit against Bob in an Ohio state court, the court can compel Bob to appear, under the "sliding scale" test, if

    a. Bob conducted substantial business with Ohio residents at his Web site.
    b. there was any interactivity with any Ohio resident at Bob's Web site.
    c. Bob's Web site was only a passive ad.
    d. any of the above.

____ 2. General Business, Inc. (GBI), has its offices in Virginia, but owns property in Maryland, where Ann files a suit against GBI concerning that property. In this suit, Maryland has

    a. diversity jurisdiction.
    b. *in personam* jurisdiction.
    c. *in rem* jurisdiction.
    d. no jurisdiction.

____ 3. National Corporation was incorporated in Delaware, has its main office in Illinois, and does business in New York. National is subject to the jurisdiction of

    a. Delaware, Illinois, and New York.
    b. Delaware and Illinois, but not New York.
    c. Delaware and New York, but not Illinois.
    d. Illinois and New York, but not Delaware.

____ 4. Ace Manufacturing, Inc., loses its suit against Best Products, Inc., and files an appeal. The appellate court is most likely to review the trial court's

    a. application of the law.
    b. consideration of the credibility of the evidence.
    c. findings of fact.
    d. interpretation of the conduct of the witnesses.

____ 5. The United States Supreme Court is required to hear John's suit against Kay if

    a. it comes from a federal court.
    b. it is an appeal.
    c. John lost in a lower court.
    d. none of the above.

____ 6. Ann sues Beth in a state trial court. Ann loses the suit. If Ann wants to appeal, the most appropriate court in which to file the appeal is

    a. a state appellate court.
    b. the nearest federal district court.
    c. the nearest federal court of appeals.
    d. the United States Supreme Court.

____ 7. Grant serves a complaint on Lee. Lee files a motion to dismiss. Lee will also need to file an answer to the complaint if

    a. the motion to dismiss is granted.
    b. the motion to dismiss is denied.
    c. Grant files a motion for judgment on the pleadings.
    d. none of the above.

____ 8. Jill and Ken are involved in an auto accident. Lyle is a passenger in Ken's car. Jill wants to ask Lyle, as a witness, some questions concerning the accident. Lyle's answers to the questions are given in

    a. a deposition.
    b. a response to interrogatories.
    c. a response to a judge's request at a pretrial conference.
    d. none of the above.

____ 9. Ron files a suit against Sue. At the trial, Ron calls and questions Tim. What happens next?

    a. Ron calls his second witness.
    b. Ron questions Tim again.
    c. Sue calls her first witness.
    d. Sue questions Tim.

____ 10. A jury returns a verdict against Gamma Corporation, in its suit against Omega, Inc. Gamma can file a motion for

    a. a directed verdict.
    b. a judgment on the pleadings.
    c. a new trial or for a judgment notwithstanding the verdict.
    d. summary judgment.

SHORT ESSAY QUESTIONS

1. What is jurisdiction? How does jurisdiction over a person or property differ from subject matter jurisdiction?

2. What permits a court to exercise jurisdiction based on contacts over the Internet?

ISSUE SPOTTERS

(Answers at the Back of the Book)

1. Ron wants to sue Art's Supply Company for Art's failure to deliver supplies that Ron needed to prepare his work for an appearance at a local Artists Fair. What must Ron establish before a court will hear the suit?

2. Carlos, a citizen of California, is injured in an automobile accident in Arizona. Alex, the driver of the other car, is a citizen of New Mexico. Carlos wants Alex to pay Carlos's $125,000 in medical expenses and car repairs. Can Carlos sue in federal court?

3. Jay is fired from his job and sues his employer. Jay loses the trial, and he appeals. The reviewing court affirms the decision of the trial court. Jay wants to appeal to the United States Supreme Court. Can the Court refuse to hear the case?

Chapter 3
Alternative and Online Dispute Resolution

WHAT THIS CHAPTER IS ABOUT

This chapter outlines alternatives to judicial resolution of legal controversies. These alternatives include negotiation, conciliation, mediation, arbitration, and online dispute resolution.

CHAPTER OUTLINE

I. THE PROBLEMS OF COST AND COMPLEXITY

Reasons for methods of alternative dispute resolution (ADR) include the complexity of litigation (complex rules, complicated facts) and its expense in time and money.

II. THE SEARCH FOR ALTERNATIVES TO LITIGATION

ADR is any procedure or device for resolving disputes other than the traditional judicial process. Besides the solutions outlined elsewhere in this chapter, proposals include—

A. CAPS ON DAMAGE AWARDS

For pain and suffering, to deter some potential litigants from suing.

B. PENALIZING THOSE WHO BRING FRIVOLOUS LAWSUITS

Rule 11 of the Federal Rules of Civil Procedure allows for sanctions against lawyers and litigants who bring frivolous lawsuits in federal courts.

C. CASE-MANAGEMENT PLANS

Require courts to place cases on different tracks, to hear simple cases sooner.

III. NEGOTIATION AND MEDIATION

Nonadversarial in nature—the goal is to find grounds for agreement.

A. NEGOTIATION

Parties come together informally, with or without attorneys, to try to settle or resolve their differences without involving independent third parties.
Forms of ADR associated with negotiation include—

1. Mini-trial

A private proceeding in which attorneys briefly argue each party's case. A third party indicates how a court would likely decide the issue.

2. Early Neutral Case Evaluation

Parties select a neutral third party (generally an expert) to evaluate their positions, with no hearing and no discovery. The evaluation is a basis for negotiating a settlement.

3. Summary Jury Trial (SJT)

Like a mini-trial, but a jury renders a nonbinding verdict. Negotiations must follow. If no settlement is reached, either side can seek a full trial.

4. Conciliation
A conciliator assists disputing parties in negotiating, communicating offers, etc. Conciliators sometimes recommend solutions.

B. MEDIATION
Parties come together informally with a mediator, who may propose solutions for the parties to consider. A mediator is often an expert in a particular field and charges a fee.

1. Advantages of Mediation
Few procedural rules; proceedings can be made to fit the parties' needs; the parties reach agreement by consent; the parties select a mediator.

2. Disadvantages of Mediation
The mediator can only help the parties reach a decision, not make a decision for them; no deadline; no threat of sanctions if a party fails to negotiate in good faith.

IV. ARBITRATION
An arbitrator—the third party hearing the dispute—decides the dispute. The decision may (or may not) be legally binding. Disputes are often arbitrated because of an arbitration clause in a contract entered into before the dispute.

A. THE FEDERAL ARBITRATION ACT (FAA) OF 1925
Provides means for enforcing whatever arbitration procedure the parties agree on. Under the FAA, the parties can ask a federal district court to—

1. Compel Arbitration
The FAA enforces any arbitration clause in a contract that involves interstate commerce (which may include business activities only slightly connected to the flow of commerce) [Section 4].

2. Confirm the Arbitrator's Decision
One party obtains a court order directing another party to comply with the terms of the arbitrator's decision [Section 9].

3. Set Aside the Arbitrator's Decision
Grounds are limited to misconduct, fraud, corruption, or abuse of power in the arbitration process; a court will not review the merits of the dispute or the arbitrator's judgment [Section 10]. (See below.)

B. STATE ARBITRATION STATUTES
The states follow the federal approach to enforce voluntary agreements to arbitrate disputes between private parties. Most states require that (1) an agreement to submit a dispute to arbitration be in writing and (2) the submission be within a certain time of the dispute (generally six months).

C. THE ARBITRATION PROCESS
Unless a statute provides otherwise, the rights and duties of the parties are set by their agreement. (For example, by including a choice-of-law clause, they may have the law of a specific state govern their agreement.)

1. Submission
Typically includes identities of the parties, nature of the dispute, monetary amounts involved, place at which arbitration is to occur, and a statement that parties intend to be bound by the arbitrator's award.

2. Hearing
The parties must decide on the issues and the arbitrator's powers. They may stipulate rules of procedure or have the arbitrator set rules. Typically, the parties present opening arguments and evidence, call and examine witnesses, and present closing arguments.

3. **Award**
This is the arbitrator's final decision. Under most statutes, an arbitrator must render an award within thirty days of the close of a hearing. In most states, the award must be in writing but does not need to state findings of fact or conclusions of law.

D. **ENFORCEMENT AND APPEAL**

1. **Enforcement of Agreements to Submit to Arbitration**
A court can decide whether or not the parties agreed to submit a particular matter to arbitration (without ruling on the issue in dispute).

2. **Setting Aside an Arbitration Award**
A losing party may appeal the arbitrator's award to a court.

   a. **Fact Findings and Legal Conclusions**
   The arbitrator's factual findings and legal conclusions are normally conclusive. Whether the arbitrator erred is no basis for setting aside an award. A court will not look at the merits of a dispute, the sufficiency of the evidence, or the arbitrator's reasoning.

   b. **Public Policy and Illegality**
   No award will be enforced if compliance would result in the commission of a crime, or conflict with or undermine public policy.

   c. **Defects in the Arbitration Process**
   An award may be set aside if—

   1) The award was the result of corruption, fraud, or other "undue means" (such as a bribe or *ex parte* communications).

   2) The arbitrator exhibited bias or corruption.

   3) The arbitrator refused to postpone the hearing despite sufficient cause, refused to hear material evidence, or otherwise acted to substantially prejudice the rights of a party.

   4) The arbitrator exceeded his or her powers or failed to use them to make a mutual, final, and definite award.

   d. **Waiver**
   A party may forfeit the right to challenge an award by failing to object to a defect in a timely manner.

E. **CONFLICTS OF LAW AND CHOICE OF LAW**
When there is a conflict between federal law and state law concerning arbitration, federal law takes precedence. Parties can choose state law to govern their arbitration agreement, however.

F. **DISADVANTAGES OF ARBITRATION**
The result can be unpredictable; arbitrators do not have to issue written opinions; arbitrators must decide disputes according to rules provided by the parties; arbitration can be as expensive as litigation; discovery is usually not available.

V. THE INTEGRATION OF ADR AND COURT PROCEDURES

A. **COURT-MANDATED ADR**
Many, if not most, federal courts require parties to attempt to settle their differences through ADR before going to trial. Many states refer certain cases to ADR. Some states compel the arbitration of certain disputes.

B. **COURT-ANNEXED ARBITRATION**
Unlike voluntary arbitration, in court-annexed arbitration—

1. **Certain Disputes Are Not Arbitrable**
    Disputes involving title to real estate or a court's equity powers are not.

2. **No Discovery Without Court Approval**
    After a hearing commences, a party seeking discovery must usually secure approval from the court that mandated the arbitration.

3. **Rules of Evidence May Be Different**
    Most states impose the same rules on arbitration hearings and trials. Others allow all relevant evidence whether or not it would be admissible at trial. Some leave it to the arbitrator to decide.

4. **A Court Can Review an Arbitrated Dispute *De Novo***
    Either party may reject an award for any reason; the case proceeds to trial, and the court considers all the evidence and legal questions as though no arbitration had occurred.

5. **Court Costs and Fees May Be Imposed**
    Many statutes impose such expenses on a party who rejects an award but does not improve his or her position by going to trial.

C. **COURT-RELATED MEDIATION**
    Mediation is often used in disputes in employment law, environmental law, product liability, and franchises. Advantages of mediation include lower cost, speed (one or two days), and resolutions that benefit both sides.

VI.   ADR FORUMS AND SERVICES

Services facilitating dispute resolution outside the courtroom are provided by government agencies and private organizations, including programs in the insurance, automobile, and securities industries. Litigants can use for-profit services to have their cases heard before former judges with jurors selected from public jury rolls and verdicts appealed to a state appellate court.

VII.   ONLINE DISPUTE RESOLUTION

Many Web sites offer online dispute resolution (ODR) services to help resolve small- to medium-sized business liability claims.

A. **WHAT LAW APPLIES IN AN ODR PROCEEDING?**
    Most ODR services do not apply the law of a specific jurisdiction. Results are based on general, common legal principles.

B. **NEGOTIATION AND MEDIATION SERVICES**

1. **Online Negotiation**
    A settlement may be negotiated through blind bidding: one party submits an offer to be shown to the other party if it falls within a previously agreed range. There is a limited time to respond.

2. **Mediation Providers—SquareTrade**
    SquareTrade resolves, as part of a free pilot program, disputes involving $100 or more between eBay customers. SquareTrade also resolves other disputes related to online transactions, using software to walk participants through a step-by-step resolution process.

C. **ARBITRATION PROGRAMS**

1. **Internet Corporation for Assigned Names and Numbers (ICANN)**
    The federal government set up ICANN as a nonprofit corporation to oversee the distribution of domain names. ICANN has issued rules and authorized organizations to resolve related disputes.

2. **Resolution Forum, Inc. (RFI)**

   RFI, a nonprofit entity associated with the Center for Legal Responsibility at South Texas College of Law, offers arbitration in an online conference room via a standard browser, using a password.

3. **Virtual Magistrate Project (VMAG)**

   VMAG resolves disputes involving users of online systems; victims of wrongful messages, postings and files; and system operators subject to complaints or similar demands. Online-related contract, intellectual property, property, and tort disputes. The goal is resolution within seventy-two hours. Appeal of a result may be made to a court.

VIII. INTERNATIONAL DISPUTE RESOLUTION

To protect themselves, parties to international contracts may include special clauses, including a forum-selection clause (stating which jurisdiction will hear a dispute), a choice-of-law clause (stating which law applies), and an arbitration clause (stating that a dispute must go first to arbitration).

TRUE-FALSE QUESTIONS

(Answers at the Back of the Book)

____   **1.** Most lawsuits go to trial.

____   **2.** In mediation, a mediator makes a decision on the matter in dispute.

____   **3.** A party to an arbitration agreement may never be compelled to arbitrate a dispute.

____   **4.** The jury verdict, in a summary jury trial, is binding.

____   **5.** A major similarity between negotiation and mediation is that no third parties are involved.

____   **6.** In binding arbitration, an arbitrator's decision is usually the final word.

____   **7.** In court-annexed arbitration, an award is final.

____   **8.** The goal of arbitration is to come to a resolution that benefits both sides in a dispute.

____   **9.** A losing party may appeal an arbitrator's award to a court.

____   **10.** ADR resolves disputes by any method other than litigation.

FILL-IN QUESTIONS

(Answers at the Back of the Book)

_____ (Arbitration/Mediation/Negotiation) is the settling of a dispute by parties meeting informally, with or without attorneys, to discuss and resolve their differences without the involvement of independent third parties. _____ (Arbitration/Mediation/Negotiation) is the settling of a dispute by parties meeting informally with a third party, _____ (an arbitrator/ a mediator/ a negotiator), who assists the parties in reaching an agreement. _____ (Arbitration/Mediation/Negotiation) is the settling of a dispute by an impartial third party, _____ (an arbitrator/a mediator/a negotiator), who does more than assist the parties in resolving their dispute—he or she renders a decision that may be legally binding.

MULTIPLE-CHOICE QUESTIONS

(Answers at the Back of the Book)

_____ 1. In Carol's suit against Don, before going to trial, the parties meet, with their attorneys, to try to resolve the dispute without a third party. This is

a. arbitration.
b. litigation.
c. mediation.
d. negotiation.

_____ 2. In Sara's suit against Tim, their attorneys present the case to a judge and jury. The jury renders an advisory verdict. The judge then meets with the parties to encourage a settlement. This is

a. a mini-trial.
b. a summary jury trial.
c. early neutral case evaluation.
d. mediation.

_____ 3. Small Business Company submits a claim against Medium Market Supplier, Inc., to an online dispute resolution forum. An appeal of this dispute may be made to a court by

a. Small only.
b. Medium only.
c. Small and Medium together only.
d. Small or Medium.

_____ 4. Pat and Don submit their dispute to binding arbitration. A court can set aside the arbitrator's award if

a. Don is not satisfied with the award.
b. Pat is not satisfied with the award.
c. the award involves at least $75,000.
d. the award violates public policy.

_____ 5. Alpha Shoes, Inc., sells to Beta Sporting Goods 1,000 pairs of hiking boots. Beta does not pay, claiming the boots are defective. They agree to mediate the dispute. Beta does not mediate in good faith. The mediator can impose

a. any sanction.
b. any sanction that a court could impose.
c. only a sanction that the parties agreed to initially.
d. no sanctions.

_____ 6. Mega Insurance Company and National Insurance, Inc., cannot agree on which of them should pay a certain claim. They submit their dispute to a mini-trial. The result will be

a. advisory only.
b. legally binding only.
c. advisory and legally binding.
d. none of the above.

_____ 7. Standard Manufacturing Company and Total Products, Inc., agree to submit their contract dispute to a summary jury trial. The verdict will be

a. advisory only.
b. legally binding only.
c. advisory and legally binding.
d. none of the above.

____ 8. Pam files a suit against Ron in a state court that requires the parties to some disputes to attempt arbitration before a trial will be held. In most states, court-annexed arbitration is *not* available

    a. only if a dispute involves title to real estate.
    b. only if a court's equity powers are involved.
    c. if a dispute involves title to real estate or if a court's equity powers are involved.
    d. none of the above.

____ 9. Don and Eve agree to dissolve their corporation but cannot agree on the division of assets. They decide to arbitrate their dispute. The advantages of arbitration include

    a. informality of proceedings, compared to litigation.
    b. lower cost than litigation.
    c. the speed with which a dispute can be resolved, compared to litigation.
    d. all of the above.

____ 10. Kim and Lee agree to dissolve their partnership but cannot agree on the division of assets and profits. They decide to mediate their dispute. The advantages of mediation include

    a. lower cost than arbitration.
    b. resolutions that benefit both sides.
    c. the speed with which a dispute can be resolved, compared to arbitration.
    d. all of the above.

SHORT ESSAY QUESTIONS

1. What are the principal advantages and disadvantages of using mediation?

2. What are the differences between voluntary and court-annexed arbitration?

ISSUE SPOTTERS

(Answers at the Back of the Book)

1. Beth rents an apartment from Carl. When they disagree over $200 in back rent, they discuss the matter and compromise on a payment of $100. What is the basic difference between this negotiation and litigation?

2. A-One Hybrids, Inc., agrees to supply Best Farms with certain hybrids. When problems develop, Best claims that the hybrids are genetically inferior. The parties submit their dispute to Curt, an arbitrator who is an expert in genetic engineering. They give him the power to set the rules to govern the arbitration. Why are these rules likely to be less restrictive than rules governing a court proceeding?

3. Some states require that certain disputes be submitted to mediation or nonbinding arbitration. If the dispute is not resolved, or if a party disagrees with the decision of the mediator or arbitrator, will a court hear the case?

Chapter 4
Ethics and Business Decision Making

WHAT THIS CHAPTER IS ABOUT

The concepts set out in this chapter include the nature of business ethics and the relationship between ethics and business. Ultimately, the goal of this chapter is to provide you with basic tools for analyzing ethical issues in a business context.

CHAPTER OUTLINE

I. **BUSINESS ETHICS**
    Ethics is the study of what constitutes right and wrong behavior. Ethics focuses on morality and the application of moral principles in everyday life.

    A. **WHAT IS BUSINESS ETHICS?**
        Business ethics focuses on what constitutes ethical behavior in the world of business. Business ethics is *not* a separate kind of ethics.

    B. **WHY IS BUSINESS ETHICS IMPORTANT?**
        An understanding of business ethics is important to the long-run viability of a business, the well being of its officers and directors, and the welfare of its employees.

II. **SETTING THE RIGHT ETHICAL TONE**
    Some unethical conduct is founded on the lack of sanctions.

    A. **THE IMPORTANCE OF ETHICAL LEADERSHIP**
        Management must set and apply ethical standards to which they are committed. Employees will likely follow their example. Ethical conduct can be furthered by not tolerating unethical behavior, setting realistic employee goals, and periodic employee review.

    B. **CREATING ETHICAL CODES OF CONDUCT**
        Most large corporations have codes of conduct that indicate the firm's commitment to legal compliance and to the welfare of those who are affected by corporate decisions and practices. Large firms may also emphasize ethics in other ways (for example, with training programs).

    C. **CORPORATE COMPLIANCE PROGRAMS**
        Components of a comprehensive corporate ethical-compliance program include an ethical code of conduct, an ethics committee, training programs, and internal audits to monitor compliance. These components should be integrated. The Sarbanes-Oxley Act of 2002 requires firms to set up confidential systems for employees to report suspected illegal or unethical financial practices.

    D. **CONFLICTS AND TRADE-OFFS**
        A firm's duty to its shareholders should be weighed against duties to others who may have a greater stake in a particular decision. For example, an employer should consider whether it has an ethical duty to loyal, long-term employees not to replace them with workers who will accept lower pay and whether this duty prevails over a duty to improve profitability by restructuring.

III. **DEFYING THE RULES: THE ENRON CASE**
    Unethical conduct resulted in the single largest bankruptcy of a U.S. business firm.

A. THE UNETHICAL CONDUCT
Managers took advantage of accounting standards to overestimate future earnings, which resulted in inflated reports of current earnings. To maintain these exaggerations, the company created subsidiaries to which it could shift unreported losses and assets with inflated values. Many of these shifts occurred outside the U.S. to avoid federal income taxes. When questioned, management refused to investigate and reveal financial improprieties.

B. WHO WAS AFFECTED
This misconduct affected the firm's managers, employees, suppliers, and shareholders, and the community and society in general.

IV. BUSINESS ETHICS AND THE LAW
The minimal acceptable standard for ethical business behavior is compliance with the law. Ethical standards, such as those in a company's policies or codes of ethics, must also guide decisions.

A. LAWS REGULATING BUSINESS
Because there are many laws regulating business, it is possible to violate one without realizing it. Ignorance of the law is no excuse.

B. "GRAY AREAS"
There are many "gray areas" in which it is difficult to predict how a court will rule. For example, if a consumer's misuse of a product harms the consumer, should the manufacturer bear the responsibility? The best course is to act responsibly and in good faith.

C. TECHNOLOGICAL DEVELOPMENTS AND LEGAL UNCERTAINTIES
How laws apply in the context of cyberspace is not certain.

V. APPROACHES TO ETHICAL REASONING
Ethical reasoning is the process by which an individual examines a situation according to his or her moral convictions or ethical standards. Fundamental ethical reasoning approaches include the following.

A. DUTY-BASED ETHICS

1. Religious Ethical Standards
Religious standards provide that when an act is prohibited by religious teachings, it is unethical and should not be undertaken, regardless of the consequences. Religious standards also involve compassion.

2. Kantian Ethics
Immanual Kant believed that people should be respected because they are qualitatively different from other physical objects. Kant's *categorical imperative* is that individuals should evaluate their actions in light of what would happen if everyone acted the same way.

3. Principle of Rights
According to the principle that persons have rights (to life and liberty, for example), a key factor in determining whether a business decision is ethical is how that decision affects the rights of others, including employees, customers and society.

B. OUTCOME-BASED ETHICS
Utilitarianism is a belief that an action is ethical if it produces the greatest good for the greatest number. This approach is often criticized, because it tends to reduce the welfare of people to plus and minus signs on a cost-benefit worksheet.

VI. BUSINESS ETHICS ON A GLOBAL LEVEL

A. MONITORING THE EMPLOYMENT PRACTICES OF FOREIGN SUPPLIERS
Concerns include the treatment of foreign workers who make goods imported and sold in the United States by U.S. firms. Should a U.S firm refuse to deal with certain suppliers or monitor their workplaces to make sure that the workers are not being mistreated?

B. THE FOREIGN CORRUPT PRACTICES ACT
The Foreign Corrupt Practices Act (FCPA) of 1977 applies to—

1. U.S. Companies
Including their directors, officers, shareholders, employees, and agents.

a. What Is Prohibited
The FCPA prohibits the bribery of most foreign government officials to get an official to act in an official capacity to provide business opportunities.

b. What Is Permitted
The FCPA permits payments to (1) minor officials whose duties are ministerial, (2) foreign officials if the payments are lawful in the foreign country, or (3) private foreign companies or other third parties unless the U.S. firm knows payments will be made to a foreign government.

2. Accountants

a. What Is Required
All companies must (1) keep detailed records that "accurately and fairly" reflect the company's financial activities and (2) have an accounting system that provides "reasonable assurance" that all transactions are accounted for and legal.

b. What Is Prohibited
The FCPA prohibits false statements to accountants and false entries in accounts.

3. Penalties
Firms: fines up to $2 million. Officers or directors: fines up to $100,000 (cannot be paid by the company); imprisonment up to five years.

C. OTHER NATIONS
A treaty signed by members of the Organization for Economic Cooperation and Development makes the bribery of foreign officials a crime.

TRUE-FALSE QUESTIONS

(Answers at the Back of the Book)

____ 1. Ethics is the study of what constitutes right and wrong behavior.

____ 2. A background in business ethics is as important as knowledge of specific laws.

____ 3. The *minimal* acceptable standard for ethical behavior is compliance with the law.

____ 4. According to utilitarianism, it does not matter how many people benefit from an act.

____ 5. The best course towards accomplishing legal and ethical behavior is to act responsibly and in good faith.

____ 6. The ethics of a particular act is always clear.

____ 7. To foster ethical behavior among employees, managers should apply ethical standards to which they are committed.

____ 8. If an act is legal, it is ethical.

____ 9. The roles that women play in other countries can present ethical problems for U.S. firms doing business internationally.

____ 10. Bribery of public officials is only an ethical issue.

FILL-IN QUESTIONS

(Answers at the Back of the Book)

_____ (Religious standards/ Kantian ethics/ The principle of rights) provide that when an act is prohibited by religious teachings, it is unethical and should not be undertaken, regardless of the consequences. According to _____ (religious standards/ Kantian ethics/ the principle of rights), individuals should evaluate their actions in light of what would happen if everyone acted the same way. According to _____ (religious standards/ Kantian ethics/ the principle of rights), a key factor in determining whether a business decision is ethical is how that decision affects the rights of others.

MULTIPLE-CHOICE QUESTIONS

(Answers at the Back of the Book)

____   1.   Beth is a marketing executive for Consumer Goods Company. Compared to Beth's personal actions, her business actions require the application of ethical standards that are

a. more complex.
b. simpler.
c. the same.
d. none of the above.

____   2.   Pat, an employee of Quality Products, Inc., takes a duty-based approach to ethics. Pat believes that regardless of the consequences, he must

a. avoid unethical behavior.
b. conform to society's standards.
c. place his employer's interest first.
d. produce the greatest good for the most people.

____   3.   Joy adopts religious ethical standards. These involve an element of

a. compassion.
b. cost-benefit analysis.
c. discretion.
d. utilitarianism.

____   4.   Eve, an employee of Fine Sales Company, takes an outcome-based approach to ethics. Eve believes that she must

a. avoid unethical behavior.
b. conform to society's standards.
c. place her employer's interest first.
d. produce the greatest good for the most people.

____   5.   In a debate, Ed's best criticism of utilitarianism is that it

a. encourages unethical behavior.
b. fosters conformance with society's standards.
c. mandates acting in an employer's best interest.
d. results in human costs many persons find unacceptable.

_____ 6. In resolving an ethical problem, in most cases a decision by a business firm will have a negative effect on

a. one group as opposed to another.
b. the firm's competitors.
c. the government.
d. none of the above.

_____ 7. Ethical standards would most likely be considered to have been violated if Acme Services, Inc., represents to Best Production Company that certain services will be performed for a stated fee, but it is apparent at the time of the representation that

a. Acme cannot perform the services alone.
b. the actual charge will be substantially higher.
c. the actual charge will be substantially lower.
d. the fee is a competitive bid.

_____ 8. Tina, the president of United Sales, Inc., tries to ensure that United's actions are legal and ethical. To ensure this result, the best course of Tina and United is to act in

a. good faith.
b. ignorance of the law.
c. regard for the firm's shareholders only.
d. their own self interest.

_____ 9. Alan, an executive with Beta Corporation, follows the "principle of rights" theory, under which an action may be ethical depending on how it affects

a. the right determination under a cost-benefit analysis.
b. the right of Alan to maintain his dignity.
c. the right of Beta to make a profit.
d. the rights of others.

_____ 10. Gamma, Inc., a U.S. corporation, makes a side payment to the minister of commerce of another country for a favorable business contract. In the United States, this payment would be considered

a. illegal only.
b. unethical only.
c. illegal and unethical.
d. none of the above.

SHORT ESSAY QUESTIONS

What is the difference between legal and ethical standards? How are legal standards affected by ethical standards?

ISSUE SPOTTERS

(Answers at the Back of the Book)

1. If, like Robin Hood, a person robs the rich to pay the poor, does his or her benevolent intent make his or her actions ethical?

2.   Delta Tools, Inc., markets a product that under some circumstances is capable of seriously injuring consumers. Does Delta owe an ethical duty to remove this product from the market, even if the injuries result only from misuse?

3.   Acme Corporation decides to respond to what it sees as a moral obligation to correct for past discrimination by adjusting pay differences among its employees. Does this raise an ethical conflict between Acme's employees? Between Acme and its employees? Between Acme and its shareholders?

CUMULATIVE HYPOTHETICAL PROBLEM FOR UNIT ONE—INCLUDING CHAPTERS 1–4

(Answers at the Back of the Book)

Computer Data, Inc. (CDI), incorporated and based in California, signs a contract with Digital Products Corporation (DPC), incorporated and based in Arizona, to make and sell customized software for DPC to, in turn, sell to its clients. CDI ships defective software to DPC, which sells it to Eagle Distribution Corporation. The defective software causes losses to Eagle estimated at $100,000.

____   1.   Eagle and DPC enter into mediation. In mediation, the parties

a.   may come to an agreement by mutual consent.
b.   must accept a winner-take-all result.
c.   settle their dispute without the assistance of a third party.
d.   submit their dispute to a mediator for a legally binding decision.

____   2.   Eagle is located in Tennessee. Eagle could file a suit against DPC in

a.   Arizona only.
b.   Tennessee only.
c.   a federal court only.
d.   Arizona, Tennessee, or a federal court.

____   3.   Eagle files a suit against DPC, seeking the amount of its losses as damages. Damages is a remedy

a.   at law.
b.   in equity.
c.   at law or in equity, depending on how the plaintiff phrases its complaint.
d.   at law or in equity, depending on whether there was any actual "damage."

____   4.   Federal authorities file charges against CDI, alleging that the shipment of defective software violated a federal statute. CDI asks the court to exercise its power of judicial review. This means that the court can review

a.   the actions of the federal authorities and declare them excessive.
b.   the charges against CDI and declare them unfounded.
c.   the statute and declare it unconstitutional.
d.   the totality of the situation and declare it unethical.

____   5.   CDI's managers evaluate the shipment of defective software in terms of CDI's ethical obligations, if any. In other words, CDI's managers are considering the firm's

a.   legal liability.
b.   maximum profitability.
c.   optimum profitability.
d.   right or wrong behavior.

QUESTIONS ON THE FOCUS ON LEGAL REASONING FOR UNIT ONE— *PAVLOVICH V. SUPERIOR COURT*

(Answers at the Back of the Book)

_____ 1. In light of the majority's opinion in *Pavlovich v. Superior Court,* a court could most likely exercise jurisdiction over a non-resident defendant based on

a. an interactive exchange of data or a transaction of business through a Web site.
b. a posting of information on a Web site that is available to anyone.
c. a posting of information on a Web site with the intent to harm businesses in the jurisdiction.
d. a resident's visit to the non-resident's passive Web site.

_____ 2. In the dissent's opinion, a court could exercise jurisdiction over a non-resident defendant based on

a. an interactive exchange of data or a transaction of business through a Web site.
b. a posting of information on a Web site that is available to anyone.
c. a posting of information on a Web site with the intent to harm businesses in the jurisdiction.
d. a resident's visit to the non-resident's passive Web site.

_____ 3. Under the majority's holding, a plaintiff connected to

a. the computer industry could sue any defendant in California.
b. the financial industry could sue any defendant in New York.
c. the movie industry could sue a California resident in California.
d. the potato industry could sue any defendant in Idaho.

QUESTIONS ON THE FOCUS ON ETHICS FOR UNIT ONE— ETHICS AND THE LEGAL ENVIRONMENT OF BUSINESS

(Answers at the Back of the Book)

_____ 1. The managers of Standard Products Company (SPC) evaluate its sale of possibly defective goods in terms of its ethical obligations, if any. In other words, the managers are considering SPC's

a. legal liability.
b. maximum profitability.
c. optimum profitability.
d. right or wrong behavior.

_____ 2. Obstacles to ethical business behavior by SPC's managers include

a. co-workers' dissent to unethical decisions.
b. legislative determinations as to what is in society's best interest.
c. the accountability of SPC to society for the firm's actions.
d. the collectivity of corporate decision making.

_____ 3. If SPC conducts its operations ethically, there will be a likely increase in its

a. future profits, goodwill, and reputation.
b. future profits only.
c. good will only.
d. reputation only.

Chapter 5
Constitutional Law

WHAT THIS CHAPTER IS ABOUT

This chapter emphasizes that the Constitution is the supreme law in this country and discusses some of the constitutional limits on the law. Neither Congress nor any state may pass a law in conflict with the Constitution. To sustain a federal law or action, a specific federal power must be found in the Constitution. A state has inherent power to enact laws that have a reasonable relationship to the welfare of its citizens.

CHAPTER OUTLINE

I. **THE CONSTITUTIONAL POWERS OF GOVERNMENT**

   A. **FEDERAL FORM OF GOVERNMENT**
   In a federal form of government (the United States), the states form a union and sovereign power is divided between a central authority and the states.

   1. **Relation between State and Federal Powers**
   Neither the national government nor a state government is superior to the other except within areas of exclusive authority granted under the Constitution. The courts determine the nature and scope of state and federal powers.

   2. **Relations among the States**

   a. **The Privileges and Immunities Clauses**
   The Constitution (Article IV, Section 2) requires each state to provide the citizens of other states the same privileges and immunities it provides its own citizens. A state cannot treat nonresidents engaged in basic, essential activities differently without substantial justification. The Fourteenth Amendment prohibits a state from infringing on the privileges or immunities (such as the right to travel) of U.S. citizens.

   b. **The Full Faith and Credit Clause**
   The Constitution (Article IV, Section 1) requires that property and contract rights established by the law in one state be honored by other states.

   B. **THE SEPARATION OF POWERS**
   Under the Constitution, the legislative branch makes the laws, the executive branch enforces the laws, and the judicial branch interprets the laws. Each branch has some power to limit the actions of the other two.

   C. **THE COMMERCE CLAUSE**
   The Constitution (Article I, Section 8) gives Congress the power to regulate commerce among the states.

   1. **The Commerce Power Today**
   The national government can regulate every commercial enterprise in the United States. The United States Supreme Court has held, however, that this does not justify regulation of areas that have "nothing to do with commerce."

2. **The Regulatory Powers of the States**
States possess police powers (the right to regulate private activities to protect or promote the public order, health, safety, morals, and general welfare). Statutes covering almost every aspect of life have been enacted under the police powers.

3. **The "Dormant" Commerce Clause**
When state laws impinge on interstate commerce, courts balance the state's interest in regulating a certain matter against the burden on interstate commerce. State laws that *substantially* interfere with interstate commerce violate the commerce clause.

D. **THE SUPREMACY CLAUSE AND FEDERAL PREEMPTION**
The Constitution (Article IV) provides that the Constitution, laws, and treaties of the United States are the supreme law of the land. When federal and state laws are in direct conflict, the state law is rendered invalid. If Congress chooses to act exclusively in an area in which states have concurrent power, the federal law takes precedence over a state law on the same subject. It can be difficult to predict how a court will interpret congressional intent, however.

E. **THE TAXING AND SPENDING POWERS**

1. **The Taxing Power**
The Constitution (Article I, Section 8) gives Congress the power to levy taxes, but Congress may not tax some states and exempt others. Any tax that is a valid revenue-raising measure will be upheld.

2. **The Spending Power**
The Constitution (Article I, Section 8) gives Congress the power to spend the money it raises with its taxing power. This involves policy choices, with which taxpayers may disagree. Congress can spend funds to promote any objective, so long as it does not violate the Bill of Rights.

II. BUSINESS AND THE BILL OF RIGHTS
The first ten amendments to the Constitution protect individuals and businesses against some interference by the federal government. Under the due process clause of the Fourteenth Amendment, many rights also apply to the states.

A. **FREEDOM OF SPEECH**
The First Amendment guaranty of freedom of speech applies to the federal and state governments.

1. **Protected Speech**
Includes symbolic speech—nonverbal expressions, such as gestures, articles of clothing, some acts and so on. Governments can regulate the time, place, and manner of speech.

2. **Speech with Limited Protection**

a. **Commercial Speech**
A state restriction on commercial speech, such as advertising, is valid as long as it (1) seeks to implement a substantial government interest, (2) directly advances that interest, and (3) goes no further than necessary to accomplish its objective.

b. **Corporate Political Speech**
States can prohibit corporations from using corporate funds for independent expressions of opinion about political candidates.

3. **Unprotected Speech**

a. **Defamatory Speech**
Speech that harms the good reputation of another. Such speech can take the form of libel (if it is in writing) or slander (if it is oral).

    b. Lewd and Obscene Speech
    States can ban child pornography. One court has banned lewd speech and pornographic pinups in the workplace.

    c. "Fighting Words"
    Words that are likely to incite others to violence.

    d. Online Obscenity
    Attempts to regulate obscene materials on the Internet have been challenged, and some have been struck, as unconstitutional.

B. FREEDOM OF RELIGION
Under the First Amendment, the government may not establish a religion (the establishment clause) nor prohibit the exercise of religion (the free exercise clause).

    1. The Establishment Clause
    The government cannot show a preference for one religion over another, but must accommodate all religions. Sunday "closing laws" (restrictions on commercial acts on Sunday) have been upheld on the ground it is a legitimate government function to provide a day of rest.

    2. The Free Exercise Clause
    A law that infringes on the free exercise of religion in public places must be justified by a compelling state interest. Employers must reasonably accommodate the religious practices of their employees.

C. SEARCHES AND SEIZURES
Under the Fourth Amendment, law enforcement and other government officers cannot conduct unreasonable searches or seizures.

    1. Search Warrant
    An officer must obtain a search warrant before searching or seizing private property. It must describe what is to be searched or seized.

        a. Probable Cause
        To obtain a warrant, the officer must convince a judge that there is **probable cause** (evidence that would convince a reasonable person a search or seizure is justified).

        b. General and Neutral Enforcement Plan
        To obtain a warrant to inspect business premises, government inspectors must have probable cause, but the standard is different: a general and neutral enforcement plan is enough.

    2. No Search Warrant
    No warrant is required for seizures of spoiled or contaminated food or searches of businesses in highly regulated industries. General manufacturing is not considered a highly regulated industry.

D. SELF-INCRIMINATION
Under the Fifth Amendment, no person can be compelled to give testimony that might subject him or her to a criminal prosecution.

    1. Sole Proprietors
    Individuals who own their own businesses and have not incorporated cannot be compelled to produce their business records.

    2. Partnerships and Corporations
    Partnerships and corporations *can* be compelled to produce their business records, even if the records incriminate the persons who constitute the business entity.

III. DUE PROCESS AND EQUAL PROTECTION

A. DUE PROCESS

Both the Fifth and the Fourteenth Amendments provide that no person shall be deprived "of life, liberty, or property, without due process of law."

1. Procedural Due Process

Any government decision to take away the life, liberty, or property of an individual must include procedural safeguards to ensure fairness.

2. Substantive Due Process

Substantive due process focuses on the content (substance) of legislation.

a. Compelling Interest Test

A statute can restrict an individual's fundamental right (such as all First Amendment rights) only if the statute promotes a compelling or overriding governmental interest.

b. Rational Basis Test

Restrictions on business activities must relate rationally to a legitimate government purpose. Most business regulations qualify.

B. EQUAL PROTECTION

The Fourteenth Amendment prohibits a state from denying any person "the equal protection of the laws." The due process clause of the Fifth Amendment applies the equal protection clause to the federal government.

1. What Equal Protection Means

Equal protection means that the government must treat similarly situated individuals in a similar manner. If a law distinguishes among individuals, the basis for the distinction (classification) is examined.

a. Strict Scrutiny

A law that inhibits some persons' exercise of a fundamental right or a classification based on a suspect trait must be necessary to promote a compelling state interest.

b. Intermediate Scrutiny

Laws using classifications based on gender or legitimacy must be substantially related to important government objectives.

c. The "Rational Basis" Test

In matters of economic or social welfare, the classification will be considered valid if there is any conceivable rational basis on which it might relate to any legitimate government interest.

2. The Difference between Substantive Due Process and Equal Protection

A law that limits the liberty of *all* persons to do something may violate substantive due process. A law that limits the liberty of only *some* persons may violate equal protection.

C. PRIVACY RIGHTS

There is no specific guarantee of this right, but it is derived from guarantees in the First, Third, Fourth, Fifth, and Ninth Amendments. There are a number of federal statutes that protect privacy in certain areas.

TRUE-FALSE QUESTIONS

(Answers at the Back of the Book)

____ 1. A federal form of government is one in which a central authority holds all power.

____ 2. The president can hold acts of Congress and of the courts unconstitutional.

____ 3. Congress can regulate any activity that substantially affects commerce.

____ 4. A state law that substantially impinges on interstate commerce is unconstitutional.

____ 5. When there is a direct conflict between a federal law and a state law, the federal law is invalid.

____ 6. If a tax is reasonable, it is within the federal taxing power.

____ 7. The Bill of Rights protects individuals against various types of interference by the federal government only.

____ 8. Any restriction on commercial speech is unconstitutional.

____ 9. Due process and equal protection are different terms for the same thing.

____ 10. A right to privacy is not specifically guaranteed in the U.S. Constitution.

FILL-IN QUESTIONS

(Answers at the Back of the Book)

Police power is possessed by the _____ (federal government/states). Police power refers to the right of the _____ (federal government/states) to regulate private activities to protect or promote the public order, health, safety, morals, and general welfare. Building codes, licensing requirements, and many other _____ (federal/state) statutes have been enacted under the police power.

MULTIPLE-CHOICE QUESTIONS

(Answers at the Back of the Book)

____ 1. Of the three branches of the federal government provided by the Constitution, the branch that makes the laws is

a. the administrative branch.
b. the executive branch.
c. the judicial branch.
d. the legislative branch.

____ 2. Under the commerce clause, Congress can regulate

a. any commercial activity in the United States.
b. any noncommercial activity in the United States.
c. both a and b.
d. none of the above.

____ 3. A business challenges a state law in court, claiming that it unlawfully interferes with interstate commerce. The court will consider

a. only the state's interest in regulating the matter.
b. only the burden that the law places on interstate commerce.
c. the state's interest in regulating the matter and the burden that the law places on interstate commerce.
d. none of the above.

____   4.   A state statute that bans corporations from making political contributions individuals can make is likely unconstitutional under

    a.   the commerce clause.
    b.   the First Amendment.
    c.   the supremacy clause.
    d.   none of the above.

____   5.   A state statute that bans certain advertising practices to prevent consumers from being misled is likely unconstitutional under

    a.   the commerce clause.
    b.   the First Amendment.
    c.   the supremacy clause.
    d.   none of the above.

____   6.   Procedures that are used to decide whether to take life, liberty, or property are the focus of constitutional provisions covering

    a.   equal protection.
    b.   procedural due process.
    c.   substantive due process.
    d.   the right to privacy.

____   7.   A law that limits the liberty of all persons to engage in a certain activity may violate constitutional provisions covering

    a.   equal protection.
    b.   procedural due process.
    c.   substantive due process.
    d.   the right to privacy.

____   8.   A law that restricts most vendors from doing business in a heavily trafficked area might be upheld under constitutional provisions covering

    a.   equal protection.
    b.   procedural due process.
    c.   substantive due process.
    d.   the right to privacy.

____   9.   Congress enacts a law covering airports. If a state enacts a law that directly conflicts with this federal law

    a.   both laws are valid.
    b.   neither law is valid.
    c.   the federal law takes precedence.
    d.   the state law takes precedence.

____   10.   Under the First Amendment, protected speech includes

    a.   dissemination of obscene materials.
    b.   "fighting words."
    c.   speech that harms the good reputation of another.
    d.   none of the above.

SHORT ESSAY QUESTIONS

1.   What is the effect of the supremacy clause?

2.   What is the significance of the commerce clause?

ISSUE SPOTTERS

(Answers at the Back of the Book)

1.   Can a state, in the interest of energy conservation, ban all advertising by power utilities if conservation could be accomplished by less restrictive means? Why or why not?

2.   Would a state law imposing a fifteen-year term of imprisonment without allowing a trial on all businesspersons who appear in their own television commercials be a violation of substantive due process? Would it violate procedural due process?

3.   Would it be a violation of equal protection for a state to impose a higher tax on out-of-state companies doing business in the state than it imposes on in-state companies if the only reason for the tax is to protect the local firms from out-of-state competition?

Chapter 6
Administrative Law

WHAT THIS CHAPTER IS ABOUT

Federal, state, and local administrative agencies regulate virtually every aspect of a business's operation. Agencies' rules, orders, and decisions make up the body of administrative law. How agencies function is the subject of this chapter.

CHAPTER OUTLINE

I. AGENCY CREATION AND POWERS
Congress delegates some of its authority to make and implement laws, particularly in highly technical areas, to administrative agencies.

A. ENABLING LEGISLATION
To create an agency, Congress passes enabling legislation, which specifies the powers of the agency.

B. TYPES OF AGENCIES

1. Executive Agencies
Includes cabinet departments and their subagencies. Subject to the authority of the president, who can appoint and remove their officers.

2. Independent Regulatory Agencies
Includes agencies outside the major executive departments. Their officers serve for fixed terms and cannot be removed without just cause.

C. AGENCY POWERS AND THE CONSTITUTION
Agency powers include functions associated with the legislature (rulemaking), executive branch (enforcement), and courts (adjudication). Under Article I of the Constitution and the delegation doctrine, Congress has the power to establish agencies to create rules for implementing laws.

II. ADMINISTRATIVE PROCESS
Rulemaking, investigation, and adjudication make up the administrative process. The Administrative Procedure Act (APA) of 1946 imposes procedural requirements that agencies must follow.

A. RULEMAKING
Rulemaking is the formulation of new regulations. Legislative rules, or substantive rules, are as legally binding as the laws that Congress makes. Interpretive rules are not binding but indicate how an agency will apply a certain statute.

1. Notice of the Proposed Rulemaking
An agency begins by publishing, in the *Federal Register*, a notice that states where and when proceedings will be held, terms or subject matter of the proposed rule, and the agency's authority for making the rule.

2. Comment Period
Interested parties can express their views. An agency must respond to significant comments by modifying the final rule or explaining, in a statement accompanying the final rule, why it did not.

3. The Final Rule
The agency publishes the final rule in the *Federal Register*. The final rule has binding legal effect unless overturned by a court.

B. INVESTIGATION
Agencies must have knowledge of facts and circumstances pertinent to proposed rules. Agencies must also obtain information and investigate conduct to ascertain whether its rules are being violated.

1. Inspections and Tests
Through on-site inspections and testing, agencies gather information to prove a regulatory violation or to correct or prevent a bad condition.

2. Subpoenas
A subpoena *ad testificandum* is an order to a witness to appear at a hearing. A subpoena *duces tecum* is an order to a party to hand over records or other documents. Limits on agency demands for information through these subpoenas, and otherwise, include—

a. An investigation must have a legitimate purpose.

b. The information that is sought must be relevant.

c. Demands must be specific.

d. The party from whom the information is sought must not be unduly burdened by the request.

3. Search Warrants
A search warrant directs an officer to search a specific place for a specific item and present it to the agency.

a. Fourth Amendment
The Fourth Amendment protects against unreasonable searches and seizures by requiring that in most instances a physical search must be conducted under the authority of a search warrant.

b. Warrantless Searches
Warrants are not required to conduct searches in businesses in highly regulated industries, in certain hazardous operations, and in emergencies.

C. ADJUDICATION
Adjudication involves the resolution of disputes by an agency.

1. Negotiated Settlements
The purpose of negotiation is (1) for agencies: to eliminate the need for further proceedings and (2) for parties subject to regulation: to avoid publicity and the expense of litigation.

2. Formal Complaints
If there is no settlement, the agency may issue a formal complaint. The party charged in the complaint may respond with an answer. The case may go before an administrative law judge (ALJ).

3. The Role of an Administrative Law Judge (ALJ)
The ALJ presides over the hearing. The ALJ has the power to administer oaths, take testimony, rule on questions of evidence, and make determinations of fact. An ALJ works for the agency, but must be unbiased. Certain safeguards in the APA prevent bias and promote fairness.

4. Hearing Procedures
Procedures vary widely from agency to agency. Agencies exercise substantial discretion over the type of procedures used. A formal hearing resembles a trial, but more items and testimony are admissible in an administrative hearing.

5. **Agency Orders**
   After a hearing, the ALJ issues an initial order. Either side may appeal to the commission that governs the agency and ultimately to a federal appeals court. If there is no appeal or review, the initial order becomes final.

III. LIMITATIONS ON AGENCY POWERS
Because of the concentration of so much authority in administrative agencies, the three branches of the government exercise control over agency powers.

A. JUDICIAL CONTROLS
The APA provides for judicial review of most agency decisions.

1. **Requirements for Judicial Review**

   a. The action must be reviewable (under the APA, agency actions are presumed reviewable).

   b. Under the ripeness doctrine, the case must be "ripe for review," which requires—

      1) The party must have standing (a direct stake in the outcome).

      2) The party must have exhausted all administrative remedies.

      3) An actual controversy must be at issue.

2. **Scope of Review**
   In most cases, a court defers to the facts as found in an agency proceeding. A court will review whether an agency has —

   a. Exceeded its authority under its enabling legislation.

   b. Improperly interpreted laws applicable to the action under review.

   c. Violated any constitutional provisions.

   d. Failed to act in accord with procedural requirements.

   e. Taken actions that were arbitrary, capricious, or an abuse of discretion. (Actions taken willfully, unreasonably, and without considering the facts violate the "arbitrary and capricious" test.)

   f. Reached conclusions not supported by substantial evidence.

B. EXECUTIVE CONTROLS
The president may veto enabling legislation or subsequent modifications to agency authority that Congress seeks to enact. The president appoints and removes many federal officers, including those in charge of agencies.

C. LEGISLATIVE CONTROLS
Congress can give power to an agency, take power away, reduce or increase agency finances, abolish an agency, investigate the implementation of the laws, investigate agencies, and affect policy through individual legislators' attempts to help their constituents deal with agencies.

IV. PUBLIC ACCOUNTABILITY

A. FREEDOM OF INFORMATION ACT (FOIA) OF 1966
The federal government must disclose certain records to any person on request. A failure to comply may be challenged in federal district court.

B. GOVERNMENT-IN-THE-SUNSHINE ACT OF 1976
Requires (1) that "every portion of every meeting of an agency" that is headed by a "collegial body" is open to "public observation" and (2) procedures to ensure that the public is provided with adequate advance notice of meetings and agendas (with exceptions).

C. REGULATORY FLEXIBILITY ACT OF 1980
Whenever a new regulation will have a "significant impact upon a substantial number of small entities," the agency must conduct a regulatory flexibility analysis. The analysis must measure the cost imposed by the rule on small businesses and must consider less burdensome alternatives.

D. SMALL BUSINESS REGULATORY ENFORCEMENT FAIRNESS ACT
Under this act, passed in 1996—

1. **Congress Reviews New Federal Regulations**
Congress reviews new regulations for at least sixty days before they take effect. Opponents have time to present arguments to Congress.

2. **Agencies Must Issue "Plain English" Guides**
Agencies must prepare guides that explain how small businesses can comply with their regulations.

3. **Regional Boards Rate Federal Agencies**
The National Enforcement Ombudsman receives comments from small businesses about agencies. Based on the comments, Regional Small Business Fairness Boards rate the agencies.

4. **Small Businesses May Recover Expenses and Fees**
Small businesses may recover expenses and legal fees from the government if an agency makes excessive demands for fines or penalties.

V. STATE ADMINISTRATIVE AGENCIES
A state agency often parallels a federal agency, providing similar services on a local basis. The supremacy clause requires that the federal agency's operation prevail over an inconsistent state agency's action. State court judicial review of state agency decisions parallels federal court review of federal agency decisions.

TRUE-FALSE QUESTIONS

(Answers at the Back of the Book)

1. Enabling legislation specifies the powers of an agency.

2. Most federal agencies are part of the executive branch of government.

3. To create an agency, Congress enacts enabling legislation.

4. Agency rules are not as legally binding as the laws that Congress enacts.

5. After an agency adjudication, the administrative law judge's order must be appealed to become final.

6. Congress has no power to influence agency policy.

7. The Administrative Procedure Act provides for judicial review of most agency actions.

8. When a new regulation will have a significant impact on a substantial number of small entities, an analysis must be conducted to measure the cost imposed on small businesses.

9. State administrative agency operations prevail over federal agency actions.

10. An agency cannot conduct a search without a warrant.

FILL-IN QUESTIONS

(Answers at the Back of the Book)

The rulemaking process begins with the publication in the _____ (*Congressional Record/Federal Register*) of a notice of the proposed rulemaking. The agency may conduct a public hearing at which it presents evidence to justify the proposed rule, and _____ (anyone/no one) may present opposing evidence. The agency _____ (must/need not) respond to significant comments. After the hearing, the agency publishes the final draft of the rule in the _____ (*Congressional Record/Federal Register*).

MULTIPLE-CHOICE QUESTIONS

(Answers at the Back of the Book)

____ 1. Ann, a congressperson, believes a new federal agency is needed to perform a certain function. Congress has the power to establish an agency to

   a. adjudicate disputes arising from rules only.
   b. make rules only.
   c. adjudicate disputes arising from rules and make rules.
   d. none of the above.

____ 2. Like other federal agencies, the Securities and Exchange Commission may obtain information concerning activities and organizations that it oversees by compelling disclosure through

   a. a search only.
   b. a subpoena only.
   c. a search or a subpoena.
   d. neither a search nor a subpoena.

____ 3. In making rules, the procedures of the Equal Employment Opportunity Commission and other federal agencies normally includes

   a. notice and opportunity for comments by interested parties only.
   b. publication of the final draft of the rule only.
   c. notice and opportunity for comments by interested parties, and publication of the final draft of the rule.
   d. none of the above.

____ 4. The Occupational Safety and Health Administration (OSHA) issues a subpoena for Alpha Corporation to hand over its files. Alpha's possible defenses against the subpoena include

   a. OSHA cannot issue a subpoena.
   b. OSHA is a federal agency, but Alpha only does business locally.
   c. OSHA's request is not specific enough.
   d. OSHA's request violates Alpha's right to privacy.

____ 5. The National Oceanic and Atmospheric Administration (NOAA) is a federal agency. To limit the authority of NOAA, the president can

   a. abolish NOAA.
   b. take away NOAA's power.
   c. refuse to appropriate funds to NOAA.
   d. veto legislative modifications to NOAA's authority.

____   6.   The Federal Energy Regulatory Commission (FERC) wants to close a series of its meetings to the public. To open the meetings, a citizen could sue the FERC under

   a.   the Freedom of Information Act.
   b.   the Government-in-the-Sunshine Act.
   c.   the Regulatory Flexibility Act.
   d.   the Small Business Regulatory Enforcement Fairness Act.

____   7.   The U.S. Fish and Wildlife Service orders Ed to stop using a certain type of fishing net from his boat. To appeal this order to a court, Ed must

   a.   appeal simultaneously to the agency and the court.
   b.   bypass all administrative remedies and appeal directly to the court.
   c.   exhaust all administrative remedies.
   d.   ignore the agency and continue using the net.

____   8.   The Federal Trade Commission (FTC) issues an order relating to the advertising of Great Sales, Inc. Great Sales appeals the order to a court. The court may review whether the FTC's action is

   a.   arbitrary, capricious, or an abuse of discretion.
   b.   discourteous, disrespectful, or dissatisfying to one or more parties.
   c.   flippant, wanton, or in disregard of social norms.
   d.   impious, non-utilitarian, or in violation of ethical precepts.

____   9.   The Environmental Protection Agency (EPA) publishes notice of a proposed rule. When comments are received about the rule, the EPA must respond to

   a.   all of the comments.
   b.   any significant comments that bear directly on the proposed rule.
   c.   only comments by businesses engaged in interstate commerce.
   d.   only comments by businesses that will be affected by the rule.

____   10.   Mary is an administrative law judge (ALJ) for the National Labor Relations Board. In hearing a case, Mary has the authority to make

   a.   decisions binding on the federal courts.
   b.   determinations of fact.
   c.   new laws.
   d.   new rules.

SHORT ESSAY QUESTIONS

1.   What are the conditions to judicial review of an agency enforcement action?

2.   How does Congress hold agency authority in check?

ISSUE SPOTTERS

(Answers at the Back of the Book)

1.   The Securities and Exchange Commission (SEC) makes rules regarding what disclosures must be made in a stock prospectus, prosecutes and adjudicates alleged violations, and prescribes punishment. This gives the SEC considerable power. What checks are there against this power?

2.   The U.S. Department of Transportation (DOT) sometimes hears an appeal from a party whose contract with the DOT is canceled. An administrative law judge (ALJ), who works for the DOT, hears this appeal. What safeguards promote the ALJ's fairness?

3.   The U.S. Department of Justice holds formal hearings concerning the deportation and exclusion of immigrants. How do such formal hearings resemble a trial? How are they different?

Chapter 7
Criminal Law and Cyber Crimes

WHAT THIS CHAPTER IS ABOUT

This chapter defines what makes an act a crime, describes crimes, lists defenses to crimes, and outlines criminal procedure. Sanctions for crimes are different from those for torts or breaches of contract. Another difference between civil and criminal law is that individuals can bring civil suits but only the government can prosecute criminals.

CHAPTER OUTLINE

I.   CIVIL LAW AND CRIMINAL LAW

A. CIVIL LAW
Civil law consists of the duties that exist between persons or between citizens and their governments, excluding the duty not to commit crimes.

B. CRIMINAL LAW
A crime is a wrong against society proclaimed in a statute and, if committed, punishable by society through fines, imprisonment, or death. Crimes are offenses against society as a whole (some torts are also crimes) and are prosecuted by public officials, not victims. In a criminal trial, the state must prove its case beyond a reasonable doubt.

II. CLASSIFICATION OF CRIMES
Felonies are serious crimes punishable by death or by imprisonment in a federal or state penitentiary for more than a year. A crime that is not a felony is a misdemeanor—punishable by a fine or by confinement (in a local jail) for up to a year. Petty offenses are minor misdemeanors.

III. THE ESSENTIALS OF CRIMINAL LIABILITY
Two elements must exist for a person to be convicted of a crime:

A. THE CRIMINAL ACT (*ACTUS REUS*)
A criminal statute prohibits certain behavior—an act of commission (doing something) or an act of omission (not doing something that is a legal duty).

B. STATE OF MIND (INTENT TO COMMIT A CRIME, OR *MENS REA*)
The mental state required to establish criminal guilt depends on the crime.

IV. CORPORATE CRIMINAL LIABILITY
Corporations are liable for (1) crimes committed by their agents and employees within the course and scope of employment, (2) failing to perform a specific affirmative duty imposed by law, or (3) crimes authorized, commanded, committed, or recklessly tolerated by a firm's high managerial agents. Directors and officers are personally liable for crimes they commit and may be liable for the actions of employees under their supervision.

V.   TYPES OF CRIMES

A. VIOLENT CRIME
These include murder, rape, assault and battery (see Chapter 12), and *robbery* (forcefully and unlawfully taking personal property from another). Classified by degree, depending on intent, weapon, and victim's suffering.

B. PROPERTY CRIME

Robbery could also be in this category.

1. **Burglary**

   Unlawful entry into a building with the intent to commit a felony.

2. **Larceny**

   Wrongfully taking and carrying away another's personal property with the intent of depriving the owner permanently of the property (without force or intimidation, which are elements of robbery).

   a. **Property**

      Property includes computer programs, computer time, trade secrets, cellular phone numbers, long-distance phone time, and natural gas.

   b. **Grand Larceny and Petit Larceny**

      In some states, grand larceny is a felony and petit larceny a misdemeanor. The difference depends on the value of the property taken.

3. **Arson**

   The willful and malicious burning, by fire or explosion, of a building (and in some states, personal property) owned by another. Every state has a statute that covers burning a building to collect insurance.

4. **Receiving Stolen Goods**

   The recipient need not know the identity of the true owner of the goods.

5. **Forgery**

   Fraudulently making or altering any writing in a way that changes the legal rights and liabilities of another.

6. **Obtaining Goods by False Pretenses**

   Obtaining goods through fraud or deceit.

C. PUBLIC ORDER CRIME

Examples: public drunkenness, prostitution, gambling, and illegal drug use.

D. WHITE-COLLAR CRIME

1. **Embezzlement**

   Fraudulently appropriating another's property or money by one who has been entrusted with it (without force or intimidation).

2. **Mail and Wire Fraud**

   a. **The Crime**

      It is a federal crime to (1) mail or cause someone else to mail something written, printed, or photocopied for the purpose of executing (2) a scheme to defraud (even if no one is defrauded). Also a crime to use wire, radio, or television transmissions to defraud.

   b. **The Punishment**

      Fine of up to $1,000, imprisonment for up to five years, or both. If the violation affects a financial institution, the fine may be up to $1 million, the imprisonment up to thirty years, or both.

3. **Bribery**

   a. **Bribery of Public Officials**

      Attempting to influence a public official to act in a way that serves a private interest by offering the official a bribe. Committed when the bribe (anything the recipient considers valuable) is offered.

  b. Commercial Bribery
   Attempting, by a bribe, to obtain proprietary information, cover up an inferior product, or secure new business.

  c. Bribery of Foreign Officials
   Attempting, by bribing foreign officials, to obtain business contracts. Banned by the Foreign Corrupt Practices Act of 1977 (see Chapter 4).

 4. Bankruptcy Fraud
  Filing a false claim against a debtor; fraudulently transferring assets to favored parties; or fraudulently concealing property before or after a petition for bankruptcy is filed.

 5. Insider Trading
  Using inside information (information not available to the general public) about a publicly traded corporation to profit from the purchase or sale of the corporation's securities (see Chapter 28).

 6. Theft of Trade Secrets
  Under the Economic Espionage Act of 1996, it is a federal crime to steal trade secrets, or to knowingly buy or possess another's stolen secrets. Penalties include up to ten years' imprisonment, fines up to $500,000 (individual) or $5 million (corporation), and forfeiture of property.

E. ORGANIZED CRIME

 1. Money Laundering
  Transferring the proceeds of crime through legitimate businesses. Financial institutions must report transactions of more than $10,000.

 2. RICO
  Two offenses under the Racketeer Influenced and Corrupt Organizations Act (RICO) of 1970 constitutes "racketeering activity."

  a. Activities Prohibited by RICO
   (1) Use income from racketeering to buy an interest in an enterprise, (2) acquire or maintain such an interest through racketeering activity' (3) conduct or participate in an enterprise through racketeering activity, or 4) conspire to do any of the above.

  b. Civil Liability
   Civil penalties include divestiture of a defendant's interest in a business or dissolution of the business. Private individuals can recover treble damages, plus attorneys' fees, for business injuries.

  c. Criminal Liability
   RICO can be used to attack white-collar crime. Penalties include fines of up to $25,000 per violation, imprisonment for up to 20 years, or both.

VI. DEFENSES TO CRIMINAL LIABILITY

A. INFANCY
 Cases involving persons who have not reached the age of majority are handled in juvenile courts. In some states, a child over a certain age (usually fourteen) and charged with a felony may be tried in an adult court.

B. INTOXICATION
 Involuntary intoxication is a defense to a crime if it makes a person incapable of understanding that the act committed was wrong or incapable of obeying the law. *Voluntary* intoxication may be a defense if the person was so intoxicated as to lack the required state of mind.

C. INSANITY

1. **The *M'Naughten* Test**

   Some states use this test: a person is not responsible if at the time of the offense, he or she did not know the nature and quality of the act or did not know that the act was wrong.

2. **The Irresistible Impulse Test**

   Some states use this test: a person operating under an irresistible impulse may know an act is wrong but cannot refrain from doing it.

3. **The Model Penal Code Test**

   Most federal courts and some states use this test: a person is not responsible for criminal conduct if at the time, as a result of mental disease or defect, the person lacks substantial capacity either to appreciate the wrongfulness of the conduct or to conform his or her conduct to the law.

D. **MISTAKE**

1. **Mistake of Fact**

   Defense if it negates the mental state necessary to commit a crime.

2. **Mistake of Law**

   A person not knowing a law was broken may have a defense if (1) the law was not published or reasonably made known to the public or (2) the person relied on an official statement of the law that was wrong.

E. **CONSENT**

Defense if it cancels the harm that the law is designed to prevent, unless the law forbids an act without regard to the victim's consent. Normally applies only cases involving property crimes.

F. **DURESS**

1. **What Duress Is**

   When a person's threat induces another person to perform an act that he or she would not otherwise perform.

2. **When Duress Is a Defense**

   (1) The threat is one of serious bodily harm, (2) the threat is immediate and inescapable, (3) the threatened harm is greater than the harm caused by the crime, (4) the defendant is involved through no fault of his or her own, and (5) the crime is not murder.

G. **JUSTIFIABLE USE OF FORCE**

1. **Nondeadly Force**

   People can use as much nondeadly force as seems necessary to protect themselves, their dwellings, or other property or to prevent a crime.

2. **Deadly Force**

   Can be used in self-defense if there is a reasonable belief that imminent death or serious bodily harm will otherwise result, if the attacker is using unlawful force, and if the defender did not provoke the attack.

H. **NECESSITY**

A defendant may be relieved of liability if his or her criminal act was necessary to prevent an even greater harm.

I. **ENTRAPMENT**

When a law enforcement agent suggests that a crime be committed, pressures or induces an individual to commit it, and arrests the individual for it.

J. **STATUTE OF LIMITATIONS**

Provides that the state has only a certain amount of time to prosecute a crime. Most statutes of limitations do not apply to murder.

K. IMMUNITY

A state can grant immunity from prosecution or agree to prosecute for a less serious offense in exchange for information. This is often part of a plea bargain between the defendant and the prosecutor.

VII. CRIMINAL PROCEDURES

A. CONSTITUTIONAL SAFEGUARDS

Most of these safeguards apply not only in federal but also in state courts by virtue of the due process clause of the Fourteenth Amendment.

1. Fourth Amendment

Protection from unreasonable searches and seizures. No warrants for a search or an arrest can be issued without probable cause.

2. Fifth Amendment

No one can be deprived of "life, liberty, or property without due process of law." No one can be tried twice (double jeopardy) for the same offense. No one can be required to incriminate himself or herself.

3. Sixth Amendment

Guarantees a speedy trial, trial by jury, a public trial, the right to confront witnesses, and the right to a lawyer in some proceedings.

4. Eighth Amendment

Prohibits excessive bail and fines, and cruel and unusual punishment.

B. THE EXCLUSIONARY RULE

Evidence obtained in violation of the Fourth, Fifth, and Sixth Amendments, as well as all "fruit of the poisonous tree" (evidence derived from illegally obtained evidence), must be excluded.

C. THE *MIRANDA* RULE

1. Rights

A person in custody to be interrogated must be informed (1) he or she has the right to remain silent, (2) anything said can and will be used against him or her in court, (3) he or she has the right to consult with an attorney, and (4) if he or she is indigent, a lawyer will be appointed.

2. Exceptions

Rights can be waived. "Public safety" may warrant admissibility. If other evidence justifies a conviction, it will not be overturned if confession was coerced. A suspect must assertively state that he or she wants a lawyer, to exercise the right.

D. CRIMINAL PROCESS

1. Arrest

Requires a warrant based on probable cause (a substantial likelihood that the person has committed or is about to commit a crime). To make an arrest without a warrant, an officer must also have probable cause.

2. Indictment or Information

A formal charge is called an indictment if issued by a grand jury and an information if issued by a public prosecutor.

3. Trial

Criminal trial procedures are similar to those of a civil trial, but the standard of proof is higher: the prosecutor must establish guilt beyond a reasonable doubt.

4. Federal Sentencing Guidelines
Possible penalties for federal crimes. Sentence is based on a defendant's criminal record, seriousness of the offense, and other factors.

VIII. CYBER CRIME

A. CYBER THEFT
Computers make it possible for employees, and others, to commit crimes (such as fraud) involving serious financial losses. The Internet has made identity theft and crimes committed with stolen identities easier.

B. CYBER STALKING
Harassing a person in cyberspace (such as via e-mail). Prohibited by federal law and most states. Some states require a "credible threat" that puts the person in reasonable fear for his or her safety or the safety of the person's family.

C. HACKING
Using one computer to break into another. Often part of cyber theft.

D. CYBER TERRORISM
Exploiting computers for such serious impacts as the exploding of a "bomb" to shut down a central computer.

E. PROSECUTING CYBER CRIMES
Jurisdictional issues and the anonymous nature of technology can hinder the investigation and prosecution of crimes committed in cyberspace.

1. The Computer Fraud and Abuse Act
The Computer Access Device and Computer Fraud and Abuse Act of 1984 provides for criminal prosecution of a person who accesses a computer online, without authority, to obtain classified, restricted, or protected data (restricted government info, financial records, etc.), or attempts to do. Penalties include fines and up to five years' imprisonment.

2. Other Federal Statutes
Electronic Fund Transfer Act of 1978, Anticounterfeiting Consumer Protection Act of 1996, National Stolen Property Act of 1988, and more.

TRUE-FALSE QUESTIONS

(Answers at the Back of the Book)

_____ 1.   Only the government prosecutes criminal defendants.

_____ 2.   A crime punishable by imprisonment is a felony.

_____ 3.   Burglary involves taking another's personal property from his or her person or immediate presence.

_____ 4.   Embezzlement requires physically taking property for another's possession.

_____ 5.   Stealing a computer program is larceny.

_____ 6.   Offering a bribe is only one element of the crime of bribery.

_____ 7.   Receiving stolen goods is a crime only if the recipient knows the true owner.

_____ 8.   Generally, a person is not responsible for a criminal act if, as a result of a mental defect, he or she lacked substantial capacity to appreciate the wrongfulness of the act or to conform the conduct to the law.

____ **9.** A person who accesses a computer online, without authorization, to obtain protected data commits a federal crime.

____ **10.** RICO is often used to prosecute acts classified as white-collar crimes.

FILL-IN QUESTIONS

(Answers at the Back of the Book)

Specific constitutional safeguards for those accused of crimes apply in all federal courts, and most of them also apply in state courts under the due process clause of the Fourteenth Amendment. The safeguards include (1) the Fourth Amendment protection from _____ (unexpected/unreasonable) searches and seizures, (2) the Fourth Amendment requirement that no warrants for a search or an arrest can be issued without _____ (probable/possible) cause, (3) the Fifth Amendment requirement that no one can be deprived of "life, liberty, or property without _____ (consent/due process of law)," (4) the Fifth Amendment prohibition against double _____ (immunity/jeopardy), (5) the Sixth Amendment guaranties of a speedy _____ (appeal/trial), _____ _____ (appeal to/trial by) a jury, a public trial, the right to confront _____ (counsel/witnesses), and the right to legal counsel, and (6) the Eighth Amendment prohibitions against excessive _____(bail/bail and fines) and cruel and unusual punishment.

MULTIPLE-CHOICE QUESTIONS

(Answers at the Back of the Book)

____ **1.** Carl wrongfully takes a box from a Delta, Inc., shipping container, puts it in his truck, and drives away. This is

a. burglary.
b. embezzlement.
c. forgery.
d. larceny.

____ **2.** Nora is charged with the commission of a crime. For a conviction, most crimes require

a. only a specified state of mind or intent on the part of the actor.
b. only the performance of a prohibited act.
c. a specified state of mind and performance of a prohibited act.
d. none of the above.

____ **3.** Adam signs Beth's name, without her consent, to the back of a check payable to Beth. This is

a. burglary.
b. embezzlement.
c. forgery.
d. larceny.

____ **4.** Owen, a bank teller, deposits into his account checks that bank customers give to him to deposit into their accounts. This is

a. burglary.
b. embezzlement.
c. forgery.
d. larceny.

_____ 5. Jay is charged with the commission of a crime. For a conviction, Jay must be found guilty beyond

    a. a clear and convincing doubt.
    b. all doubt.
    c. a preponderance of doubt.
    d. a reasonable doubt.

_____ 6. Nick is charged with the crime of mail fraud. For a conviction, Nick must be found to have

    a. had a scheme to defraud.
    b. used the mails.
    c. had a scheme to defraud and used the mails.
    d. none of the above.

_____ 7. Sue, a government agent, arrests Tim for the commission of a crime. Tim claims that Sue entrapped him. This is a valid defense if Sue

    a. did not tell Tim that she was a government agent.
    b. pressured Tim into committing the crime.
    c. set a trap for Tim, who was looking to commit the crime.
    d. was predisposed to commit the crime.

_____ 8. John is arrested on suspicion of the commission of a crime. Individuals who are arrested must be told of their right to

    a. confront witnesses.
    b. protection against unreasonable searches.
    c. remain silent.
    d. trial by jury.

_____ 9. While away from her business, Kate is arrested on suspicion of commission of a crime. At Kate's trial, under the exclusionary rule

    a. biased individuals must be excluded from the jury.
    b. business records must be excluded from admission as evidence.
    c. illegally obtained evidence must be excluded from admission as evidence.
    d. the arresting officer must be excluded from testifying.

_____ 10. Eve is arrested on suspicion of commission of a crime. A grand jury issues a formal charge against her. This is

    a. an arraignment.
    b. an indictment.
    c. an information.
    d. an inquisition.

SHORT ESSAY QUESTIONS

1. What are some of the significant differences between criminal law and civil law?

2. What constitutes criminal liability under the Racketeer Influenced and Corrupt Organizations Act (RICO) of 1968 and what are the penalties?

ISSUE SPOTTERS

(Answers at the Back of the Book)

1. Bob drives off in Fred's car mistakenly believing that it is his. Is this theft?

2. Ellen takes her roommate's credit card, intending to charge expenses that she incurs on a vacation. Her first stop is a gas station, where she uses the card to pay for gas. With respect to the gas station, has she committed a crime? If so, what is it?

3. Ben downloads consumer credit files from a computer of Consumer Credit Agency, without permission, over the Internet. Ben sells the data to Donna. Has Ben committed a crime? If so, what is it?

Chapter 8
International and Comparative Law

WHAT THIS CHAPTER IS ABOUT

This chapter notes sources of international law, some of the ways in which U.S. businesspersons do business in foreign countries, and how that business is regulated. This chapter also compares the legal systems of various nations and specific legal concepts and principles related to contracts, torts, and employment relationships.

CHAPTER OUTLINE

I. **INTERNATIONAL LAW**
To facilitate commerce, sovereign nations agree to be governed in certain respects by international law.

A. **SOURCES OF INTERNATIONAL LAW**

1. **International Customs**
These are customs that evolved among nations in their relations with each other. "[E]vidence of a general practice accepted as law" [Article 38(1) of the Statute of the International Court of Justice].

2. **Treaties and International Agreements**
A treaty is an agreement or contract between two or more nations that must be authorized and ratified by the supreme power of each nation. A bilateral agreement occurs when only two nations form an agreement; multilateral agreements are those formed by several nations.

3. **International Organizations and Conferences**
Composed mainly of nations (such as the United Nations); usually established by treaty; such entities adopt resolutions that require particular behavior of nations (such as the 1980 United Nations Convention on Contracts for the International Sale of Goods).

B. **LEGAL PRINCIPLES AND DOCTRINES**
The following are based on courtesy and respect and are applied in the interest of maintaining harmony among nations.

1. **The Principle of Comity**
One nation defers and gives effect to the laws and judicial decrees of another country, so long as those laws and judicial decrees are consistent with the law and public policy of the accommodating nation.

2. **The Act of State Doctrine**
A doctrine under which the judicial branch of one country will not examine the validity of public acts committed by a recognized foreign government within its own territory. Often used in cases involving—

a. **Expropriation**
This occurs when a government seizes a privately owned business or goods for a proper public purpose and pays just compensation.

b. **Confiscation**
This occurs when a government seizes private property for an illegal purpose or without just compensation.

3. **The Doctrine of Sovereign Immunity**
   Exempts foreign nations from the jurisdiction of domestic courts. In the United States, the Foreign Sovereign Immunities Act (FSIA) of 1976 exclusively governs the circumstances in which an action may be brought against a foreign nation.

   a. **When Is a Foreign State Subject to U.S. Jurisdiction?**
      When it has waived its immunity, or when the action is based on commercial activity in the U.S. by the foreign state [Section 1605].

   b. **What Entities Fall within the Category of Foreign State?**
      A political subdivision and an instrumentality (an agency or entity acting for the state) [Section 1603].

   c. **What Is a Commercial Activity?**
      Courts decide whether an activity is governmental or commercial.

II. DOING BUSINESS INTERNATIONALLY

A. INTERNATIONAL BUSINESS OPERATIONS

1. **Exporting**
   The simplest way to do business internationally is to export to foreign markets. *Direct exporting*: signing a sales contract with a foreign buyer. *Indirect exporting*: selling directly to consumers through a foreign agent or foreign distributor.

2. **Manufacturing Abroad**
   A domestic firm can establish a manufacturing plant abroad by—

   a. **Licensing**
      A firm may license its technology to a foreign manufacturer to avoid the process, product, or formula being pirated. The foreign firm agrees to keep the technology secret and to pay royalties for its use.

   b. **Franchising**
      Franchising (see Chapter 16) is a form of licensing in which the owner of a trademark, trade name, or copyright conditions its use in the selling of goods or services.

   c. **Investing in a Wholly Owned Subsidiary or a Joint Venture**
      When a wholly owned subsidiary is established, the domestic firm retains ownership of the foreign facilities and control over the entire operation. In a joint venture, a domestic firm and one or more foreign firms share responsibilities, profits, and liabilities.

B. REGULATION OF INTERNATIONAL BUSINESS ACTIVITIES

1. **Investing**
   For property confiscated by a government without just compensation, few remedies are available. Many countries guarantee compensation to foreign investors in their constitutions, statutes, or treaties. Some countries provide insurance for their citizens' investments abroad.

2. **Export Control**

   a. **Restricting Exports**
      Under the Constitution, Congress cannot tax exports, but may set quotas. Under the Export Administration Act of 1979, restrictions can be imposed on the flow of technologically advanced products and technical data.

   b. **Stimulating Exports**
      Devices to stimulate exports include incentives and subsidies.

3. **Import Control**

Laws prohibit, for example, importing illegal drugs and agricultural products that pose dangers to domestic crops or animals.

a. **Quotas and Tariffs**

Quotas limit how much can be imported. Tariffs are taxes on imports (a percentage of the value or a flat rate per unit).

b. **Antidumping Duties**

A tariff (duty) may be assessed on imports to prevent dumping (sales of imported goods at "less than fair value," usually determined by prices in the exporting country).

4. **International Organizations and Agreements**

a. **World Trade Organization (WTO)**

This the principal instrument for regulating international trade. Each member country agrees to grant *most-favored-nation status* to other members (the most favorable treatment with regard to trade).

b. **European Union (EU)**

The EU is a regional trade association that minimizes trade barriers among its European member nations.

c. **North American Free Trade Agreement (NAFTA)**

NAFTA created a regional trading unit consisting of Mexico, the United States, and Canada. The goal is to eliminate tariffs in the region on substantially all goods over a period of fifteen to twenty years, while retaining tariffs on goods imported from other countries.

III. COMPARATIVE LAW

Comparative law is the study of legal systems and laws across nations.

A. COMPARATIVE LEGAL SYSTEMS

1. **Common Law and Civil Law Systems**

Legal systems are generally divided into common law and civil law systems.

a. **Common Law Systems**

Common law systems are based on case law. These systems exist in countries that were once a part of the British Empire (such as Australia, India, and the United States). The judges of different common law nations have produced differing common law principles.

b. **Civil Law Systems**

Civil law systems are based on codified law (statutes). Courts interpret the code and apply the rules without developing their own laws. Civil law systems exist in most European nations, in Latin American, African, and Asian countries that were colonies of those nations; Japan; South Africa; Muslim countries; and Louisiana.

c. **Similarities between Common and Civil Law Systems**

Much of the law in a common law system is statutory. In a civil law system, judges must develop some law because codes cannot address every issue.

d. **Differences among Common Law Systems**

The judges of different common law nations have produced differing common law principles. For example, the principles governing contracts differ in the United States and India.

e. **Differences among Civil Law Systems**
The French code sets out general principles of law; the German code is more specific. In some Middle Eastern countries, the code is grounded in religious, Islamic directives, known as *shari'a*. This makes it difficult to change.

B. JUDGES AND PROCEDURES
In all countries, the primary function of judges is the resolution of litigation.

1. Differences among Judges
In the United States, a judge normally does not actively participate in a trial, but in many countries, judges are involved, such as by questioning witnesses. In the United States, a federal judge is less likely to be influenced by politics (he or she serves for life and cannot be removed by impeachment except in extreme cases). In India, judges ruling contrary to the prime minister have been transferred or demoted.

2. Differences among Procedures
The procedures employed to resolve cases varies from country to country. For example, in Saudi Arabia, a defendant can "demand the oath"—swear before God that he did not do what he is charged with doing—and be released.

C. NATIONAL LAWS COMPARED
Even when statutory language is similar, application of the law varies among nations.

1. Tort Law
Tort law allows persons to recover damages for harms or injuries caused by the wrongful actions of others (see Chapters 12 and 13).

a. Failure to Act
In Germany, one is normally not liable for failing to rescue someone in distress. Some nations provide liability for negligent omissions.

b. Damages
Swiss and Turkish courts reduce damages if an award of full damages would cause undue hardship to a party who was found negligent. In some nations of northern Africa, different amounts of damages are awarded depending on the type of tort.

c. Statutes of Limitations
Generally, the period is longer than in the United States.

d. Burden of Proof
In the United States, the burden of proof is on the plaintiff. In Russia, the defendant must prove that he or she was not at fault.

2. Contract Law
For requirements of contracts in the United States, see Chapters 9 and 10. Generally, the laws of other nations are similar.

a. United Nations Convention for the International Sale of Goods (CISG)
Some contract law has been internationalized through the CISG, but parties can agree to apply other law.

b. Agreement (Offer and Acceptance)
In Germany, a written offer must be held open for a reasonable time, unless the offer states otherwise. Oral offers must be accepted immediately or they expire. In Mexico, if a time for acceptance is not stated in an offer, the offer is deemed held open for three days (plus whatever time is necessary for the mails).

    c. **Consideration**
In Germany, consideration is not required for a contract to be binding—agreements to make gifts may thus be enforceable by the recipient. In India, some contracts are lawful in the absence of consideration, such as promises in exchange for a past act.

    d. **Remedies**
Germany's typical remedy for breach of contract is specific performance (breaching party does what was promised). In the United States, this is granted only if the remedy of damages (money) is inadequate.

    e. **Defenses**
Defenses include lack of a writing (United States, Saudi Arabia) or witnesses (Saudi Arabia), and lack of consideration (India).

3. Employment Law
Under the employment-at-will doctrine (see Chapter 20), employers can hire and fire employees "at will" (for any reason or no reason).

    a. **Reasons for Discharging Employees**
Employers may fire employees without notice only for causes such as violence, imprisonment, excessive absenteeism, or lying on a job application (Taiwan), or if the worker commits a criminal offense, loses a license or other employment qualification, or seriously breaches his or her duties (Poland).

    b. **Discharge Procedures**
In some countries, to discharge an employee for cause, an employer must first submit the proposed discharge to mediators (France) or a committee (Egypt).

    c. **Wages and Benefits**
Wages are typically lower in other countries, but workers are often entitled to more paid time off.

    d. **Equal Employment Opportunity**
In Indonesia, Japan, and Mexico, employers cannot discriminate against employees or job applicants on some bases. Discrimination is not prohibited in Argentina, Brazil, Egypt, or Turkey.

D. CULTURAL AND BUSINESS TRADITIONS

1. Communication
Language differences and different understandings of body movements, gestures, facial expressions, colors, and numbers can confound efforts to do business abroad. For example, advertising slogans translated word-for-word may be nonsense in other languages.

2. Ethics

    a. **Gift Giving and Bribery**
In many countries, gift giving is common among companies or between companies and government. U.S. firms are prohibited from offering payments to foreign officials to secure favorable contracts (see Chapter 4). Payments to minor officials to, for example, facilitate paperwork are not prohibited.

    b. **Women in Business**
Some countries reject any role for women professionals. Others impose cultural restrictions. For this reason, a U.S. company may be reluctant to assign women to work overseas. Equal employment opportunity is a basic policy in the United States, however (see Chapter 21).

TRUE-FALSE QUESTIONS

(Answers at the Back of the Book)

____ 1. All nations must give effect to the laws of all other nations.

____ 2. Under the act of state doctrine, foreign nations are subject to the jurisdiction of U.S. courts.

____ 3. Under the doctrine of sovereign immunity, foreign nations are subject to the jurisdiction of U.S. courts.

____ 4. The Foreign Sovereign Immunities Act states the circumstances in which the United States can be sued in foreign courts.

____ 5. A member of the World Trade Organization must usually grant other members most-favored nation status, with regard to trade.

____ 6. U.S. firms are prohibited from offering payments to foreign officials to secure favorable contracts.

____ 7. Legal systems are generally divided into criminal law and civil law systems.

____ 8. In all countries, the primary function of judges is the resolution of litigation.

____ 9. All international contracts are subject exclusively to the CISG.

____ 10. Congress cannot tax exports.

FILL-IN QUESTIONS

(Answers at the Back of the Book)

_____ (A confiscation/An expropriation) occurs when a national government seizes a privately owned business or privately owned goods for a proper public purpose. _____ (A confiscation/An expropriation) occurs when the taking is made for an illegal purpose. When _____ _____ (a confiscation/an expropriation) occurs, the government pays just compensation. When _____ (a confiscation/an expropriation) occurs, the government does not pay just compensation.

MULTIPLE-CHOICE QUESTIONS

(Answers at the Back of the Book)

____ 1. Kenya issues bonds to finance the construction of an international airport. Kenya sells some of the bonds in the United States to Larry. A terrorist group destroys the airport, and Kenya refuses to pay interest or principal on the bonds. Larry files suit in a U.S court. The court will hear the suit if Kenya

a. in effect confiscated Larry's funds when it refused to pay on the bonds.
b. in effect expropriated Larry's funds when it refused to pay on the bonds.
c. is a "foreign state" and selling bonds is a "commercial activity."
d. none of the above.

____ 2. To install new computers in government offices, Mexico accepts bids from U.S. firms, including Alpha, Inc., and Beta Corporation. Alpha wins the contract. Beta sues Alpha in a U.S. court, on the ground that its sole shareholder is the brother of the wife of Mexico's minister of commerce. The U.S. court

a. cannot rule on the legality of the contract under the act of state doctrine.
b. cannot rule on the legality of the contract under the principle of commercial relations.
c. must hold the contract illegal under the act of state doctrine.
d. must hold the contract illegal under the principle of commercial relations.

____   **3.**   A U.S. buyer breaches a contract with a Polish seller. The seller sues in a Polish court and wins damages, but the buyer's assets are in the United States. A U.S. court may enforce the judgment under

a. the act of state doctrine.
b. the doctrine of sovereign immunity.
c. the principle of comity.
d. the principle of commercial relations.

____   **4.**   Digital, Inc., makes supercomputers that feature advanced technology. To inhibit Digital's export of its products to other countries, Congress can

a. confiscate all profits on exported supercomputers.
b. expropriate all profits on exported supercomputers.
c. set quotas on exported supercomputers.
d. tax exported supercomputers.

____   **5.**   MotorCorp manufactures cars in the United States. To boost the sales of MotorCorp and other domestic car manufacturers, Congress can

a. only set quotas on imported vehicles.
b. only tax imported vehicles.
c. set quotas and tax imports.
d. none of the above.

____   **6.**   The United States has a common law legal system. Common law systems are based on

a. administrative rules and regulations.
b. case law.
c. codified law.
d. executive pronouncements.

____   **7.**   France has a civil law legal system. Civil law systems are based on

a. administrative rules and regulations.
b. case law.
c. codified law.
d. executive pronouncements.

____   **8.**   Nora is a judge in the United States. As a U.S. judge, Nora normally

a. actively participates in a trial.
b. does not actively participate in a trial.
c. is expected to question witnesses in a trial.
d. is influenced by politics.

____   **9.**   Adam and Beth are citizens of different countries. A dispute arises between the two parties concerning their contract. In the area of contract law

a. some of the basic principles are similar among nations, but some are very different.
b. there are so few differences among nations that the law is, for all practical purposes, uniform.
c. there are no basic principles that any two nations share.
d. there is a law enforced by the United Nations that applies to all international contracts.

____   **10.** Maria believes that she is a victim of employment discrimination. Discrimination in employment is

    a. not prohibited in any country.
    b. prohibited in all countries.
    c. prohibited in some countries.
    d. required in all countries.

SHORT ESSAY QUESTIONS

1. In what ways may a company conduct international business?

2. How does the Foreign Sovereign Immunities Act affect commercial activities by foreign governments?

ISSUE SPOTTERS

(Answers at the Back of the Book)

1. Cafe Rojo, Ltd., a Colombian firm, agrees to sell coffee beans to Java Corporation, a U.S. company. Java accepts the beans, but refuses to pay. Cafe Rojo sues Java in a Colombian court and is awarded damages, but Java's assets are in the United States. Under what circumstances would a U.S. court enforce the Colombian court's judgment?

2. Hi-Cola Corporation, a U.S. company, markets a popular soft drink. The formula is secret, but with careful chemical analysis, its ingredients could be discovered. What can Hi-Cola do to prevent its product from being pirated abroad?

3. Gems International, Ltd., is a foreign firm that has a 12-percent share of the U.S. market for diamonds. To capture a larger share, Gems offers its products at a below-cost discount to U.S. buyers (and inflates the prices in its own country to make up the difference). How can this attempt to undersell U.S. businesses be defeated?

CUMULATIVE HYPOTHETICAL PROBLEM
FOR UNIT TWO—INCLUDING CHAPTERS 5–8

(Answers at the Back of the Book)

GPS, Inc., designs and sells the technology for advanced global positioning systems that can be used to pinpoint the location of virtually any person or object.

____   **1.** As a for-profit corporation that does business in interstate commerce, GPS may be subject to regulations issued by

    a. federal administrative agencies only.
    b. state administrative agencies in states in which Beta does business only.
    c. federal agencies or state agencies in states in which Beta does business.
    d. none of the above.

____   **2.** During an investigation into GPS's activities, a court orders GPS to provide its business records. As a corporation, GPS can

    a. be compelled to provide only records that do *not* incriminate its officers.
    b. be compelled to provide records that incriminate its officers.
    c. refuse to provide records that incriminate its officers.
    d. refuse to provide *any* business records.

_____ 3. After the investigation into GPS's activities, some of its officers are suspected of having committed crimes. As a corporation, GPS can

a. be fined or denied certain privileges if it is held criminally liable.
b. be imprisoned if it is held criminally liable.
c. be fined, denied privileges, or imprisoned if it is held criminally liable.
d. not be found to be criminally liable.

_____ 4. To limit GPS's export of its technology to foreign countries, Congress can

a. confiscate any profit on the export of GPS products.
b. restrict the export of GPS products.
c. tax the export of GPS products.
d. confiscate, restrict, and tax.

_____ 5. Congress enacts a law that affects GPS, which challenges the law on the basis of equal protection. This means that GPS claims the law

a. does not include sufficient procedural safeguards.
b. limits the liberty of *all* persons in a way that is unconstitutional.
c. limits the liberty of *some* persons in a way that is unconstitutional.
d. unduly burdens interstate commerce.

QUESTIONS ON THE FOCUS ON LEGAL REASONING FOR UNIT TWO—
KASKY V. NIKE, INC.

(Answers at the Back of the Book)

_____ 1. In *Kasky v. Nike, Inc.*, in the majority's opinion, commercial speech is distinguished from other speech in part by

a. its capacity to inform the public.
b. its contribution to the marketplace of ideas.
c. its inherent worth.
d. the identity of the speaker.

_____ 2. In the dissent's opinion, commercial speech should be distinguished from other speech by

a. its capacity to inform the public.
b. its content.
c. its inherent worth in the marketplace of ideas.
d. the identity of the speaker.

_____ 3. According to the majority, its holding regarding the defendant would have a chilling effect on

a. commercial speech only.
b. public debate only.
c. commercial speech and public debate.
d. none of the above.

QUESTIONS ON THE FOCUS ON ETHICS FOR UNIT TWO— THE PUBLIC AND INTERNATIONAL ENVIRONMENT

(Answers at the Back of the Book)

____ 1. In making, interpreting, and applying the law of the public environment and the law of the international environment

a. conceptions of fairness, justice, and equality do not differ among individuals.
b. practical considerations provide sufficient guidance.
c. there is always a broad social consensus over legal issues.
d. value judgments must be made.

____ 2. Alpha Corporation wants to use its resources to influence the political process with respect to issues that do not relate to Alpha's business. Alpha's state attempts to block this use of resources. In a challenge to this state action, under the First Amendment the most important question is whether

a. Alpha and other corporations are protected by the free speech clause.
b. Alpha should leverage political power through its economic skills.
c. Alpha's speech is political in nature.
d. Alpha's speech relates to an economic matter.

____ 3. The Environmental Protection Agency (EPA) may inspect Beta Company's plant

a. only if a regulatory violation is occurring.
b. only if Beta is in an industry subject to extensive regulation.
c. only if the EPA is obtaining private information for regulatory purposes.
d. none of the above.

Chapter 9
Contract Formation

WHAT THIS CHAPTER IS ABOUT

Contract law concerns the formation and keeping of promises, the excuses our society accepts for breaking such promises, and what promises are considered contrary to public policy and therefore legally void. This chapter introduces the basic terms and concepts of contract law.

CHAPTER OUTLINE

I.   THE FUNCTION OF CONTRACT LAW

  A. ENFORCE PROMISES
  Contract law assures the parties to private agreements that the promises they make will be enforceable. Without the framework that the law provides, businesspersons could rely only on the good faith of others to keep their promises.

  B. AVOID PROBLEMS
  The rules of contract law are often followed in business agreements to avoid potential problems.

  C. SUPPORT THE EXISTENCE OF A MARKET ECONOMY
  Businesspersons can usually rely on the good faith of others to keep their promises, but when price changes or adverse economic factors make it costly to comply with a promise, good faith may not be enough.

II. DEFINITION OF A CONTRACT

  A. WHAT A CONTRACT IS
  A *contract* is a promise for the breach of which the law gives a remedy or the performance of which the law recognizes as a duty (that is, an agreement that can be enforced in court). Two or more parties form a contract by promising to perform or refrain from performing some act now or in the future.

  B. THE OBJECTIVE THEORY OF CONTRACTS
  Intention to enter into a contract is judged by objective (outward) facts as interpreted by a reasonable person, rather than by a party's subjective intention. Objective facts include (1) what the party said when entering into the contract, (2) how the party acted or appeared, and (3) the circumstances surrounding the transaction.

III. ELEMENTS OF A CONTRACT

  A. REQUIREMENTS OF A VALID CONTRACT

    1. Agreement
    This requirement includes an offer and an acceptance. One party must offer to enter into a legal agreement, and another party must accept the offer.

    2. Consideration
    Promises must be supported by legally sufficient and bargained-for consideration.

3. Contractual Capacity
This includes characteristics that qualify the parties to a contract as competent.

4. Legality
A contract's purpose must be to accomplish a goal that is not against public policy.

B. DEFENSES TO THE ENFORCEABILITY OF A CONTRACT

1. Genuineness of Assent
The apparent consent of both parties must be genuine.

2. Form
A contract must be in whatever form the law requires (some contracts must be in writing).

IV. TYPES OF CONTRACTS

A. BILATERAL VERSUS UNILATERAL CONTRACTS
Bilateral contract—a promise for a promise (to accept the offer, the offeree need only promise to perform). *Unilateral contract*—a promise for an act (the offeree can accept only by completing performance).

B. EXPRESS VERSUS IMPLIED CONTRACTS
Express contract—the terms of the agreement are fully and explicitly stated in words (oral or written). *Implied contract*—implied from the conduct of the parties.

C. QUASI CONTRACTS—CONTRACTS IMPLIED IN LAW
In the absence of an actual contract, a court imposes a quasi contract to avoid the unjust enrichment of one party at the expense of another (unless there is an actual contract that covers the area in controversy).

D. EXECUTED VERSUS EXECUTORY CONTRACTS
Executed contract—a contract that has been fully performed on both sides. *Executory contract*—a contract that has not been fully performed by one or more of the parties.

E. VALID, VOID, VOIDABLE, AND UNENFORCEABLE CONTRACTS
Valid contract—has all elements necessary to entitle at least one party to enforce it. *Void contract*—produces no legal obligations on the part of any of the parties. *Voidable contract*—valid contract that can be avoided by one or more of the parties. *Unenforceable contract*—contract that cannot be enforced because of certain legal defenses.

V. AGREEMENT

A. REQUIREMENTS OF THE OFFER
An offer is a promise or commitment to do or refrain from doing some specified thing in the future. The elements for an offer to be effective are—

1. Intention of the Offeror
The offeror must intend to be bound by the offer. Intent is determined by what a reasonable person in the offeree's position would conclude the offeror's words and actions meant.

a. Expressions and Statements that Are Not Offers
These include (1) expressions of opinion, (2) statements of intention, (3) preliminary negotiations, and (4) advertisements, catalogues, price lists, and circulars.

b. Agreements to Agree
Agreements to agree to a material term of a contract at some future date may be enforced if the parties clearly intended to be bound.

2. **Definiteness of Terms**
    All major terms must be stated with reasonable definiteness in the offer (or, if the offeror directs, in the offeree's acceptance). Courts are sometimes willing to supply a missing term when the parties have clearly manifested an intent to form a contract.

3. **Communication of the Offer**
    The offer must be communicated to the offeree.

B. TERMINATION OF THE OFFER

1. **Termination by Action of the Parties**

    a. **Revocation of the Offer by the Offeror**
        The offeror can revoke an offer by express repudiation or by performance of acts that are inconsistent with the offer and that are made known to the offeree. A revocation becomes effective when the offeree or offeree's agent actually receives it.

    b. **Irrevocable Offers**

        1) **Option Contract**
            A promise to hold an offer open for a specified period of time (if no time is specified, a reasonable time is implied).

        2) **Detrimental Reliance**
            An offer may be irrevocable if the offeree justifiably relies on it to his or her detriment. Many courts will not allow an offeror to revoke an offer after the offeree has performed some substantial part of his or her duties under a unilateral contract.

    c. **Rejection of the Offer by the Offeree**
        An offer may be rejected by words or conduct evidencing an intent not to accept the offer. Asking about an offer is not rejecting it. Rejection is effective only on its receipt by the offeror or the offeror's agent.

    d. **Counteroffer by the Offeree**
        The offeree's attempt to include different terms is a rejection of the original offer and a simultaneous making of a new offer. The *mirror image rule* requires the acceptance to match the offer exactly.

2. **Termination by Operation of Law**
    An offer terminates automatically when the time specified in the offer has passed (if no time is specified, a reasonable time is implied).

C. ACCEPTANCE
The offeree must accept the offer unequivocally.

1. **Silence as Acceptance**
    Silence can constitute acceptance if (1) an offeree receives the benefit of offered services even though he or she had an opportunity to reject them and knew that they were offered with the expectation of compensation, or (2) the offeree had prior dealings with the offeror that led the offeror to understand that silence will constitute acceptance.

2. **Communication of Acceptance**
    A bilateral contract is formed when acceptance is communicated (must be timely). In a unilateral contract, communication is unnecessary, unless the offeror requests notice or has no adequate means of determining if the act has been performed, or the law requires notice.

3. **Technology and Acceptance Rules**
   Generally, on the Internet, the mailbox rule is not needed because online acceptances are instantaneous (see Chapter 11).

VI. CONSIDERATION

Consideration is the value given in return for a promise.

A. ELEMENTS OF CONSIDERATION

1. **A Bargained-for Exchange**
   The promise must induce the value, and the value must induce the promise. Situations that lack this element include "past" consideration (promises made with respect to events that have already taken place are unenforceable).

2. **Something of Legal Value**
   Something of legal value must be given in exchange for a promise. It may be a return promise. If it is performance, it may be (1) an act (other than a promise); (2) a forbearance (refraining from action); or (3) the creation, modification, or destruction of a legal relation.

   a. **Adequacy of Consideration**
      Generally, a court will not evaluate the adequacy of consideration (the fairness of a bargain), unless it is so grossly inadequate as to "shock the conscience" of the court.

   b. **Preexisting Duty Rule and Past Consideration**
      A promise to do what one already has a legal duty to do does not constitute consideration. A promise made in return for an event that has already occurred also lacks consideration.

B. PROMISSORY ESTOPPEL

In some states, a promisor cannot assert a lack of consideration as a defense if (1) a promise given by one party induces another party to rely (justifiably) on that promise to his or her detriment, and (2) the promisor knew or had reason to believe that the promisee would likely be induced to change position (in a substantial way).

VII. CAPACITY

Persons who are minors, intoxicated, or mentally incompetent but not yet adjudicated officially as such, have capacity to enter into a contract; but they can normally avoid liability under the contract.

VIII. LEGALITY

To be enforceable, a contract must not violate any statutes or public policy. A covenant not to compete, for example, to be enforceable, must be no more restrictive than necessary to protect a legitimate business interest.

IX. GENUINENESS OF ASSENT

A. MISTAKES

1. **Bilateral (Mutual) Mistakes**
   When both parties make a mistake as to a material fact, either party can rescind the contract. The same rule applies if the parties attach materially different meanings to a word or term in the contract that may be subject to more than one reasonable interpretation.

2. **Unilateral Mistakes of Fact**
   A unilateral mistake as to a material fact does not afford a mistaken party relief. Exceptions: include (1) if the other party knows or should know of the mistake or (2) if the mistake is due to a mathematical error and is done inadvertently and without gross negligence.

B. FRAUDULENT MISREPRESENTATION

If an innocent party is fraudulently induced to enter into a contract, the contract normally can be avoided. Fraud consists of: (1) misrepresentation of a material fact, (2) an intent to deceive, and (3) the innocent party's justifiable reliance on the misrepresentation. To collect damages, a party must also have suffered an injury.

C. NONFRAUDULENT MISREPRESENTATION

If a person misrepresents a material fact without the intent to defraud (he or she believes the statement to be true), the person may be guilty of innocent or negligent misrepresentation. The party who relied on the statement to his or her detriment can rescind the contract.

D. UNDUE INFLUENCE

Occurs when a contract enriches a party at the expense of another who is dominated by the enriched party. The contract is voidable. The essential feature is that the party taken advantage of does not exercise free will.

E. DURESS

Duress involves forcing a party to enter into a contract by threatening the party with a wrongful act. The threatened act must be wrongful or illegal.

F. ADHESION CONTRACTS AND UNCONSCIONABILITY

To avoid a contract, an adhering party must show that the parties had substantially unequal bargaining positions and that enforcement would be unfair or oppressive.

X.   STATUTE OF FRAUDS

The Statute of Frauds stipulates what types of contracts must be in writing to be enforceable. If a contract is not in writing, it is not void but the Statute of Frauds is a defense to its enforcement.

A. CONTRACTS THAT MUST BE IN WRITING TO BE ENFORCEABLE

Contracts involving interests in land, contracts that cannot be performed within one year of formation, collateral promises, promises made in consideration of marriage, contracts for sale of goods priced at $500 or more.

B. EXCEPTION

An oral contract may be enforced if (1) a promisor makes a promise on which the promisee justifiably relies to his or her detriment, (2) the reliance was foreseeable to the promisor, and (3) injustice can be avoided only by enforcing the promise.

XI.   THIRD PARTY RIGHTS

A. ASSIGNMENTS

The transfer of a contract right to a third person is an assignment.

1. Rights That Cannot Be Assigned

Rights cannot be assigned if a statute prohibits assignment, a contract is personal (unless all that remains is a money payment), the assignment materially increases or alters the risk or duties of the obligor, or the contract provides that it cannot be assigned.

2. Exceptions

A contract cannot prevent an assignment of (1) a right to receive money, (2) rights in real property, (3) rights in negotiable instruments (checks and notes), or (4) a right to receive damages for breach of a sales contract or for payment of an amount owed under the contract (even if the contract prohibits it).

B. DELEGATIONS

Duties are not assigned; they are delegated. A delegation does not relieve the delegator of the obligation to perform if the delegatee fails to perform.

1. **Duties That Cannot Be Delegated**
   Any duty can be delegated unless (1) performance depends on the personal skill or talents of the obligor, (2) special trust has been placed in the obligor, (3) performance by a third party will vary materially from that expected by the obligee, or (4) the contract prohibits it.

2. **Effect of a Delegation**
   The obligee must accept performance from the delegatee, unless the duty is one that cannot be delegated. If the delegatee fails to perform, the delegator is still liable.

C. **THIRD PARTY BENEFICIARIES**
   There are two types of third party beneficiaries: intended and incidental. An intended beneficiary is one for whose benefit a contract is made; if the contract is breached, he or she can sue the promisor. The benefit that an incidental beneficiary receives from a contract between other parties is unintentional; an incidental beneficiary cannot enforce the contract.

TRUE-FALSE QUESTIONS

(Answers at the Back of the Book)

F **1.** All promises are legal contracts.

T **2.** An agreement includes an offer and an acceptance.

F **3.** All rights under a contract can be assigned.

F **4.** A contract providing that one party is to pay another "a fair share of the profits" is enforceable.

F **5.** Normally, courts evaluate the adequacy of consideration even if the consideration is legally sufficient.

T **6.** A promise to do what one already has a legal duty to do is not legally sufficient consideration under most circumstances.

T **7.** A minor may generally disaffirm a contract entered into with an adult.

T **8.** Under a mistake of fact, a contract can sometimes be avoided.

F **9.** A contract for a transfer of an interest in land need not be in writing to be enforceable.

T **10.** Only intended beneficiaries acquire legal rights in a contract.

FILL-IN QUESTIONS

(Answers at the Back of the Book)

Whether or not a party intended to enter into a contract is determined by the ___objective___ (objective/subjective) theory of contracts. The theory is that a party's intention to enter into a contract is judged by _____ (objective/subjective) facts as they would be interpreted by a reasonable person. Relevant facts include: (1) what the party said; (2) what the party _____ (did/secretly believed); and (3) the _____ (circumstances surrounding/party's personal thoughts concerning) the transaction. Generally, courts examine facts in _____ (a particular transaction/similar transactions) to determine whether the parties made a contract and, if so, what its terms are.

MULTIPLE-CHOICE QUESTIONS

(Answers at the Back of the Book)

 1. Ed questions whether there is consideration for his contract with Fran. Consideration has two elements—there must be a bargained-for exchange and the value of whatever is exchanged must be

   a. adequately sufficient.
   b. definitely sufficient.
   c. economically sufficient.
   d. legally sufficient.

 2. Ann claims that she and Brian entered into a contract. The intent to enter into a contract is determined with reference to

   a. the apparent theory of contracts.
   b. the objective theory of contracts.
   c. the personal theory of contracts.
   d. the subjective theory of contracts.

 3. Before opening her new sports merchandise store, Kay places an ad in the newspaper showing cross-training shoes at certain prices. Within hours of opening for business, the store is sold out of some of the shoes. In this situation

   a. Kay has made an offer to the people reading the ad.
   b. Kay has made a contract with the people reading the ad.
   c. Kay has made an invitation seeking offers.
   d. Any customer who demands goods advertised and tenders the money is entitled to them.

 4. Alpha Properties, Inc., makes an offer in a letter to Bob to sell a certain lot for $5,000, with the offer to stay open for thirty days. Bob would prefer to pay $4,000, if Alpha would sell at that price. To leave room for negotiation without rejecting the offer, Bob should reply

   a. "I will not pay $5,000."
   b. "Will you take $4,000?"
   c. "I will pay $4,000."
   d. "I will pay $4,500."

 5. Metro Transport asks for bids on a construction project. Metro estimates that the cost will be $200,000. Most bids are about $200,000, but A&B Construction bids $150,000. In adding a column of figures, A&B mistakenly omitted a $50,000 item. Because Metro had reason to know of the mistake

   a. A&B can avoid the contract because Metro knew of the errors.
   b. A&B can avoid the contract because the errors were the result of negligence.
   c. Metro can enforce the contract because the errors were unilateral.
   d. Metro can enforce the contract because the errors were material.

 6. Kay offers to buy a book owned by Lee for $40. Lee accepts and hands the book to Kay. The transfer and delivery of the book constitute performance. Is this performance consideration for Kay's promise?

   a. Yes, because Kay sought it in exchange for her promise, and Lee gave it in exchange for that promise.
   b. Yes, because performance always constitutes consideration.
   c. No, because Lee already had a duty to hand the book to Kay.
   d. No, because performance never constitutes consideration.

7. Diane, a doctor, renders aid to Earl, who is injured. Diane can recover the cost from Earl

    a. even if Earl was not aware of Diane's help.
    b. only if Earl was aware of Diane's help.
    c. only if Earl was aware of Diane's help and survives.
    d. only if Earl was not aware of Diane's help.

8. Eve, a sixteen-year-old minor, buys a car from Fine Autos and wrecks it. To disaffirm the contract and satisfy a duty of restitution, Eve must

    a. only return the car.
    b. only pay for the damage.
    c. return the car and pay for the damage.
    d. none of the above.

9. Alpha Properties and Beta Corporation enter into an oral contract for the sale of a warehouse. Before Beta takes possession, this contract is enforceable by

    a. Alpha only.
    b. Beta only.
    c. Alpha or Beta.
    d. none of the above.

10. Jill insures her warehouse under a policy with Kappa Insurance Company. Jill assigns the policy to Lyle, who also owns a warehouse. Kappa's best argument against the assignment of the policy is that

    a. it did not consent to the assignment.
    b. it was not paid for the assignment.
    c. the assignment will materially alter its risk.
    d. this is a personal service contract.

SHORT ESSAY QUESTIONS

1. What are the basic elements of a contract?

2. What are the elements of fraudulent misrepresentation?

ISSUE SPOTTERS

(Answers at the Back of the Book)

1. Jill signs and returns a letter from Kyle, referring to a book and its price. When Kyle delivers the book, Jill sends it back, claiming that they have no contract. Kyle claims they do. What standard determines whether these parties have a contract?

2. Mary makes an offer to Neal in a fax. Neal indicates his acceptance in a return fax. When is Neal's acceptance effective?

3. Before Paula starts her first year of college, Ross promises to pay her $5,000 if she graduates. She goes to college, borrowing and spending more than $5,000. At the start of her last semester, she reminds Ross of the promise. Ross sends her a note that says, "I revoke the promise." Is Ross's promise binding?

Chapter 10
Contract Performance, Breach, and Remedies

WHAT THIS CHAPTER IS ABOUT

This chapter begins with a discussion of performance and discharge of contracts. Performance of a contract discharges it. Discharging a contract terminates it. Breach of contract is the failure to perform what a party is under a duty to perform. When this happens, the nonbreaching party can choose one or more remedies.

CHAPTER OUTLINE

I.   **PERFORMANCE AND DISCHARGE**

   A. **CONDITIONS**
      If performance is contingent on a condition and the condition is not satisfied, the obligations of the parties are discharged.

   B. **DISCHARGE BY PERFORMANCE**
      Most contracts are discharged by the parties' doing what they promised.

      1. **Tender of Performance**
         Discharge can be accomplished by an unconditional offer to perform by one who is ready, willing, and able to do so. If the other party then refuses to perform, the party making the tender can sue for breach.

      2. **Degree of Performance Required**

         a. **Complete Performance**
            Express conditions fully occur in all aspects. Any deviation operates as a discharge.

         b. **Substantial Performance**
            Performance that does not vary greatly from the performance promised in the contract. The other party is obligated to perform (but may obtain damages for the deviations).

         c. **Performance to the Satisfaction of One of the Parties**
            When the subject matter of the contract is personal, performance must actually satisfy the party (a condition precedent). Contracts involving mechanical fitness, utility, or marketability need only be performed to the satisfaction of a reasonable person.

         d. **Performance to the Satisfaction of a Third Party**
            When the satisfaction of a third party is required, most courts require the work to be satisfactory to a reasonable person.

      3. **Material Breach of Contract**
         A breach of contract is the nonperformance of a contractual duty. A breach is material when performance is not at least substantial; the nonbreaching party is excused from performing. If a breach is minor, the nonbreaching party's duty to perform may be suspended.

4. Time for Performance

If a specific time is stated, the parties must perform by that time. If no time is stated, a reasonable time is implied. If time is construed to be "of the essence," a deadline must be complied with. Otherwise, a delay will not destroy the performing party's right to payment.

C. DISCHARGE BY AGREEMENT

1. Discharge by Rescission

Rescission is the process by which a contract is canceled and the parties are returned to the positions they occupied prior to forming it.

2. Discharge by Novation

A novation occurs when the parties to a contract agree to substitute a third party for one of the original parties.

3. Discharge by Substituted Agreement

A settlement agreement worked out as a compromise in a genuine dispute substitutes as a new contract (there is no third party).

4. Discharge by Accord and Satisfaction

The parties agree to accept performance that is different from the performance originally promised.

D. DISCHARGE BY OPERATION OF LAW

1. Alteration of the Contract

An innocent party can treat a contract as discharged if the other party materially alters a term (such as quantity or price) without consent.

2. Statutes of Limitations

Statutes of limitations limit the period during which a party can sue based on a breach of contract.

3. Bankruptcy

A discharge in bankruptcy (see Chapter 15) will ordinarily bar enforcement of most of a debtor's contracts.

4. Discharge by Impossibility or Impracticability

a. Objective Impossibility of Performance

A contract may be discharged if, after it is made, performance becomes objectively impossible (death or incapacity of one of the parties, specific subject matter of the contract is destroyed, or change in the law that renders performance illegal.)

b. Commercial Impracticability

Performance may be excused if it becomes much more difficult or expensive than contemplated when the contract was formed.

c. Frustration of Purpose

A contract will be discharged if supervening circumstances make it impossible to attain the purpose the parties had in mind.

d. Temporary Impossibility

An event that makes it temporarily impossible to perform will suspend performance until the impossibility ceases.

II.   BREACH OF CONTRACT AND REMEDIES

A. DAMAGES

Damages compensate a nonbreaching party for the loss of a bargain and, under special circumstances, for additional losses. Generally, the party is placed in the position he or she would have occupied if the contract been performed.

1. Types of Damages

a. Compensatory Damages

Compensatory damages compensate a party for the loss of a bargain. Incidental damages (expenses caused directly by a breach, such as the cost to obtain performance from another source) may also be recovered.

1) Contract for a Sale of Goods

The usual measure is the difference between the contract price and the market price. If the buyer breaches and the seller has not yet made the goods, the measure is lost profits.

2) Contract for a Sale of Land

If specific performance is unavailable, or if the buyer breaches, the measure of damages is usually the difference between the land's contract price and its market price.

b. Consequential Damages

Consequential damages give the injured party the entire benefit of the bargain—foreseeable losses caused by special circumstances beyond the contract. The losses flow from the consequences of the breach.

c. Punitive Damages

Punitive damages punish and deter wrongdoing.

d. Nominal Damages

Nominal damages recognize wrongdoing when no monetary loss is shown.

2. Mitigation of Damages

The nonbreaching party has a duty to mitigate damages. For example, persons whose employment has been wrongfully terminated have a duty to seek other jobs. The damages they receive are their salaries, less the income they received (or would have received) in similar jobs.

3. Liquidated Damages versus Penalties

a. Liquidated Damages

A liquidated damages provision specifies a certain amount to be paid in the event of a breach. Such provisions are enforceable.

b. Penalties

Penalties specify a certain amount to be paid in the event of a breach (to penalize the breaching party). Such provisions are not enforceable.

B. RESCISSION AND RESTITUTION

1. Rescission

Rescission is an action to undo a contract—to return the contracting parties to the positions they occupied before the transaction. If fraud, mistake, duress, undue influence, misrepresentation, lack of capacity, or a party's failure to perform is present, unilateral rescission is available. Rescission may also be available by statute.

2. Restitution

To rescind a contract, the parties must make restitution by returning to each other goods, property, or money previously conveyed.

C. SPECIFIC PERFORMANCE

This remedy calls for the performance of the act promised in the contract.

1. When Specific Performance Is Available

Damages must be an inadequate remedy. If goods are unique, a court will decree specific performance. Specific performance is granted to a buyer in a contract for the sale of land (every parcel of land is unique).

2. When Specific Performance Is Not Available

Contracts for a sale of goods (other than unique goods) rarely qualify, because substantially identical goods can be bought or sold elsewhere. Courts normally refuse to grant specific performance of personal service contracts.

D. REFORMATION

This remedy is used when the parties have imperfectly expressed their agreement in writing. It allows the contract to be rewritten to reflect the parties' true intentions.

E. RECOVERY BASED ON QUASI CONTRACT

Quasi contract provides a basis for relief when no enforceable contract exists. The courts use this theory to prevent unjust enrichment. The law implies a promise to pay the reasonable value (fair market value) for benefits received by the party accepting the benefits.

F. ELECTION OF REMEDIES DOCTRINE

A nonbreaching party must choose which remedy to pursue. This doctrine has been eliminated in contracts for sales of goods [UCC 2–703, 2–711]. Remedies under the UCC are cumulative.

G. WAIVER OF BREACH

A nonbreaching party may be willing to accept a defective performance of the contract. This relinquishment of a right to full performance is a waiver. A waiver keeps the contract going, but the nonbreaching party can recover damages caused by defective or less-than-full performance.

H. CONTRACT PROVISIONS LIMITING REMEDIES

1. Exculpatory Clauses

A provision excluding liability for fraudulent or intentional injury or for illegal acts will not be enforced. An exculpatory clause for negligence contained in a contract made between parties who have roughly equal bargaining positions usually will be enforced.

2. Limitation-of-Liability Clauses

A clause excluding liability for negligence may be enforced.

TRUE-FALSE QUESTIONS

(Answers at the Back of the Book)

T 1. Complete performance occurs when a contract's conditions fully occur.

F 2. A material breach of contract does not excuse the nonbreaching party from further performance.

F 3. An executory contract cannot be rescinded.

T 4. Objective impossibility discharges a contract.

T 5. If a contract does not require a certain time for performance, a reasonable time will be implied.

T 6. Damages are designed to compensate a nonbreaching party for the loss of a bargain.

F 7. Liquidated damages are uncertain in amount.

F 8. Quasi-contractual recovery is possible only when there is an enforceable contract.

T 9. Consequential damages are foreseeable damages that arise from a party's breach of a contract.

F 10. Specific performance is the usual remedy when one party has breached a contract for a sale of goods.

FILL-IN QUESTIONS

(Answers at the Back of the Book)

Most contracts are discharged by performance—by doing what was promised. Any contract can be discharged by agreement of the parties. _____ (Rescission/Novation) is the process by which a contract is canceled and the parties are returned to the positions they occupied before forming it. _____ (Rescission/Novation) substitutes a new party for an original party by agreement of all the parties. _____ (Substitution of a new contract/Accord and satisfaction) revokes and discharges a prior contract. _____ (A substitution/An accord) suspends a contractual duty that has not been discharged. Once the _____ (substitution/accord) is performed, the original contractual obligation is discharged.

MULTIPLE-CHOICE QUESTIONS

(Answers at the Back of the Book)

D 1. Adam contracts with Beth to deliver Beth's goods to her customers. This contract will, like most contracts, be discharged by

   a. accord and satisfaction.
   b. agreement.
   c. operation of law.
   d. performance.

C 2. Don contracts to build a store for Pat for $500,000, with payments to be in installments of $50,000 as building progresses. Don finishes the store except for a cover over a compressor on the roof. A cover can be installed for $500. Pat refuses to pay the last installment. If Don's breach is not material

   a. Don has a claim against Pat for $50,000.
   b. Pat has a claim against Don for damages for Don's breach of his duty to put a cover over the compressor.
   c. both a and b.
   d. none of the above.

D 3. Tony and Carol contract for the sale of Tony's business. Carol gives Tony a down payment, and Tony gives Carol the keys to one of his stores. Before the contract is fully performed, however, they agree to return the down payment and keys, and cancel the sale. This is

   a. an accord and satisfaction.
   b. an alteration of contract.
   c. a novation.
   d. a rescission.

4. Eve contracts with Frank to act as his personal financial planner. Eve's duties under this contract will be discharged if

a. Frank declares bankruptcy.
b. it becomes illegal for Eve to provide the service.
c. the cost of providing the service doubles.
d. none of the above.

5. Lee and Mary want Nick to replace Lee as a party to their contract. They can best accomplish this by agreeing to

a. an accord and satisfaction.
b. an assignment.
c. a novation.
d. a nullification.

6. Sue contracts to deliver Tom's products to his customers for $1,500, payable in advance. Tom pays the money, but Sue fails to perform. Tom can

a. rescind the contract.
b. obtain restitution of the $1,500 but not rescind the contract.
c. rescind the contract and obtain restitution of the $1,500.
d. none of the above.

7. Eagle Corporation contracts to sell to Frosty Malts, Inc., six steel mixers for $5,000. When Eagle fails to deliver, Frosty buys mixers from Great Company, for $6,500. Frosty's measure of damages is

a. $6,500.
b. $5,000.
c. $1,500 plus incident al damages.
d. nothing.

8. Dave contracts with Paul to buy a computer for $1,000. Dave tells Paul that if it is not delivered on Monday, he will lose $2,000 in business. Paul ships the computer late. Dave can recover

a. $3,000.
b. $2,000.
c. $1,000.
d. nothing.

9. Jay agrees to sell an acre of land to Kim for $5,000. Kim Jay fails to go through with the deal, when the market price of the land is $7,000. If Kim cannot obtain the land through specific performance, Kim may recover

a. $7,000.
b. $5,000.
c. $2,000.
d. nothing.

10. Ken orally agrees to build three barns for Lora. He builds the first barn, but she fails to pay him. To redress the breach, Ken's best option is

a. damages.
b. quasi-contractual recovery.
c. rescission.
d. specific performance.

SHORT ESSAY QUESTIONS

1. What effect does a material breach have on the nonbreaching party? What is the effect of a nonmaterial breach?

2. What are damages designed to do in a breach of contract situation?

ISSUE SPOTTERS

(Answers at the Back of the Book)

1. Eagle Construction contracts with Fred to build a store. The work is to begin on May 1 and be done by November 1, so that Fred can open for the holiday buying season. Eagle does not finish until November 15. Fred opens but, due to the delay, loses some sales. Is Fred's duty to pay for the construction of the store discharged?

2. Lyle contracts to sell his ranch to Mary, who is to take possession on June 1. Lyle delays the transfer until August 1. Mary incurs expenses in providing for livestock that she bought for the ranch. When they made the contract, Lyle had no reason to know of the livestock. Is Lyle liable for Mary's expenses in providing for the cattle?

3. Excel Engineering, Inc., signs a contract to design a jet for Flight, Inc. The contract excludes liability for errors in the design and construction of the jet. An error in design causes the jet to crash. Is the clause that excluded liability enforceable?

Chapter 11
Sales, Leases, and E-Contracts

WHAT THIS CHAPTER IS ABOUT

The Uniform Commercial Code (UCC) provides a framework of rules to deal with all the phases arising in an ordinary sales transaction from start to finish—from sale to payment. This chapter outlines the principles of UCC Article 2 and Article 2A.

CHAPTER OUTLINE

I.   THE SCOPE OF ARTICLE 2—SALES OF GOODS

Article 2 governs contracts for sales of goods. A *sale* is "the passing of title from the seller to the buyer for a price" [UCC 2–106(1)]. *Title* is the formal right of ownership of property. The price may be payable in money, goods, services, or land. *Goods* are tangible and movable.

II.   THE SCOPE OF ARTICLE 2A—LEASES

Article 2A governs contracts for leases of goods. A *lease agreement* is the bargain of the lessor and lessee, in their words and deeds, including course of dealing, usage of trade, and course of performance [UCC 2A–103(k)].

III. THE AMENDMENTS TO ARTICLES 2 AND 2A

Amendments have been proposed to update these articles to accommodate e-commerce.

IV. THE FORMATION OF SALES AND LEASE CONTRACTS

The following sections summarize how UCC provisions *change* the effect of the common law of contracts.

A.   OFFER

Verbal exchanges, correspondence, and the actions of the parties may not reveal exactly when a binding contractual obligation arises. An agreement sufficient to constitute a contract can exist even if the moment of its making is undetermined [UCC 2–204(2), 2A–204(2)].

1.   Open Terms

A sales contract will not fail for indefiniteness, even if one or more terms are left open, as long as (1) the parties intended to make a contract and (2) there is a reasonably certain basis for the court to grant an appropriate remedy [UCC 2–204(3), 2A–204(3)]. (Without a quantity term, there is no basis for a remedy.)

2.   Merchant's Firm Offer

If a merchant gives assurances in a signed writing that an offer will remain open, the offer is irrevocable, without consideration for the stated period of time, or if no definite period is specified, for a reasonable period (not more than three months) [UCC 2–205, 2A–205].

B.   ACCEPTANCE

1.   Promise to Ship or Prompt Shipment

The UCC permits acceptance of an offer to buy goods for current or prompt shipment by either a promise to ship or prompt shipment of goods to the buyer [UCC 2–206(1)(b)]. Shipment of nonconforming goods is both an acceptance and a breach.

2. **Communication of Acceptance**
To accept a unilateral offer, the offeree must notify the offeror of performance within a reasonable time if the offeror would not otherwise know [UCC 2–206(2), 2A–206(2)].

3. **Additional Terms**
If the offeree's response indicates a definite acceptance of the offer, a contract is formed, even if the acceptance includes terms in addition to, or different from, the original offer [UCC 2–207(1)]. If both parties are merchants, the terms may become part of the contract [UCC 2–207(2)].

V.   CONSIDERATION

An agreement modifying a contract or lease needs no consideration to be binding [UCC 2–209(1), 2A–208(1)]. Modification must be sought in good faith [UCC 1–203]. Good faith in a merchant is honesty in fact and observance of reasonable commercial standards of fair dealing in the trade [UCC 2–103(1)(b)].

VI.   THE STATUTE OF FRAUDS

To be enforceable, a sales contract must be in writing if the goods are $500 or more and a lease if the payments are $1,000 or more [UCC 2–201, 2A–201].

A. SPECIAL RULES FOR CONTRACTS BETWEEN MERCHANTS

The requirement of a writing is satisfied if one merchant sends a signed written confirmation to the other, unless the merchant who receives the confirmation gives written notice of objection within ten days of receipt.

B. EXCEPTIONS

An oral contract for a sale or lease that should otherwise be in writing will be enforceable if [UCC 2–201(3), 2A–201(4)] (1) manufacture of special goods has begun, (2) party against whom enforcement is sought admits in court proceedings a contract was made, or (3) payment is made and accepted or goods are received and accepted (enforceable to that extent).

VII. TITLE, RISK, AND INSURABLE INTEREST

A. IDENTIFICATION

Identification is the designation of goods as the subject matter of the contract. For an interest in goods to pass from seller to buyer or lessor to lessee, the goods must (1) exist and (2) be identified as the goods subject to the contract.

B. WHEN TITLE PASSES

1. **According to the Parties' Agreement**
Parties can agree on when and under what conditions title will pass.

2. **At the Time and Place at Which the Seller Performs**
If the parties do not specify a time, title passes on delivery [UCC 2–401(2)]. Delivery terms determine when this occurs.

C. RISK OF LOSS

The question of who suffers a financial risk if goods are damaged, destroyed, or lost is resolved mostly under UCC 2–509 and 2A–219.

1. **Passage of Risk of Loss under the Parties' Agreement**
Risk of loss can be assigned in the parties' agreement if at the time, the goods are in existence and identified to the contract.

2. **Passage of Risk of Loss absent a Breach of Contract**
In the absence of agreement, risk of loss generally passes to buyer or lessee when seller or lessor delivers or tenders delivery of the goods.

a. **Delivery *with* Movement of the Goods**
When goods are to be delivered by truck or other paid transport, in a shipment contract risk passes to buyer or lessee when goods are delivered to a carrier. In a destination contract, risk passes to buyer or lessee when goods are tendered at the destination.

b. **Delivery *without* Movement of the Goods**
When goods are to be picked up from seller or lessor by buyer or lessee, if seller or lessor is a merchant, risk passes only on buyer's or lessee's taking possession. If seller or lessor is not a merchant, risk passes on seller's or lessor's tender of delivery.

3. **Risk of Loss in a Breached Sales Contract**
Generally, the party in breach bears the risk of loss.

D. **INSURABLE INTEREST**
A buyer or lessee has an insurable interest in goods the moment they are identified to the contract [UCC 2–501(1), 2A–218(1)]. A seller or lessor has an insurable interest in goods as long as he or she retains title or holds a security interest in the goods [UCC 2–501(2), 2A–218(3)].

VIII. PERFORMANCE OF SALES AND LEASE CONTRACTS

The UCC imposes on the performance of all sales or lease contract an obligation of good faith (honesty, and in the case of a merchant the observance of reasonable commercial standards of fair dealing in the trade) [UCC 2–103(b)].

A. **OBLIGATION OF THE SELLER OR LESSOR—PERFECT TENDER OF DELIVERY**
Seller or lessor must have and hold goods that conform exactly to the description in the contract at buyer's or lessee's disposal and give buyer or lessee notice to take delivery [UCC 2–503(1), 2A–508(1)]. If goods or tender fail in any respect, buyer or lessee can accept the goods, reject them, or accept part and reject part [UCC 2–601, 2A–509]. Exceptions—

1. **Agreement of the Parties**
For example, parties may agree that seller or lessor can repair or replace any defective goods within a reasonable time.

2. **Cure**
If nonconforming goods are rejected, seller or lessor can notify buyer or lessee of intent to repair or replace the goods and can then do so in the contract time for performance [UCC 2–508, 2A–513].

3. **Substitution of Carriers**
When an agreed-on manner of delivery becomes impracticable or unavailable through no fault of either party, a commercially reasonable substitute is sufficient [UCC 2–614(1)].

4. **Commercial Impracticability**
Delay or nondelivery is not a breach if performance is impracticable "by the occurrence of a contingency the nonoccurrence of which was a basic assumption on which the contract was made" [UCC 2–615(a), 2A–405(a)]. Seller must give notice.

5. **Destruction of Identified Goods**
When goods are destroyed (through no fault of a party) before risk passes, parties are excused from performance [UCC 2–613(a), 2A–221]. If goods are only partially destroyed, a buyer can treat a contract as void or accept damaged goods with a price allowance.

B. **OBLIGATIONS OF THE BUYER OR LESSEE**
Buyer or lessee must (1) furnish facilities reasonably suited for receipt of the goods [UCC 2–503] and (2) make payment at time and place of delivery, even if it is the same as the place of shipment [UCC 2–310(a), 2A–516(1)].

C. ANTICIPATORY REPUDIATION

A party can (1) treat a repudiation as a final breach by pursuing a remedy or (2) wait, hoping that the repudiating party will decide to honor the contract [UCC 2–610, 2A–402]. If the party decides to wait, the breaching party can retract the repudiation [UCC 2–611, 2A–403].

IX. REMEDIES FOR BREACH OF SALES AND LEASE CONTRACTS

A. REMEDIES OF THE SELLER OR LESSOR

1. **The Right to Withhold Delivery**
   Seller or lessor can withhold delivery if buyer or lessee wrongfully rejects or revokes acceptance, fails to pay, or repudiates [UCC 2–703, 2A–523].

2. **The Right to Resell or Dispose of the Goods**
   If seller or lessor still has the goods and buyer or lessee breaches or repudiates the contract, seller or lessor can resell or otherwise dispose of the goods, holding buyer or lessee liable for any loss [UCC 2–703(d), 2–706(1), 2A–523(1)(e), 2A–527(1)].

3. **The Right to Recover the Purchase Price or Lease Payments Due**
   Seller or lessor can bring an action for the price if he or she is unable to resell [UCC 2–709(1), 2A–529(1)]. The buyer gets the goods, unless the seller or lessor disposes of them before collection of the judgment (with the proceeds credited to the buyer).

4. **The Right to Recover Damages**
   If buyer or lessee repudiates a contract or wrongfully refuses to accept, seller or lessor can recover the difference between the contract price and the market price (at the time and place of tender), plus incidental damages [UCC 2–708, 2A–528]. If the market price is less than the contract price, seller or lessor gets lost profits.

B. REMEDIES OF THE BUYER OR LESSEE

1. **The Right of Cover**
   Buyer or lessee can obtain cover (substitute goods) and then sue for damages. The measure of damages is the difference between the cost of cover and the contract price, plus incidental and consequential damages, minus expenses saved by the breach [UCC 2–712, 2–715, 2A–518, 2A–520].

2. **The Right to Obtain Specific Performance**
   Buyer or lessee can obtain specific performance if goods are unique [UCC 2–716(1), 2A–521(1)].

3. **The Right to Recover Damages**
   The measure is the difference between the contract price and, when buyer or lessee learned of the breach, the market price (at the place of delivery), plus incidental and consequential damages, minus expenses saved by the breach [UCC 2–713, 2A–519].

4. **The Right to Reject the Goods**
   If goods or tender fails to conform to the contract, buyer or lessee can reject them. If some of the goods conform, buyer or lessee can keep those and reject the rest [UCC 2–601, 2A–509].

5. **The Right to Recover Damages for Accepted Goods**
   Notice of a breach must be within a reasonable time [UCC 2–607, 2A–516]. The measure of damages is the difference between value of goods as accepted and value if they had been as promised [UCC 2–714(2), 2A–519(4)].

6. **The Right to Revoke Acceptance**
   Acceptance can be revoked if a nonconformity substantially impairs the value of the goods *and* is either not seasonably cured or is difficult to discover [UCC 2–608, 2A–517]. Notice must be given to

seller or lessor before goods have undergone substantial change (not caused by their own defects, such as spoilage) [UCC 2–608(2), 2A–517(4)].

X.   SALES AND LEASE WARRANTIES

A. WARRANTIES OF TITLE

1. Sellers
Sellers warrant (1) they have good title to the goods and transfer of title is rightful [UCC 2–312(1)(a)]; (2) goods are free of a security interest or other lien of which buyer has no knowledge [UCC 2–312(1)(b)]; and (3) goods are free of any third person's patent, trademark, or copyright claims [UCC 2–312(3)].

2. Lessors
Lessors warrant (1) no third party will interfere with the lessee's use of the goods and (2) the goods are free of any third person's patent, trademark, or copyright claims [UCC 2A–211].

3. Disclaimers
Title warranty can be disclaimed or modified only by specific language (although circumstances in a sale may indicate clearly that no assurance of title is being made [UCC 2–312(2)]). In a lease, a disclaimer must be specific, in writing, and conspicuous [UCC 2A–214(4)].

B. EXPRESS WARRANTIES

1. When Express Warranties Arise
Seller or lessor warrants that goods will conform to [UCC 2–313, 2A–210] (1) affirmations or promises of fact (on a label or in a contract, an ad, a brochure, etc.); (2) descriptions (for example, on a label or in a contract, an ad, a brochure, etc.); and (3) samples or models.

2. Statements of Opinion and Value
A statement that relates to the value or worth of goods or a statement of opinion or recommendation about goods is not an express warranty [UCC 2–313(2), 2A–210(2)], unless seller or lessor is an expert and gives an opinion as an expert.

3. Disclaimers
Seller can avoid making express warranties by not promising or affirming anything, describing the goods, or using of a sample or model [UCC 2–313]. A written disclaimer in clear and conspicuous language, called to buyer or lessee's attention, can negate all oral warranties not included in the written contract [UCC 2–316(1), 2A–214(1)].

C. IMPLIED WARRANTIES
An implied warranty is derived by implication or inference from the nature of a transaction or the relative situations or circumstances of the parties.

1. Implied Warranty of Merchantability
This warranty automatically arises in every sale or lease of goods by a merchant who deals in such goods. Goods that are merchantable are "reasonably fit for the ordinary purposes for which such goods are used" [UCC 2–314, 2A–212].

2. Implied Warranty of Fitness for a Particular Purpose
Arises when a seller or lessor knows or has reason to know particular purpose for which buyer or lessee will use goods and knows buyer or lessee is relying on seller or lessor to select suitable goods [UCC 2–315, 2A–213]. Goods can be merchantable but not fit for a particular purpose.

3. Implied Warranty—Dealing, Performance, or Trade Usage
When the parties know a well-recognized trade custom, it is inferred that they intended it to apply to their contract [UCC 2–314, 2A–212].

4. **Disclaimers**
Implied warranties can be disclaimed by the expression "as is" or a similar phrase [UCC 2–316(3)(a), 2A–214(3)(a)]. Implied warranty of fitness for a particular purpose: disclaimer must be in writing and be conspicuous. Implied warranty of merchantability: disclaimer must mention merchantability; if it is in writing, it must be conspicuous.

XI.   E-CONTRACTS

These include contracts entered into in e-commerce, whether business-to-business (B2B) or business-to-consumer (B2C), and contracts involving the computer industry.

A.   ONLINE CONTRACT FORMATION

Disputes arising from contracts entered into online concern the terms and the parties' assent to them.

1. **Online Offers**
Terms should be conspicuous and clearly spelled out. On a Web site, this can be done with a link to a separate page that contains the details. Subjects include remedies, forum selection, payment, taxes, refund and return policies, disclaimers, and privacy policies. A click-on acceptance box should also be included.

2. **Online Acceptances**

   a. **Click-On Agreements**
   This is when a buyer, completing a transaction on a computer, indicates his or her assent to be bound by the terms of the offer by clicking on a button that says, for example, "I agree." The terms may appear on a Web site through which a buyer obtains goods or services, or on a computer screen when software is loaded.

   b. **Browse-Wrap Terms**
   These do not require a user to assent to the terms before going ahead with an online transaction. Offerors of these terms generally assert that they are binding without the user's active consent. Critics argue that a user should at least be required to navigate past the terms before they should be considered binding.

B.   E-SIGNATURES

How are e-signatures created and verified, and what is their legal effect?

1. **E-Signature Technologies**
This most common method involves the use of asymmetric (different) cryptographic keys, which provide private code for one party and public software for another party, who reads the code to verify the first party's identity. A cybernotary issues the keys.

2. **State Laws Governing E-Signatures**
Most states have laws governing e-signatures, although the laws are not uniform. The Uniform Electronic Transactions Act (UETA), issued in 1999, was an attempt by the National Conference of Commissioners on Uniform State Laws and the American Law Institute to create more uniformity.

3. **Federal Law on E-Signatures and E-Documents**

   a. **The E-SIGN Act**
   In 2000, Congress enacted the Electronic Signatures in Global and National Commerce (E-SIGN) Act to provide no contract, record, or signature may be denied legal effect solely because it is in an electronic form. Some documents are excluded (such as those under UCC Articles 3, 4, and 9).

   b. **Preemption**
   If a state enacts the UETA without modifying it, the E-SIGN Act does not preempt it. The E-SIGN Act preempts modified versions of the UETA to the extent that they are inconsistent with the E-SIGN Act.

C. THE UNIFORM ELECTRONIC TRANSACTIONS ACT

1. **What the UETA Does**

   The UETA removes barriers to e-commerce by giving the same legal effect to e-records and e-signatures as to paper documents and signatures.

2. **The Scope and Applicability of the UETA**

   The UETA applies only to e-records and e-signatures in a transaction (an interaction between two or more people relating to business, commercial, or government activities). It does not apply to laws governing wills or testamentary trusts, the UCC (except Articles 2 and 2A), the UCITA, and other laws excluded by states that adopt the UETA, or to agreements that opt out of its provisions.

D. THE UNIFORM COMPUTER INFORMATION TRANSACTIONS ACT

UCC Article 2 could not be applied to most transactions involving software, so alternatives were proposed. The National Conference of Commissioners on Uniform State Laws and the American Law Institute issued the Uniform Computer Information Transactions Act (UCITA).

1. **The Scope and Applicability of the UCITA**

   The UCITA covers contracts to license or buy software, and contracts that give access to, or allow the distribution of, computer information ("information in electronic form obtained from or through use of a computer, or that is in digital or equivalent form capable of being processed by a computer" [UCITA 102(10)].

2. **Parties Can Opt Out**

   The UCITA applies in the absence of an agreement to the contrary, but parties can waive or vary any or all of it.

TRUE-FALSE QUESTIONS

(Answers at the Back of the Book)

____ 1. Article 2 of the UCC governs sales of goods.

____ 2. The UCC governs sales of services and real estate.

____ 3. Before an interest in specific goods can pass from a seller to a buyer, the goods must exist and be identified to the contract.

____ 4. If a seller is a merchant, the risk of loss passes when a buyer takes possession of the goods.

____ 5. The duties and obligations of the parties to a contract include those specified in their agreement.

____ 6. Unless the parties agree otherwise, a buyer or lessee must pay for goods in advance.

____ 7. If a buyer or lessee wrongfully refuses to accept or pay for conforming goods, the seller or lessor can recover damages.

____ 8. If a seller or lessor wrongfully refuses to deliver conforming goods, the buyer or lessee can recover damages.

____ 9. A contract cannot include both an implied warranty and an express warranty.

____ 10. A click-on agreement is not normally enforced.

FILL-IN QUESTIONS

(Answers at the Back of the Book)

A seller's obligations include holding _____ (conforming/nonconforming) goods at a buyer's disposal _____ (and/or) giving notice reasonably necessary for the buyer to take delivery. The _____ (seller/buyer) must make payment at the time and place of _____ (delivery/receipt) of the goods _____ (even if/unless) the parties have agreed otherwise.

MULTIPLE-CHOICE QUESTIONS

(Answers at the Back of the Book)

____ 1. A-One Products Corporation and Best Manufacturing, Inc., enter into a contract for a sale of goods that does not include a price term. In a suit between A-One and Best over this contract and the price, a court will

   a. determine a reasonable price.
   b. impose the lowest market price for the goods.
   c. refuse to enforce the agreement.
   d. return the parties to the positions they held before the contract.

____ 2. Coastal Sales Corporation sends its purchase order form to Delta Products, Inc., for sixty display stands. Delta responds with its own form. Additional terms in Delta's form automatically become part of the contract unless

   a. Coastal objects to the new terms within a reasonable period of time.
   b. Coastal's form expressly required acceptance of its terms.
   c. the additional terms materially alter the original contract.
   d. any of the above.

____ 3. Best Products Corporation agrees to ship one hundred calculators to International Engineering, Inc. (IEI). Before the calculators arrive at IEI's offices, they are lost. The most important factor in determining who bears the risk of loss is

   a. how the calculators were lost.
   b. the contract's shipping terms.
   c. the method by which the calculators were shipped.
   d. title to the calculators.

____ 4. Standard Goods, Inc., ships fifty defective hard drives to Top Business Corporation. Top rejects the drives and ships them back to Standard, via United Transport, Inc. The drives are lost in transit. The loss is suffered by

   a. Standard.
   b. Top.
   c. United.
   d. none of the above.

____ 5. Athletic Goods, Inc. (AGI), agrees to sell sports equipment to Bob's Sports Store. Before the time for performance, AGI tells Bob that it will not deliver. This is

   a. anticipatory repudiation.
   b. assurance and cooperation.
   c. commercial impracticability.
   d. perfect tender.

____ 6. Standard Office Products orders one hundred computers from National Suppliers. Unless the parties agree otherwise, National's obligation to Standard is to

    a. deliver the computers to a common carrier.
    b. deliver the computers to Standard's place of business.
    c. hold conforming goods and give notice for Standard to take delivery.
    d. set aside conforming goods for Standard's inspection before delivery.

____ 7. Gamma Corporation agrees to sell the updated version of its word-processing software to Omega Company. Gamma delivers an outdated version of the program. Omega's remedies may include

    a. recovering damages only.
    b. rejecting part or all of the goods, or revoking acceptance only.
    c. recovering damages, rejecting the goods, or revoking acceptance.
    d. none of the above.

____ 8. E-Equip, Inc., agrees to lease ten servers to Office Company. When E-Equip tries to deliver, Office refuses to accept. There is nothing wrong with the servers. E-Equip sues Office, seeking damages. E-Equip is entitled to the difference between

    a. the contract price and the market price.
    b. the market price and E-Equip's lost profits.
    c. E-Equip's lost profits and the contract price.
    d. none of the above.

____ 9. Great Furniture Company makes and sells furniture. To avoid liability for most implied warranties, their sales agreements should note that their goods are sold

    a. "as is."
    b. by a merchant.
    c. for cash only.
    d. in perfect condition.

____ 10. American Sales Company and B2C Corporation enter into a contract over the Internet. The contract says nothing about the UETA. The UETA applies to

    a. none of the contract.
    b. only the part of the contract that does not involve computer information.
    c. only the part of the contract that involves computer information.
    d. the entire contract.

STARBUCKS COFFEE COMPANY
INTERNATIONAL SALES CONTRACT
APPLICATIONS

(Answers at the Back of the Book)

The following hypothetical situation and multiple-choice questions relate to your text's fold-out exhibit of the international sales contract used by Starbucks Coffee Company. In that contract, Starbucks orders five hundred tons of coffee at $10 per pound from XYZ Co.

____ 1. Starbucks and XYZ would have an enforceable contract even if they did *not* state in writing

    a. the amount of coffee ordered.
    b. the price of the coffee.
    c. both a and b.
    d. none of the above.

____ **2.** If Starbucks and XYZ did not include a "DESCRIPTION" of the coffee as "High grown Mexican Altura," then the delivered coffee must met

   a. Starbuck's subjective expectations of their quality.
   b. Starbuck's description of the goods in ads, on labels, and so on.
   c. XYZ's description of the goods in ads, on labels, and so on.
   d. XYZ's subjective belief in their quality.

____ **3.** Starbucks's incentive to pay on time, according to the terms of this contract, is the clause titled

   a. CLAIMS.
   b. GUARANTEE.
   c. PAYMENT.
   d. PRICE.

____ **4.** XYZ's incentive to deliver coffee that conforms to the contract is the clause titled

   a. CLAIMS.
   b. GUARANTEE.
   c. PAYMENT.
   d. PRICE.

____ **5.** Under this contract, until the coffee is delivered to its destination, the party who bears the risk of loss is

   a. Bonded Public Warehouse.
   b. Green Coffee Association
   c. Starbucks.
   d. XYZ.

SHORT ESSAY QUESTIONS

1. For purposes of the UCC, who is a merchant?

2. What is the difference between the implied warranty of merchantability and the implied warranty of fitness for a particular purpose?

ISSUE SPOTTERS

(Answers at the Back of the Book)

1. E-Design, Inc., orders 150 computer desks. Fine Supplies, Inc., ships 150 printer stands. Is this an acceptance of the offer or a counteroffer? If it is an acceptance, is it a breach of the contract? What if Fine told E-Design it was sending printer stands as "an accommodation"?

2. Market Distributors, Inc., contracts to sell to National Motor Company (NMC) 10,000 cogwheels at $1 each to be delivered to NMC's factory in Detroit on May 1. Market knows that NMC will use the cogwheels to manufacture specialty motors and that NMC's operation will be at a standstill if it does not receive the goods. When Market fails to deliver, the price of cogwheels in Detroit is $1.20 each. NMC's operation shuts down. NMC sues Market. What is NMC entitled to?

3. Owen loves Phat Foods, which are cholesterol-rich. When Owen is diagnosed as suffering from heart disease, he sues Phat Foods Company, on the ground that its foods are not fit to eat in violation of the implied warranty of merchantability. Is it likely that the court will agree with Owen?

Chapter 12
Torts and Cyber Torts

WHAT THIS CHAPTER IS ABOUT

The law of *torts* is concerned with a person's wrongful conduct that causes injury to another. *Tort* is French for "wrong." For acts that cause physical injury or that interfere with physical security and freedom of movement, tort law provides remedies, typically damages (money).

This chapter outlines intentional torts, including torts that are more specifically related to business, and negligence. Strict liability, another part of tort law, is outlined in Chapter 13.

CHAPTER OUTLINE

I. THE BASIS OF TORT LAW
Tort law recognizes that some acts are wrong because they cause physical injuries to persons or property, interfere with others' security or freedom, or harm certain intangible interests, such as privacy or reputation.

II. INTENTIONAL TORTS AGAINST PERSONS AND BUSINESS RELATIONSHIPS
Intentional torts involve acts that were intended or could be expected to bring about consequences that are the basis of the tort. A tortfeasor (one committing a tort) must intend to commit an act, the consequences of which interfere with the personal or business interests of another in a way not permitted by law.

A. ASSAULT AND BATTERY

1. Assault
An assault is an intentional act that creates in another person a reasonable apprehension or fear of immediate harmful or offensive contact.

2. Battery
A battery is an intentional and harmful or offensive physical contact. Physical injury need not occur. Whether the contact is offensive is determined by the reasonable person standard.

3. Compensation
A plaintiff may be compensated for emotional harm or loss of reputation resulting from a battery, as well as for physical harm.

4. Defenses to Assault and Battery

a. Consent
When a person consents to an act that damages him or her, there is generally no liability for the damage.

b. Self-Defense
An individual who is defending his or her life or physical well being can claim self-defense.

c. Defense of Others
An individual can act in a reasonable manner to protect others who are in real or apparent danger.

d. **Defense of Property**

Reasonable force may be used in attempting to remove intruders from one's home, although force that is likely to cause death or great bodily injury can never be used just to protect property.

B. FALSE IMPRISONMENT

1. **What False Imprisonment Is**

False imprisonment is the intentional confinement or restraint of another person without justification. The confinement can be accomplished through the use of physical barriers, physical restraint, or threats of physical force.

2. **The Defense of Probable Cause**

In some states, a merchant is justified in delaying a suspected shoplifter if the merchant has probable cause. The detention must be conducted in a reasonable manner and for only a reasonable length of time.

C. INTENTIONAL INFLICTION OF EMOTIONAL DISTRESS

Infliction of emotional distress is an intentional act that amounts to extreme and outrageous conduct resulting in severe emotional distress to another (a few states require physical symptoms). Repeated annoyance, with threats (such as extreme methods of debt collection), is one way to commit this tort.

D. DEFAMATION

Defamation is wrongfully hurting another's good reputation through false statements. Doing it orally is slander; doing it in writing is libel.

1. **The Publication Requirement**

The statement must be published (communicated to a third party). Anyone who republishes or repeats a defamatory statement is liable.

2. **Types of False Utterances that Are Torts *Per Se***

Proof of injury is not required when one falsely states that another has a loathsome communicable disease, has committed improprieties while engaging in a profession or trade, or has committed or been imprisoned for a serious crime, or that an unmarried woman is unchaste.

3. **Defenses to Defamation**

a. **Truth**

The statement is true. It must be true in whole, not in part.

b. **Privileged Speech**

The statement is privileged: absolute (made in a judicial or legislative proceeding) or qualified (for example, made by one corporate director to another and was about corporate business).

c. **Public Figures**

The statement is about a public figure, made in a public medium, and related to a matter of general public interest. To recover damages, a public figure must prove a statement was made with actual malice (knowledge of its falsity or reckless disregard for the truth).

E. INVASION OF PRIVACY

Four acts qualify as invasions of privacy:

1. The use of a person's name, picture, or other likeness for commercial purposes without permission. (This is appropriation—see below.)

2. Intrusion on an individual's affairs or seclusion.

3. Publication of information that places a person in a false light.

4. Public disclosure of private facts about an individual that an ordinary person would find objectionable.

F. APPROPRIATION

The use of one person's name or likeness by another, without permission and for the benefit of the user, is appropriation. An individual's right to privacy includes the right to the exclusive use of his or her identity.

G. FRAUDULENT MISREPRESENTATION

Fraud is the use of misrepresentation and deceit for personal gain. Puffery (seller's talk) is not fraud. The elements of fraudulent misrepresentation are—

1. A misrepresentation of material facts or conditions with knowledge that they are false or with reckless disregard for the truth.

2. An intent to induce another to rely on the misrepresentation.

3. Justifiable reliance by the deceived party.

4. Damages suffered as a result of the reliance.

5. A causal connection between the misrepresentation and the injury.

H. WRONGFUL INTERFERENCE

Torts involving wrongful interference with another's business rights generally fall into the two categories outlined here.

1. **Wrongful Interference with a Contractual Relationship**
   This occurs when one party induces another to break a contract. Simply reaping the benefits of a broken contract is not enough. Elements include:

   a. A contract between two parties.

   b. A third party's knowledge of the contract.

   c. The third party's intentionally causing either of the two parties to break the contract. The third party's bad faith or harmful intent is immaterial, but the purpose of the interference must be to advance the third party's economic interest.

2. **Wrongful Interference with a Business Relationship**
   If there are two shoe stores in a mall, placing an employee of Store A in front of Store B to divert customers to Store A is wrongful interference with a business relationship (an unfair trade practice).

3. **Defenses to Wrongful Interference**
   A person is not liable if the interference is justified or permissible (such as bona fide competitive behavior).

III. INTENTIONAL TORTS AGAINST PROPERTY

A. TRESPASS TO LAND

This occurs if a person, without permission, enters onto, above, or below the surface of land owned by another; causes anything to enter onto the land; or remains on the land or permits anything to remain on it.

1. **Trespass Criteria, Rights, and Duties**
   Posted signs *expressly* establish trespass. Entering onto property to commit an illegal act *impliedly* does so. Trespassers are liable for any property damage. Owners may have a duty to post notice of any danger.

2. Defenses against Trespass to Land
Defenses against trespass include that the trespass was warranted or that the purported owner had no right to possess the land in question.

B. TRESPASS TO PERSONAL PROPERTY
Occurs when an individual unlawfully harms the personal property of another or interferes with an owner's right to exclusive possession and enjoyment. Defenses include that the interference was warranted.

C. CONVERSION

1. What Conversion Is
Conversion is an act depriving an owner of personal property without the owner's permission and without just cause. This is the civil side of crimes related to theft. Buying stolen goods is conversion.

2. Defenses
Defenses to conversion include that the purported owner does not own the property or does not have a right to possess it that is superior to the right of the holder. Necessity is also a defense.

D. DISPARAGEMENT OF PROPERTY
Disparagement of property occurs when economically injurious falsehoods are made about another's product or ownership of property. It is a general term for torts that can be specifically referred to as slander of quality (product) or slander of title (ownership of property).

IV. NEGLIGENCE

A. THE ELEMENTS OF NEGLIGENCE

1. What Negligence Is
Negligence is someone's failure to live up to a required duty of care, causing injury. The breach of the duty must create a risk of certain harmful consequences, whether or not that was the intent.

2. The Elements of Negligence
(1) A duty of care, (2) breach of the duty of care, (3) damage or injury as a result of the breach, and (4) the breach causes the damage or injury.

B. THE DUTY OF CARE AND ITS BREACH

1. The Reasonable Person Standard
The duty of care is measured by the reasonable person standard (how a reasonable person would have acted in the same circumstances).

2. Duty of Landowners
Owners are expected to use reasonable care (guard against some risks and warn of others) to protect persons coming onto their property.

3. Duty of Professionals
A professional's duty is consistent with his or her knowledge, skill, and intelligence, including what is reasonable for that professional.

4. Factors for Determining a Breach of the Duty of Care
The nature of the act (whether it is outrageous or commonplace), the manner in which the act is performed (cautiously versus heedlessly), and the nature of the injury (whether it is serious or slight). Note: failing to rescue a stranger in peril is *not* a breach of a duty of care.

C. THE INJURY REQUIREMENT AND DAMAGES

To recover damages (receive compensation), the plaintiff must have suffered some loss, harm, wrong, or invasion of a protected interest. Punitive damages (to punish the wrongdoer and deter others) may also be awarded.

D. CAUSATION

1. Causation in Fact

The breach of the duty of care must cause the injury—that is, "but for" the wrongful act, the injury would not have occurred.

2. Proximate Cause

There must be a connection between the act and the injury strong enough to justify imposing liability. Generally, the harm or the victim of the harm must have been foreseeable in light of all of the circumstances.

E. DEFENSES TO NEGLIGENCE

1. Assumption of Risk

A plaintiff who voluntarily enters into a risky situation, knowing the risk, cannot recover. This does not include a risk different from or greater than the risk normally involved in the situation.

2. Superseding Cause

A superseding intervening force breaks the connection between the breach of the duty of care and the injury or damage. Taking a defensive action (such as swerving to avoid an oncoming car) does not break the connection. Nor does someone else's attempt to rescue the injured party.

3. Contributory Negligence

In some states, a plaintiff cannot recover for an injury if he or she was negligent. The last-clear-chance doctrine allows a negligent plaintiff to recover if the defendant had the last chance to avoid the damage.

4. Comparative Negligence

In most states, the plaintiff's and the defendant's negligence is compared and liability prorated. Some states allow a plaintiff to recover even if his or her fault is greater than the defendant's. In many states, the plaintiff gets nothing if he or she is more than 50 percent at fault.

F. SPECIAL NEGLIGENCE DOCTRINES AND STATUTES

1. *Res Ipsa Loquitur*

If negligence is very difficult to prove, a court may infer it, and the defendant must prove he or she was *not* negligent. This is only if the event causing the harm is one that normally does not occur in the absence of negligence and is caused by something within the defendant's control.

2. Negligence *Per Se*

A person who violates a statute providing for a criminal penalty is liable when the violation causes another to be injured, if (1) the statute sets out a standard of conduct, and when, where, and of whom it is expected; (2) the injured person is in the class protected by the statute; and (3) the statute was designed to prevent the type of injury suffered.

3. "Danger Invites Rescue" Doctrine

A person who endangers another is liable for injuries to third persons attempting to rescue the endangered party.

4. Special Negligence Statutes

Good Samaritan statutes protect those who aid others from being sued for negligence. Dram shop acts impose liability on bar owners for injuries caused by intoxicated persons who are served by those owners. A statute may impose liability on social hosts for acts of their guests.

V.   CYBER TORTS

A. DEFAMATION ONLINE
Under the Communications Decency Act of 1996, Internet service providers (ISPs) are not liable for the defamatory remarks of those who use their services.

B. SPAM
Spam is junk e-mail. Some states ban or regulate its use, which may constitute trespass to personal property. The First Amendment may also limit what the government can do to restrict it.

TRUE-FALSE QUESTIONS

(Answers at the Back of the Book)

T   1.   To commit an intentional tort, a person must intend the consequences of his or her act or know with substantial certainty that certain consequences will result.

F   2.   A reasonable apprehension or fear of harmful or offensive contact at some time in the future is an assault.

T   3.   A defamatory statement must be communicated to a third party to be actionable.

F   4.   Puffery is fraud.

T   5.   Depriving an owner of personal property without permission and without just cause, to place it in another's service, is conversion.

F   6.   To determine whether a duty of care has been breached, a judge asks how he or she would have acted in the same circumstances.

F   7.   Disparagement of property is another term for appropriation.

F   8.   Bona fide competitive behavior can constitute wrongful interference with a contractual relationship.

T   9.   Internet service providers are not normally liable for the defamatory remarks of those who use their services.

F   10.   The government cannot regulate spam.

FILL-IN QUESTIONS

(Answers at the Back of the Book)

1.   Basic defenses to _____ (negligence/intentional torts) include comparative negligence, contributory negligence, and assumption of risk.

2.   One who voluntarily and knowingly enters into a risky situation normally cannot recover damages. This is the _____ (defense of contributory negligence/defense of assumption of risk).

3.   When both parties' failure to use reasonable care combines to cause injury, in some states the injured party's recovery is precluded by his or her own negligence. This is the _____ (comparative/contributory) negligence doctrine.

4.   When both parties' failure to use reasonable care combines to cause injury, in most states damages are reduced by a percentage that represents the degree of the plaintiff's negligence. This is the _____ (comparative/contributory) negligence doctrine.

MULTIPLE-CHOICE QUESTIONS

(Answers at the Back of the Book)

1. Driving his car negligently, Paul crashes into a telephone pole. The pole falls, smashing through the roof of a house onto Karl, who is sitting inside. Karl dies. But for Paul's negligence, Karl would not have died. Regarding Karl's death, Paul's crash is the

    a. cause in fact.
    b. intervening cause.
    c. proximate cause.
    d. superseding cause.

2. Joe shoves Kay, who falls and suffers a concussion. This is an intentional tort

    a. if Joe had a bad motive for shoving Kay.
    b. if Joe intended to shove Kay.
    c. if Kay was afraid of Joe.
    d. only if Joe intended that Kay suffer a concussion.

3. Alan, the owner of Beta Computer Store, detains Cathy, a customer, whom Alan suspects of shoplifting. This is false imprisonment if

    a. Alan detains Cathy for an unreasonably long time.
    b. Cathy did not shoplift.
    c. Cathy has probable cause to suspect Alan of deceit.
    d. Cathy protests her innocence.

4. Best Box Company advertises so effectively that National Products, Inc., stops doing business with Average Packages Corporation. Best is liable for

    a. appropriation.
    b. wrongful interference with a business relationship.
    c. wrongful interference with a contractual relationship.
    d. none of the above.

5. Gil sends a letter to Holly in which he falsely accuses her of embezzling from her employer. This is defamation only if the letter is read by

    a. any third person.
    b. Gil.
    c. Holly.
    d. Holly's employer.

6. Internet Services, Inc. (ISI), is an Internet service provider. ISI does not create, but disseminates, a defamatory statement by Jill, its customer, about Ron. Liability for the remark may be imposed on

    a. ISI and Jill.
    b. ISI or Jill, but not both.
    c. ISI only.
    d. Jill only.

7. Lee, a salesperson for Midsize Corporation, causes a car accident while on business. Lee and Midsize are liable to all persons

    a. who are injured.
    b. who do not have insurance to pay for their injuries.
    c. whose injuries could have been reasonably foreseen.
    d. with whom Lee was doing business.

8. Fred drives across Gail's land. This is a trespass to land only if

a. Fred damages the land.
b. Fred does not have Gail's permission to drive on her land.
c. Fred makes disparaging remarks about Gail's land.
d. Gail is aware of Fred's driving on her land.

9. To protect its customers and other business invitees, Grocers Market must warn them of

a. hidden dangers.
b. obvious dangers.
c. hidden and obvious dangers.
d. none of the above.

10. Online Services Company (OSC) is an Internet service provider. Ads Unlimited, Inc., sends spam to OSC's customers, some of whom then cancel OSC's services. Ads Unlimited is liable for

a. battery.
b. conversion.
c. infliction of emotional distress.
d. trespass to personal property.

SHORT ESSAY QUESTIONS

1. What is a *tort*?

2. Identify and describe the elements of a cause of action based on negligence.

ISSUE SPOTTERS

(Answers at the Back of the Book)

1. Adam kisses the sleeve of Eve's blouse, to which she did not consent and which she finds offensive. Is Adam guilty of a tort?

2. If a student takes another student's business law textbook as a practical joke and hides it for several days before the final examination, has a tort been committed?

3. After less than a year in business, Superior Club surpasses Ordinary Club in number of members. Superior's marketing strategies attract many Ordinary members, who then change clubs. Does Ordinary have any recourse against Superior?

Chapter 13
Strict Liability and Product Liability

WHAT THIS CHAPTER IS ABOUT

Strict liability is liability for injury imposed for reasons other than fault. Manufacturers, processors, and sellers may be liable to consumers, users, and bystanders for physical harm or property damage caused by defective goods. This is *product liability*.

CHAPTER OUTLINE

I. STRICT LIABILITY

A. ABNORMALLY DANGEROUS ACTIVITIES
The basis for imposing strict liability on an abnormally dangerous activity is that the activity creates an extreme risk. Balancing the risk against the potential for harm, it is fair to ask the person engaged in the activity to pay for injury caused by that activity.

B. OTHER APPLICATIONS OF STRICT LIABILITY
A person who keeps a dangerous animal is strictly liable for any harm inflicted by the animal. A significant application of strict liability is in the area of product liability (discussed below).

II. PRODUCT LIABILITY
Product liability may be based on negligence, misrepresentation, or strict liability. It may also be based on warranty law (see Chapter 11).

A. PRODUCT LIABILITY BASED ON NEGLIGENCE
If the failure to exercise reasonable care in the making or marketing of a product causes an injury, the basis of liability is negligence.

   1. **Manufacturer's Duty of Care**
   Due care must be exercised in designing, assembling, and testing a product; selecting materials; inspecting and testing products bought for use in the final product; and placing warnings on the label to inform users of dangers of which an ordinary person might not be aware.

   2. **Privity of Contract between Plaintiff and Defendant Is Not Required**

   3. **Violation of Statutory Duty**
   Manufacturers have statutory duties, such as those relating to labeling. Violation of a statutory duty may be negligence *per se* (see Chapter 12).

B. PRODUCT LIABILITY BASED ON MISREPRESENTATION
If misrepresentation causes injury, there may be liability if it (1) is of a material fact, (2) is intended to induce a buyer's reliance, and (3) the buyer relies on it.

   1. **Proof of Defects Not Required**
   Plaintiff does not have to show product was defective or malfunctioned.

   2. **Fraudulent Misrepresentation**
   Occurs when misrepresentation is done knowingly or with reckless disregard for the facts (such as intentionally concealing defects).

3. **Nonfraudulent Misrepresentation**
   Occurs when a merchant innocently misrepresents the character or quality of goods (the misrepresentation need not be done knowingly).

III. STRICT PRODUCT LIABILITY
A defendant may be held liable for the result of his or her act regardless of intention or exercise of reasonable care (see Chapter 12).

A. PUBLIC POLICY
Public policy assumes that (1) consumers should be protected from unsafe products, (2) manufacturers and distributors should not escape liability solely for lack of privity, and (3) sellers and lessors are in a better position to bear the cost of injuries caused by their products.

B. THE REQUIREMENTS FOR STRICT PRODUCT LIABILITY
Under the *Restatement (Second) of Torts*, Section 402A—

1. **Product Is in a Defective Condition When the Defendant Sells It**

2. **Defendant Is Normally in the Business of Selling the Product**

3. **Defect Makes the Product Unreasonably Dangerous**
   A product may be so defective if either—

   a. **Product Is Dangerous beyond the Ordinary Consumer's Expectation**
      There may have been a flaw in the manufacturing process that led to some defective products being marketed, or a perfectly made product may not have had adequate warning on the label.

   b. **There Is a Less Dangerous, Economically Feasible Alternative that the Manufacturer Failed to Use**
      A manufacturer may have failed to design a safe product.

4. **Plaintiff Incurs Harm to Self or Property by Use of the Product**

5. **Defect Is the Proximate Cause of the Harm**

6. **Product Was Not Substantially Changed After It Was Sold**
   Between the time the product was sold and the time of the injury.

C. PRODUCT DEFECTS
The *Restatement (Third) of Torts: Products Liability* categorizes defects as—

1. **Manufacturing Defects**
   A manufacturing defect occurs when a product departs from its intended design even though all possible care was taken (strict liability).

2. **Design Defects**
   A design defect exists when a foreseeable risk of harm posed by a product could have been reduced by use of a reasonable alternative design and the omission makes the product unreasonably unsafe. A court would consider such factors as consumer expectations and warnings.

3. **Warning Defects**
   A warning defect happens when a reasonable warning could have reduced a product's foreseeable risk of harm and its omission makes the product unreasonably unsafe. Factors include the content and comprehensibility of a warning, and the expected users.

D. MARKET-SHARE LIABILITY
Some courts hold that all firms that manufactured and distributed DES (diethylstilbestrol) during a certain period are liable for injuries in proportion to the firms' respective shares of the market.

E. OTHER APPLICATIONS OF STRICT PRODUCT LIABILITY

1. **Who May Be Liable**
Sellers of goods, including manufacturers, processors, assemblers, packagers, bottlers, wholesalers, distributors, and retailers may be liable. Suppliers of component parts and lessors may be liable for injuries caused by defective products.

2. **Strict Liability Extends to Bystanders**
All courts extend strict liability to cover injured bystanders (limited in some cases to those whose injuries are reasonably foreseeable).

IV. DEFENSES TO PRODUCT LIABILITY

A. ASSUMPTION OF RISK
In some states, this is a defense if (1) plaintiff knew and appreciated the risk created by the defect and (2) plaintiff voluntarily engaged in the risk, event though it was unreasonable to do so.

B. PRODUCT MISUSE
The use must not be the one for which the product was designed, and the misuse must not be reasonably foreseeable.

C. COMPARATIVE NEGLIGENCE (FAULT)
Most states consider a plaintiff's actions in apportioning liability.

D. COMMONLY KNOWN DANGERS
Failing to warn against such a danger is not ground for liability.

E. STATUTES OF LIMITATIONS
A statute of limitations provides that an action must be brought within a specified period of time after the cause of action accrues (after some damage occurs or after a harmed party discovers the damage).

F. STATUTES OF REPOSE
A statute of repose limits the time in which a suit can be filed. It runs from an earlier date and for a longer time than a statute of limitations.

G. TYPE OF INJURY OR LOSS
Some courts limit recovery to personal injuries. Recovery for economic loss is rarely available.

H. TYPE OF GOODS OR LACK OF RECOGNITION
Some states limit the application of strict liability to new goods. Some states refuse to recognize the doctrine of strict liability.

TRUE-FALSE QUESTIONS
(Answers at the Back of the Book)

____ 1. Strict liability is imposed for reasons other than fault.

____ 2. Under the doctrine of strict liability, a defendant is liable for the results of his or her acts only if he or she intended those results.

____ 3. A product liability suit may be based on a warranty theory.

____ 4. Product liability is imposed only if a defect in the design or construction of a product causes an injury.

____ 5. Suppliers are generally required to design products that are safe when misused or that include some protective device.

____ 6. Privity of contract between the plaintiff and defendant is required to bring a product liability suit based on negligence.

____ 7. One of the requirements for a product liability suit based on strict liability is a failure to exercise due care.

____ 8. In many states, the plaintiff's negligence is a defense that may be raised in a product liability suit based on strict liability.

____ 9. A manufacturer has a duty to warn about risks that are obvious or commonly known.

____ 10. Assumption of risk can be raised as a defense in a product liability suit.

FILL-IN QUESTIONS

(Answers at the Back of the Book)

Statutes of limitations and statutes of repose restrict the time within which an action may be brought. A statute of _____ (limitations/repose) typically provides a specified period after a cause of action accrues within which an action must be brought. Sometimes the running of this period _____ (does not begin until/ends when) the injured party discovers, or should have discovered, the injury. A statute of _____ (limitations/repose) provides a time limit on filing a claim, whether or not a cause of action has accrued, so that a defendant will not be vulnerable to a lawsuit indefinitely. Usually, a statute of _____ (limitations/repose) begins to run at an earlier date and runs for a longer time than a statute of _____ (limitations/repose).

MULTIPLE-CHOICE QUESTIONS

(Answers at the Back of the Book)

1. A bridge's design is defective and soon after completion it begins to sway in the wind. Everyone stays off, except Carl, who wants to show off. Carl falls from the bridge and sues its manufacturer, who can raise the defense of

    a. assumption of risk.
    b. commonly known danger.
    c. product misuse.
    d. none of the above.

2. Sport Supplies sells a treadmill to John without warning him of the fact, known to Sport, that the safety shut-off device does not work. In using the treadmill, John discovers the defect. Later, while running on the treadmill, John's shoelace is caught in the gears, which do not shut off, and his foot is injured. If John sues Sport on the ground of strict liability in a jurisdiction that recognizes comparative negligence, Sport may be

    a. entirely liable, because Sport was comparatively negligent.
    b. partially liable, because Sport was comparatively negligent.
    c. entirely liable, because John was comparatively negligent.
    d. not liable, because John was comparatively negligent.

3. SmithCo supplies Jones, Inc., with components for its products. Jones assembles the components and sells the assembled products to consumers. Lee buys and uses one of the products and is injured due to a defective component. In a suit based on strict liability, Lee may recover damages from

    a. SmithCo only.
    b. Jones only.
    c. either SmithCo or Jones.
    d. none of the above.

4. Standard Manufacturing Corporation makes appliances. To satisfy its liability for injuries to consumers harmed by defective Standard appliances, Standard can pass the costs on to

   a. consumers in the form of higher prices.
   b. other makers of appliances in the form of market-share liability.
   c. suppliers in the form of kickbacks.
   d. the government in the form of direct payments.

____ 5. Alpha Products, Inc., makes bicycles. Carla is injured while riding an Alpha bike and files a suit against the maker for product liability based on misrepresentation. To succeed, Carla must show that

   a. Alpha did not use due care with respect to making the bike.
   b. Alpha misrepresented a material fact regarding the bike, on which Carla relied.
   c. Carla did not abuse or misuse the bike.
   d. Carla was in privity of contract with Alpha.

____ 6. Kitchen Products, Inc. (KPI), makes knives. Jay is injured while using a KPI knife, and sues the maker for product liability based on negligence. KPI could successfully defend against the suit by showing that

   a. Jay's injury resulted from a commonly known danger.
   b. Jay misused the knife in a foreseeable way.
   c. KPI did not sell the knife to Jay.
   d. the knife was not altered after KPI sold it.

____ 7. Standard Tools, Inc., makes and sells tools. Tina is injured as a result of using a Standard tool. Tina sues Standard for product liability based on strict liability. To succeed, Tina must prove that Standard

   a. was in privity of contract with Tina.
   b. did not use care with respect to the tool.
   c. misrepresented a material fact regarding the tool on which Tina relied.
   d. none of the above.

____ 8. Yard Work, Inc., makes and sells garden tools. Under the *Restatement (Second) of Torts*, a tool could be unreasonably dangerous

   a. only if, in making the tool, Yard Work failed to use a less dangerous but economically feasible alternative.
   b. only if the tool is dangerous beyond the ordinary consumer's expectation.
   c. if, in making the tool, Yard Work failed to use a less dangerous but economically feasible alternative or if the tool is dangerous beyond the ordinary consumer's expectation.
   d. none of the above.

____ 9. Fran is in Green's Grocery store when a bottle of Hi Cola on a nearby shelf explodes, injuring her. She can recover from the manufacturer of Hi Cola only if she can show that

   a. she did not assume the risk of the explosive bottle of Hi Cola.
   b. she intended to buy the explosive bottle of Hi Cola.
   c. she was injured due to a defect in the product.
   d. the manufacturer failed to use due care in making the bottle of Hi Cola.

____ 10. Omega Electronics, Inc., designs and makes CD players. In a product liability suit based on negligence, Omega could be liable for violating its duty of care with respect to a player's

   a. design only.
   b. manufacture only.
   c. design or manufacture.
   d. none of the above.

SHORT ESSAY QUESTIONS

1.   What distinguishes strict liability as a theory for recovery in a product liability case from other bases for recovery?

2.   How defective must a product be to support a cause of action in strict liability?

ISSUE SPOTTERS

(Answers at the Back of the Book)

1.   Delta Corporation makes tire rims, which it sells to Eagle Vehicles, Inc., to put on its cars. One set of rims is defective, which an inspection would reveal. Eagle does not inspect the rims. The car is sold to Fast Auto Sales. Greg buys the car, which is soon in an accident caused by the defective rims and in which Greg is injured. Is Eagle liable?

2.   Real Chocolate Company makes a box of candy, which it sells to Sweet Things, Inc., a distributor. Sweet sells the box to a Tasty Candy store, where Jill buys it. Jill gives it to Ken, who breaks a tooth on a stone the same size and color of a piece of the candy. If Real, Sweet, and Tasty were not negligent, can they be liable for the injury?

3.   Good Lock Company makes automobile door locks. Premier Motors Corporation installs the locks on Premier cars. Doug buys a Premier car. While driving home, Doug does not wear a seat belt. In a one-car accident, he is thrown from the car when the door flies open and is killed. In a suit based on strict liability, could Good and Premier claim that Doug's failure to wear a seat belt contributed to his death?

Chapter 14
Intellectual Property and Internet Law

WHAT THIS CHAPTER IS ABOUT

Intellectual property consists of the products of intellectual, creative processes. The law of trademarks, patents, copyrights, and related concepts protect many of these products (such as inventions, books, software, movies, and songs). The first parts of this chapter outline these laws. The last part of the chapter covers the protection of intellectual property in cyberspace.

CHAPTER OUTLINE

I. TRADEMARKS AND RELATED PROPERTY

A. TRADEMARKS
The Lanham Act protects trademarks at the federal level. Many states also have statutes that protect trademarks.

1. What a Trademark Is
A distinctive mark, motto, device, or emblem that a manufacturer stamps, prints, or otherwise affixes to the goods it produces to distinguish them from the goods of other manufacturers.

2. The Federal Trademark Dilution Act of 1995
Prohibits **dilution** (unauthorized use of marks on goods or services, even if they do not compete directly with products whose marks are copied).

3. Trademark Registration
A trademark may be registered with a state or the federal government. Trademarks do not need to be registered to be protected.

a. Requirements for Federal Registration
A trademark may be filed with the U.S. Patent and Trademark Office on the basis of (1) use or (2) the intent to use the mark within six months (which may be extended to thirty months).

b. Renewal of Federal Registration
Between the fifth and sixth years and then every ten years (twenty years for marks registered before 1990).

4. Requirements for Trademark Protection
The extent to which the law protects a trademark is normally determined by how distinctive the mark is.

a. Fanciful, Arbitrary, or Suggestive Trademarks
Generally considered the most distinctive trademarks.

b. Descriptive Terms, Geographic Terms, and Personal Names
Not inherently distinctive and not protected until they acquire a secondary meaning (which means that customers associate the mark with the source of a product)

c. Generic Terms
Terms such as *bicycle* or *computer* receive no protection, even if they acquire secondary meaning.

> **5. Trademark Infringement**
> When a trademark is copied to a substantial degree or used in its entirety by another, the trademark is infringed.

B. TRADE DRESS

Trade dress is the image and appearance of a product, and is subject to the same protection as trademarks.

C. SERVICE, CERTIFICATION, AND COLLECTIVE MARKS

The same policies and restrictions that apply to trademarks normally apply to service, certification, and collective marks.

> **1. Service Marks**
> Used to distinguish the services of one person or company from those of another. Registered in the same manner as trademarks.

> **2. Certification Marks**
> Used by one or more persons, other than the owner, to certify the region, materials, quality, mode of manufacture, or accuracy of the owner's goods or services.

> **3. Collective Marks**
> Certification marks used by members of a cooperative, association, or other organization.

D. TRADE NAMES

Used to indicate part or all of a business's name. Trade names cannot be registered with the federal government but may be protected under the common law if they are used as trademarks or service marks.

II.   CYBER MARKS

A. ANTICYBERSQUATTING LEGISLATION

The Anticybersquatting Consumer Reform Act (ACRA) of 1999 amended the Lanham Act to make cybersquatting clearly illegal. Bad faith intent is an element (the ACRA lists "bad faith" factors). Damages may be awarded.

B. META TAGS

Meta tags are words in a Web site's key-word field that determine the site's appearance in search engine results. Using others' marks as tags without permission constitutes trademark infringement.

C. DILUTION IN THE ONLINE WORLD

Using a mark, without permission, in a way that diminishes its distinctive quality. Tech-related cases have concerned the use of marks as domain names and spamming under another's logo.

III.   PATENTS

A. WHAT A PATENT IS

A grant from the federal government that conveys and secures to an inventor the exclusive right to make, use, and sell an invention for a period of twenty years (fourteen years for a design).

B. REQUIREMENTS FOR A PATENT

An invention, discovery, or design must be genuine, novel, useful, and not obvious in light of the technology of the time. A patent is given to the first person to invent a product, not to the first person to file for a patent.

C. PATENT INFRINGEMENT

Patent infringement is making, using, or selling another's patented design, product, or process without the patent owner's permission. The owner may obtain an injunction, damages, destruction of all infringing copies, attorneys' fees, and court costs.

D. PATENTS FOR SOFTWARE

The basis for software is often a mathematical equation or formula, which is not patentable, but a patent can be obtained for a process that incorporates a computer program.

E. PATENTS FOR BUSINESS PROCESSES

Business processes are patentable (laws of nature, natural phenomena, and abstract ideas are not patentable).

IV. COPYRIGHTS

A. WHAT A COPYRIGHT IS

An intangible right granted by statute to the author or originator of certain literary or artistic productions. Protection is automatic; registration is not required.

B. COPYRIGHT PROTECTION

Automatic for the life of the author plus fifty years. Copyrights owned by publishing houses expire seventy-five years from the date of publication or a hundred years from the date of creation, whichever is first. For works by more than one author, copyright expires fifty years after the death of the last surviving author.

C. WHAT IS PROTECTED EXPRESSION?

To be protected, under Section 102 of the Copyright Act a work must meet these requirements—

1. Fit a Certain Category

It must be a (1) literary work; (2) musical work; (3) dramatic work; (4) pantomime or choreographic work; (5) pictorial, graphic, or sculptural work; (6) film or other audiovisual work; or (7) a sound recording. The Copyright Act also protects computer software and architectural plans.

2. Be Fixed in a Durable Medium

From which it can be perceived, reproduced, or communicated.

3. Be Original

A compilation of facts (formed by the collection and assembling of preexisting materials of data) is copyrightable if it is original.

D. WHAT IS NOT PROTECTED

Ideas, facts, and related concepts are not protected. If an idea and an expression cannot be separated, the expression cannot be copyrighted.

E. COPYRIGHT INFRINGEMENT

A copyright is infringed if a work is copied without the copyright holder's permission. A copy does not have to be exactly the same as the original—copying a substantial part of the original is enough.

1. Penalties

Actual damages (based on the harm to the copyright holder); damages under the Copyright Act, not to exceed $150,000; and criminal proceedings (which may result in fines or imprisonment).

2. Exception—Fair Use Doctrine

The Copyright Act permits the fair use of a work for purposes such as criticism, comment, news reporting, teaching (including multiple copies for classroom use), scholarship, or research.

F. COPYRIGHT PROTECTION FOR SOFTWARE

The Computer Software Copyright Act of 1980 provides protection.

1. What Is Protected

The binary object code (the part of a software program readable only by computer); the source code (the part of a program readable by people); and the program structure, sequence, and organization.

2. **What May or May Not Be Protected**
The "look and feel"—the general appearance, command structure, video images, menus, windows, and other displays—of a program.

V. COPYRIGHTS IN DIGITAL INFORMATION

Copyright law is important in cyberspace in part because the nature of the Internet means that data is "copied" before being transferred online.

A. THE COPYRIGHT ACT OF 1976
Copyright law requires the copyright holder's permission to sell a "copy" of a work. For these purposes, loading a file or program into a computer's random access memory (RAM) is the making of a "copy."

B. NO ELECTRONIC THEFT ACT OF 1997
Extends criminal liability to the exchange of pirated, copyrighted materials, even if no profit is realized from the exchange, and to the unauthorized copying of works for personal use.

C. DIGITAL MILLENNIUM COPYRIGHT ACT OF 1998
Imposes penalties on anyone who circumvents encryption software or other technological anti-piracy protection. Also prohibits the manufacture, import, sale, or distribution of devices or services for circumvention. ISP s are not liable for their customers' violations.

D. MP3 AND FILE-SHARING TECHNOLOGY
MP3 file compression and music file sharing occur over the Internet through peer-to-peer (P2P) networking. Doing this without the permission of the owner of the music's copyright is infringement.

VI. TRADE SECRETS

A. WHAT A TRADE SECRET IS
Customer lists, formulas, plans, research and development, pricing information, marketing techniques, production techniques, and generally anything that provides an opportunity to obtain an advantage over competitors who do not know or use it.

B. TRADE SECRET PROTECTION
Protection of trade secrets extends both to ideas and their expression. Liability extends to those who misappropriate trade secrets by any means. Trade secret theft is also a federal crime.

C. TRADE SECRETS IN CYBERSPACE
The nature of technology (especially e-mail) undercuts a firm's ability to protect its confidential information, including trade secrets.

VII. LICENSING

Permitting the use of a mark, copyright, patent, or trade secret for certain purposes. Use for other purposes is a breach of the license agreement. Licensing of computer information is discussed in Chapter 11.

VIII. INTERNATIONAL PROTECTION

A. THE BERNE CONVENTION
The Berne Convention is an international copyright treaty.

1. **For Citizens of Countries That Have Signed the Berne Convention**
If, for example, an American writes a book, the copyright in the book is recognized by every country that has signed the convention.

2. **For Citizens of Other Countries**
If a citizen of a country that has not signed the convention publishes a book first in a country that has signed, all other countries that have signed the convention recognize that author's copyright.

B. THE TRIPS AGREEMENT

Trade-Related Aspects of Intellectual Property Rights (TRIPS) Agreement is part of the agreement creating the World Trade Organization (WTO). Each member nation must not discriminate (in administration, regulation, or adjudication of intellectual property rights) against owners of such rights.

TRUE-FALSE QUESTIONS

(Answers at the Back of the Book)

____   1.   To receive a patent, an applicant must show that an invention is genuine, novel, useful, and not obvious in light of current technology.

____   2.   To obtain a copyright, an author must show that a work is genuine, novel, useful, and not a copy of a current copyrighted work.

____   3.   In determining whether the use of a copyrighted work is infringement under the fair use doctrine, one factor is the effect of that use on the market for the copyrighted work.

____   4.   A personal name is protected under trademark law if it acquires a secondary meaning.

____   5.   A formula for a chemical compound is not a trade secret.

____   6.   A trade name, like a trademark, can be registered with the federal government.

____   7.   A copy must be exactly the same as an original work to infringe on its copyright.

____   8.   Only the *intentional* use of another's trademark is trademark infringement.

____   9.   Using another's trademark in a domain name without permission violates federal law.

____   10.   Trademark dilution requires proof that consumers are likely to be confused by the unauthorized use of the mark.

FILL-IN QUESTIONS

(Answers at the Back of the Book)

Copyright protection is automatic for the life of the author of a work plus _____ (70/95/120) years. Copyrights owned by publishing houses expire _____ (70/95/120) years from the date of the publication of a work or _____ (70/95/120) years from the date of its creation, whichever is first. For works by more than one author, a copyright expires _____ (70/95/120) years after the death of the last surviving author.

MULTIPLE-CHOICE QUESTIONS

(Answers at the Back of the Book)

____   1.   Alpha, Inc., makes computer chips identical to Beta Corporation's patented chip, except for slight differences in the "look," without Beta's permission. This is

a. copyright infringement.
b. patent infringement.
c. trademark infringement.
d. none of the above.

____   2. Omega, Inc., uses a trademark on its products that no one, including Omega, has registered with the government. Under federal trademark law, Omega

a. can register the mark for protection.
b. cannot register a mark that has been used in commerce.
c. is guilty of trademark infringement.
d. must postpone registration until the mark has been out of use for three years.

____   3. Ken invents a light bulb that lasts longer than ordinary bulbs and applies for a patent. If the patent is granted, the invention will be protected

a. for ten years.
b. for twenty years.
c. for Ken's life plus seventy years.
d. forever.

____   4. The graphics used in "Grave Raiders," a computer game, are protected by

a. copyright law.
b. patent law.
c. trademark law.
d. trade secrets law.

____   5. Production techniques used to make "Grave Raiders," a computer game, are protected by

a. copyright law.
b. patent law.
c. trademark law.
d. trade secrets law.

____   6. National Products Company uses USA Goods, Inc.'s trademark in National's advertising without USA's permission. This is

a. copyright infringement.
b. patent infringement.
c. trademark infringement.
d. none of the above.

____   7. Clothes made by workers who are members of the Clothes Makers Union are sold with tags that identify this fact. This is a

a. certification mark.
b. collective mark.
c. service mark.
d. trade name.

____   8. Tony owns Antonio's, a pub in a small town in Iowa. Universal Dining, Inc., opens a chain of pizza places in California called "Antonio's" and, without Tony's consent, uses "antoniosincalifornia" as part of the URL for the chain's Web site. This is

a. copyright infringement.
b. cybersquatting.
c. trademark dilution.
d. none of the above.

___   **9.** Data Corporation created and sells "Economix," financial computer software. Data's copyright in Economix is best protected under

    a. the Berne Convention.
    b. the Paris Convention.
    c. the TRIPS Agreement.
    d. none of the above.

___   **10.** International Media, Inc. (IMI), publishes *Opinion* magazine, which contains an article by Carl. Without Carl's permission, IMI puts the article into an online database. This is

    a. copyright infringement.
    b. patent infringement.
    c. trademark infringement.
    d. none of the above.

SHORT ESSAY QUESTIONS

1. What does a copyright protect?

2. What is a trade secret and how is it protected?

ISSUE SPOTTERS

(Answers at the Back of the Book)

1. Delta Company discovers that it can extract data from the computer of Gamma, Inc., its major competitor, by making a series of phone calls over a high-speed modem. When Delta uses its discovery to extract Gamma's customer list, without permission, what recourse does Gamma have?

2. Global Products develops, patents, and markets software. World Copies, Inc., sells Global's software without the maker's permission. Is this patent infringement? If so, how might Global save the cost of suing World for infringement and at the same time profit from World's sales?

3. Eagle Corporation began marketing software in 1990 under the mark "Eagle." In 2002, Eagle.com, Inc., a different company selling different products, begins to use "eagle" as part of its URL and registers it as a domain name. Can Eagle Corporation stop this use of "eagle"? If so, what must the company show?

Chapter 15
Creditor-Debtor Relations and Bankruptcy

WHAT THIS CHAPTER IS ABOUT

This chapter covers bankruptcy law. Congressional authority to regulate bankruptcies comes from Article I, Section 8, of the U.S. Constitution. Bankruptcy law (1) protects a debtor by giving him or her a fresh start and (2) ensures equitable treatment to creditors competing for a debtor's assets.

CHAPTER OUTLINE

I.   **LAWS ASSISTING CREDITORS**

   A. MECHANIC'S LIEN
   A *mechanic's lien* is placed by a creditor on real property when a person contracts for labor, services, or material to make improvements on the property but does not immediately pay for the improvements.

   B. ARTISAN'S LIEN
   An *artisan's lien* is a security device by which a creditor can recover from a debtor for labor and materials furnished in the repair of personal property.

   C. JUDICIAL LIENS
   A debt must be past due before a creditor can commence legal action. Once an action is brought, the debtor's property may be seized to satisfy the debt.

   1. Attachment
   Attachment is a court-ordered seizure and taking into custody of property before the entry of a final judgment for a past-due debt.

   2. Writ of Execution
   A *writ of execution* is an order, usually issued by the clerk of the court, directing the sheriff to seize and sell any of the debtor's nonexempt property within the court's geographical jurisdiction.

   D. GARNISHMENT
   Garnishment is when a creditor collects a debt by seizing property of the debtor (such as wages or money in a bank account) that is being held by a third party (such as an employer or a bank).

   E. MORTGAGE FORECLOSURE
   A mortgagor can foreclose on the mortgaged property if the debtor defaults. The usual method is a judicial sale. The proceeds are applied to the debt.

   1. Equity of Redemption
   A mortgagor can redeem the property any time before the sale (and, in some states, within a certain period of time after the sale).

   2. Deficiency Judgment
   If the proceeds do not cover the foreclosure costs and the debt, the mortgagee can recover the difference from the mortgagor by obtaining a deficiency judgment (in a separate legal action after the foreclosure).

II. SURETYSHIP AND GUARANTY

A. SURETYSHIP
Suretyship is a promise by a third person to be responsible for a debtor's obligation. It does not have to be in writing. A surety is primarily liable: a creditor can demand payment from the surety the moment the debt is due.

B. GUARANTY
A *guaranty* is a promise to be secondarily liable for the debt or default of another. A guarantor pays only after the debtor defaults and the creditor has made an attempt to collect from the debtor. A guaranty must be in writing to be enforceable unless the main-purpose exception applies.

C. DEFENSES OF THE SURETY AND THE GUARANTOR
The surety (guarantor) can be discharged from the obligation to pay in the following ways.

1. **The Contract between the Debtor and the Creditor Is Modified**
   Without obtaining the consent of the surety (guarantor), a gratuitous surety is discharged completely and a compensated surety is discharged to the extent that the surety suffers a loss.

2. **The Principal Obligation Is Paid or Valid Tender Is Made**

3. **Most of the Defenses of the Principal Debtor**
   Defenses that a surety cannot use include the debtor's incapacity or bankruptcy, and the statute of limitations.

4. **A Surety or Guarantor's Own Defenses**
   These include fraud by a creditor to induce a surety (guarantor) to guarantee a debt (such as the creditor's failure to inform the surety of facts that would substantially increase the surety's risk).

5. **A Creditor's Surrender or Impairment of the Collateral**
   Without the surety's (guarantor's) consent, this releases the surety to the extent of any loss suffered from the creditor's actions.

D. RIGHTS OF THE SURETY AND THE GUARANTOR
If a surety (guarantor) pays the debt, he or she may have the following rights.

1. **The Right of Subrogation**
   A surety (guarantor) may pursue any remedies that were available to the creditor against the debtor.

2. **The Right of Reimbursement**
   A surety is entitled to receive from the debtor all outlays made on behalf of the suretyship arrangement.

3. **The Right of Contribution**
   A surety who pays more than his or her proportionate share on a debtor's default is entitled to recover from the co-sureties the amount paid above the surety's obligation.

III. PROTECTION FOR DEBTORS

A. PROPERTY EXEMPT FROM CREDITORS' ACTIONS
In most states, certain property is exempt from execution or attachment.

1. **Homestead**
   Each state permits a debtor to retain a family home (in some states only if the debtor has a family) in total or to a specified dollar amount.

2. **Personal Property**
    Often exempt: household furniture up to a specified dollar amount; clothing and other personal possessions; a vehicle (or vehicles) (up to a specified dollar amount); certain animals, usually livestock but including pets; and equipment that the debtor uses in a business or trade.

B. **SPECIAL PROTECTION FOR CONSUMER DEBTORS**
    A Federal Trade Commission rule limits the rights of a holder in due course (HDC) who holds a negotiable promissory note executed by a consumer as part of a consumer transaction. Other laws include the Truth-in-Lending Act, which protects consumers by requiring creditors to disclose certain information when making loans (see Chapter 23).

IV. BANKRUPTCY AND REORGANIZATION

A. **THE GOALS OF BANKRUPTCY LAW**
    Federal bankruptcy law has two goals: to protect a debtor by freeing him or her from creditors' claims to make a fresh start and to insure fair treatment to creditors competing for the debtor's assets.

B. **BANKRUPTCY PROCEEDINGS**
    Bankruptcy proceedings are held in federal bankruptcy courts. Current law is based on the Bankruptcy Reform Act of 1978 (the Bankruptcy Code, or the Code). Relief can be granted under the Code's Chapter 7, Chapter 11, Chapter 12, or Chapter 13.

V. CHAPTER 7 LIQUIDATION

This is the most familiar type of bankruptcy proceeding. A debtor declares his or her debts and gives all assets to a trustee, who sells the nonexempt assets and distributes the proceeds to creditors.

A. **WHO CAN FILE FOR A LIQUIDATION**
    Any "person"—individuals, partnerships, and corporations (spouses can file jointly)—except railroads, insurance companies, banks, savings and loan associations, and credit unions.

B. **FILING THE PETITION**

1. **Voluntary Bankruptcy**

    a. **The Debtor Files a Petition with the Court**
        The petition includes schedules (lists) of (1) creditors and the debt to each, (2) the debtor's financial affairs, (3) the debtor's property, and (4) current income and expenses.

    b. **Filing of the Petition Constitutes an Order for Relief**
        The clerk of the court must give the trustee and creditors notice of the order within not more than twenty days.

    c. **Substantial Abuse**
        A court can dismiss a petition if granting it would constitute substantial abuse (if the debtor seeks only an advantage over creditors and his or her financial situation does not warrant a discharge of debts) [11 U.S.C. Section 707(b)].

2. **Involuntary Bankruptcy**
    A debtor's creditors can force the debtor into bankruptcy proceedings.

    a. **Who Can Be Forced into Involuntary Proceedings**
        A debtor with twelve or more creditors, three or more of whom (with unsecured claims of at least $11,625) file a petition. A debtor with fewer than twelve creditors, one or more of whom (with a claim of $11,625) files. Not a farmer or a charitable institution.

b. When an Order for Relief Will Be Entered

If the debtor does not challenge the petition, the debtor is generally not paying debts as they come due, or a receiver, assignee, or custodian took possession of the debtor's property within 120 days before the petition was filed.

C. AUTOMATIC STAY

When a petition is filed, an automatic stay suspends all action by creditors against the debtor. The adequate protection doctrine protects secured creditors by requiring payments, or other collateral or relief, to the extent that the stay may cause the value of their collateral to decrease.

D. PROPERTY OF THE ESTATE

1. What Property Is Included in the Debtor's Estate

Interests in property presently held; community property; property transferred in a transaction voidable by the trustee; proceeds and profits; after-acquired property; interests in gifts, inheritances, property settlements, and life insurance death proceeds to which the debtor becomes entitled within 180 days after filing.

2. What Property Is Not Included

Property acquired after the filing of the petition except as noted above.

E. CREDITORS' MEETING AND CLAIMS

Within "not less than ten days or more than thirty days," the court calls a meeting of creditors, at which the debtor answers questions. Within ninety days of the meeting, a creditor must file a proof of claim. The proof lists the creditor's name and address, as well as the amount of the debt.

F. EXEMPTIONS

1. Federal Law

Exempts such property as interests in a residence to $17,425, a motor vehicle to $2,775, household goods to $9,300, and tools of a trade to $1,750, and the rights to receive Social Security and other benefits.

2. State Law

Most states preclude the use of federal exemptions; others allow a debtor to choose between state and federal. State exemptions may include different value limits and exempt different property.

G. THE TRUSTEE

After the order for relief, an interim trustee is appointed to preside over the debtor's property until the first meeting of creditors, when a permanent trustee is elected. A trustee's duty is to collect and reduce to money the property of the estate and distribute the proceeds.

1. Trustee's Powers

A trustee has the same rights as (1) a lien creditor with priority over an unperfected secured party and (2) a bona fide purchaser of real property from the debtor.

2. Voidable Rights

A trustee can use any reason (fraud, duress, etc.) that a debtor can use to obtain the return of property.

3. Preferences

A trustee can recover payments made or property transferred (or the value of the property if a preferred creditor has sold it to an innocent third party) by a debtor (1) within ninety days before the petition and (2) for a preexisting debt.

a. Insiders or Fraud

If a creditor is an insider (partner, corporate officer, relative) or a transfer is fraudulent, a trustee may recover transfers made within one year before filing.

> **b. Transfers That Are Not Preferences**
> Payment for services rendered within ten to fifteen days before the payment; payment received in the ordinary course of business (such as payment of a phone bill); transfer of property up to $600.

> **4. Liens on Debtor's Property**
> A trustee can avoid statutory liens that first became effective when the bankruptcy petition was filed or the debtor became insolvent, and any lien against a bona fide purchaser that was not enforceable on the date of the filing.

> **5. Fraudulent Transfers**
> A trustee can avoid fraudulent transfers made within one year of the filing of the petition or if they were made with the intent to delay, defraud, or hinder a creditor. Transfers for less than reasonably equivalent consideration may also be avoided if, by making them, the debtor became insolvent or was left in business with little capital.

H. DISTRIBUTION OF PROPERTY
Any amount remaining after the property is distributed to creditors is turned over to the debtor.

> **1. Distribution to Secured Creditors**
> Within thirty days of the petition or before the first creditors' meeting (whichever is first), a debtor must state whether he or she will retain secured collateral (or claim it as exempt, etc.). The trustee must enforce the statement within forty-five days. If the collateral does not cover the debt, the secured creditor is an unsecured creditor for the difference.

> **2. Distribution to Unsecured Creditors**
> Paid in the order of priority. Each class is paid before the next class is entitled to anything. The order of priority is—
>
> a. Administrative expenses (court costs, trustee and attorney fees).
> b. In an involuntary bankruptcy, expenses incurred by the debtor in the ordinary course of business from the filing of the petition to the appointment of the trustee or the issuance of an order for relief.
> c. Unpaid wages, salaries, and commissions earned within ninety days of the petition, to $4,650 per claimant. A claim in excess is a claim of a general creditor (no. i below).
> d. Unsecured claims for contributions to employee benefit plans, limited to services performed within 180 days before the petition and $4,650 per employee.
> e. Claims by farmers and fishers, to $4,650, against storage or processing facilities.
> f. Consumer deposits to $2,100 given to the debtor before the petition to buy, lease, or rent property or services that were not received.
> g. Claims for paternity, alimony, maintenance, and support.
> h. Taxes and penalties due to the government.
> i. Claims of general creditors.

I. DISCHARGE
A discharge voids any judgment on a discharged debt and prohibits any action to collect a discharged debt. A co-debtor's liability is not affected.

> **1. Exceptions—Debts That May Not Be Discharged**
> Claims for back taxes, amounts borrowed to pay back taxes, goods obtained by fraud, debts that were not listed in the petition, alimony, child support, student loans, certain cash advances, and others.

> **2. Objections—Debtors Who May Not Receive a Discharge**
> Those who conceal property with the intent to hinder, delay, or defraud a creditor; who fail to explain a loss of assets; or who have been granted a discharge within six years of the filing of the petition.

3. **Revocation of Discharge**
    A discharge may be revoked within one year if the debtor was fraudulent or dishonest during the bankruptcy proceedings.

J. **REAFFIRMATION OF DEBT**
    A debtor's agreement to pay an otherwise dischargeable debt must be made before a discharge is granted and must usually be approved by the court. Can be rescinded within sixty days or before the discharge is granted, whichever is later.

VI.   CHAPTER 11 REORGANIZATION

The creditors and debtor formulate a plan under which the debtor pays a portion of the debts, is discharged of the rest, and continues in business.

A. **WHO IS ELIGIBLE FOR RELIEF UNDER CHAPTER 11**
    Any debtor (except a stockbroker or a commodities broker) who is eligible for Chapter 7 relief. Used most commonly by corporate debtors. The same principles apply that govern liquidation (automatic stay, etc.).

B. **WHY A CASE MAY BE DISMISSED**
    Creditors may prefer a *workout* (a privately negotiated settlement) to bankruptcy proceedings, or there may be other reasons (inability to effect a plan, unreasonable delay by the debtor that is prejudicial to creditors, etc.).

C. **DEBTOR IN POSSESSION**
    On entry of an order for relief, the debtor continues to operate his or her business as a debtor in possession (DIP). If gross mismanagement is shown, the court may appoint a trustee (or receiver) to operate the business. This may also be done if it is in the best interests of the estate.

D. **CREDITORS' COMMITTEES**
    A committee of unsecured creditors is appointed to consult with the trustee or DIP. Other committees may represent special-interest creditors. Some small businesses can avoid creditors' committees.

E. **THE REORGANIZATION PLAN**

1. **Who Can File a Plan**
    Only debtor within the first 120 days (100 days in some cases) after date of the order for relief. Any other party, if debtor does not meet the deadline or fails to obtain creditor consent within 180 days (or 160 days).

2. **What the Plan Must Do**
    Conserve and administer the debtor's assets in the hope of a return to solvency; be fair and equitable ("in the best interests of the creditors"); designate classes of claims and interests; specify the treatment to be afforded the classes; and provide an adequate means for execution.

3. **The Plan Is Submitted to Creditors for Acceptance**
    Each class adversely affected by a plan must accept it (two-thirds of the total claims must approve). If only one class accepts, the court may confirm it under the Code's cram-down provision if the plan does not discriminate unfairly against any creditors. The plan is binding on confirmation—the debtor is given a discharge from all claims not within the plan (except those that would be denied in a liquidation).

VII.   INDIVIDUALS' REPAYMENT PLANS (CHAPTER 13)

A. **WHO IS ELIGIBLE**
    Individuals (not partnerships or corporations) with regular income and unsecured debts of less than $290,525 or secured debts of less than $871,550.

B. VOLUNTARY FILING ONLY

A Chapter 13 case can be initiated by the filing of a voluntary petition only. A trustee is appointed.

C. AUTOMATIC STAY

On the filing of a petition, an automatic stay enjoins creditors from taking action against co-obligors of the debtor. If a creditor asks to vacate the stay against a co-debtor, unless written objection is filed, twenty days later the stay against the co-debtor is automatically terminated without a hearing.

D. THE REPAYMENT PLAN

The plan must provide for (1) turnover to the trustee of the debtor's future income, (2) full payment of all claims entitled to priority, and (3) the same treatment of each claim within a particular class.

1. Filing and Confirming the Plan

Only the debtor can file a plan, which the court will confirm if (1) the secured creditors accept it, (2) it provides that creditors retain their liens and the value of the property to be distributed to them is not less than the secured portion of their claims, or (3) the debtor surrenders the property securing the claim to the creditors.

2. Payments under the Plan

The time for payment must be less than three years (five years, with court approval). The payments must be timely, or the court can convert the case to a liquidation or dismiss the petition. Before completion of payments, the plan may be modified at the request of the debtor, the trustee, or an unsecured creditor.

3. Objection to the Plan

Over the objection of the trustee or an unsecured creditor, the court may approve a plan only if (1) the value of the property to be distributed is equal to the amount of the claims, or (2) all the debtor's disposable income during the plan will be used to make payments.

E. DISCHARGE

After completion of all payments, all debts provided for by the plan are discharged. A discharge obtained by fraud can be revoked within one year.

TRUE-FALSE QUESTIONS

(Answers at the Back of the Book)

____ 1. A mechanic's lien involves personal property.

____ 2. An employer can dismiss an employee due to garnishment for any one debt.

____ 3. A writ of execution is a court order to seize a debtor's property *after* the entry of a final judgment in a creditor's lawsuit against the debtor.

____ 4. A surety or guarantor is discharged from his or her obligation when the principal debtor pays the debt.

____ 5. To avoid liability on an obligation to a creditor, a surety cannot use any defenses available to the debtor.

____ 6. A debtor must be insolvent to file a voluntary petition under Chapter 7.

____ 7. The same principles cover the filing of a liquidation petition and a reorganization proceeding.

____ 8. Filing for bankruptcy under Chapter 13 is less expensive and less complicated than other bankruptcy proceedings.

____ 9. When a business debtor files for Chapter 11 protection, the debtor is not allowed to continue in business.

____ 10. No small business can avoid creditors' committees under Chapter 11.

FILL-IN QUESTIONS

(Answers at the Back of the Book)

A _____ (contract of suretyship/guaranty contract) is a promise to a creditor made by a third person to be responsible for a debtor's obligation. A _____ (guarantor/surety) is primarily liable: the creditor can hold the _____ (guarantor/surety) responsible for payment of the debt when the debt is due, without first exhausting all remedies against the debtor. A _____ (contract of suretyship/guaranty contract) also includes a promise to answer for a principal's obligation, but a _____ (guarantor/surety) is secondarily liable—that is, the principal must first default, and ordinarily, a creditor must have attempted to collect from the principal, because ordinarily a debtor would not otherwise be declared in default.

MULTIPLE-CHOICE QUESTIONS

(Answers at the Back of the Book)

____   1.   Adam borrows money from Best Credit Company. If Adam defaults, to use attachment as a remedy Best must first

a.   commence a suit against Adam.
b.   succeed in a suit against Adam.
c.   be unable to collect the amount of a judgment against Adam.
d.   all of the above.

____   2.   Ed's $2,500 debt to Owen is past due. To collect money from Ed's wages to pay the debt, Owen can use

a.   an order of receivership.
b.   a writ of attachment.
c.   a writ of execution.
d.   garnishment.

____   3.   Eve owes Fred $200,000. A court awards Fred a judgment in the amount of the debt. To satisfy the judgment, Eve's home is sold at public auction for $150,000. The state homestead exemption is $50,000. Fred gets

a. $50,000.
b. $100,000.
c. $150,000.
d.   nothing.

____   4.   Great Company wants to borrow money from First State Bank. The bank insists that Hal, Great Company's president, agree to be personally liable for payment if Great defaults. If Hal agrees, he is

a.   a guarantor only.
b.   a surety only.
c.   a guarantor and a surety.
d.   none of the above.

_____ 5. Ira and Jill agree to act as guarantors on a loan made by Ken. Ken defaults on the payments and Jill refuses to pay. If Ira pays the debt, he can recover from

    a. Ken and Jill under the right of reimbursement.
    b. Ken and Jill under the right of proportionate liability.
    c. Ken under the right of subrogation and Jill under the right of contribution.
    d. none of the above.

_____ 6. Carol is the sole proprietor of Diners Cafe, which owes debts in an amount more than Carol believes she and the cafe can repay. The creditors agree that liquidating the business would not be in their best interests. To stay in business, Carol could file for bankruptcy under

    a. Chapter 7 only.
    b. Chapter 11 only.
    c. Chapter 13 only.
    d. Chapter 11 or Chapter 13.

_____ 7. Owen files a bankruptcy petition under Chapter 7 to have his debts discharged. The debts most likely to be discharged include claims for

    a. alimony and child support.
    b. back taxes accruing within three years before the petition was filed.
    c. certain fines and penalties payable to the government.
    d. student loans, if the payment would impose undue hardship on Owen.

_____ 8. Pat files a Chapter 7 petition for a discharge in bankruptcy. Pat may be denied a discharge if Pat

    a. fails to explain a loss of assets.
    b. fails to list a debt.
    c. owes back taxes.
    d. owes child support payments.

_____ 9. Cathy and Don make down payments on goods to be received from Eagle Furniture Store. Before the goods are delivered, Eagle files for bankruptcy. Besides consumers like Cathy and Don, Eagle owes wages to its employees and taxes to the government. In what order will these debts be paid?

    a. Consumer deposits, unpaid wages, taxes
    b. Taxes, consumer deposits, unpaid wages
    c. Unpaid wages, consumer deposits, taxes
    d. Unpaid wages, taxes, consumer deposits

_____ 10. Regional Stores, Inc., files for bankruptcy. A corporation can file a petition for bankruptcy under

    a. Chapter 7 only.
    b. Chapter 11 only.
    c. Chapter 13 only.
    d. Chapter 7 or Chapter 11.

SHORT ESSAY QUESTIONS

1. What is a lien? What are the ways in which a lien can arise? What is a lienholder's priority compared to other creditors?

2.   What are the differences between contracts of suretyship and guaranty contracts?

ISSUE SPOTTERS

(Answers at the Back of the Book)

1.   Joe contracts with Larry of Midwest Roofing to fix Joe's roof. Joe pays half of the contract price in advance. Larry and Midwest complete the job, but Joe refuses to pay the rest of the price. What can Larry and Midwest do?

2.   Pat wants to borrow $10,000 from Quality Loan Company to buy a new car, but Quality refuses to lend the money unless Ron cosigns the note. Ron cosigns and makes three of the payments when Pat fails to do so. Can Ron get this money from Pat?

3.   Adam is a vice president for Beta Company. On May 1, Adam loans Beta $10,000. On June 1, the company re-pays the loan. On July 1, Beta files for bankruptcy. Carl is appointed trustee. Can Carl recover the $10,000 paid to Adam on June 1?

CUMULATIVE HYPOTHETICAL PROBLEM
FOR UNIT THREE—INCLUDING CHAPTERS 9–15

(Answers at the Back of the Book)

Adam, Beth, and Carl pool their resources to make and sell customized software. They do business under the name "Computer Data" (CD).

_____   1.   To protect the rights that CD has in the software it produces, CD's best protection is offered by

a.   bankruptcy law.
b.   intellectual property law.
c.   sales law.
d.   tort law.

_____   2.   CD sends e-mail to Doe & Roe, an accounting firm, offering to contract for its services for a certain price. The offer is sent on June 1 and is seen by Doe on June 2. The offer states that it will be open until July 1. This offer

a.   cannot be revoked because it is a firm offer.
b.   cannot be revoked because it is an option contract.
c.   could have been revoked only before Doe saw it.
d.   may be revoked any time before it is accepted.

_____   3.   Digital Products Company (DPC) writes to CD to order customized software, which it plans to sell to its customer, Eagle Corporation. CD writes to accept but adds a clause providing for interest on any overdue invoices (a common practice in the industry). If there is no further communication between the parties

a.   CD has made a counteroffer.
b.   there is a contract but without CD's added term.
c.   there is a contract that includes CD's added term.
d.   there is no contract because DPC did not expressly accept the added term.

____ 4. In the previous question, CD ships defective software to DPC, which sells it to Eagle. The defective software causes losses estimated at $100,000. With respect to Eagle, CD likely violated

  a. bankruptcy law.
  b. creditor-debtor law.
  c. intellectual property law.
  d. tort law.

____ 5. After the news about Eagle's losses is publicized, CD loses business and files a voluntary petition in bankruptcy under Chapter 11. A reorganization plan is filed with the court. The court will confirm the plan if it is accepted by

  a. CD.
  b. CD's secured creditors.
  c. CD's shareholders.
  d. CD's unsecured creditors.

QUESTIONS ON THE FOCUS ON LEGAL REASONING FOR UNIT THREE— *FORD V. TRENDWEST RESORTS, INC.*

(Answers at the Back of the Book)

____ 1. Alpha Corporation enters into an agreement to hire Bob for employment at-will. If Alpha breaches the agreement, under the holding in *Ford v. Trendwest Resorts, Inc.,* Bob is most likely to be awarded

  a. damages that represent future earnings.
  b. damages that represent lost earnings.
  c. nominal damages.
  d. nothing.

____ 2. Beta Company enters into an agreement to hire Carol for employment at-will. In the opinion of the majority in *Ford v. Trendwest Resorts, Inc.,* the agreement between Beta and Carol

  a. does not change the at-will employment relation between the parties.
  b. establishes a claim for lost wages if Beta breaches the agreement *after* Carol starts work.
  c. establishes a claim for lost wages if Beta breaches the agreement *before* Carol starts work.
  d. establishes a claim for lost wages if Beta breaches the agreement at any time.

____ 3. Gamma, Inc., enters into an agreement to hire Dan for employment at-will. In the opinion of the dissent in *Ford v. Trendwest Resorts, Inc.,* the agreement between Gamma and Dan

  a. does not change the at-will employment relation between the parties.
  b. establishes a claim for lost wages if Gamma breaches the agreement *after* Dan starts work.
  c. establishes a claim for lost wages if Gamma breaches the agreement *before* Dan starts work.
  d. establishes a claim for lost wages if Gamma breaches the agreement at any time.

QUESTIONS ON THE FOCUS ON ETHICS FOR UNIT THREE— THE COMMERCIAL ENVIRONMENT

(Answers at the Back of the Book)

____ **1.** Ann and Bill enter into a contract for Bill's services. Whether this contract is unconscionable is determined by

a. a court.
b. Ann only.
c. Bill only.
d. UCC 2–302.

____ **2.** Macro Corporation makes and sells software. Nick operates a Web site under the domain name "macro-softwaresucks.com." In Macro's suit against Nick, his best defense is that this domain is protected by

a. copyright law.
b. Nick's freedom of speech.
c. Nick's privacy rights.
d. trademark law.

____ **3.** Don is the author of *E-Murder*, a cyberspace mystery. Fourteen years after Don dies, Fran prints copies of *E-Murder* and sells them for her own profit. This may violate Don's

a. copyright.
b. freedom of speech.
c. privacy rights.
d. trademark.

Chapter 16
Sole Proprietorships, Partnerships, and Special Business Organizations

WHAT THIS CHAPTER IS ABOUT

This chapter outlines the features of sole proprietorships (the most common form of business), partnerships, and other, special business organizational forms. The chapter also discusses franchises.

CHAPTER OUTLINE

I. SOLE PROPRIETORSHIPS

The simplest form of business—the owner is the business.

A. ADVANTAGES

The proprietor takes all the profits. Easier to start than other kinds of businesses (few legal forms involved); has more flexibility (proprietor is free to make all decisions); owner pays only personal income tax on profits.

B. DISADVANTAGES

The proprietor has all the risk (unlimited liability for all debts); limited opportunity to raise capital; and the business dissolves when the owner dies.

II. PARTNERSHIPS

A. THE LAW GOVERNING PARTNERSHIPS

A partnerships arises from an agreement between two or more persons to carry on a business for profit. A partnership is governed by this agreement, the principles of agency law, and the Uniform Partnership Act (UPA) or the Revised Uniform Partnership Act (RUPA).

B. DEFINITION OF A PARTNERSHIP

1. **Elements of a Partnership**
   "[A]n association of two or more persons to carry on as co-owners a business for profit" [UPA 6(1)]. There are three essential elements:

   a. A sharing of profits or losses.
   b. A joint ownership of the business.
   c. An equal right in the management of the business.

2. **Sharing Profits Is Not Enough**
   Sharing profits from a business does not imply a partnership, if the profits were received as payment of a debt in installments, rent to a landlord profits from the joint ownership of property, etc. [UPA 7].

C. THE NATURE OF PARTNERSHIPS

1. **Partnership as an Entity**
   In many states, and under the UPA, the RUPA, and federal law, a partnership can be treated as an entity for such purposes as owning property, lawsuits in federal courts, and bankruptcy proceedings.

2. **Aggregate Theory of Partnership**
   If a partnership is not regarded as a separate entity, it is treated as an aggregate of the individual partners.

D. PARTNERSHIP FORMATION

A partnership agreement generally states an intent to create a partnership, contribute capital, share profits and losses, and participate in management.

1. **Formalities**
   A partnership agreement can be oral, written, or implied by conduct. Some must be in writing under the Statute of Frauds (see Chapter 9). Partners can agree to any terms not illegal or contrary to public policy.

2. **Duration**

   a. **Partnership for a Term**
      The agreement can specify the duration of the partnership in terms of a date or the completion of a project. Dissolution without all partners' consent before expiration is a breach of the agreement.

   b. **Partnership at Will**
      No duration is set; a partner can dissolve a partnership at any time.

3. **A Corporation as Partner**
   Many states (not the UPA) restrict the ability of corporations to become partners. In those states, courts sometimes validate such arrangements by characterizing them as joint ventures.

4. **Partnership by Estoppel**
   When parties who are not partners hold themselves out as partners and make representations that third persons rely on in dealing with them, liability is imposed on the alleged partner [UPA 16] (but not the firm).

E. PARTNERSHIP OPERATION

1. **Rights of Partners**

   a. **Management**

      1) **Ordinarily, the Majority Rules**
         "All partners have equal rights in the management and conduct of partnership business" [UPA 18]. Each partner has one vote.

      2) **When Unanimous Consent Is Required**
         Unanimous consent is required for such purposes as altering the essential nature of the firm's business, admitting new partners, entering a new business, and amending partnership articles.

   b. **Interest in the Partnership**
      Unless partners agree otherwise, profits and losses are shared equally [UPA 18(a)].

   c. **Compensation**
      Doing partnership business is a partner's duty and not compensable. On the death of a partner, a surviving partner is entitled to compensation to wind up partnership affairs [UPA 18(f)].

   d. **Inspection of Books**
      A partner has a right to complete information concerning the conduct of partnership business [UPA 20]. Partnership books must be kept at the principal business office [UPA 19].

e. **Accounting**

A partner has a right to a formal accounting (1) on dissolution [UPA 22]; (2) when the agreement provides for it; (3) when a partner is wrongfully excluded from the business, the books, or both; (4) when a partner withholds profits or benefits belonging to the firm; or (5) when circumstances "render it just and reasonable."

f. **Partner's Interest in the Firm**

A personal asset consisting of a proportionate share of the profits [UPA 26] and a return of capital [UPA 28].

g. **Partnership Property**

A partner is co-owner with his or her partners of partnership property, holding it as a tenant in partnership [UPA 25(1)].

1) **If a Partner Dies**

Surviving partners, not the heirs of the deceased, have a right of survivorship to the property (they must account to the decedent's estate for the value [UPA 25(2)(d), (e)]).

2) **Each Partner Has Equal Rights**

Each partner can possess partnership property for business purposes or in satisfaction of firm debts, but cannot sell, assign, or deal with the property other than for partnership purposes [UPA 25(2)(a), (b)], without the consent of all of the partners.

2. **Duties and Powers of Partners**

a. **Fiduciary Duties**

Partners (1) must act in good faith for the benefit of the firm, (2) cannot engage in independent competitive activities without the other partners' consent, and (3) must account to the firm for profits or benefits derived in a partnership transaction [UPA 21].

b. **General Agency Powers**

Each partner is an agent of every other partner and of the firm in carrying out partnership business [UPA 9(1)]. The character and scope of the partnership business and the customary nature of the business determine the scope of the partners' implied authority. Partners exercise all implied powers necessary to carry on the business [UPA 11].

c. **Joint Liability**

In most states, partners are jointly liable for partnership debts and contracts [UPA 15(b)] (each partner is liable for the entire debt; if one pays, the partnership or the other partners must reimburse that partner [UPA 18(b)]).

d. **Joint and Several Liability**

In some states, partners are jointly and severally liable for partnership debts and contracts [see RUPA 306]. In all states, partners are jointly and severally liable for torts and breaches of trust [UPA 15(a)].

e. **Liability of Incoming Partners**

A newly admitted partner is liable for partnership debts incurred before his or her admission only to the extent of his or her interest in the partnership [UPA 17].

F. **PARTNERSHIP TERMINATION**

Termination is caused by any change in the relations of the partners that demonstrates unwillingness or inability to carry on partnership business [UPA 29]. To continue, a partner can organize a new partnership.

1. **Dissolution**

   Occurs when a partner ceases to be associated with the business. Dissolution terminates the right of a partnership to exist as a going concern, but the partnership exists long enough to wind up its affairs.

   a. **Dissolution by Acts of the Partners**

      The partnership agreement can stipulate events that dissolve the firm. Partners can agree to dissolve the firm early. A partner's withdrawal dissolves the firm if it must be liquidated. A transfer of a partner's interest for the benefit of creditors [UPA 28] leads to judicial dissolution (see below).

   b. **Dissolution by Operation of Law**

      Dissolution is caused by the death of a partner, bankruptcy of a partner (or the firm), an event that makes it unlawful for the partnership or any partner to continue.

   c. **Dissolution by Judicial Decree**

      A court can dissolve a firm for a partner's mental incompetency, incapacity, or improper conduct; impracticality of the firm's business (can be run only at a loss); or other circumstances [UPA 32].

   d. **Notice of Dissolution**

      Intent to dissolve must be communicated to each partner. Unless the other partners have notice, a withdrawing partner will continue to be bound as a partner to all contracts created for the firm. Notice must also be given to all affected third persons.

2. **Winding Up**

   Involves collecting and preserving partnership assets, paying debts, and accounting to each partner for the value of his or her interest.

   a. **No New Obligations**

      Once dissolution has occurred and partners have been notified, they cannot create new obligations on behalf of the firm. Their only authority is to complete transactions begun but not finished.

   b. **Distribution of Assets**

      1) **UPA Distribution**

         Priority for the distribution of a partnership's assets is [UPA 40(b)]: (1) payment to third party creditors; (2) refund of loans made to or for the firm by a partner; (3) return of capital contribution to a partner; and (4) distribution of the balance, if any, to partners proportionate to their shares in the profits.

      2) **RUPA Distribution**

         Partner creditors are included among creditors who take first priority [RUPA 808]. Capital contributions and profits or losses are then calculated together to determine the amounts that the partners receive or the amounts that they must pay.

III. SPECIAL BUSINESS FORMS

A. JOINT VENTURE

A joint venture is an enterprise in which two or more persons combine their efforts or property for a single transaction or project, or a related series of transactions or projects. Unless otherwise agreed, members share profits and losses equally.

1. **Characteristics**

   Same as a partnership except: members have less implied and apparent authority; a member's death does not terminate a joint venture.

2. **Duration**

Depending on the circumstances: members specify duration, a venture terminates when the project for which it is formed is completed, or a venture is terminable at the will of any of its members.

3. **Duties, Rights, and Liabilities among Joint Venturers**

a. **Duties**

Joint venturers have the same duties as partners in a partnership.

b. **Conflicts When Members Are Competitors**

(1) Each may face a choice between disclosing trade secrets to a competitor and breaching the duty to disclose, and (2) there is potential for violation of antitrust laws (see Chapters 26 and 27).

c. **Rights**

Each joint venturer has an equal right to manage the activities of the enterprise (though control may be given to one member).

d. **Liability**

Each joint venturer is liable to third parties for the actions of the other members in pursuit of the goal of the venture.

B. **SYNDICATE**

A group of individuals financing a project; may exist as a corporation, a partnership, or no legally recognized form.

C. **JOINT STOCK COMPANY**

Usually treated like a partnership (formed by agreement, members have personal liability, etc.), but members are not agents of one another, and has many characteristics of a corporation: (1) ownership by shares of stock, (2) managed by directors and officers, and (3) perpetual existence.

D. **BUSINESS TRUST**

Legal ownership and management of the property of the business is in one or more trustees; profits are distributed to beneficiaries, who are not personally responsible for the debts of the trust. Resembles a corporation.

E. **COOPERATIVE**

A cooperative is an association that is organized to provide an economic service without profit to its members (or shareholders).

1. **Incorporated Cooperative**

Subject to state laws governing nonprofit corporations. Distributes profits to owners on the basis of their transactions with the cooperative rather than on the basis of the amount of capital they contributed.

2. **Unincorporated Cooperatives**

Often treated like partnerships. The members have joint liability for the cooperative's acts.

IV. FRANCHISES

A franchise is any arrangement in which the owner of a trademark, a trade name, or a copyright has licensed others to use it in selling goods or services.

A. **TYPES OF FRANCHISES**

1. **Distributorship**

When a manufacturer licenses a dealer to sell its product (such as an automobile dealer). Often covers an exclusive territory.

2. Chain-Style Business Operation
When a franchise operates under a franchisor's trade name and is identified as a member of a group of dealers engaged in the franchisor's business (such as most fast-food chains). The franchisee must follow standardized or prescribed methods of operations, and may be obligated to obtain supplies exclusively from the franchisor.

3. Manufacturing or Processing-Plant Arrangement
When a franchisor transmits to the franchisee the essential ingredients or formula to make a product (such as Coca-Cola), which the franchisee makes and markets according to the franchisor's standards.

B. LAWS GOVERNING FRANCHISING

1. Federal Protection for Franchisees

a. Automobile Dealers' Franchise Act of 1965
Dealership franchisees are protected from manufacturers' bad faith termination of their franchises.

b. Petroleum Marketing Practices Act (PMPA) of 1979
Prescribes the grounds and conditions under which a gasoline station franchisor may terminate or decline to renew a franchise.

c. Antitrust Laws
May apply if there is an anticompetitive agreement (see Chapters 26 and 27).

d. Federal Trade Commission (FTC) Regulations
Franchisors must disclose material facts necessary to a prospective franchisee's making an informed decision concerning a franchise.

2. State Protection for Franchisees
Similar to federal law. State deceptive practices acts may apply, as may Article 2 of the Uniform Commercial Code.

C. THE FRANCHISE CONTRACT
A franchise relationship is created by a contract between the franchisor and the franchisee.

1. Payment for the Franchise
A franchisee pays (1) a fee for the franchise license, (2) fees for products bought from or through the franchisor, (3) a percentage of sales, and (4) a percentage of advertising and administrative costs.

2. Business Premises
The agreement may specify whether the premises for the business are leased or purchased and who is to supply equipment and furnishings.

3. Location of the Franchise
The franchisor determines the territory to be served and its exclusivity.

4. Business Organization of the Franchisee
A franchisor may specify requirements for the form and capital structure of the business.

5. Quality Control
A franchisor may specify standards of operation (such as quality standards) and personnel training methods. Too much control may result in a franchisor's liability for torts of a franchisee's employees.

6. **Pricing Arrangements**
   A franchisor may require a franchisee to buy certain supplies from the franchisor at an established price. A franchisor may also set retail prices for the goods that the franchisee sells.

7. **Termination of the Franchise**
   Determined by the parties. Usually, termination must be "for cause" (such as breach of the agreement, etc.) and notice must be given. A franchisee must be given reasonable time to wind up the business.

TRUE-FALSE QUESTIONS

(Answers at the Back of the Book)

____ 1. In a sole proprietorship, the owner and the business are entirely separate.

____ 2. In a sole proprietorship, the owner receives all of the profits.

____ 3. The sharing of profits from joint ownership of property is usually enough to create a partnership.

____ 4. Unless a partnership agreement specifies otherwise, each partner has one vote in management matters.

____ 5. The liability of a partner for partnership debts is limited to the amount of capital he or she invests in the partnership.

____ 6. A joint stock company is usually treated like a partnership.

____ 7. A syndicate may exist in the form of a corporation.

____ 8. A court always determines the termination of a franchise.

____ 9. A franchisee is not subject to the franchisor's control in the area of product quality.

____ 10. The members of a joint venture have the same power as partners in a partnership to bind other members in the firm.

FILL-IN QUESTIONS

(Answers at the Back of the Book)

In most states, partners _____ (are/are not) subject to joint liability on partnership debts, contracts, and torts. Joint liability means that if a third party sues a partner on a partnership _____ (obligation/tort), the partner has the right to insist that the other partners be sued with him or her. If the third party does not sue all of the partners, those partners who are _____ (not sued/sued) cannot be required to pay a judgment. In that circumstance, the assets of the partnership _____ (can/cannot) be used to satisfy the judgment. The third party's release of one partner _____ (does not release/releases) the other partners. In most states, to bring a successful claim against a partnership on a debt or contract, a plaintiff _____ (may/must) name all the partners as defendants.

MULTIPLE-CHOICE QUESTIONS

(Answers at the Back of the Book)

____   1.   Ann owns Beta Enterprises, a sole proprietorship. Ann's liability for the obligations of the business is

a. limited by state statute.
b. limited to the amount of his original investment.
c. limited to the total amount of capital Ann invests in the business.
d. unlimited.

____   2.   Carl holds himself out as a partner of Delta Associates, a partnership, even though he has no connection to the firm. Carl obtains a personal loan based on this misrepresentation. Carl's default on the loan will result in liability on the part of

a. Carl only.
b. Delta only.
c. Carl and Delta jointly.
d. no one.

____   3.   Alan, Bill, and Carol are partners in ABC Accountants. Dissolution would be caused by

a. Alan joining another partnership.
b. Bill's interest in the partnership being attached by a court.
c. Carol being adjudicated bankrupt.
d. any partner being sued by the other partners for an accounting.

____   4.   Vicky and Warren do business as a partnership under the name United Digital. United

a. is a tax-paying entity.
b. is required to file an information return but is not a tax-paying entity.
c. pays 1/2 of the taxes if there are only two partners.
d. pays 1/3 of the taxes if there are only two partners.

____   5.   Ann, Bert, and Carol are partners in an accounting firm. Ann tells Bert and Carol that effective immediately, she is quitting the firm. Later, Bert and Carol sign a contract with a supplier. The contract is binding on

a. Bert only.
b. Bert and Carol only.
c. Ann, Bert, and Carol.
d. none of the partners.

____   6.   Alpha Corporation and Beta, Inc., form a joint venture to develop and market business software. A joint venture is

a. a corporate enterprise for a single undertaking of limited duration.
b. an association limited to no more than two persons in business for profit.
c. an association of persons engaged as co-owners in a single undertaking for profit.
d. an enterprise of numerous co-owners in a nonprofit undertaking.

____   7.   Gamma, Inc., and Omega Corporation pool their assets to form a business trust. A business trust is

a. similar to a corporation.
b. similar to a partnership.
c. a hybrid of a corporation and a partnership.
d. unlike a corporation or a partnership.

___   8.   Barb invests in a franchise with Copy Centers, Inc. The franchise agreement may require Barb to pay a percentage of Copy's

a.   administrative expenses only.
b.   advertising expenses only.
c.   administrative and advertising expenses.
d.   none of the above.

___   9.   Fran buys a franchise from Global Services, Inc. In their agreement, Global may specify

a.   requirements for the business form of the organization only.
b.   standards of operation only.
c.   requirements for the form of business and standards of operation.
d.   none of the above.

___   10.   Aaron invests in a franchise with Big Foods Corporation. With respect to the franchise, Aaron may have legal protection under

a.   federal law only.
b.   state law only.
c.   federal and state law.
d.   none of the above.

SHORT ESSAY QUESTIONS

1.   What are the rights of partners in a partnership?

2.   How do franchise agreements generally delegate price and quality controls over the franchisee's business?

ISSUE SPOTTERS

(Answers at the Back of the Book)

1.   Merit Restaurants, Inc., sells franchises. Merit imposes on its franchisees standards of operation and personnel training methods. What is the potential pitfall to Merit if it exercises too much control over its franchisees?

2.   Fred and Gail are partners in a delivery business. When business is slow, without Gail's knowledge, Fred leases the delivery vehicles as moving vans. Because the vehicles would otherwise be sitting idle in a parking lot, can Fred keep the lease money?

3.   Ace Construction and Bayside Developers form a joint venture. Central Processing and Delta Data form a joint stock company. Efficient Systems and Fast Products form an unincorporated cooperative. What do these forms of business organization have in common?

Chapter 17
Limited Liability Companies and Limited Partnerships

WHAT THIS CHAPTER IS ABOUT

This chapter sets out the law relating to relatively new business organizations: limited liability companies (LLCs), limited liability partnerships (LLPs), limited partnerships, and limited liability limited partnerships (LLLPs). The chief features of these business forms are limited liability and tax advantages.

CHAPTER OUTLINE

I. **LIMITED LIABILITY COMPANIES**
   A limited liability company (LLC) is a hybrid form of business enterprise.

   A. **GOVERNING LAW**
   State statutes govern LLCs. Despite some similarities among these state laws, less than one-fourth of the states have adopted the Uniform Limited Liability Company Act (ULLCA).

   B. **TAXATION OF AN LLC**
   An LLC is taxed as a partnership unless it chooses to be taxed as a corporation.

   C. **FOREIGN INVESTORS**
   These may become LLC members.

   D. **THE NATURE OF THE LLC**
   An LLC offers the limited liability of a corporation [ULLCA 303]. Members can bring derivative actions on the LLC's behalf [ULLCA 101]. Courts may pierce the LLC veil.

   E. **LLC FORMATION**
   Articles of organization must be filed with the state. Certain information is required. Some states require that an LLC have at least two members.

   F. **JURISDICTIONAL REQUIREMENTS**
   An LLC is a citizen of every state of which its members are citizens.

   G. **ADVANTAGES OF THE LLC**
   Taxed as a partnership; liability of members is limited to the amount of their investment; members can participate in management; corporations, partnerships, and foreign investors can be members; no limit on the number of members (in many states, one is enough).

   H. **DISADVANTAGES OF THE LLC**
   Statutory restrictions on the transfer of ownership; because the LLC is a new form, little case law exists; until uniform statutes are adopted by most states, an LLC with multistate operations may face difficulties.

   I. **THE LLC OPERATING AGREEMENT**
   Provisions relate to management, division of profits (equally if not specified otherwise), transfer of membership, what events trigger dissolution, and so on. The agreement does not have to be in writing. If there is no agreement, state statutes govern. If there is no statute, partnership law applies.

J. LLC MANAGEMENT

1. Member-Managed LLC
Unless members agree otherwise, all members participate in management and voting rights are usually proportional to capital contributions. An agreement may set governing procedures (in contrast to corporations, which are subject to specific state requirements).

2. Manager-Managed LLC
Members may designate a group to run the firm. If so, the members' interests in the firm may qualify as securities.

II.   LIMITED LIABILITY PARTNERSHIPS
Professionals may organize as a limited liability partnership (LLP) to enjoy the tax advantages of a partnership, while avoiding personal liability for the wrongdoing of other partners.

A. LIABILITY IN AN LLP
In an LLP, professionals avoid personal liability for malpractice of other partners.

1. Liability outside the State of Formation
Most states apply the law of the state in which the LLP was formed.

2. Supervising Partner's Liability
A partner who commits a wrongful act is liable for the results. Also liable is the partner who supervises the party who commits the act. Some states provide that each partner is liable only up to the proportion of his or her responsibility for the result.

B. FAMILY LIMITED LIABILITY PARTNERSHIPS
This is a limited liability partnership (LLP) in which most of the partners are related. All partners must be natural persons or persons acting in a fiduciary capacity for natural persons. Family-owned farms may benefit from the use of the family limited liability partnership (FLLP) form.

III.   LIMITED PARTNERSHIPS
Limited partnerships must include at least one general partner and one or more limited partners. General partners assume management responsibility and liability for all partnership debts.

A. FORMATION OF A LIMITED PARTNERSHIP
The partners sign a certificate of limited partnership, which requires information similar to that found in a corporate charter (see Chapter 18). The certificate is filed with the secretary of state [RULPA 101(7), 201].

B. RIGHTS AND LIABILITIES OF PARTNERS

1. Rights of Limited Partners
Essentially the same rights as general partners. Can generally assign their interests in the partnership [RULPA 702, 704]. Can also sue on behalf of the firm if general partners refuse [RULPA 1001].

2. Liabilities of Limited Partners

a. Limited Liability to Creditors of the Partnership
Limited partners are liable to the extent of any contribution that is promised to the firm or any part of a contribution that was withdrawn [RULPA 502].

b. Personal Liability for Defects in Formation

1) If a Firm Is Organized in an Improper Manner
If a limited partner fails to withdraw on discovery of the defect, he or she can be personally liable to the firm's creditors.

2) If There Is a False Statement in the Partnership Certificate
If a limited partner knows of the statement, he or she may be liable to any person who relies on it [RULPA 207].

3) How to Avoid Future Liability
File an amendment or corrected certificate or renounce an interest in the profits of the partnership [RULPA 304].

3. Limited Partners and Management
Generally, participating in management results in personal liability for partnership debt, if creditors knew of participation [RULPA 303].

C. DISSOLUTION OF THE LIMITED PARTNERSHIP

1. General Partners—Dissolution
Retirement, death, or mental incompetence of a general partner dissolves the firm, unless continued by other general partners [RULPA 801]. Illegality, expulsion, or bankruptcy of general partner dissolves a firm.

2. Limited Partners—No Dissolution
Death or assignment of interest of a limited partner does not dissolve the firm [RULPA 702, 704, 705], nor does personal bankruptcy.

3. Court Decree
A limited partnership can be dissolved by court decree [RULPA 802].

4. Priority to Assets on Dissolution
(1) Creditors, including partners who are creditors; (2) partners and former partners receive unpaid distributions of partnership assets and, except as otherwise agreed, a return on their contributions and amounts proportionate to their share of distributions [RULPA 201(a)(10), 804].

IV.   LIMITED LIABILITY LIMITED PARTNERSHIPS
This form is similar to a limited partnership, except that the liability of all partners in a limited liability limited partnership (LLLP) is limited to the amount of their investment in the firm.

V.   MAJOR BUSINESS FORMS COMPARED
To decide which form of business organization is appropriate involves the consideration of such factors as the ease of creation, the liability of the owners, tax considerations, and the need for capital. Each form has advantages and disadvantages that indicate when it is most useful.

TRUE-FALSE QUESTIONS
(Answers at the Back of the Book)

_____   1.   Most states require that a limited partnership file a certificate of limited partnership with the appropriate state office.

_____   2.   The death of a limited partner will dissolve a limited partnership.

_____   3.   A limited liability company must be formed and operated in compliance with federal law.

_____   4.   A limited liability company is a citizen of every state of which its members are citizens.

_____   5.   A limited liability company does not offer the limited liability of a corporation.

_____   6.   A limited liability partnership does not limit in any way the liability of its partners.

___   7. In a limited partnership, the liability of each partner is limited to the amount of capital he or she has invested in the partnership.

___   8. In a limited liability limited partnership, the liability of each partner is limited to the amount of capital he or she has invested in the partnership.

___   9. In a limited liability company, members do not have to participate in the management of the company.

___ 10. Most limited liability company (LLC) statutes provide that unless the members agree otherwise, all profits of the LLC will be divided equally.

FILL-IN QUESTIONS

(Answers at the Back of the Book)

Unless the participants agree otherwise, all of the _____ (members/limited partners) of a _____ (limited liability company/limited partnership) may participate in management without assuming liability for the obligations of the firm. In contrast, the _____ (members/limited partners) of a _____ (limited liability company/limited partnership) who participate in management may be personally liable for the debts of the firm.

MULTIPLE-CHOICE QUESTIONS

(Answers at the Back of the Book)

___   1. Ann is a limited partner in Beta Sales, a limited partnership. Credit Company, a Beta creditor, claims that Ann is subject to personal liability for Beta's debts because Ann has the right, as a limited partner to take control of the firm. Credit is correct about

    a. Ann's liability only.
    b. Ann's right to control the firm only.
    c. Ann's liability and Ann's right to control the firm.
    d. none of the above.

___   2. Dave is a general partner in Eagle Investments, a limited partnership. Dave pays personal income taxes on

    a. all of the firm's income.
    b. his share of the firm's income.
    c. only the amount of the firm's income that is actually paid to him.
    d. none of the above.

___   3. Adam and Beth form A&B, LLC, a limited liability company (LLC). One advantage of an LLC is that it may be taxed as

    a. a corporation.
    b. a partnership.
    c. a sole proprietorship.
    d. none of the above.

___   4. Larry is a member of Macro Services, a limited liability company. Larry is liable for the firm's debts

    a. in proportion to the total number of members in the firm.
    b. to the extent of his capital contribution.
    c. to the full extent of the debts.
    d. none of the above.

___   5. Carol and Don form E-Stuff as a limited liability company. They can participate in the firm's management

   a. only to the extent that they assume personal liability for the firm's debts.
   b. only to the extent of the amount of their investment in the firm.
   c. to any extent.
   d. to no extent.

___   6. Jack and Jill form J&J, a limited partnership. Jack is a general partner. Jill is a limited partner. Dissolution of the firm would result from Jill's

   a. assignment of her interest in the firm to a third party only.
   b. bankruptcy or death only.
   c. assignment of interest, bankruptcy, or death.
   d. none of the above.

___   7. Drs. Kay and Lyle are partners in a medical clinic, which is organized as a limited liability partnership. A court holds Lyle liable in a malpractice suit. Kay is liable

   a. in proportion to the total number of partners in the firm.
   b. to the extent of her capital contribution.
   c. to the full extent of the liability.
   d. none of the above.

___   8. Mike, Nora, and Owen want to form a limited partnership. A limited partnership must have at least

   a. one general partner and one limited partner.
   b. one general partner and two limited partners.
   c. two limited partners.
   d. none of the above.

___   9. Pete is a general partner, and Quinn is a limited partner in PQ Partners, a limited partnership. As regards PQ, Quinn has

   a. fewer rights than Pete.
   b. more rights than Pete.
   c. the same rights as Pete.
   d. none of the above.

___   10. Ron and Sara form Top Goods, LLC, a limited liability company (LLC). A disadvantage of an LLC is that

   a. its income is double taxed.
   b. its members are subject to personal liability for the firm's debts.
   c. state laws concerning limited liability companies are not yet uniform.
   d. none of the above.

SHORT ESSAY QUESTIONS

1. What are the advantages of doing business as a limited liability company?

2. Describe the following characteristics of limited partnerships: creation, sharing of profits and loses, liability, capital contribution, management, duration, assignment, and priorities on liquidation.

ISSUE SPOTTERS

(Answers at the Back of the Book)

1. Carol, Donna, and Earl are partners in an accounting firm that is a limited liability partnership. Carol is Donna's supervising partner. Donna obtains $50,000 by committing fraud against Fred, one of the firm's clients. Who may be liable for the $50,000?

2. Olga is a limited partner, and Anton is a general partner of Platinum Fitness Club, a limited partnership. Anton manages the firm. Olga has some expertise in the area and believes that she could do a better job than Anton at managing, but she abstains from becoming actively involved. Why might she choose to keep away from management activities?

3. Greg, Harry, and Ida are members of Best Products, LLC (limited liability company). What are their options with respect to the management of Best Products?

Chapter 18
Corporations

WHAT THIS CHAPTER IS ABOUT

This chapter covers corporate classifications, formation, and the rights and responsibilities of all participants—directors, officers, and shareholders. Most corporations are formed under state law, and most states follow some version of the Revised Model Business Corporation Act (RMBCA).

CHAPTER OUTLINE

I. THE NATURE OF THE CORPORATION

A. CORPORATE PERSONNEL
Shareholders elect a board of directors, which is responsible for overall management and hires corporate officers to run daily operations.

B. CORPORATE POWER
A corporation has the power to perform all acts reasonably appropriate and necessary to accomplish its purposes (except as limited by charter, statutes, or constitutions).

C. CORPORATE TAXATION
Corporate profits are taxed twice: as income to the corporation and, when distributed as dividends, as income to the shareholders.

II. CLASSIFICATION OF CORPORATIONS

A. DOMESTIC, FOREIGN, AND ALIEN CORPORATIONS
A corporation is a *domestic corporation* in the state in which it incorporated, a *foreign corporation* in other states, and an *alien corporation* in other countries. A foreign corporation normally must obtain a certificate of authority to do business in any state except its home state.

B. PUBLIC AND PRIVATE CORPORATIONS
A *public corporation* is formed by the government to meet a political or governmental purpose (such as the U.S. Postal Service). A *private corporation* is created for private benefit and is owned by private persons.

C. NONPROFIT CORPORATIONS
Corporations formed without a profit-making purpose (private hospitals, educational institutions, charities, and religious organizations).

D. CLOSE CORPORATIONS
To qualify as a *close corporation*, a firm must have a limited number of shareholders, and restrict its issue and transfer of stock.

1. Advantage
Exempt from most of the nonessential formalities of corporate operation (bylaws, annual meetings, etc. [RMBCA 7.32]).

2. Management

Resembles that of a sole proprietorship or a partnership—one or a few shareholders usually hold the positions of directors and officers.

3. Transfer of Shares

Often restricted by stipulating that shareholders offer their shares to the corporation or other shareholders before offering them to outsiders.

E. S CORPORATIONS

1. Requirements

Must be a domestic corporation; must not be a member of an affiliated group of corporations; shareholders must be individuals, estates, or certain trusts; must have thirty-five or fewer shareholders; can have only one class of stock; no shareholder can be a nonresident alien.

2. Advantages

Shareholders can use corporate losses to offset other income; only a single tax on corporate income is imposed at individual income tax rates at the shareholder level (whether or not it is distributed).

III.   CORPORATE FORMATION

A. PROMOTIONAL ACTIVITIES

Promoters take the first steps in organizing a corporation: issue a prospectus (see Chapter 28) and secure the corporate charter (see below).

1. Promoter's Liability

Promoters are personally liable on preincorporation contracts, unless the contracting party agrees otherwise. This liability continues after incorporation unless the third party releases the promoter or the corporation assumes the contract by novation (see Chapter 10).

2. Subscribers and Subscriptions

Subscribers (who agree to buy stock in a future corporation) become shareholders as soon as the corporation is formed or as soon as the corporation accepts their subscription agreement with the promoter.

a. Subscribers' Liability

A subscription is irrevocable for six months unless the parties agree otherwise [RMBCA 6.20]. In some states, a subscriber can, without liability, revoke an offer to buy before the corporation accepts.

b. Corporation's Liability

Preincorporation subscriptions are continuing offers to buy stock. On or after its formation, a corporation can choose to accept the offer.

B. INCORPORATION PROCEDURES

1. State Chartering

Some states offer more advantageous tax or incorporation provisions.

2. Articles of Incorporation

The articles include basic information about the corporation and serve as a primary source of authority for its organization and functions.

a. Corporate Name

This cannot be the same as, or deceptively similar to, the name of a corporation doing business in the state.

b. **Nature and Purpose**
The intended business activities of the corporation must be specified. Stating a general corporate purpose is usually sufficient.

c. **Duration**
A corporation can have perpetual existence in most states.

d. **Capital Structure**
The amount of stock authorized for issuance; its valuation; and other information as to equity, capital, and credit must be outlined.

e. **Internal Organization**
Management structure can be described in bylaws later.

f. **Registered Office and Agent**
Usually, the registered office is the principal office of the corporation; the agent is a person designated to receive legal documents on behalf of the corporation.

g. **Incorporators**
Incorporators (some states require only one) must sign the articles when they are submitted to the state; often this is the only duty, and they need have no other interest in the corporation.

3. **Certificate of Incorporation (Corporate Charter)**
The articles of incorporation are sent to the appropriate state official (usually the secretary of state). Many states issue a certificate of incorporation authorizing the corporation to conduct business.

IV. IMPROPER INCORPORATION

A. POSSIBLE RESULTS OF IMPROPER INCORPORATION
On the basis of improper incorporation—

1. **Shareholders May Be Personally Liable for Corporate Obligations**
A person attempting to enforce a contract or bring a tort suit against the corporation could seek to make the shareholders personally liable.

2. **Third Parties May Avoid Liability to the Corporation**
If a corporation seeks to enforce a contract, the defaulting party who learns of a defect in incorporation may be able to avoid liability.

B. *DE JURE* AND *DE FACTO* CORPORATIONS

1. *De Jure* **Existence**
This occurs if there is substantial compliance with all requirements for incorporation. In most states, the certificate of incorporation is evidence that all requirements have been met, and neither the state nor a third party can attack the corporation's existence.

2. *De Facto* **Existence**
In this situation, the existence of a corporation cannot be challenged by third persons (except the state) if (1) there is a statute under which the firm can be incorporated, (2) the parties made a good faith attempt to comply with it, and (3) the firm has attempted to do business as a corporation.

C. CORPORATION BY ESTOPPEL
If an association that is neither an actual corporation nor a *de facto* or *de jure* corporation holds itself out as being a corporation, it is estopped from denying corporate status in a lawsuit by a third party.

V. DISREGARDING THE CORPORATE ENTITY

A. PIERCING THE CORPORATE VEIL

A court may ignore the corporate structure (pierce the corporate veil) if—

1. A party is tricked or misled into dealing with the corporation rather than the individual.
2. The corporation is set up never to make a profit or always to be insolvent, or it is too thinly capitalized.
3. Statutory corporate formalities are not followed.
4. Personal and corporate interests are commingled to the extent that the corporation has no separate identity.

B. RESULT

Personal liability for corporate debts is imposed on shareholders.

VI. DIRECTORS, OFFICERS, AND SHAREHOLDERS

A. ROLE OF DIRECTORS

The board of directors governs a corporation. Officers handle daily business.

1. Election of Directors

a. Number of Directors
Set in a corporation's articles or bylaws. Corporations with fewer than fifty shareholders can eliminate the board of directors.

b. How Directors Are Chosen
The first board (appointed by the incorporators or named in the articles) serves until the first shareholders' meeting. Subsequent directors are elected by a majority vote of the shareholders.

c. Removal of Directors
A director can be removed for cause by shareholder action (or the board may have the power). In most states, a director cannot be removed without cause unless shareholders reserved the right.

2. Board of Directors' Meetings

a. Formal Minutes and Notice
A board conducts business by holding formal meetings with recorded minutes. The dates for regular meetings are usually set in the articles and bylaws or by board resolution, and no other notice is required. Special meetings require notice to all directors.

b. Quorum Requirements and Voting
Quorum requirements vary. If the firm specifies none, in most states a quorum is a majority of the number of directors authorized in the articles or bylaws. Voting is done in person, one vote per director.

3. Rights of Directors

a. Participation and Inspection
A director has a right to participate in corporate business. A director must have access to all books and records to make decisions.

b. Compensation and Indemnification
Nominal sums may be paid to directors, and there is a trend to provide more. Most states permit a corporation to indemnify a director for costs and fees in defending against corporate-related lawsuits. Many firms buy insurance to cover indemnification.

4. Management Responsibilities

a. **Areas of Responsibility**

Major policy and financial decisions; appointment, supervision, pay, and removal of officers and other managerial employees.

b. **Executive Committee**

Most states permit a board to elect an executive committee from among the directors to handle management between board meetings. The committee is limited to ordinary business matters.

B. ROLE OF CORPORATE OFFICERS AND EXECUTIVES

The board hires officers and other executive employees. Officers are agents of the corporation (see Chapter 19).

1. **Qualifications**

At the discretion of the firm; included in the articles or bylaws. A person can hold more than one office and also be a director.

2. **Rights and Duties**

Employment contracts define the rights of corporate officers and other high-level managers. The board can normally remove officers at any time (but the corporation could be liable for breach of contract). Officers' duties are the same as those of directors.

C. FIDUCIARY DUTIES OF DIRECTORS AND OFFICERS

Directors and officers are fiduciaries of the corporation.

1. **Duty of Care**

Directors and officers must act in good faith, in what they consider to be the best interests of the corporation, and with the care that an ordinarily prudent person would exercise in similar circumstances.

a. **Duty to Make Informed and Reasonable Decisions**

Directors must be informed on corporate matters and act in accord with their knowledge and training. A director can rely on information furnished by competent officers, or others, without being accused of acting in bad faith or failing to exercise due care.

b. **Duty to Exercise Reasonable Supervision**

Directors must use reasonable supervision when work is delegated.

c. **Dissenting Directors**

Directors must attend board meetings; if not, they should register a dissent to actions taken (to avoid liability for mismanagement).

2. **Duty of Loyalty**

Directors and officers cannot use corporate funds or confidential information for personal advantage. Specifically, they cannot—

a. Compete with the corporation.
b. Usurp a corporate opportunity.
c. Have an interest that conflicts with the interest of the corporation.
d. Engage in insider trading (see Chapter 28).
e. Authorize a transaction detrimental to minority shareholders.
f. Sell control over the corporation.

3. **Conflicts of Interest**

Directors and officers must disclose fully any conflict of interest that might occur in a deal involving the firm. A contract may be upheld if it was fair and reasonable to the firm when it was made, there was full disclosure of the interest of the officers or directors involved, and it was approved by a majority of disinterested directors or shareholders.

D. LIABILITY OF DIRECTORS AND OFFICERS

1. The Business Judgment Rule

Honest mistakes of judgment and poor business decisions do not make directors and officers liable to the firm for poor results, if the decision complies with management's fiduciary duties, has a reasonable basis, and is within managerial authority and the power of the corporation.

2. Liability for Torts and Crimes

Directors and officers are personally liable for their torts and crimes, and may be liable for those of subordinates.

E. ROLE OF SHAREHOLDERS

1. Shareholders' Powers

Shareholders own the corporation, approve fundamental corporate changes, and elect and remove directors.

2. Shareholders' Meetings

Regular meetings must be annual; special meetings can be called for urgent matters. Notice of a special meeting must state the purpose.

3. Shareholder Voting

a. Quorum Requirements

At the meeting, a quorum must be present. A majority vote of the shares present is required to pass resolutions. Fundamental changes require a higher percentage. Each common shareholder has one vote per share. The articles can exclude or limit voting rights.

b. Cumulative Voting

With this method, the number of members of the board to be elected is multiplied by the total number of voting shares. This is the number of votes a shareholder has and can be cast for one or more nominees.

c. Shareholder Voting Agreement

A group of shareholders can agree to vote their shares together. A shareholder can vote by proxy. Any person can solicit proxies.

d. Voting Trust

Exists when legal title (recorded ownership on the corporate books) is transferred to a trustee who is responsible for voting the shares. The shareholder retains all other ownership rights.

F. RIGHTS OF SHAREHOLDERS

1. Stock Certificates

Notice of shareholder meetings, dividends, and corporate reports are distributed to owners listed in the corporate books, not on the basis of possession of stock certificates (which most states do not require).

2. Preemptive Rights

Usually apply only to additional, newly issued stock sold for cash and must be exercised within a specified time (usually thirty days). When new shares are issued, each shareholder is given *stock warrants* (transferable options to acquire a certain number of shares at a stated price).

3. Dividends

Dividends can be paid in cash, property, or stock. Once declared, a cash dividend is a corporate debt. Dividends are payable only from (1) retained earnings, (2) current net profits, or (3) any surplus.

a. **Illegal Dividends**
   A dividend paid when a corporation is insolvent is illegal and must be repaid. A dividend paid from an unauthorized account or causing a corporation to become insolvent may have to be repaid. In any case, the directors can be held personally liable.

b. **If the Directors Fail to Declare a Dividend**
   Shareholders can ask a court to compel a declaration of a dividend, but to issue such an order, the court must find that the directors' conduct was an abuse of discretion.

4. **Inspection Rights**
   Shareholders (or their attorney, accountant, or agent) can inspect and copy corporate books and records for a proper purpose, if the request is made in advance. This right can be denied to prevent harassment or to protect confidential corporate information.

5. **Transfer of Shares**
   Any restrictions on transferability must be noted on the face of a stock certificate. Restrictions must be reasonable—for example, a right of first refusal remains with the corporation or the shareholders for only a specified time or a reasonable time.

6. **Rights on Dissolution**
   Shareholders can petition a court to dissolve a firm if—

   a. The directors are deadlocked, shareholders are unable to break the deadlock, and there is or could be irreparable injury to the firm.
   b. The acts of the directors or those in control of the corporation are illegal, oppressive, or fraudulent.
   c. Corporate assets are being misapplied or wasted.
   d. The shareholders are deadlocked in voting power and have failed, for a specified period (usually two annual meetings), to elect successors to directors.

7. **Shareholder's Derivative Suit**
   If directors fail to sue in the corporate name to redress a wrong suffered by the firm, shareholders can do so (after complaining to the board). Any recovery normally goes into the corporate treasury.

G. **LIABILITY OF SHAREHOLDERS**
   In most cases, if a corporation fails, shareholders lose only their investment. Exceptions include (see also Chapter 28)—

   1. **Stock-Subscription Agreements**
      Once an agreement is accepted, any refusal to pay is a breach, resulting in personal liability.

   2. **Watered Stock**
      In most cases, a shareholder who receives watered stock (stock sold by a corporation for less than par value) must pay the difference to the corporation. In some states, such shareholders may be liable to creditors of the corporation for unpaid corporate debts.

H. **DUTIES OF MAJORITY SHAREHOLDERS**
   A single shareholder (or a few acting together) who owns enough shares to control the corporation owes a fiduciary duty to the minority shareholders and creditors when they sell their shares.

TRUE-FALSE QUESTIONS

(Answers at the Back of the Book)

____ **1.** A foreign corporation is a corporation formed in another country but doing business in the United States.

____ **2.** S corporations cannot avoid federal taxes at the corporate level.

____   **3.**   The business judgment rule immunizes officers from liability for poor decisions that were made in good faith.

____   **4.**   An officer is a fiduciary of a corporation.

____   **5.**   Preemptive rights entitle shareholders to bring a derivative suit against the corporation.

____   **6.**   Damages recovered in a shareholder's derivative suit are paid to the shareholder who brought the suit.

____   **7.**   Generally, shareholders are not personally responsible for the debts of the corporation.

____   **8.**   Directors, but not officers, owe a duty of loyalty to the corporation.

____   **9.**   The business judgment rule makes a director liable for losses to the firm in most cases.

____   **10.**   Shareholders may vote to remove members of the board of directors.

FILL-IN QUESTIONS

(Answers at the Back of the Book)

A stock certificate may be lost or destroyed, _____ (and ownership is/but ownership is not) destroyed with it. A new certificate _____ (can/cannot) be issued to replace one that has been lost or destroyed. Notice of meetings, dividends, and operational and financial reports are all distributed according to the individual _____
_____ (in possession of the certificate/recorded as the owner in the corporation's books).

MULTIPLE-CHOICE QUESTIONS

(Answers at the Back of the Book)

____   **1.**   Adam and Beth want to incorporate to sell computers. The first step in the incorporation procedure is to

   a.   file the articles of incorporation.
   b.   hold the first organizational meeting.
   c.   obtain a corporate charter.
   d.   select a state in which to incorporate.

____   **2.**   Responsibility for the overall management of Beta, Inc., a corporation, is entrusted to

   a.   the board of directors.
   b.   the corporate officers and managers.
   c.   the owners of the corporation.
   d.   the promoters of the corporation.

____   **3.**   Delta Company is a private, for-profit corporation that (1) was formed for the purpose of marketing business office software, (2) is owned by ten shareholders, (3) is subject to double taxation, and (4) has made no public offering of its shares. Delta is

   a.   a close corporation.
   b.   a nonprofit corporation.
   c.   an S corporation.
   d.   a professional corporation.

____ **4.** Jill is a shareholder of Kappa Company. As a shareholder, Jill does *not* have a right to

a. dividends.
b. inspect corporate books and records.
c. sue the corporation.
d. transfer shares.

____ **5.** Don and Eve are officers of Fine Products Corporation. As officers, their rights are set out in

a. Don and Eve's employment contracts.
b. international agreements.
c. state corporation statutes.
d. the firm's certificate of authority.

____ **6.** The management of National Brands, Inc., is at odds with the shareholders over some recent decisions. The shareholders may file a shareholders' derivative suit to

a. compel dissolution of National.
b. compel payment of a properly declared dividend.
c. enforce a right to inspect corporate records.
d. recover damages from the management for an *ultra vires* act.

____ **7.** Jiffy Corporation uses cumulative voting in its elections of directors. Kay owns 3,000 Jiffy shares. At an annual meeting at which three directors are to be elected, Mary may cast for any one candidate

a. 1,000 votes.
b. 3,000 votes.
c. 9,000 votes.
d. 27,000 votes.

____ **8.** Local Business Corporation invests in intrastate businesses. In Local's state, as in most states, the minimum number of directors that must be present before its board can transact business is

a. all of the directors authorized in the articles.
b. a majority of the number authorized in the articles or bylaws.
c. any odd number.
d. none of the above.

____ **9.** Micro Company makes and sells computer chips. Like most corporations, Micro's officers are hired by the company's

a. directors.
b. incorporators.
c. officers.
d. shareholders.

____ **10.** Kate is a shareholder of Local Delivery, Inc. A court might "pierce the corporate veil" and hold her personally liable for Local's debts if

a. Kate's personal interests are commingled with Local's interests to the extent that Local has no separate identity.
b. Local calls too many shareholders' meetings.
c. Local is overcapitalized.
d. none of the above.

SHORT ESSAY QUESTIONS

1. How do the duty of care and the duty of loyalty govern the conduct of directors and officers in a corporation?

2. What are the rights of the shareholders of a corporation?

ISSUE SPOTTERS

(Answers at the Back of the Book)

1. Macro Corporation is formed in one state, but does business through sales representatives in another state, in which it has no office or warehouse. Can the latter exercise jurisdiction over Macro?

2. Alpha Corporation's board of directors, who include Beth and Carl (officers of the firm), is deadlocked over whether to market a new product. Dan, a minority shareholder, suspects that Beth and Carl are taking advantage of the deadlock to use corporate assets (offices, equipment, supplies, staff time) to initiate a competing enterprise. Can Dan intervene?

3. Beta Corporation has an opportunity to buy stock in Gamma, Inc. The directors decide that, instead of Beta buying the stock, the directors will buy it. Frank, a Beta shareholder, learns of the purchase and wants to sue the directors on Beta's behalf. Can he do it?

CUMULATIVE HYPOTHETICAL PROBLEM FOR UNIT FOUR—INCLUDING CHAPTERS 16–18

(Answers at the Back of the Book)

Adam, Beth, and Carl are sole proprietors who decide to pool their resources to produce and maintain an Internet portal Web site, "i-World."

_____ 1. Adam, Beth, and Carl decide to form a partnership. They transfer their business assets and liabilities to the firm and start business on May 1, 2003. The parties execute a formal partnership agreement on July 1. The partnership began its existence

    a. on May 1.
    b. on July 1.
    c. when each partner's individual creditors consented to the asset transfer.
    d. when the parties initially decided to form a partnership.

_____ 2. After six months in operation, Adam, Beth, and Carl decide to change the form of their partnership to a limited partnership. To form a limited partnership, they must

    a. accept limited liability for all of the partners.
    b. create the firm according to specific statutory requirements.
    c. designate one general partner to be a limited partner.
    d. each make a capital contribution.

_____ 3. Adam, Beth, and Carl's i-World is very successful. In March 2004, they decide to incorporate. The articles of incorporation must include all of the following except

    a. the name of a registered agent.
    b. the name of the corporation.
    c. the names of the incorporators.
    d. the names of the initial officers.

____ **4.** Adam is a director of i-World. Adam has a right to

a. compensation.
b. participation.
c. preemption.
d. none of the above.

____ **5.** The board of directors of i-World announces a cash dividend. This dividend may *not* be paid from

a. accumulated surplus.
b. gross profits.
c. net profits.
d. retained earnings.

QUESTIONS ON THE FOCUS ON LEGAL REASONING FOR UNIT FOUR—
SEVEN SPRINGS FARM, INC. V. CROKER

(Answers at the Back of the Book)

____ **1.** Micro Company's shareholders are subject to a stock-transfer restriction agreement that defines *shareholder* to include only individual shareholders (not Micro) and that gives the shareholders a right of first refusal. Micro wants to merge with National Corporation. According to the majority's opinion in *Seven Springs Farm, Inc. v. Croker*, this stock-transfer restriction agreement

a. applies to any fundamental corporate actions.
b. applies to this merger.
c. does not apply to any fundamental corporate actions.
d. does not apply to this merger.

____ **2.** In the dissent's opinion, the stock-transfer restriction agreement mentioned in the previous question

a. applies to any fundamental corporate actions.
b. applies to this merger.
c. does not apply to any fundamental corporate actions.
d. does not apply to this merger.

____ **3.** Under the majority's holding, Micro's shareholders could obtain cash for their shares

a. by selling their shares subject to aright of first refusal only.
b. by way of a merger only.
c. by selling their shares subject to aright of first refusal or by way of a merger.
d. none of the above.

QUESTIONS ON THE FOCUS ON ETHICS FOR UNIT FOUR—
THE BUSINESS ENVIRONMENT

(Answers at the Back of the Book)

____ **1.** Donna is an officer with Eagle, Inc. Donna finds herself in a position to acquire assets that would benefit Eagle if acquired in its name. If Donna usurps this opportunity, she may violate the duty of

a. acting in one's own interest.
b. agency.
c. care.
d. loyalty.

____ 2. Frank is a director of Great Sale Corporation. Ordinarily, Frank owes fiduciary duties only to

    a. Great Sale's corporate personnel.
    b. Great Sale's creditors.
    c. Great Sale's shareholders.
    d. himself.

____ 3. Burt is an employee of Cathy, a franchisee of Diners Restaurants, Inc. The franchisor may be liable for Burt's torts committed within the scope of his employment under the principles of

    a. acting in one's own interest.
    b. agency.
    c. care.
    d. loyalty.

Chapter 19
Agency

WHAT THIS CHAPTER IS ABOUT

This chapter covers agency relationships, including how they are formed and the duties involved. Agency relationships are essential to a corporation, which can function and enter into contracts only through its agents.

CHAPTER OUTLINE

I. AGENCY RELATIONSHIPS

In an agency relationship, the parties agree that the agent will act on behalf and instead of the principal in negotiating and transacting business with third persons.

A. EMPLOYER-EMPLOYEE RELATIONSHIPS

Normally, all employees who deal with third parties are deemed to be agents. Statutes covering workers' compensation and so on apply only to employer-employee relationships.

B. EMPLOYER–INDEPENDENT CONTRACTOR RELATIONSHIPS

Those who hire independent contractors have no control over the details of their physical performance. Independent contractors can be agents.

C. DETERMINING EMPLOYEE STATUS

The greater an employer's control over the work, the more likely it is that the worker is an employee. Another key factor is whether the employer withholds taxes from payments to the worker and pays unemployment and Social Security taxes covering the worker.

II. FORMATION OF THE AGENCY RELATIONSHIP

Consideration is not required. A principal must have capacity to contract, but anyone can be an agent. An agency can be created for any legal purpose.

A. AGENCY BY AGREEMENT

Normally, an agency must be based on an agreement that the agent will act for the principal. Such an agreement can be an express written contract or can be implied by conduct.

B. AGENCY BY RATIFICATION

A person who is not an agent (or who is an agent acting outside the scope of his or her authority) may make a contract on behalf of another (a principal). If the principal approves or affirms that contract by word or by action, an agency relationship is created by ratification.

C. AGENCY BY ESTOPPEL

1. The Principal's Actions

When a principal causes a third person to believe that another person is his or her agent, and the third person deals with the supposed agent, the principal is estopped to deny the agency relationship.

2. The Third Party's Reasonable Belief
The third person must prove that he or she reasonably believed that an agency relationship existed and that the agent had authority—that an ordinary, prudent person familiar with business practice and custom would have been justified in concluding that the agent had authority.

D. AGENCY BY OPERATION OF LAW
A court may find an agency relationship in the absence of a formal agreement. This may occur in family relationships or in an emergency, when the agent's failure to act outside the scope of his or her authority would cause the principal substantial loss.

III. DUTIES OF AGENTS AND PRINCIPALS
The principal-agent relationship is fiduciary.

A. AGENT'S DUTIES TO PRINCIPAL

1. Performance
An agent must use reasonable diligence and skill (the degree of skill of a reasonable person under similar circumstances), unless an agent claims special skills (such as those of an accountant), in which case the agent is expected to use those skills.

2. Notification
An agent must notify the principal of all matters concerning the agency. Notice to the agent is considered to be notice to the principal.

3. Loyalty
An agent must act solely for the benefit of the principal (not in the interest of the agent or a third party).

a. Confidentiality
Any information or knowledge acquired through the agency relationship is confidential. It cannot be disclosed during the agency or after its termination.

b. Agent's Loyalty Must Be Undivided
An agent employed by a principal to buy cannot buy from himself or herself, and an agent employed to sell cannot become the purchaser, without the principal's consent.

4. Obedience
When an agent acts on behalf of the principal, the agent must follow all lawful instructions of the principal. Exceptions include emergencies and instances in which instructions are not clearly stated.

5. Accounting
An agent must keep and make available to the principal an account of everything received and paid out on behalf of the principal. An agent must keep separate accounts for the principal's funds.

B. PRINCIPAL'S DUTIES TO AGENT

1. Compensation
A principal must pay an agent for services rendered (unless the agent does not act for money). Payment must be timely. If no amount has been agreed to, the principal owes the customary amount for such services.

2. Reimbursement and Indemnification
A principal must (1) reimburse the agent for money paid at the principal's request or for necessary expenses and (2) indemnify an agent for liability incurred because of authorized acts.

3. Cooperation
A principal must cooperate with and assist an agent in performing his or her duties. The principal must do nothing to prevent performance.

4. **Safe Working Conditions**
   A principal must provide safe working conditions.

IV. RIGHTS AND REMEDIES OF AGENTS AND PRINCIPALS

If one party violates his or her duty to the other, remedies available to the party not in breach arise out of contract and tort law, and include damages, termination of the agency, injunction, and accounting.

A. AGENT'S RIGHTS AND REMEDIES AGAINST PRINCIPAL

For every duty of the principal, an agent has a corresponding right. Breach of a duty by the principal follows normal contract and tort remedies. If the relation is not contractual, an agent has no right to specific performance (but can recover for past services and future damages).

B. PRINCIPAL'S RIGHTS AND REMEDIES AGAINST AGENT

1. **Constructive Trust**
   A court imposes a constructive trust if an agent retains benefits or profits that belong to the principal or takes advantage of the agency to obtain property the principal wants to buy. The court declares that the agent holds money or property on behalf of the principal.

2. **Avoidance**
   If an agent breaches an agency agreement under a contract, the principal has a right to avoid any contract entered into with the agent.

3. **Indemnification**
   A third party can sue a principal for an agent's negligence, and in certain situations the principal can sue the agent. The same is true if the agent violates the principal's instructions.

V. SCOPE OF AN AGENT'S AUTHORITY

A principal's liability in a contract with a third party arises from the authority given the agent to enter contracts on the principal's behalf.

A. EXPRESS AUTHORITY

Express authority may be oral or in writing. Under the equal dignity rule in most states, if the contract being executed is or must be in writing, the agent's authority must also be in writing. Exceptions: a corporate executive doing ordinary business does not need written authority from the corporation, and an agent acting in the presence of the principal does not need written authority.

B. IMPLIED AUTHORITY

Conferred by custom, can be inferred from the position an agent occupies, or is implied as reasonably necessary to carry out express authority.

C. APPARENT AUTHORITY AND ESTOPPEL

An agent has apparent authority when a principal, by word or action, causes a third party reasonably to believe that an agent has authority, though the agent has no authority. The principal may be estopped from denying it if the third party changes position in reliance.

D. EMERGENCY POWERS

If an emergency demands action by the agent, but the agent is unable to communicate with the principal, the agent has emergency power.

E. RATIFICATION

A principal can ratify an unauthorized contract or act, if he or she is aware of all material facts. Ratification can be done expressly or impliedly (by accepting the benefits of a transaction). An entire transaction must be ratified; a principal cannot affirm only part.

1. **Effect of Ratification Without Knowing All the Facts**
   If the third party acts in reliance to his or her detriment on the apparent ratification, the principal can repudiate but must reimburse the third party's costs.

2. **Effect of Ratification**
   Ratification binds the principal to the agent's act and treats it as if it had been authorized from the outset.

3. **Effect of No Ratification**
   There is no contract binding the principal; the third party's agreement with the agent is an unaccepted offer; the agent may be liable to the third party for misrepresenting his or her authority.

VI. LIABILITY FOR CONTRACTS
Who is liable to third parties for contracts formed by an agent?

A. DEFINITIONS

1. **Disclosed Principal**
   This is a principal whose identity is known by the third party when the contract is made.

2. **Partially Disclosed Principal**
   This is a principal whose identity is not known by the third party, but the third party knows the agent is or may be acting for a principal when the contract is made.

3. **Undisclosed Principal**
   This is a principal whose identity is totally unknown by the third party, who also does not know that the agent is acting in an agency capacity at the time of the contract.

B. IF AN AGENT ACTS WITHIN THE SCOPE OF HIS OR HER AUTHORITY

1. **Disclosed Principal**
   If a principal's identity is known to a third party when an agent makes a contract, the principal is liable. The agent is not liable.

2. **Partially Disclosed Principal**
   The principal is liable. In most states, the agent is also liable (but is entitled to indemnification by the principal).

3. **Undisclosed Principal**
   The principal and the agent are liable. Exceptions—

   a. The principal was expressly excluded as a party in the contract.
   b. The contract is a negotiable instrument (check or note).
   c. The performance of the agent is personal to the contract.
   d. The third party would not have contracted with the principal had the third party known his or her identity, the agent or the principal knew this, and the third party rescinds the contract.

C. IF THE AGENT HAS NO AUTHORITY
The principal is not liable in contract to a third party. The agent is liable, for breach of the implied warranty of authority (not on breach of the contract), unless the third party knew the agent did not have authority.

D. ACTIONS BY E-AGENTS
E-agents include semi-autonomous computer programs capable of executing specific tasks. How much authority do e-agents have? Generally, any party who uses an e-agent is bound by the e-agent's operations whether or not the principal was aware of them.

VII. LIABILITY FOR AGENT'S TORTS

An agent is liable to third parties for his or her torts. Is the principal liable?

A. PRINCIPAL'S TORTIOUS CONDUCT

A principal may be liable for harm resulting from the principal's negligence or recklessness (giving improper instructions; authorizing the use of improper materials or tools; establishing improper rules; or failing to prevent others' tortious conduct while they are on the principal's property or using the principal's equipment, materials, or tools).

B. PRINCIPAL'S AUTHORIZATION OF AGENT'S TORTIOUS CONDUCT

A principal who authorizes an agent to commit a tortious act may be liable.

C. LIABILITY FOR AGENT'S MISREPRESENTATION

1. Fraudulent Misrepresentation

If a principal has given an agent authority to make statements and the agent makes false claims, the principal is liable. If an agent appears to be acting within the scope of authority in taking advantage of a third party, the principal who placed the agent in that position is liable.

2. Innocent Misrepresentation

When a principal knows that an agent does not have all the facts but does not correct the agent's or the third party's impressions, the principal is liable.

D. LIABILITY FOR AGENT'S NEGLIGENCE

Under the doctrine of *respondeat superior*, an employer is liable for harm caused (negligently or intentionally) to a third party by an employee acting within the scope of employment, without regard to the personal fault of the employer. This is known as *vicarious liability.*

1. Determining the Scope of Employment

a. Factors

In determining whether an act is within the scope of employment, a court considers—

1) the time, place, and purpose of the act.
2) whether the act was authorized by the employer.
3) whether the act is one commonly performed by employees on behalf of their employers.
4) whether the employer's interest was advanced by the act.
5) whether the private interests of the employee were involved.
6) whether the employer furnished the means by which an injury was inflicted.
7) whether the employer had reason to know that the employee would do the act in question.
8) whether the act involved the commission of a serious crime.

b. Travel and Commuting

The travel of those whose jobs require it is considered within the scope of employment for the duration of the trip, including the return. An employee going to and from work or meals is usually considered outside the scope of employment.

2. Employer's Liability for Agent's Torts outside the Scope of Employment

An employer who knows or should know that an employee has a propensity for committing tortious acts is liable for the acts even if they are outside the scope of employment. Also, an employer is liable for permitting an employee to engage in reckless acts that can injure others.

3. Agent's Liability for His or Her Own Torts

An employee is liable for his or her own torts. An employee who commits a tort at the employer's direction can be liable with the employer, even if he or she was unaware of the wrongfulness of the act.

VIII.   LIABILITY FOR INDEPENDENT CONTRACTOR'S TORTS

An employer is not liable for physical harm caused to a third person by the tortious act of an independent contractor (except in cases of hazardous activities such as blasting operations, the transportation of highly volatile chemicals, and the use of poisonous gases, in which strict liability is imposed).

IX.   LIABILITY FOR AGENT'S CRIMES

A principal is not liable for an agent's crime, unless the principal participated. In some jurisdictions, a principal may be liable for an agent's violating, in the course and scope of employment, such regulations as those governing sanitation, prices, weights, and the sale of liquor.

X.   TERMINATION OF AN AGENCY

A.   TERMINATION BY ACT OF THE PARTIES

An agency ends when the time specified in the agreement expires, its purpose is achieved, a specified event occurs, or by mutual agreement. Both parties have the *power* to terminate an agency, but they may not have the *right* and may therefore be liable for breach of contract.

B.   TERMINATION BY OPERATION OF LAW

Circumstances under which an agency terminates by operation of law include death of insanity of either party, destruction of the subject matter of the agency, changed circumstances, bankruptcy of either party, and war between the principal's and agent's countries.

C.   NOTICE REQUIRED FOR TERMINATION

If an agency terminates by operation of law because of death, insanity, or some other unforeseen circumstance, there is no duty to notify third persons, unless the agent's authority is coupled with an interest. If the parties themselves terminate the agency, the principal must inform any third parties who know of the agency that it has ended.

TRUE-FALSE QUESTIONS

(Answers at the Back of the Book)

____   1.   Unless the parties agree otherwise, a principal must pay for an agent's services.

____   2.   A principal can never avoid a contract entered into with an agent.

____   3.   A third party cannot sue a principal for an agent's negligence.

____   4.   An agent must keep separate accounts for the principal's funds.

____   5.   Information obtained through an agency relationship is confidential.

____   6.   If an agent acts within the scope of authority, a *disclosed* principal is liable to a third party for contracts made by the agent.

____   7.   If an agent acts within the scope of authority, an *undisclosed* principal is liable to a third party for contracts made by the agent.

____   8.   An employer is liable for *any* harm caused to a third party by an employee acting within the scope of employment.

____   9.   Both parties to an agency have the right to terminate the agency at any time.

____   10.   An e-agent is a person.

FILL-IN QUESTIONS

(Answers at the Back of the Book)

An agent's use of reasonable diligence and skill is part of the agent's duty of _____ (obedience/performance). Informing a principal of all material matters that come to the agent's attention concerning the subject matter of the agency is an aspect of the agent's duty of _____ (accounting/notification). Acting solely for the benefit of the principal and not in the interest of the agent or a third party is part of the agent's duty of _____ (loyalty/performance). Following all lawful and clearly stated instructions of the principal is an aspect of the agent's duty of _____ (loyalty/obedience). If an agent is required to keep and make available to the principal a record of all property and money received and paid out on behalf of the principal, this is part of the agent's duty of _____ (accounting/notification).

MULTIPLE-CHOICE QUESTIONS

(Answers at the Back of the Book)

____ 1. Home Interiors, Inc. (HII), tells Jan, whose business is purchasing for others, to select and buy $200 worth of certain goods and ship them to HII's office. Jan buys the goods from Brand Name Products Store and ships them as directed, keeping an account for the expense in HII's name. HII and Jan

   a. do not have an agency relationship, because Jan's business is buying for others.
   b. do not have an agency relationship, because Jan did not indicate that she was acting for Baron.
   c. do not have an agency relationship, because their agreement is not in writing.
   d. have an agency relationship.

____ 2. Greg, a salesperson at Home Electronics Company, tells Irma, a customer, "Buy your computer here, and I'll set it up for less than what Home would charge." Irma buys the computer, Greg sets it up, and Irma pays Greg, who keeps the money. Greg has breached the duty of

   a. loyalty.
   b. notification.
   c. obedience.
   d. performance.

____ 3. Ann gives Bill the impression that Carol is Ann's agent, when in fact she is not. Bill deals with Carol as Ann's agent. Regarding any agency relationship, Ann

   a. can deny it.
   b. can deny it to the extent of any injury suffered by Bill.
   c. can deny it to the extent of any liability that might be imposed on Ann.
   d. cannot deny it.

____ 4. Pat asks Quinn, a real estate broker, to sell her land. Quinn learns that Retail Mall Corporation (RMC) is willing to pay a high price for the land. Without telling Pat about RMC, Quinn says that he will buy the land himself. Instead, however, Pat sells the land to Sam. Quinn sues Pat. Quinn will

   a. lose, because Pat was not Quinn's principal.
   b. lose, because Quinn breached his duty to Pat.
   c. win, because Pat breached her duty to Quinn.
   d. win, because Quinn was never Pat's agent.

____ 5. Kay acts within the scope of her authority to enter into a contract with First National Bank on behalf of Kay's undisclosed principal, Digital Engineering, Inc. Digital is

   a. liable on the contract only if Digital ratifies the contract.
   b. liable on the contract only if Digital's identity is later disclosed.
   c. liable on the contract under the stated circumstances.
   d. not liable on the contract.

____ 6. Security Guns & Ammo, Inc., directs its salespersons never to load a gun during a sale. Bert, a salesperson, loads a gun during a sale. The gun fires, negligently injuring Kathy, who is in the store. Security is

   a. not liable, because Bert was not acting within the scope of employment.
   b. not liable, because employers are not responsible for their employees' torts.
   c. liable under the doctrine of *respondeat superior*.
   d. liable under the doctrine of *res ipsa loquitur*.

____ 7. Smith Petroleum, Inc., contracts to sell oil to Jones Petrochemicals, telling Jones that it is acting on behalf of "a rich Saudi Arabian who doesn't want his identity known." Smith signs the contract, "Smith, as agent only." In fact, Smith is acting on its own. If the contract is breached, Smith may

   a. not be liable, because Smith signed the contract as an agent.
   b. not be liable, unless Jones knew Smith did not have authority to act.
   c. be liable, unless Jones knew Smith did not have authority to act.
   d. be liable, because Smith signed the contract as an agent.

____ 8. National Manufacturing, Inc., employs Mark as an assembly worker. While attempting, without National's knowledge, to steal a forklift from National's property, Mark has an accident, negligently injuring Pam. Pam can recover from

   a. National only.
   b. Mark only.
   c. National and Mark.
   d. none of the above.

____ 9. Standard Delivery Company employs Tina as a driver. While driving within the scope of employment, Tina causes an accident in which Vic is injured. Vic can recover from

   a. Standard only.
   b. Tina only.
   c. Standard or Tina.
   d. none of the above

____ 10. American Grocers, Inc., employs Jill to buy and install a computer system for American's distribution network. When the system is set up and running, the agency

   a. terminates automatically.
   b. terminates after fourteen days.
   c. continues for one year.
   d. continues indefinitely.

SHORT ESSAY QUESTIONS

1. What are the chief differences among the relationships of principal and agent, employer and employee, and employer and independent contractor? What are the factors that indicate whether an individual is an employee or an independent contractor?

2. Identify and describe the categories of authority by which an agent can bind a principal and a third party in contract.

ISSUE SPOTTERS

(Answers at the Back of the Book)

1. Don contracts with Eve to buy a certain horse for Eve, who asks Don not to reveal her identity. Don makes a deal with Farm Stables, the owner of the horse, and makes a down payment. Eve fails to pay the rest of the price. Farm Stables sues Don for breach of contract. Can Don hold Eve liable for whatever damages he has to pay?

2. Alpha Corporation wants to build a new mall on a specific tract of land. Alpha enters into a contract with Beth to buy the land. When Beth learns the difference between the price that Alpha is willing to pay and the price at which the owner is willing to sell, she wants to buy the land and sell it to Alpha herself. Can she do this?

3. Ann, owner of Best Goods Company, employs Cathy as an administrative assistant. In Ann's absence, and without authority, Cathy represents herself as Ann and signs a promissory note in Ann's name. In what circumstance is Ann liable on the note?

Chapter 20
Employment Relationships

WHAT THIS CHAPTER IS ABOUT

This chapter outlines some of the most significant laws regulating employment relationships. Other significant laws regulating the workplace—those prohibiting employment discrimination and those regulating labor unions—are dealt with in Chapters 21 and 22.

CHAPTER OUTLINE

I. EMPLOYMENT AT WILL

Under the employment at-will doctrine, either the employer or the employee may terminate an employment relationship at any time and for any reason (unless a contract or the law provides to the contrary).

A. WRONGFUL DISCHARGE

An employer cannot fire an employee in violation of an employment contract or a federal or state statute. If so, the employee may bring an action for wrongful discharge.

B. EXCEPTIONS TO THE EMPLOYMENT-AT-WILL DOCTRINE

1. Exceptions Based on Contract Theory

Some courts have held that an implied contract exists between an employer and an employee (if, for example, a personnel manual states that no employee will be fired without good cause). A few states have held all employment contracts contain an implied covenant of good faith.

2. Exceptions Based on Tort Theory

Discharge may give rise to a tort action (based on fraud, for example) for wrongful discharge.

3. Exceptions Based on Public Policy

An employer may not fire a worker for reasons that violate a public policy of the jurisdiction (for example, for refusing to violate the law). This policy must be expressed clearly in statutory law. Some state and federal statutes protect whistleblowers from retaliation. The False Claims Reform Act of 1986 gives a whistleblower 15 to 25 percent of proceeds recovered from fraud.

II. WAGE-HOUR LAWS

Davis-Bacon Act of 1931 requires "prevailing wages" for employees of some government contractors. Walsh-Healey Act of 1936 requires minimum wage and overtime for employees of some government contractors. Fair Labor Standards Act of 1938 (FLSA) covers all employees and regulates—

A. CHILD LABOR

Children under fourteen can deliver newspapers, work for their parents, and work in entertainment and agriculture. Children fourteen and older cannot work in hazardous occupations.

B. MAXIMUM HOURS

Employees who work more than forty hours per week must be paid no less than one and a half times their regular pay for all hours over forty. Executives, administrative employees, professional employees, and outside salespersons are exempt.

C. MINIMUM WAGE

A specified amount (periodically revised) must be paid to employees in covered industries. Wages include the reasonable cost to furnish employees with board, lodging, and other facilities.

III. WORKER HEALTH AND SAFETY

A. OCCUPATIONAL SAFETY AND HEALTH ACT OF 1970

Attempts to ensure safe and healthful work conditions for most employees.

1. **Enforcement Agencies**

   a. **Occupational Safety and Health Administration (OSHA)**
   Inspects workplaces and issues safety standards, including standards covering employee exposure to harmful substances.

   b. **National Institute for Occupational Safety and Health**
   Researches safety and health problems and recommends standards for OSHA to adopt.

   c. **Occupational Safety and Health Review Commission**
   Hears appeals from actions taken by OSHA administrators.

2. **Procedures and Violations**
   Employees file complaints of OSHA violations (employers cannot retaliate); employers must keep injury and illness records; employers must file accident reports directly to OSHA. Penalties are limited.

B. STATE WORKERS' COMPENSATION LAWS

State laws establish procedure for compensating workers injured on the job.

1. **No State Covers All Employees**
   Often excluded are domestic workers, agricultural workers, temporary employees, and employees of common carriers.

2. **Requirements for Recovery**
   There must be an employment relationship, and the injury must be accidental and occur on the job or in the course of employment.

3. **Filing a Claim**
   An employee must notify the employer of an injury (usually within thirty days), and file a claim with a state agency within a certain period (sixty days to two years) from the time the injury is first noticed.

4. **Acceptance of Workers' Compensation Benefits Bars Suits**
   An employee's acceptance of benefits bars the employee from suing for injuries caused by the employer's negligence.

IV. INCOME SECURITY

A. SOCIAL SECURITY

The Social Security Act of 1935 provides for payments to persons who are retired, widowed, disabled, etc. Employers and employees must contribute under the Federal Insurance Contributions Act (FICA).

B. MEDICARE

A health insurance program administered by the Social Security Administration for people sixty-five years of age and older and for some under sixty-five who are disabled.

C. PRIVATE PENSION PLANS
The Employee Retirement Income Security Act (ERISA) of 1974 empowers the Labor Management Services Administration of the U.S. Department of Labor to oversee operators of private pension funds.

1. Vesting
Generally, employee contributions to pension plans vest immediately; employee rights to employer contributions vest after five years.

2. Investing
Pension-fund managers must be cautious in investing and refrain from investing more than 10 percent of the fund in securities of the employer.

D. UNEMPLOYMENT COMPENSATION
The Federal Unemployment Tax Act of 1935 created a state system that provides unemployment compensation to eligible individuals.

V. COBRA
The Consolidated Omnibus Budget Reconciliation Act (COBRA) of 1985 prohibits the elimination of a worker's medical, optical, or dental insurance on the termination of most workers' employment. Coverage must continue for up to 18 months (29 months in some cases). A worker pays the premium plus 2 percent.

VI. FAMILY AND MEDICAL LEAVE ACT (FMLA) OF 1993
Employers with fifty or more employees must provide them with up to twelve weeks of family or medical leave during any twelve-month period, continue health-care coverage during the leave, and guarantee employment in the same, or a comparable, position when the employee returns to work.

VII. EMPLOYEE PRIVACY RIGHTS
A right to privacy has been inferred from constitutional guarantees provided by the First, Third, Fourth, Fifth, and Ninth Amendments to the Constitution. Tort law, state constitutions, and some federal and state statutes also provide some privacy rights.

A. ELECTRONIC MONITORING IN THE WORKPLACE

1. Laws Protecting Employee Privacy Rights
The Electronic Communications Privacy Act (ECPA) of 1986 bars the interception of any wire or electronic communication or the disclosure or use of information obtained by interception. Excepted is employers' monitoring of *business* telephone conversations.

2. Factors Considered by the Courts in Employee Privacy Cases
If an employee brings a tort action for invasion of privacy (see Chapter 12), a court may weigh the employee's reasonable expectation of privacy against the employer's need for surveillance. This may depend on whether the employee was aware of the monitoring.

3. Privacy Expectations and E-Mail Systems
In cases involving e-mail, it has not seemed to matter whether employees were aware of being monitored.

B. OTHER TYPES OF MONITORING

1. Lie-Detector Tests
Under the Employee Polygraph Protection Act of 1988, most employers cannot, among other things, require, request, or suggest that employees or applicants take lie-detector tests, except when investigating theft, including theft of trade secrets.

2. Drug Testing

a. **Protection for the Privacy Rights of Private Employees**
Some state constitutions may prohibit private employers from testing for drugs. State statutes may restrict drug testing by private employers. Other sources of protection include collective bargaining agreements and tort actions for invasion of privacy.

b. **Protection for Government Employees**
Constitutional limitations (the Fourth Amendment) apply. Drug tests have been upheld when there was a reasonable basis for suspecting employees of using drugs, or when drug use could threaten public safety.

3. **AIDS Testing**
Some state laws restrict AIDS testing. The federal Americans with Disabilities Act of 1990 and other statutes protect employees or applicants who have tested positive from discrimination.

4. **Genetic Testing**
This may violate the Americans with Disabilities Act of 1990 or other privacy provisions.

5. **Screening Procedures**
A key factor in determining whether preemployment screening tests violate privacy rights is whether there is a connection between the questions and the job for which an applicant is applying.

VIII. EMPLOYMENT-RELATED IMMIGRATION LAWS

A. **IMMIGRATION REFORM AND CONTROL ACT (IRCA) OF 1986**
The IRCA prohibits employers from hiring illegal immigrants.

B. **IMMIGRATION ACT OF 1990**
Employers recruiting workers from other countries must complete a certification process, satisfy the U.S. Department of Labor that there is a shortage of qualified U.S. workers to perform the work, and show that bringing aliens into this country will not adversely affect the labor market.

TRUE-FALSE QUESTIONS

(Answers at the Back of the Book)

_____ 1. Drug testing by private employers is permitted.

_____ 2. There are no exceptions to the employment "at will" doctrine.

_____ 3. Employers are required to establish retirement plans for their employees.

_____ 4. Federal wage-hour laws cover all employers engaged in interstate commerce.

_____ 5. Whistleblower statutes protect employers from workers' disclosure of the employer's wrongdoing.

_____ 6. Under federal law, employers can monitor employees' personal communications.

_____ 7. Workers' compensation laws cover all employees in all states.

_____ 8. Except in investigating theft, employers cannot tell employees or job applicants take lie-detector tests.

_____ 9. Children fourteen and older can work in hazardous occupations.

_____ 10. There is no prohibition against employers' hiring illegal immigrants.

FILL-IN QUESTIONS

(Answers at the Back of the Book)

Under the employment-at-will doctrine, _____ (either/neither) party may terminate an employment relationship at any time and for any reason _____ (unless/even if) a contract provides to the contrary. An employee who is fired in violation of a federal or state statute _____ (may/may not) bring an action for wrongful discharge. _____ (Some/No) courts have held that an implied contract exists between an employer and an employee. _____ (All/A few states) have held that all employment contracts contain an implied covenant of good faith. An employer _____ (may/may not) fire a worker for reasons that violate a public policy of the jurisdiction.

MULTIPLE-CHOICE QUESTIONS

(Answers at the Back of the Book)

____ 1. Fast Jack is a fast-food restaurant. To verify Fast Jack's compliance with statutes governing employees' wages and hours, personnel records should be checked against the provisions of

a. the Fair Labor Standards Act.
b. the Family and Medical Leave Act.
c. the National Labor Relations Act.
d. the Taft-Hartley Act.

____ 2. Interstate Distributors, Inc., is investigating losses due to theft. Without violating employees' rights of privacy, Interstate may

a. monitor all employee phone conversations only.
b. require employees to take polygraph tests only.
c. monitor all employee phone conversations and require employees to take polygraph tests.
d. none of the above.

____ 3. Ron, an employee of Standard Company, is injured. For Ron to receive *workers' compensation*, the injury must be

a. accidental and arise out of a preexisting disease or condition.
b. accidental and occur on the job or in the course of employment.
c. intentional and arise out of a preexisting disease or condition.
d. intentional and occur on the job or in the course of employment.

____ 4. U.S. Goods, Inc. (USG), recruits workers from other countries to work in its U.S. plant. Under the Immigration Act of 1990, USG must show

a. only that bringing aliens into the country will not adversely affect the labor market in the area.
b. only that there is a shortage of qualified U.S. workers to perform the work.
c. that there is a shortage of qualified U.S. workers to perform the work and that bringing aliens into the country will not adversely affect the labor market in the area.
d. none of the above.

____ 5. Mary is an employee of National Sales Company. Both Mary and National make contributions to the federal social security system under

a. the Employment Retirement Income Security Act.
b. the Federal Insurance Contributions Act.
c. the Federal Unemployment Tax Act.
d. none of the above.

___ 6. Eagle, Inc., sets up a pension fund for its employees. Eagle's operation of the fund is regulated by

    a. the Employment Retirement Income Security Act.
    b. the Federal Insurance Contributions Act.
    c. the Federal Unemployment Tax Act.
    d. none of the above.

___ 7. ABC Corporation provides health insurance for its 150 employees, including Dian. When Dian takes twelve weeks' leave to care for her child, she

    a. can collect "leave pay" equal to twelve weeks' health insurance coverage.
    b. can continue her heath insurance at ABC's expense.
    c. can continue her heath insurance at her expense.
    d. loses her heath insurance immediately on taking leave.

___ 8. Mega Corporation provides health insurance for its employees. When Mega closes one of its offices and terminates the employees, the employees

    a. can collect "severance pay" equal to twelve weeks' of health insurance coverage.
    b. can continue their heath insurance at Mega's expense.
    c. can continue their heath insurance at their expense.
    d. lose their heath insurance immediately on termination of employment.

___ 9. Adam works for Beta Company as an at-will employee. This employment may be terminated at any time by

    a. Adam only.
    b. Beta only.
    c. Adam or Beta.
    d. none of the above.

___ 10. Delta Company is a private employer that wants to test its employees for drug use. This testing may be limited or prohibited by

    a. a state constitution.
    b. a state statute.
    c. a state constitution or a state statute.
    d. none of the above.

SHORT ESSAY QUESTIONS

1. What is the employment-at-will doctrine? What are its exceptions?

2. What protection do employees have from the financial impact of retirement, disability, death, hospitalization, and unemployment?

ISSUE SPOTTERS

(Answers at the Back of the Book)

1. Associated Services Company (ASC) issues an employee handbook that states employees will be discharged only for good cause. One day, Bob, an ASC supervisor, says to Carl, "I don't like your looks. You're fired." Is ASC liable for breach of contract?

2.   Workers' compensation laws establish a procedure for compensating workers who are injured on the job. Instead of suing, an injured worker files a claim with the appropriate state agency. For the employee to obtain compensation, does the injury have to have been caused by the employer's negligence?

3.   Carl, a waiter at Diners Cafe, notices that the kitchen staff is not wearing protective gloves while preparing food, a violation of state law. Carl reports this to the manager, but no steps are taken. Carl tells Donna, who works for *Eagle News*, a local paper. *Eagle* runs a story on the violation. Business at Diners is cut in half. Can Diners fire Carl?

Chapter 21
Employment Discrimination

WHAT THIS CHAPTER IS ABOUT

The law restricts employers and unions from discriminating against workers on the basis of race, color, religion, national origin, gender, age, or handicap. A class of persons defined by one or more of these criteria is a *protected class*. This chapter outlines these laws.

CHAPTER OUTLINE

I. **TITLE VII OF THE CIVIL RIGHTS ACT OF 1964**
   Prohibits employment discrimination against employees, applicants, and union members on the basis of race, color, national origin, religion, and gender.

   A. **WHO IS SUBJECT TO TITLE VII?**
      Employers with fifteen or more employees, labor unions with fifteen or more members, labor unions that operate hiring halls, employment agencies, and federal, state, and local agencies.

   B. **PROCEDURES UNDER TITLE VII**
      (1) A victim files a claim with the Equal Employment Opportunity Commission (EEOC); (2) the EEOC investigates and seeks a voluntary settlement; (3) if no settlement is reached, the EEOC may sue the employer; (4) if the EEOC chooses not to sue, the victim may file a lawsuit.

   C. **INTENTIONAL AND UNINTENTIONAL DISCRIMINATION**
      Title VII prohibits both intentional and unintentional discrimination.

      1. **Disparate-Treatment Discrimination**
         This is intentional discrimination by an employer against an employee.

         a. *Prima Facie* **Case—Plaintiff's Side of the Case**
            Plaintiff must show (1) he or she is a member of a protected class, (2) he or she applied and was qualified for the job, (3) he or she was rejected by the employer, (4) the employer continued to seek applicants or filled the job with a person not in a protected class.

         b. **Defense—Employer's Side of the Case**
            Employer must articulate a legal reason for not hiring the plaintiff. To prevail, the plaintiff must show that the employer's reason is a pretext and that discriminatory intent motivated the decision.

      2. **Disparate-Impact Discrimination**

         a. **Types of Disparate-Impact Discrimination**
            Disparate-impact discrimination results if, because of a requirement or hiring practice—

            1) an employer's work force does not reflect the percentage of members of protected classes that characterizes qualified individuals in the local labor market, or

            2) members of protected class are excluded from employer's work force at substantially higher rate than nonmembers (under EEOC's "four-fifths rule," selection rate for protected class must be at least 80 percent of rate for group with the highest rate).

b. *Prima Facie* **Case—Plaintiff's Side of the Case**
Plaintiff must show a connection between a requirement or practice and a disparity; no evidence of discriminatory intent is needed.

D. DISCRIMINATION BASED ON RACE, COLOR, AND NATIONAL ORIGIN
Employers cannot effectively discriminate against employees on the basis of race, color, national origin, or religion (absent a substantial, demonstrable relationship between the trait and the job, etc.).

E. DISCRIMINATION BASED ON RELIGION
Title VII prohibits employers and unions from discriminating against persons because of their religions.

F. DISCRIMINATION BASED ON GENDER
Employers cannot discriminate against employees on the basis of gender (unless the gender of the applicant can be proved essential to the job, etc.). The Pregnancy Discrimination Act of 1978 amended Title VII: employees affected by pregnancy or related conditions must be treated the same as persons not so affected but similar in ability to work.

G. SEXUAL HARASSMENT

1. Forms of Harassment
(1) *Quid pro quo* harassment: when promotions, etc., are doled out on the basis of sexual favors; (2) hostile-environment harassment: when an employee is subjected to offensive sexual comments, etc.

2. Harassment by Supervisors, Co-Workers, or Nonemployees

a. When an Employer May Be Liable
If anyone (employee or nonemployee) harasses an employee, and the employer knew, or should have known, and failed to take immediate corrective action, the employer may be liable. To be liable for a supervisor's harassment, the supervisor must have taken a tangible employment action against the employee.

b. Employer's Defense
(1) Employer took "reasonable care to prevent and correct promptly any sexually harassing behavior," and (2) employee suing for harassment failed to follow employer's policies and procedures.

H. ONLINE HARASSMENT
Employers may avoid liability if they take prompt remedial action. Privacy rights must be considered if the action includes electronic monitoring of employees.

I. REMEDIES UNDER TITLE VII
Remedies include reinstatement, back pay, retroactive promotions, and damages.

1. Damages
Compensatory damages are available only in cases of intentional discrimination. Punitive damages are available only if an employer acted with malice or reckless indifference

2. Limitations
Total damages are limited to specific amounts against specific employers (from $50,000 against those with one hundred or fewer employees to $300,000 against those with more than five hundred employees).

II.   EQUAL PAY ACT OF 1963
Prohibits gender-based discrimination in wages for equal work (work requiring equal skill, effort, and responsibility under similar conditions). Different wages are acceptable because of any factor but gender (seniority, merit, etc.).

III. DISCRIMINATION BASED ON AGE

A. AGE DISCRIMINATION IN EMPLOYMENT ACT (ADEA) OF 1967
Prohibits employment discrimination on the basis of age (including mandatory retirement), by employers with twenty or more employees, against individuals forty years of age or older. Administered by the EEOC, but private causes of action are also possible.

B. PRINCIPLES ARE SIMILAR TO TITLE VII
Requires the establishment of a *prima facie* case: plaintiff must show that he or she was (1) forty or older, (2) qualified for a position, and (3) rejected in circumstances that infer discrimination. The employer must articulate a legal reason; the plaintiff may show it is a pretext.

C. STATE EMPLOYEES
Under the Eleventh Amendment to the Constitution, a state is immune from suits brought by private individuals in federal court unless the state consents to the suit. A state agency sued by a state employee for age discrimination may have the suit dismissed on this ground.

IV. DISCRIMINATION BASED ON DISABILITY
Under the Americans with Disabilities Act (ADA) of 1990, an employer cannot refuse to hire a person who is qualified but disabled. Covered are all employers (except the states) with fifteen or more employees.

A. PROCEDURES AND REMEDIES UNDER THE ADA

1. Procedures
A plaintiff must show he or she (1) has a disability, (2) is otherwise qualified for a job and (3) was excluded solely because of the disability. A suit may be filed only after a claim is pursued through the EEOC (which may file a suit even if the employee agrees to arbitration).

2. Remedies
These include reinstatement, back pay, some compensatory and punitive damages (for intentional discrimination), and certain other relief. Repeat violators may be fined up to $100,000.

B. WHAT IS A DISABILITY?
"(1) [A] physical or mental impairment that substantially limits one or more of the major life activities . . . ; (2) a record of such impairment; or (3) being regarded as having such an impairment." Includes AIDS, morbid obesity, etc.; not homosexuality or kleptomania.

C. REASONABLE ACCOMMODATION
For a person with a disability, an employer may have to make a reasonable accommodation (more flexible working hours, new job assignment, different training materials or procedures)—but not an accommodation that will cause *undue hardship* ("significant difficulty or expense").

1. Job Applications
The application process must be accessible to those with disabilities.

2. Preemployment Physical Exams
Employers cannot require a disabled person to take a preemployment physical (unless all applicants do). Disqualification must be from problems that render a person unable to perform the job.

3. Dangerous Workers
An employer need not hire disabled workers who would pose a "direct threat to the health or safety" of co-workers or to themselves.

4. Substance Abusers
The ADA protects addicts who have completed or are in supervised rehabilitation, and alcoholics to the extent of equal treatment.

5. **Health-Insurance Plans**

Workers with disabilities must be given equal access to insurance plans provided to other workers. If a plan includes a disability-based distinction, an employer must show (1) limiting coverage keeps the plan financially sound, (2) coverage would otherwise be too expensive for many workers, or (3) the distinction is justified by the risk and costs.

V. DEFENSES TO EMPLOYMENT DISCRIMINATION

The first defense is to assert that the plaintiff did not prove discrimination. If discrimination is proved, an employer may attempt to justify it as—

A. BUSINESS NECESSITY

An employer may show that there is a legitimate connection between a job requirement that discriminates and job performance.

B. BONA FIDE OCCUPATIONAL QUALIFICATION (BFOQ)

Another defense applies when discrimination against a protected class is essential to a job—that is, when a particular trait is a BFOQ. Generally restricted to cases in which gender is essential. Race can never be a BFOQ.

C. SENIORITY SYSTEMS

An employer with a history of discrimination may have no members of protected classes or disabled workers in upper-level positions. If no present intent to discriminate is shown, and promotions, etc., are distributed according to a fair seniority system, the employer has a good defense.

D. AFTER-ACQUIRED EVIDENCE

An employer who discovers, after discharging an employee, that the worker engaged in misconduct in applying for the job or while on the job may use that misconduct to limit the amount of damages to the plaintiff.

VI. AFFIRMATIVE ACTION

An affirmative action program attempts to make up for past discrimination by giving members of protected classes preferential treatment in hiring or promotion. Such an employment program cannot use quotas or preferences for unqualified persons, and once it has succeeded, it must be changed or dropped.

VII. STATE LAWS PROHIBITING DISCRIMINATION

Most states have statutes that prohibit the kinds of discrimination prohibited under federal law. Also, state laws often protect individuals, such as those under forty years of age or those who work at very small firms, who are not protected under federal law, and may provide for damages in addition to those allowed under federal law.

TRUE-FALSE QUESTIONS

(Answers at the Back of the Book)

____ 1. Once an affirmative action program has succeeded, it must be changed or dropped.

____ 2. In a sexual harassment case, an employer cannot be held liable for the actions of an employee.

____ 3. In a sexual harassment case, an employer cannot be held liable for the actions of a nonemployee.

____ 4. Women affected by pregnancy must be treated for all job-related purposes the same as persons not so affected but similar in ability to work.

____ 5. Employment discrimination against persons with a physical or mental impairment that substantially limits their everyday activities is prohibited.

____   6. Discrimination complaints brought under federal law must be filed with the Equal Opportunity Employment Commission.

____   7. If the Equal Employment Opportunity Commission decides not to investigate a claim, the victim has no other option.

____   8. All employers are subject to Title VII of the Civil Rights Act of 1964.

____   9. Disparate-treatment discrimination occurs when an employer intentionally discriminates against an employee.

____   10. Title VII prohibits employers and unions from discriminating against persons because of their religions.

FILL-IN QUESTIONS

(Answers at the Back of the Book)

The Equal Employment Opportunity Commission (EEOC) monitors compliance with the federal antidiscrimination laws. The EEOC _____ (can/cannot) sue organizations that violate these laws. A victim files a claim with the EEOC, which investigates and _____ _____ (must sue/may sue if a settlement between the parties is not reached). If the EEOC does not sue, the victim may sue. On proof of discrimination, a victim may be awarded _____ _____ (reinstatement and back pay/reinstatement, back pay, and retroactive promotions).

MULTIPLE-CHOICE QUESTIONS

(Answers at the Back of the Book)

____   1. Ann is an employee of Beta Communications Corporation. Ann attempts to resolve a gender-based discrimination claim with Beta, whose representative denies the claim. Ann's next best step is to

a. ask the Equal Opportunity Employment Commission whether a claim is justified.
b. file a lawsuit.
c. forget about the matter.
d. secretly sabotage company operations for revenge.

____   2. Bob and Carol work for Delta Company. Bob is Carol's supervisor. During work, Bob touches Carol in ways that she perceives as sexually offensive. Carol resists the advances. Bob cuts her pay. Delta is

a. liable, because Bob's conduct constituted sexual harassment.
b. liable, because Carol resisted Bob's advances.
c. not liable, because Bob's conduct was not job-related.
d. not liable, because Carol resisted Bob's advances.

____   3. Under the Age Discrimination in Employment Act of 1967, Alpha Corporation is prohibited from

a. committing unintentional age discrimination.
b. forcing an employee to retire.
c. terminating an employee between the ages of sixty-five and seventy for cause.
d. terminating an employee as part of a rational business decision.

____ 4. Kay, who is hearing impaired, applies for a position with Local Company. Kay is qualified but is refused the job and sues Local. To succeed under the Americans with Disabilities Act, Kay must show that

    a. Kay was willing to make a "reasonable accommodation" for Local.
    b. Kay would not have to accept "significant additional costs" to work for Local.
    c. Local refused to make a "reasonable accommodation" for Kay.
    d. Local would not have to accept "significant additional costs" to hire Kay.

____ 5. Omega Sales, Inc., promotes employees on the basis of color. Employees with darker skin color are passed over in favor of those with lighter skin color, regardless of their race. This is prohibited by

    a. the Americans with Disabilities Act of 1990.
    b. the Equal Pay Act of 1963.
    c. Title VII of the Civil Rights Act of 1964.
    d. none of the above.

____ 6. Curt, personnel director for Digital Products, Inc., prefers to hire Asian Americans, because "they're smarter and work harder" than other minorities. This is prohibited by

    a. the Age Discrimination in Employment Act of 1967.
    b. the Americans with Disabilities Act of 1990.
    c. Title VII of the Civil Rights Act of 1964 .
    d. none of the above.

____ 7. Greg and Holly work for Interstate Services, Inc. (ISI), as electrical engineers. Greg is paid more than Holly because, according to ISI, he is a man with a family to support. This is prohibited by

    a. the Age Discrimination in Employment Act of 1967.
    b. the Americans with Disabilities Act of 1990.
    c. the Equal Pay Act of 1963.
    d. none of the above.

____ 8. Donna applies to Eagle Corporation for an administrative assistant's job, which requires certain typing skills. Donna cannot type but tells Eagle that she is willing to learn. Eagle does not hire Donna, who later sues. To successfully defend against the suit under Title VII, Eagle must show that

    a. being a member of the majority is a BFOQ.
    b. Donna was not willing to learn to type.
    c. Eagle has a valid business necessity defense.
    d. Eagle's work force reflects the same percentage of members of a protected class that characterizes qualified individuals in the local labor market.

____ 9. Standard Corporation terminates Tom, who sues on the basis of age discrimination. To succeed under the Age Discrimination in Employment Act, Tom must show that at the time of the discharge, he was

    a. forty or older.
    b. forty or younger.
    c. replaced with someone forty or older.
    d. replaced with someone forty or younger.

____ 10. National Company requires job applicants to pass certain physical tests. Only a few female applicants can pass the tests, but it they pass, they are hired. To successfully defend against a suit on this basis under Title VII, National must show that

    a. any discrimination is not intentional.
    b. being a male is a BFOQ.
    c. passing the tests is a business necessity.
    d. some men cannot pass the tests.

SHORT ESSAY QUESTIONS

1. Compare and contrast disparate-treatment discrimination and disparate-impact discrimination, and Title VII's response to each in the context of employment.

2. What does the Americans with Disabilities Act require employers to do?

ISSUE SPOTTERS

(Answers at the Back of the Book)

1. Phil applies for a job at Quality Corporation for which he is well qualified, but for which he is rejected. Quality continues to seek applicants and eventually fills the position with a person who is not a member of a minority. Could Phil succeed in a suit against Quality for discrimination?

2. Ruth is a supervisor for Subs & Suds, a restaurant. Tim is a Subs employee. The owner announces that some employees will be discharged. Ruth tells Tim that if he has sex with her, he can keep his job. Is this sexual harassment?

3. Paula, a disabled person, applies for a job at Quantity Corporation for which she is well qualified, but for which she is rejected. Quantity continues to seek applicants and eventually fills the position with a person who is not disabled. Could Paula succeed in a suit against Quantity for discrimination?

Chapter 22
Labor Law

WHAT THIS CHAPTER IS ABOUT

This chapter outlines labor law and legal recognition of the right to form unions, the process of unionizing a company, the process of collective bargaining, and labor practices considered fair and unfair under federal law.

CHAPTER OUTLINE

I. FEDERAL LABOR LAW
All employers whose businesses involve or affect interstate commerce are subject to these laws. Agricultural workers and domestic servants are excluded.

A. NORRIS-LAGUARDIA ACT OF 1932
This law restricts federal courts' power to issue injunctions against unions engaged in peaceful strikes, picketing, and boycotts.

B. NATIONAL LABOR RELATIONS ACT OF 1935 (NLRA)
The NLRA established the right of employees to bargain collectively and to strike; prescribed unfair employer practices; created the NLRB to oversee union elections, prevent employers from engaging in unfair practices, investigate employers in response to employee charges of unfair labor practices, issue cease-and-desist orders.

C. LABOR-MANAGEMENT RELATIONS ACT OF 1947 (TAFT-HARTLEY ACT)
This act prohibits unions from refusing to bargain with employers, engaging in certain types of picketing, featherbedding, and other unfair union practices. Expressly preserves union shops, but allows states to pass right-to-work laws, which make it illegal to require union membership for employment.

D. LABOR-MANAGEMENT REPORTING AND DISCLOSURE ACT OF 1959
This law requires regular elections of union officers, under secret ballot; prohibits ex-convicts and Communists from holding union office; makes union officials accountable for union property; allows members to participate in union meetings, nominate officers, vote in proceedings.

II. THE DECISION TO FORM OR TO SELECT A UNION

A. PRELIMINARY ORGANIZING

1. Workers Sign Authorization Cards
A majority of the relevant workers must sign authorization cards, which state that they want a certain union to represent the workforce.

2. The Employer Is Asked to Recognize the Union
If the employer refuses, unionizers must present authorization cards from at least 30 percent of the workers to the NLRB regional office with a petition for an election.

B. APPROPRIATE BARGAINING UNIT
The NLRB determines this, which requires a mutuality of interest among the workers to be represented. Mutuality of interest requires—

1. **Job Similarity**
   Similar levels of skill, wages, benefits, working conditions.

2. **Work-Site Proximity**
   It may be a problem if the workers are at many different sites.

3. **No Management Employees**
   Members of management cannot be part of a union.

C. **MOVING TOWARD CERTIFICATION**
   If no other union has been certified within the past twelve months to represent the workers, the NLRB schedules an election.

III. **UNION ELECTION**
   The NLRB supervises the election.

A. **UNION ELECTION CAMPAIGN**

1. **Employer Limits**
   Employers may limit the campaign activities of union supporters (such as where on company property and when campaigning may occur).

2. **Restrictions on Employer Limits**
   An employer may prohibit *all* solicitation during work time or in certain places but may not prohibit *only* union solicitation. Workers also have a right to a reasonable opportunity to campaign (nonworking areas on the employer's property during nonworking time).

B. **MANAGEMENT ELECTION CAMPAIGN**

1. **Employer Advantages**
   Employers may campaign on company property on company time without giving union supporters an opportunity for rebuttal.

2. **Restrictions on Employer Advantages**

   a. **No Threats**
      An employer may not make threats of reprisals if employees vote to unionize. Employers may not question individual workers about their positions on unionization.

   b. **No Last-minute Speeches**
      An employer cannot make an election speech on company time to assembled workers within twenty-four hours of an election, unless employees attend voluntarily on their own time.

   c. **No Surveillance**
      An employer may not undertake certain types of surveillance of workers or even create the impression of observing workers.

3. **NLRB Options**
   If the employer commits an unfair labor practice, the NLRB may invalidate an election (order a new election; direct the employer to recognize the union).

C. **DECERTIFICATION ELECTION**
   May be sought by employees, by a petition to the NLRB, with a showing of 30 percent employee support and no certification within the past year.

D. **ELECTION RESULTS**
   If a fair election is held and the union wins, the NLRB will certify the union as the exclusive bargaining representative of the workers polled.

IV.   COLLECTIVE BARGAINING

The central legal right of a union is to serve as the sole representative of the group of workers in bargaining with the employer over the workers' rights.

A.   SUBJECTS OF BARGAINING

1.   Appropriate Subjects

a.   Terms and Conditions of Employment
Wages, hours of work, safety rules, insurance coverage, pension and other benefits plans, procedures for discipline, and procedures for grievances against the company.

b.   Decision to Relocate a Plant
An employer must bargain over relocation if it does not involve a basic change in the nature of the operation (with exceptions).

2.   Illegal Subjects
These include featherbedding (hiring unnecessary excess workers) and a closed shop (requiring union membership as a condition of employment).

3.   Possible Subjects
Management may choose to bargain over decisions otherwise within its discretion (such as severance pay or rights of transfer to other plants in the event of plant shut-down) to obtain concessions on other subjects.

B.   NO UNILATERAL CHANGES DURING BARGAINING
Management may not make unilateral changes in important working conditions, such as wages or hours of employment, unless bargaining reaches an impasse or in cases of business necessity.

C.   GOOD FAITH BARGAINING

1.   Bad Faith Bargaining Is an Unfair Labor Practice
Includes refusing to meet with union representatives; excessive delaying tactics; insisting on unreasonable contract terms; engaging in a campaign to undermine the union; constantly shifting positions on disputed terms; sending bargainers who lack authority to commit to a contract.

2.   Options If a Party Refuses to Bargain in Good Faith
The NLRB can order a party to bargain in good faith. The other party may be excused from bargaining.

V.   STRIKES

When bargaining reaches an impasse, the union may call a strike to pressure the employer to make concessions.

A.   THE RIGHT TO STRIKE
The right to strike is guaranteed by the NLRA, within limits, and strike activities, such as picketing, are protected by the First Amendment. Nonworkers have a right to participate in picketing. Workers can also refuse to cross a picket line of fellow workers who are engaged in a lawful strike.

B.   ILLEGAL STRIKES
Illegal strikes include violent strikes, massed picketing, sitdown strikes, and—

1.   Secondary Boycotts
Picketing cannot be directed against a secondary employer, but common situs picketing (at site occupied by both primary and secondary employers) is permitted.

2. **Hot-Cargo Agreements**
Employers cannot agree with unions not to handle, use, or deal in non-union-produced goods of other employers.

3. **Wildcat Strikes**
A minority of employees cannot call their own strike.

4. **Strikes That Threaten National Health or Safety**
These strikes are not illegal, but to encourage their settlement, the president of the United States can obtain an injunction to last for eighty days, during which the government can work to produce a settlement.

5. **Strikes That Contravene No-strike Clauses in Previous Collective Bargaining Agreements**

C. **REPLACEMENT WORKERS**
An employer may hire substitute workers to replace strikers.

D. **RIGHTS OF STRIKERS AFTER A STRIKE**
Strikers have no right to return to their jobs (but former strikers must be given preference to any vacancies and also retain their seniority rights) unless the strike is due to employer unfair labor practice.

VI. LOCKOUTS

An employer can shut down to prevent employees from working, but may not use a lockout to break a union and pressure employees into decertification.

VII. UNFAIR LABOR PRACTICES

A. **EMPLOYER'S UNFAIR PRACTICES**

1. **Refusal to Recognize Union and Negotiate**
For one year after certification, it is presumed that the union enjoys majority support; after this period, the presumption is can be rebutted. With evidence to support a good faith belief that union has no majority support, an employer can refuse to recognize the union.

2. **Interference in Union Activities**
An employer may not interfere with, restrain, or coerce employees in the exercise of their rights to form a union and bargain collectively.

3. **Domination of Unions**
The NLRA forbids company unions and other forms of employer domination of workers' unions.

4. **Discrimination against Union Employees**
Employers cannot discriminate against union workers (in layoffs, hiring, or closing a union plant).

B. **UNION'S UNFAIR PRACTICES**

1. **Secondary Boycotts**

2. **Discrimination against Nonunion Workers**
A union cannot threaten employees with violence, use economic coercion, picket, or otherwise discriminate (or influence employers to discriminate) against workers who refuse to join a union.

3. **Featherbedding**

4. **Picketing to Coerce Unionization without Majority Support**

5. **Refusal to Bargain in Good Faith with Employer**

6. **Excessive Fees or Dues**
    A nonunion employee subject to a union shop clause who must pay dues cannot be required to contribute to causes or to lobby politicians.

VIII. RIGHTS OF NONUNION EMPLOYEES

A. CONCERTED ACTIVITY
This activity must be for employees' mutual aid regarding wages, hours, or terms and conditions of employment. A single employee's action may be protected if it is taken for the benefit of other employees and the employee discussed it with other approving workers.

B. SAFETY
An employee can walk off the job if he or she has a good faith belief that working conditions are abnormally dangerous.

C. EMPLOYEE COMMITTEES
The central problem with employee committees is that they may become the functional equivalent of a union that is dominated by management. Thus, these committees cannot perform union functions.

TRUE-FALSE QUESTIONS

(Answers at the Back of the Book)

____ 1. Employers can agree with unions not to handle, use, or deal in non-union-produced goods.

____ 2. Management serves as the representative of workers in bargaining with a union.

____ 3. Federal labor law protects employees' rights to strike, to picket, and to boycott.

____ 4. Employees have no right to engage in collective bargaining through elected representatives.

____ 5. Similarity of workers' jobs is a factor in determining which workers are to be represented by a union.

____ 6. Supervisors and managers cannot be members of a union.

____ 7. An employer cannot consider union participation as a criterion for deciding which workers to hire.

____ 8. An employer can use a lockout to break a union and pressure employees into decertifying it.

____ 9. An employer may make unilateral changes in important working conditions if bargaining negotiations reach an impasse.

____ 10. If an employer commits an unfair labor practice during a union election campaign, the election may be invalidated.

FILL-IN QUESTIONS

(Answers at the Back of the Book)

Peaceful strikes, picketing, and boycotts are protected under the _____
_____ (National Labor Relations/Norris-LaGuardia) Act, which also restricts federal courts in enjoining unions engaged in peaceful strikes. Employees' rights to organize, to engage in collective bargaining through elected representatives, and to engage in concerted activities for those and other purposes were established in the _____ (National Labor Relations/Norris-LaGuardia) Act. Requiring union membership as a condition of employment is prohibited by the Labor-Management _____ (Relations/Reporting and Disclosure) Act. This act also _____ (allows/prohibits) requiring workers to join the union after a certain time on the job. This act

also _____ (allows/prohibits) laws making it illegal to require union membership for continued employment.

MULTIPLE-CHOICE QUESTIONS

(Answers at the Back of the Book)

____ 1. Standard Manufacturer, Inc., refuses to pay its workers for time spent on union activities. This violates

   a. the Labor-Management Relations Act.
   b. the National Labor Relations Act.
   c. the Norris-LaGuardia Act.
   d. none of the above.

____ 2. The employees of Top Products, Inc. (TPI), designate United Machinists Union (UMU) as their bargaining representative. TPI refuses to bargain with UMU and fires several workers for "choosing the wrong side." This violates

   a. the Labor-Management Relations Act.
   b. the National Labor Relations Act.
   c. the Norris-LaGuardia Act.
   d. none of the above.

____ 3. During a union election campaign, Alpha Company asks its employees to openly declare their views on the union, so that "everyone knows where everyone stands." This is an unfair labor practice

   a. only if it is a condition of continued employment.
   b. only if the employees do not want to do it.
   c. under any circumstances.
   d. under no circumstances.

____ 4. Assembly Workers of America (AWA) represents employees of Beta Company. During collective bargaining, AWA wants to negotiate changes to Beta's health insurance plan and safety rules. Beta can refuse to bargain over changes to

   a. the plan only.
   b. the rules only.
   c. the plan and the rules.
   d. none of the above.

____ 5. Federated Union Workers (FUW) represents employees of Gamma Company. During collective bargaining, FUW wants to negotiate to the closure of a Gamma plant and the procedure for employee grievances. Gamma can refuse to negotiate over

   a. the closure only.
   b. the procedure only.
   c. the closure and the procedure.
   d. none of the above.

____ 6. Metalcraft Employees Union (MEU) represents workers of National Production Company. Bargaining reaches an impasse, and MEU calls a strike. Strikers circle the plant to prevent nonunion workers from entering. This is an unfair labor practice

   a. only if the nonunion workers are replacements.
   b. only if the nonunion workers are supervisors.
   c. under any circumstances.
   d. under no circumstances.

___ 7. Consolidated Employees Union (CEU) represents workers of Delta Company. Bargaining reaches an impasse, and CEU calls a strike. During the strike, it would be an unfair labor practice

   a. only to send nonworkers to picket Delta's plant.
   b. only to set up a twenty-four hour picket line around Delta's plant.
   c. to send nonworkers to picket and to set up a twenty-four hour picket line around Delta's plant.
   d. none of the above.

___ 8. During a union election campaign at Omega Corporation, Omega may *not*

   a. campaign against the union.
   b. give a speech against the union within twenty-hours of the election.
   c. limit the campaign activities of union supporters.
   d. none of the above.

___ 9. During a union election campaign at Eagle Corporation, Eagle may *not*

   a. designate where and when campaigning may occur.
   b. prohibit all solicitation during work time.
   c. promise to hire more workers if the union loses the election.
   d. threaten employees with the loss of their jobs if the union wins the election.

___ 10. National Workers Union (NWU) represents the employees of Office Company, Inc. NWU calls an economic strike, and Office hires replacement workers. After the strike

   a. the former strikers must be rehired and the replacement workers must be retained.
   b. the former strikers must be rehired and the replacement workers must be terminated.
   c. the replacement workers must be terminated whether or not the former strikers are rehired.
   d. none of the above.

SHORT ESSAY QUESTIONS

1. What are the four basic federal labor laws and what do they provide?

2. Which types of strikes are illegal?

ISSUE SPOTTERS

(Answers at the Back of the Book)

1.   Ann applies for work with Beta Company, which tells her that it requires union membership as a condition of employment. Ann applies for work with Omega, Inc., which does not require union membership as a condition of employment but requires employees to join a union after six months on the job. Are these conditions legal?

2.   Beth, an employee of Computer Digital, Inc. (CDI), is a vocal union advocate. CDI fires Beth, on the ground that she did not work the exact hours reported on her time card—although CDI has never discharged an employee for this reason. Can CDI be required to prove that it did not have a discriminatory motive in discharging Beth?

3.   Tasty Bakery has five nonunion employees. The employees discuss working conditions with Tasty, which refuses to make any changes. The employees agree that one of them should walk out in protest. When the employee walks out, Tasty fires him. Has Tasty committed an unfair labor practice?

CUMULATIVE HYPOTHETICAL PROBLEM FOR UNIT FIVE—INCLUDING CHAPTERS 19–22

(Answers at the Back of the Book)

Donna, Earl, Frank, Gail, Hal, Ira, Jane, Karen, Larry, and Mike work for International Sales Corporation (ISC).

_____ 1. Donna, who works in ISC's warehouse, is injured on the job. Donna may NOT collect workers' compensation benefits if she

    a. files a civil suit against a third party based on the injury.
    b. intentionally caused her own injury.
    c. was injured as a result of a co-worker's act.
    d. worked for ISC for less than sixty days.

_____ 2. Earl retires from ISC at the age of sixty-five. Frank retires at sixty-seven. Because of a disability, Gail, after fifteen years, is unable to continue working for ISC. Hal is discharged from ISC as part of a reduction in force. All of the following benefits are part of Social Security EXCEPT

    a. Earl's government retirement payments.
    b. Frank's Medicare payments.
    c. Gail's government disability payments.
    d. Hal's unemployment benefits.

_____ 3. Ira works for ISC as a sales representative at a salary of $3,000 per month, plus a 10 percent commission. As ISC's agent, Ira

    a. cannot be dismissed during the six-month period without cause.
    b. cannot enforce the agency unless it is in writing and signed by Delta.
    c. is an agent coupled with an interest.
    d. must act solely in Delta's interest in matters concerning Delta's business.

_____ 4. Four employees file suits against ISC, alleging discrimination. Title VII of the Civil Rights Act of 1964 covers all of the following EXCEPT Jane's suit alleging discrimination on the basis of

    a. age.
    b. gender.
    c. race.
    d. religion.

_____ 5. Karen, an ISC manager, wants to institute a policy of mandatory retirement for all employees at age sixty-four. Larry, an ISC manager, wants to discharge Mike, who is age sixty-seven, for cause. Under federal anti-discrimination law

    a. only Karen's wish can be granted.
    b. only Larry's wish can be granted.
    c. both Karen's and Larry's wishes can be granted.
    d. none of the above.

QUESTIONS ON THE FOCUS ON LEGAL REASONING FOR UNIT FIVE— *REDI-FLOORS, INC. V. SONENBERG CO.*

(Answers at the Back of the Book)

____   1.   Nora contracts with Owen on behalf of Nora's principal Pat, without disclosing Pat's identity. Under the holding in *Redi-Floors, Inc. v. Sonenberg Co.*, Owen could pursue a breach of contract claim against

a. Nora only.
b. Pat only.
c. Nora and Pat jointly.
d. Nora or Pat, but not both.

____   2.   In the previous question, suppose that Owen files claims jointly against Nora and Pat, and that this is unsuccessful. In the opinion of the majority in *Redi-Floors, Inc. v. Sonenberg Co.*, Owen might be able to maintain an action solely against Nora if the court

a. directed a verdict in Nora's favor.
b. directed a verdict in Pat's favor.
c. issued a written judgment order in Nora's favor.
d. issued a written judgment order in Pat's favor.

____   3.   Under the facts in the previous questions, according to the reasoning of the dissent in *Redi-Floors, Inc. v. Sonenberg Co.*, Owen could not subsequently maintain an action solely against Nora because the court

a. directed a verdict in Nora's favor.
b. directed a verdict in Pat's favor.
c. issued a written judgment order in Nora's favor.
d. issued a written judgment order in Pat's favor.

QUESTIONS ON THE FOCUS ON ETHICS FOR UNIT FIVE— THE EMPLOYMENT ENVIRONMENT

(Answers at the Back of the Book)

____   1.   Eve is Fred's agent. Ethics would prevent Eve from

a. being loyal to Fred.
b. disclosing Eve's interest in property being bought by Fred.
c. profiting from the agency relation with Fred's consent
d. representing Gary in a transaction with Fred.

____   2.   Harry is Irma's agent. Ethics might prescribe otherwise, but Harry's legal duties to Irma do *not* include

a. compensation.
b. cooperation.
c. loyalty.
d. reimbursement.

____ **3.** Jack offers Kay a job in a distant state. Kay accepts and moves her family. One month later, Kay is terminated without cause. Absent an employment contract or a personnel manual, Jack may be held to have violated

   a. the employment-at-will doctrine.
   b. the one-year exception to the employment-at-will doctrine.
   c. the public-policy exception to the employment-at-will doctrine.
   d. none of the above.

Chapter 23
Consumer Protection

WHAT THIS CHAPTER IS ABOUT

Federal and state laws protect consumers from unfair trade practices, unsafe products, discriminatory or unreasonable credit requirements, and other problems related to consumer transactions. This chapter focuses on *federal* consumer law.

CHAPTER OUTLINE

I. DECEPTIVE ADVERTISING

The Federal Trade Commission Act of 1914 created the Federal Trade Commission (FTC) to prevent unfair and deceptive trade practices. *Deceptive advertising* is advertising that would mislead a consumer.

A. ADVERTISING THAT IS DECEPTIVE
Scientifically untrue claims; misleading half-truths; bait-and-switch ads (if a seller refuses to show an advertised item, fails to have adequate quantities on hand, fails to promise to deliver within a reasonable time, or discourages employees from selling the item.).

B. ADVERTISING THAT IS NOT DECEPTIVE
Puffing (vague generalities, obvious exaggeration).

C. ONLINE DECEPTIVE ADVERTISING
The same laws that apply to other forms of advertising apply to online ads, under FTC guidelines.

D. FTC ACTIONS AGAINST DECEPTIVE ADVERTISING
If the FTC believes that an ad is unfair or deceptive, it sends a complaint to the advertiser, who may settle. If not, the FTC can, after a hearing, issue a cease-and-desist order or require counteradvertising.

E. TELEMARKETING AND ELECTRONIC ADVERTISING

1. **Telephone Consumer Protection Act (TCPA) of 1991**
   The TCPA prohibits (1) phone solicitation using an automatic dialing system or a prerecorded voice and (2) transmission of ads via fax without the recipient's permission. Consumers can recover actual losses or $500, whichever is greater, for each violation. If a defendant willfully or knowingly violated the act, a court can award treble damages.

2. **Telemarketing and Consumer Fraud and Abuse Prevention Act of 1994**
   This act authorized the FTC to set rules for telemarketing and bring actions against fraudulent telemarketers. The FTC's Telemarketing Sales Rule of 1995 makes it illegal to misrepresent information and requires disclosure.

F. STATE LAWS
Most states also have laws regulating phone solicitation.

II. LABELING AND PACKAGING

A. FAIR PACKAGING AND LABELING ACT OF 1966
This act requires that product labels identify the product; net quantity of contents; quantity of servings, if the number of servings is stated; manufacturer; packager or distributor. The appropriate federal agency can require more (such as fat content).

B. OTHER FEDERAL LAWS
Other federal statutes included the Fur Products Labeling Act of 1951, the Wool Products Labeling Act of 1939, the Flammable Fabrics Act of 1953, and the Smokeless Tobacco Health Education Act of 1986.

III. SALES
Federal agencies that regulate sales include the FTC and the Federal Reserve Board of Governors (Regulation Z governs credit provisions in sales contracts). All states have some form of consumer protection laws.

A. DOOR-TO-DOOR SALES
States' "cooling-off" laws permit a buyer to rescind a door-to-door purchase within a certain time. The FTC has a three-day period. The FTC requires a seller to notify a buyer of the right to cancel (if the sale is in Spanish, notice must be in Spanish).

B. TELEPHONE AND MAIL-ORDER SALES
Consumers are partly protected by federal laws prohibiting mail fraud and by state law that parallels federal law.

1. FTC "Mail or Telephone Order Merchandise Rule" of 1993
For goods bought via phone lines or through the mail, merchants must ship orders within the time promised in their ads, notify consumers when orders cannot be shipped on time, and issue a refund within a specified time if a consumer cancels an order.

2. Postal Reorganization Act of 1970
Unsolicited merchandise sent by the mail may be retained, used, discarded, or disposed of, without obligation to the sender.

C. ONLINE SALES
The same federal and state laws that apply to other media generally protect consumers online.

IV. CREDIT PROTECTION

A. TRUTH-IN-LENDING ACT (TILA) OF 1968
The TILA, administered by the Federal Reserve Board, requires the disclosure of credit terms.

1. Who Is Subject to the TILA?
Creditors who, in the ordinary course of business, lend money or sell goods on credit to consumers, or arrange for credit for consumers, are subject to the TILA.

2. What Does the TILA Require?
Under Regulation Z, in any transaction involving a sales contract in which payment is to be made in more than four installments, a lender must disclose all the credit terms clearly and conspicuously.

3. Equal Credit Opportunity Act of 1974
This act prohibits (1) denial of credit on the basis of race, religion, national origin, color, sex, marital status, age and (2) credit discrimination based on whether an individual receives certain forms of income.

4. Credit-Card Rules
Liability of a cardholder is $50 per card for unauthorized charges made before the issuer is notified the card is lost. An issuer cannot bill for unauthorized charges if a card was improperly issued. To withhold payment for a faulty product, a cardholder must use specific procedures.

5. Consumer Leasing Act of 1988
Those who lease consumer goods in the ordinary course of their business, if the goods are priced at $25,000 or less and the lease term exceeds four months, must disclose all material terms in writing.

B. FAIR CREDIT REPORTING ACT (FCRA) OF 1970

1. **What the FCRA Provides**
    Consumer credit reporting agencies may issue credit reports only for certain purposes (extension of credit, etc.); a consumer who is denied credit, or is charged more than others would be, on the basis of a report must be notified of the fact and of the agency that issued the report.

2. **Consumers Can Have Inaccurate Information Deleted**
    If a consumer discovers that the report contains inaccurate information, the agency must delete it within a reasonable period of time.

C. **FAIR DEBT COLLECTION PRACTICES ACT (FDCPA) OF 1977**
    Applies only to debt-collection agencies that, usually for a percentage of the amount owed, attempt to collect debts on behalf of someone else.

1. **What the FDCPA Prohibits**

    a. Contacting the debtor at the debtor's place of employment if the employer objects.

    b. Contacting the debtor during inconvenient times or at any time if an attorney represents the debtor.

    c. Contacting third parties other than the debtor's parents, spouse, or financial advisor about payment unless a court agrees.

    d. Using harassment, or false and misleading information.

    e. Contacting the debtor any time after the debtor refuses to pay the debt, except to advise the debtor of further action to be taken.

2. **What the FDCPA Requires**
    Collection agencies must give a debtor notice that he or she has thirty days to dispute the debt and request written verification of it.

3. **Remedies**
    A debt collector may be liable for actual damages, plus additional damages not to exceed $1,000 and attorneys' fees.

D. **GARNISHMENT OF WAGES**
    To collect a debt, a creditor may use garnishment, which involves attaching a debtor's assets that are in the possession of a third party (employer, bank). The debtor must be notified and have an opportunity to respond. The amount that may be garnished is limited.

V. CONSUMER HEALTH AND SAFETY

A. **FOOD AND DRUGS**
    The Federal Food, Drug, and Cosmetic Act (FFDCA) of 1938 sets food standards, levels of additives, classifications of food and food ads; regulates medical devices. Drugs must be shown to be effective and safe. Enforced by the Food and Drug Administration (FDA).

B. **CONSUMER PRODUCT SAFETY**
    The Consumer Product Safety Act of 1972 includes a scheme for the regulation of consumer products and safety by the Consumer Product Safety Commission (CPSC). The CPSC—

1. Conducts research on product safety.

2. Sets standards for consumer products and bans the manufacture and sale of a product that is potentially hazardous to consumers.

3. Removes from the market any products imminently hazardous and requires manufacturers to report on any products already sold or intended for sale if the products have proved to be hazardous.

4. Administers other product safety legislation.

VI. STATE CONSUMER PROTECTION LAWS

State laws (typically directed at deceptive trade practices) may provide more protection for consumers than do federal laws. The Uniform Consumer Credit Code (UCCC) includes sections on truth in lending, fine-print clauses, and so on, but has been adopted in part in only a few states.

TRUE-FALSE QUESTIONS

(Answers at the Back of the Book)

_____ **1.** Advertising will be deemed deceptive if a consumer would be misled by the advertising claim.

_____ **2.** In general, labels must be accurate.

_____ **3.** A consumer cannot rescind a contract freely entered into.

_____ **4.** The TILA applies to creditors who, in the ordinary course of business, sell goods on credit to consumers.

_____ **5.** Misinformation in a consumer's credit file cannot be deleted.

_____ **6.** Consumers may have more protection under state laws than federal laws.

_____ **7.** The Fair Debt Collection Practices Act applies to anyone who attempts to collect a debt.

_____ **8.** There are no federal agencies that regulate sales.

_____ **9.** One who leases consumer goods in the ordinary course of business does not have to disclose any material terms in writing.

_____ **10.** An advertiser cannot fax ads to consumers without their permission.

FILL-IN QUESTIONS

(Answers at the Back of the Book)

The Truth-in-Lending Act contains provisions regarding credit cards. One provision limits the liability of the cardholder to _____ ($50/$500) per card for unauthorized charges made _____ (after/before) the credit card issuer is notified that the card has been lost. Another provision _____ (allows/prohibits) a credit card company _____ (from billing/to bill) a consumer for any unauthorized charges _____ (unless/if) the credit card was improperly issued by the company.

MULTIPLE-CHOICE QUESTIONS

(Answers at the Back of the Book)

_____ **1.** Rich Foods Company advertises that its cereal, "Fiber Rich," reduces cholesterol. After an investigation and a hearing, the FTC finds no evidence to support the claim. To correct the public's impression of Fiber Rich, the most appropriate action would be

a. a cease-and-desist order.
b. a civil fine.
c. a criminal fine.
d. counteradvertising.

____ 2. ABC Corporation sells a variety of consumer products. Generally, the labels on its products must

a. only be accurate.
b. only use words as they are ordinarily understood by consumers.
c. be accurate and use words as they are ordinarily understood by consumers.
d. none of the above.

____ 3. Maria speaks Spanish, but not English. Nick comes to her home and, after a presentation in Spanish, sells her a vacuum cleaner. He hands her a paper that contains only in English a notice of the right to cancel a sale within three days. This transaction is

a. proper, because the seller gave the buyer notice of her rights.
b. not proper, because the deal was in Spanish but the notice was in English.
c. proper, because ignorance of your rights is no defense.
d. not proper, because ignorance of your rights is a defense.

____ 4. Ed takes out a student loan from First National Bank. After graduation, Ed goes to work, but he does not make payments on the loan. The bank agrees with Good Collection Agency (GCA) that if GCA collects the debt, it can keep a percentage of the amount. To collect the debt, GCA can contact

a. Ed at his place of employment, even if his employer objects.
b. Ed at unusual or inconvenient times or any time if he retains an attorney.
c. Ed only to advise him of further action that GCA will take.
d. third parties, including Ed's parents, unless ordered otherwise by a court.

____ 5. The ordinary business of Ace Credit Company is to lend money to consumers. Ace must disclose all credit terms clearly and conspicuously in

a. all credit transactions.
b. any credit transaction in which payments are to be made in more than four installments.
c. any credit transaction in which payments are to be made in more than one installment.
d. no credit transaction.

____ 6. Eve borrows money to buy a car and to pay for repairs to the roof of her house. She also buys furniture in a transaction financed by the seller whom she will repay in installments. If all of the parties are subject to the Truth-in-Lending Act, Regulation Z applies to

a. the car loan only.
b. the home improvement loan only.
c. the retail installment sale only.
d. the car loan, the home improvement loan, and the retail installment sale.

____ 7. National Foods, Inc., sells breakfast cereals. National must include on the packages

a. the identity of the product only.
b. the net quantity of the contents and the number of servings only.
c. the identity of the product, the net quantity of the contents, and the number of servings.
d. none of the above.

____ 8. General Tobacco Corporation (GTC) sells tobacco products. On the packages of its smokeless tobacco products, GTC must include warnings about health hazards associated with

a. cigarettes.
b. smokeless products.
c. tobacco products generally.
d. none of the above.

____ 9. Best Toy Company begins marketing a new toy that is highly flammable. The Consumer Product Safety Commission may

   a. ban the toy's future manufacture and sale only.
   b. order that the toy be removed from the market only.
   c. ban the toy's future manufacture and sale, and order that the toy be removed from the market.
   d. none of the above.

____ 10. Ann receives an unsolicited credit card in the mail and tosses it on her desk. Without Ann's permission, her roommate uses the card to buy new clothes for $1,000. Ann is liable for

   a. $1,000.
   b. $500.
   c. $50.
   d. none of the above.

SHORT ESSAY QUESTIONS

1. What are some of the more common deceptive advertising techniques and the ways in which the FTC may deal with such conduct?

2. What are the primary provisions of the Truth-In-Lending Act?

ISSUE SPOTTERS

(Answers at the Back of the Book)

1. Alpha Electronics, Inc., advertises Beta computers at a low price. Alpha keeps only a few in stock and tells its sales staff to switch consumers attracted by the price to more expensive brands. Alpha tells its staff that if all else fails, refuse to show the Betas, and if a consumer insists on buying one, do not promise delivery. Has Alpha violated a law?

2. Carol buys a notebook computer from Alpha Electronics. She pays for it with her credit card. When it proves defective, she asks Alpha to repair or replace it, but Alpha refuses. What can Carol do?

3. ABC Pharmaceuticals, Inc., believes it has developed a new drug that will be effective in the treatment of AIDS patients. The drug has had only limited testing, but ABC wants to make the drug widely available as soon as possible. To market the drug, what must ABC show the Food and Drug Administration?

Chapter 24
Environmental Law

WHAT THIS CHAPTER IS ABOUT

This chapter covers environmental law, which is the law that relates to environmental protection—common law actions and federal statutes and regulations.

CHAPTER OUTLINE

I. COMMON LAW ACTIONS

A. NUISANCE
Persons cannot use their property in a way that unreasonably interferes with others' rights to use or enjoy their own property. An injured party may be awarded damages or an injunction.

B. NEGLIGENCE AND STRICT LIABILITY
A business that fails to use reasonable care may be liable to a party whose injury was foreseeable. Businesses that engage in ultrahazardous activities are strictly liable for whatever injuries the activities cause.

II. STATE AND LOCAL REGULATION
States regulate the environment through zoning or more direct regulation. City, county, and other local governments control some aspects through zoning laws, waste removal and disposal regulations, aesthetic ordinances, and so on.

III. FEDERAL REGULATION

A. ENVIRONMENTAL REGULATORY AGENCIES
The Environmental Protection Agency (EPA) coordinates federal environmental responsibilities and administers most federal environmental policies and statutes. State and local agencies implement environmental statutes and regulations. Citizens can sue to enforce environmental regulations.

B. ENVIRONMENTAL IMPACT STATEMENTS
The National Environmental Policy Act (NEPA) of 1969 requires all federal agencies to consider environmental factors in making significant decisions.

1. When an Environmental Impact Statement Must Be Prepared
Whenever a major federal action significantly affects the quality of the environment. An action qualifies as *major* if it involves a substantial commitment of resources (monetary or otherwise). An action is *federal* if a federal agency has the power to control it.

2. What an EIS Must Analyze
(1) The impact on the environment that the action will have, (2) any adverse effects to the environment and alternative actions that might be taken, and (3) irreversible effects the action might generate.

3. When an Agency Decides That an EIS Is Unnecessary
It must issue a statement supporting this conclusion.

C. OTHER FEDERAL LAWS

Other federal laws that require the consideration of environmental values in agency decision-making include the Fish and Wildlife Coordination Act of 1958 and the Endangered Species Act of 1973.

IV.   AIR POLLUTION

The Clean Air Act of 1963 (and amendments) is the basis for regulation.

A. MOBILE SOURCES

Regulations governing air pollution from automobiles and other mobile sources specify standards and time schedules. For example, under the 1990 amendments to the Clean Air Act—

1. New Automobiles' Exhaust

Manufacturers had to cut emission of nitrogen oxide by 60 percent and emission of other pollutants by 35 percent. Other sets of emission controls became or will become effective in 2004 and 2007.

2. EPA Action

If a vehicle does not meet the standards, the EPA can order a recall and repair or replacement of pollution-control devices.

3. Sport Utility Vehicles and Light Trucks

These vehicles are now subject to the same standards as cars.

4. Gasoline

Service stations must sell gasoline with higher oxygen content.

5. New Standards

The EPA attempts to update these and other standards when new scientific evidence is available.

B. STATIONARY SOURCES

The EPA sets air quality standards for stationary sources (such as industrial plants), and the states formulate plans to achieve them. For example, under the 1990 amendments to the Clean Air Act—

1. Major New Sources

These must use the maximum achievable control technology (MACT) to reduce emissions from the combustion of fossil fuels (coal and oil).

2. 110 of the Oldest Coal-burning Power Plants in the United States

These were to cut emissions by 40 percent by the year 2001 to reduce acid rain.

3. Utilities

Utilities were granted "credits" to emit certain amounts of sulfur dioxide, and those that emit less can sell their credits to other polluters.

4. Other Factories and Businesses

These were to reduce emissions to cut ground-level ozone in 96 cities by 2005. Production of chlorofluorocarbons, carbon tetrachloride, and methyl chloroform (linked to depleting the ozone layer) must stop.

5. Hazardous Air Pollutants

Industrial emissions of 189 specific hazardous air pollutants must be reduced through MACT. Certain landfills must install air-pollution collection and control systems.

C. PENALTIES

Civil penalties include assessments of up to $25,000 per day, or an amount equal to a violator's economic benefits from noncompliance, plus up to $5,000 per day for other violations. Criminal penalties include fines of up to $1 million and imprisonment of up to two years. Private citizens can sue.

V.   WATER POLLUTION

A. NAVIGABLE WATERS
The Clean Water Act of 1972 amended the Federal Water Pollution Control Act (FWPCA) of 1948 to provide—

1. **Goals**
    The goals of the statutes are to (1) make waters safe for swimming, (2) protect fish and wildlife, and (3) eliminate the discharge of pollutants into the water.

2. **Limits on Discharges Based on Best Available Control Technology**
    Time schedules (extended by amendment in 1977 and by the Water Quality Act of 1987) limit discharges of pollutants.

3. **Permits**
    Municipal and industrial polluters must obtain permits before discharging wastes into navigable waters, which include wetlands.

4. **Penalties and Remedies**
    Civil penalties include assessments of from $10,000 per day (up to $25,000 per violation) to $25,000 per day. Criminal penalties include fines of $2,500 per day to $1 million total and one to fifteen years' imprisonment. Injunctions, damages, and clean-up costs can be imposed.

B. DRINKING WATER
The Safe Drinking Water Act of 1974 requires the EPA to set maximum levels for pollutants in public water systems. Operators must come as close as possible to the standards using the best available technology.

C. OCEAN DUMPING
The Marine Protection, Research, and Sanctuaries Act of 1972—

1. **Radiological Waste and Other Materials**
    Dumping of radiological, chemical, and biological warfare agents, and high-level radioactive waste is prohibited. Transporting and dumping other materials (with exceptions) requires a permit.

2. **Penalties**
    Civil penalties include assessments of not more than $50,000 or revocation or suspension of a permit. Criminal penalties include fines of up to $50,000, imprisonment for not more than a year, or both. Injunctions can be imposed.

D. OIL POLLUTION
The Oil Pollution Act of 1990 provides that any oil facility, oil shipper, vessel owner, or vessel operator that discharges oil may be liable for clean-up costs, damages, and fines of up to $25,000 per day.

VI. NOISE POLLUTION
Under Noise Control Act of 1972, the EPA sets maximum levels for noise. The act requires use of the best available technology. Injunctions may be imposed. Penalties include fines up to $50,000 per day and up to two years' imprisonment.

VII. TOXIC CHEMICALS

A. PESTICIDES AND HERBICIDES

1. **Federal Insecticide, Fungicide, and Rodenticide Act (FIFRA) of 1947**

    a. **Registration, Certification, and Use**
        Pesticides and herbicides must be (1) registered before they can be sold, (2) certified and used only for approved applications, and (3) used in limited quantities when applied to food crops.

b. **Labels**

Include directions for the use of a pesticide or herbicide, warnings to protect human health and the environment, a statement of treatment in the case of poisoning, and a list of the ingredients.

c. **Penalties**

For registrants and producers: suspension or cancellation of registration, up to a $50,000 fine, imprisonment up to one year. For commercial dealers: up to a $25,000 fine, imprisonment up to one year. For private users: a $1,000 fine, imprisonment up to thirty days.

2. **"Reasonable Certainty of No Harm"**

To remain on the market, a pesticide must have a "reasonable certainty of no harm" (one-in-a-million risk to people of cancer from exposure). Grocery stores must display brochures about pesticides in food.

B. **TOXIC SUBSTANCES**

Under the Toxic Substances Control Act of 1976, for substances that potentially pose an imminent hazard or an unreasonable risk of injury to health or the environment, the EPA may require special labeling, set production quotas, or limit or prohibit the use of a substance.

VIII. HAZARDOUS WASTES

A. **RESOURCE CONSERVATION AND RECOVERY ACT (RCRA) OF 1976**

The EPA determines which forms of solid waste are hazardous, and sets requirements for disposal, storage, and treatment. Penalties include up to $25,000 (civil) per violation, $50,000 (criminal) per day, imprisonment up to two years (may be doubled for repeaters), and up to $250,000 and fifteen years for knowingly violating the RCRA and endangering another's life.

B. **SUPERFUND**

The Comprehensive Environmental Response, Compensation, and Liability Act (CERCLA) of 1980 regulates the clean-up of leaking hazardous waste disposal sites. If a release or a threatened release occurs, the EPA can clean up a site and recover the cost from—

1. **Potentially Responsible Parties**

(1) The person who generated the wastes disposed of at the site, (2) the person who transported the wastes to the site, (3) the person who owned or operated the site at the time of the disposal, or (4) the current owner or operator.

2. **Joint and Several Liability**

One party can be charged with the entire cost (which that party may recover in a contribution action against others).

IX. GLOBAL ENVIRONMENTAL ISSUES

These include cross-border pollution and global warming. The Kyoto Protocol, which has been ratified by 160 nations (but not the United States), established reductions for different countries and regions in emissions of gases linked to global warming.

TRUE-FALSE QUESTIONS

(Answers at the Back of the Book)

____ 1. No common law doctrines apply against polluters today.

____ 2. Local governments can control some aspects of the environment through zoning laws.

____ 3. Under federal environmental laws, there is a single standard for all polluters and all pollutants.

____ 4. The Toxic Substances Control Act of 1976 regulates the clean up of leaking hazardous waste disposal sites.

____ 5. The Environmental Protection Agency (EPA) can clean up a release of hazardous waste at a hazardous waste disposal site and recover the entire cost from the site's owner or operator.

____ 6. States may restrict discharge of chemicals into the water or air.

____ 7. A party who violates the Clean Air Act may realize economic benefits from the noncompliance.

____ 8. The Environmental Protection Agency sets limits on discharges of pollutants into water.

____ 9. A party who only transports hazardous waste to a hazardous waste disposal site cannot be held liable for any costs to clean up the site.

____ 10. The Environmental Protection Agency sets maximum levels for noise.

FILL-IN QUESTIONS

(Answers at the Back of the Book)

The National Environmental Policy Act requires _____ (federal/state and local) agencies to prepare environmental impact statements (EIS) when major _____ (federal/state and local) actions significantly affect the quality of the environment. An EIS analyzes (1) the _____ (environmental impact that an action will have/environment's impact on a project), (2) any adverse effects to the _____ (environment/project) and alternative courses of action, and (3) irreversible effects that _____ (an action might cause to the environment/the environment might cause to the project). If an agency decides that an EIS is unnecessary, it must issue a statement announcing that decision _____ (and reasons/but it need not provide reasons) supporting the conclusion.

MULTIPLE-CHOICE QUESTIONS

(Answers at the Back of the Book)

____ 1. The U.S. Department of the Interior's approval of coal mining operations in several eastern states requires an environmental impact statement

a. only because it affects the quality of the environment.
b. only because it is "major."
c. only because it is "federal."
d. because it affects the quality of the environment, is "major," and is "federal."

____ 2. Standard Utility's new power plant burns fossil fuels. As a major new source of possible pollution, the plant must use

a. the all-pollution elimination control technology.
b. the best available control technology.
c. the maximum achievable control technology.
d. the most affordable control technology.

___ 3. National Motors Corporation (NMC) makes sport utility vehicles (SUVs). Under the Clean Air Act, NMC is required to makes its SUVs comply with standards that, with respect to automobile exhaust emissions, are

    a. different but neither more nor less strict.
    b. less strict.
    c. more strict.
    d. the same.

___ 4. Eagle Industries, Inc., fails to obtain a permit before discharging waste into navigable waters. Under the Clean Water Act, Eagle can be required

    a. only to clean up the pollution.
    b. only to pay for the cost of cleaning up the pollution.
    c. to clean up the pollution or pay for the cost of doing so.
    d. none of the above.

___ 5. Petro, Inc., ships unlabeled containers of hazardous waste to off-site facilities for disposal. If the containers later leak, Petro could be found to have violated

    a. the Comprehensive Environmental Response, Compensation, and Liability Act (CERCLA) only.
    b. the Resource Conservation and Recovery Act (RCRA) only.
    c. CERCLA and the RCRA.
    d. none of the above.

___ 6. Beta Company operates a hazardous waste storage facility. If Beta buries unlabeled containers without determining their contents and the containers leak, Beta could be found to have violated

    a. the Comprehensive Environmental Response, Compensation, and Liability Act (CERCLA) only.
    b. the Resource Conservation and Recovery Act (RCRA) only.
    c. CERCLA and the RCRA.
    d. none of the above.

___ 7. The U.S. Department of the Interior approves minor landscaping around a federal courthouse in St. Louis. This does *not* require an environmental impact statement

    a. only because it does not affect the quality of the environment.
    b. only because it is not "major."
    c. only because it is not "federal."
    d. because it does not affect the quality of the environment, is not "major," and is not "federal."

___ 8. Federated Industrial Corporation's factories emit toxic air pollutants. Under the Clean Air Act and EPA regulations, Federated is required to

    a. eliminate all air polluting emissions.
    b. install emission control equipment on its products.
    c. reduce emissions by installing the maximum achievable control technology.
    d. remove all pollutants from its factories.

___ 9. Alpha Development Company owns wetlands that it wants to fill in and develop as a site for homes. Under the Clean Water Act, before filling and dredging, Alpha must obtain a permit from

    a. no one.
    b. the Army Corps of Engineers.
    c. the EPA.
    d. the U.S. Department of the Navy.

_____ **10.** Gamma Company owns a hazardous waste disposal site that it sells to Omega Properties, Inc. Later, the EPA discovers a leak at the site and cleans it up. The EPA can recover the cost from

a. Gamma only.
b. Omega only.
c. Gamma or Omega.
d. none of the above.

SHORT ESSAY QUESTIONS

1. What does the National Environmental Policy Act require?

2. What federal laws regulate toxic chemicals?

ISSUE SPOTTERS

(Answers at the Back of the Book)

1. ChemCorp generates hazardous wastes from its operations. Central Trucking Company transports those wastes to Intrastate Disposal, Inc., which owns a hazardous waste disposal site. Intrastate sells the property on which the disposal site is located to ABC Properties, Inc. If the EPA cleans up the site, from whom can it recover the cost?

2. ABC Company's plant emits smoke and fumes. ABC's operation includes a short railway system, and trucks enter and exit the grounds continuously. Constant vibrations from the trains and trucks rattle a nearby residential neighborhood. The residents sue ABC. Are there any reasons that the court might *refuse* to enjoin ABC's operation?

3. What federal agencies have authority to regulate environmental matters?

Chapter 25
Land-Use Control and Real Property

WHAT THIS CHAPTER IS ABOUT

This chapter covers the nature of real property and the nature of ownership rights in real property. The chapter also outlines the right of the government to take private land for public use, zoning laws, and other restrictions on ownership, including easements and profits.

CHAPTER OUTLINE

I. THE NATURE OF REAL PROPERTY
Real property consists of land and the buildings, plants, and trees that it contains. It is immovable.

A. LAND
Land includes the soil on the surface of the earth, natural products or artificial structures attached to it, the water on or under it, and the air space above.

B. AIR SPACE AND SUBSURFACE RIGHTS
Limitations on air rights or subsurface rights normally have to be indicated on the document transferring title at the time of purchase.

1. Air Rights
Flights over private land do not normally violate the property owners' rights (unless they interfere with the enjoyment and use of the land).

2. Subsurface Rights
Ownership of the surface can be separated from ownership of the subsurface. In excavating, if a subsurface owner causes the land to subside, he or she may be liable to the owner of the surface.

C. PLANT LIFE AND VEGETATION
A sale of land with growing crops on it includes them, unless otherwise agreed. When crops are sold separately, they are personal property (governed by the Uniform Commercial Code [UCC 2–107(2)]).

D. FIXTURES
Personal property so closely associated with certain real property that it is viewed as part of it (such as plumbing in a building). Fixtures are included in a sale of land unless a contract provides otherwise.

1. Factors in Determining Whether an Item is a Fixture
The intent of the parties, whether the item can be removed without damaging the real property, and whether the item is sufficiently adapted so as to have become a part of the real property.

2. Trade Fixtures
Trade fixtures are fixtures installed for a commercial purpose by a tenant, whose property it remains, unless removal would irreparably damage the real property.

II. OWNERSHIP INTERESTS IN REAL PROPERTY

A. FEE SIMPLE

1. **Fee Simple Absolute**

   A fee simple owner has the most rights possible—to give the property away, sell it, transfer it by will, use it for virtually any purpose, and possess it to the exclusion of all the world—potentially forever.

2. **Fee Simple Defeasible**

   This is conditional ownership. If the condition is not met, the land reverts to the original owner. A conveyance of a fee simple defeasible usually includes the words as long as, until, while, or during ("to A, as long as the property is used for a school").

B. **LIFE ESTATE**

   This lasts for the life of a specified individual ("to A for his life"). A life tenant can use the land (but cannot commit waste), mortgage the life estate, and create liens, easements, and leases (but not longer than the life defining the estate).

C. **FUTURE INTEREST**

   This is a residuary interest that an owner retains to retake possession if condition of the fee simple defeasible is not met or when the life estate ends.

1. **Reversions and Remainders**

   If the owner retains ownership of a future interest, it is a reversionary interest. If the owner transfers rights in a future interest to another, it is a remainder ("to A for life, then to B").

2. **Executory Interest**

   This is an interest that does not take effect immediately on the expiration of another interest ("to A for life and one year after A's death to B").

D. **LEASEHOLD ESTATES**

   A leasehold estate is created when an owner or landlord conveys the right to possess and use property to a tenant for a certain period of time.

1. **Tenancy for Years**

   This is created by contract (which can sometimes be oral) by which property is leased for a specific period (a month, a year, a period of years). At the end of the period, the lease ends (without notice). If the tenant dies during the lease, the lease interest passes to the tenant's heirs.

2. **Periodic Tenancy**

   This is created by a lease specifying only that rent is to be paid at certain intervals. It can arise if a landlord allows a tenant for years to hold over. It automatically renews unless terminated (on one period's notice).

3. **Tenancy at Will**

   This is a tenancy for as long as the landlord and tenant agree. It exists when a tenant for years retains possession after termination with the landlord's consent before payment of the next rent (when it becomes a periodic tenancy). It terminates on the death of either party.

4. **Tenancy at Sufferance**

   This is the possession of land without right (without the owner's permission).

E. **CONCURRENT OWNERSHIP**

1. **Tenancy in Common**

   Each of two or more persons owns an undivided portion of the property. The portions need not be equal. On death, a tenant's interest passes to his or her heirs. Most states presume that a co-tenancy is a tenancy in common unless there is a clear intention to establish a joint tenancy.

2. **Joint Tenancy**
   Each of two or more persons owns an undivided interest in the property; a deceased joint tenant's interest passes to the surviving joint tenant or tenants. This can be terminated at any time before a joint tenant's death by gift, by sale, or by partition (divided into equal parts).

3. **Tenancy by the Entirety**
   This is created by a transfer of real property to a husband and wife; neither spouse can transfer separately his or her interest during his or her life. In some states, this tenancy has been effectively abolished. A divorce, either spouse's death, or mutual agreement will terminate it.

4. **Community Property**
   Each spouse owns an undivided half interest in property acquired by either spouse during their marriage (except property acquired by gift or inheritance). This is recognized in only some states, on divorce the property is divided equally in a few states and at a court's discretion in others.

III. PRIVATE CONTROL OF LAND USE

A. NONPOSSESSORY INTERESTS

1. **Easements and Profits**
   Easement: the right of a person to make limited use of another person's land without taking anything from the property. *Profit*: the right to go onto another's land and take away a part or product of the land.

   a. **Creation of an Easement or Profit**
      These may be created by deed, will, contract, implication, necessity, or prescription.

   b. **Effect of a Sale of Property**
      The benefit of an easement or profit goes with the land. The burden goes with the land only if the new owner recognizes it, or knew or should have known of it.

   c. **Termination of an Easement or Profit**
      Terminates when deeded back to the owner of the land that is burdened; its owner becomes the owner of the property burdened; or it is abandoned with the intent to relinquish the right to it.

2. **Licenses**
   A license is a revocable right of a person to come onto another person's land.

B. RESTRICTIVE COVENANTS

1. **Covenants Running with the Land**
   A covenant runs with the land (the original parties and their successors are entitled to its benefit or burdened with its obligation) if—

   a. It is created in a written agreement (usually the document that conveys the land).
   b. Parties intend that it run with the land (agreement states that all promisor's "successors, heirs, or assigns" will be bound).
   c. Covenant touches and concerns the land (limits on burdened land must have some connection to the land).
   d. Original parties are in privity of estate when covenant is created.

2. **Illegal Restrictive Covenants**
   A covenant cannot be discriminatory.

IV. PUBLIC CONTROL OF LAND USE

A. POLICE POWER
A state can regulate uses of land within its jurisdiction.

1. **General Plans**

   Land-use laws typically follow a local government general plan, which may be supplemented by special, area, or community plans.

2. **Zoning Laws**

   Divide an area into districts to which land-use regulations apply.

   a. **Types of Restrictions**

      Use restrictions: kind of use (commercial, residential). Structural restrictions: engineering features and architectural design.

   b. **Variances**

      An owner can obtain a variance if (1) it is impossible to realize a reasonable return on the land as zoned, (2) the ordinance adversely affects only the owner (not all owners), (3) granting a variance will not substantially alter the essential character of the zoned area.

3. **Other Regulations**

   Subdivision regulations: local requirements for dedication of land for schools, etc. Growth-management ordinances: limit building permits.

4. **Limits on the State's Power**

   A regulation cannot be (1) confiscatory (or the owner must be paid just compensation); (2) arbitrary or unreasonable (taking without due process under the Fourteenth Amendment); or (3) discriminatory, under the Fourteenth Amendment.

B. **EMINENT DOMAIN**

   The government can take private property for public use. To obtain title, a condemnation proceeding is brought. The Fifth Amendment requires that just compensation be paid for a taking; thus, in a separate proceeding a court determines the land's fair value (usually market value) to pay the owner.

TRUE-FALSE QUESTIONS

(Answers at the Back of the Book)

____   1. A fee simple absolute is potentially infinite in duration and can be disposed of by deed or by will.

____   2. The owner of a life estate has the same rights as a fee simple owner.

____   3. An easement allows a person to use land and take something from it, but a profit allows a person only to use land.

____   4. The government can take private property for *public* use without just compensation.

____   5. The government can take private property for *private* uses only.

____   6. A periodic tenancy is a tenancy for a specified period of time, such as a month, a year, or a period of years.

____   7. To obtain a variance, a landowner must show that his or her alternative use of the land would substantially alter its essential character.

____   8. A license is a revocable right of a person to come onto another person's land.

____   9. Real property consists of, in part, land and the buildings on it.

____   10. The interest of a tenant in common passes to his or her heirs on the tenant's death.

FILL-IN QUESTIONS

(Answers at the Back of the Book)

1. An owner in fee simple absolute who conveys the estate to another in fee simple defeasible retains _____ (a possibility of reverter/an executory interest). If the conditions of the conveyance are not met, the _____ (next designated heir/original owner) takes ownership of the estate.

2. An owner in fee simple who conveys the estate to another as a life estate retains a _____ (remainder/reversion). When a life estate is conveyed, the grantor has not disposed of the interest in the land remaining after the grantee's life, and thus, the grantor retains a _____ (remainder/reversion) that will become possessory on the grantee's death.

MULTIPLE-CHOICE QUESTIONS

(Answers at the Back of the Book)

____ 1. Lou owns two hundred acres next to Mark's mill. Lou sells to Mark the privilege of removing timber from his land to refine into lumber. The privilege of removing the timber is

a. a license.
b. an easement.
c. a profit.
d. none of the above.

____ 2. Evan owns an apartment building in fee simple. This means that Evan can

a. give the building away, but not sell it or transfer it by will.
b. sell the building or transfer it by a will, but cannot give it away.
c. give the building away, sell it, or transfer it by will.
d. none of the above.

____ 3. Jan sells the eastern half of her land to Ken. According to the deed, Ken agrees to maintain a fence along the common boundary. Later, Jan sells the rest of her land to Lee, and Ken sells his land to Molly. Under the deed, Molly agrees to maintain the fence. If Lee sues Molly to repair the fence, Lee will

a. win, because the covenant runs with the land to Lee and Molly through Jan and Ken.
b. win, because Lee bought his half of Jan's land before Molly bought her half.
c. lose, because the original covenant was in the deed given by Jan to Ken.
d. lose, because there is no privity between Lee and Molly.

____ 4. Dan owns a half-acre of land fronting on Eagle Lake. Fred owns the property behind Dan's land. No road runs to Dan's land, but Fred's driveway runs between a road and Dan's property, so Dan uses Fred's driveway. The right-of-way that Dan has across Fred's property is

a. a license.
b. an easement.
c. a profit.
d. none of the above.

____ 5. Susan signs a lease for an apartment, agreeing to make rental payments before the fifth of each month. The lease does not specify a termination date. This tenancy is

a. a periodic tenancy.
b. a tenancy at sufferance.
c. a tenancy at will.
d. a tenancy for years.

___   6.   Sam owns an acre of land on Red River. The federal government dams the river. A lake forms behind the dam, covering Sam's land. The federal government owes Sam

    a. just compensation.
    b. land of equivalent value.
    c. private use of the lake.
    d. none of the above.

___   7.   Alpha Corporation wants to convert a warehouse near Bay City into a shopping mall and to construct an apartment tower on adjacent land. Local policy concerning growth, and building requirements and restrictions can be found in Bay City's

    a. area and general development plans only.
    b. zoning ordinances only.
    c. area and development plans, and zoning ordinances.
    d. none of the above.

___   8.   Beta Construction, Inc., wants to develop a suburban tract, subdividing the land to build single-family homes. Formation of the subdivision and such public facilities as streets and schools are responsibilities of

    a. Beta only.
    b. the local agency that oversees the zoning process only.
    c. Beta and the local agency that oversees the zoning process.
    d. none of the above.

___   9.   Gamma Company buys forty acres of land to build a corporate complex. After construction begins, the county zones the surrounding, undeveloped area for a nature preserve, in which it includes 75 percent of Gamma's land. The county owes Gamma

    a. just compensation.
    b. land of equivalent value.
    c. private use of the preserve.
    d. none of the above.

___   10.   Adam wants to convert a residential duplex into a small office building. The duplex is in an area zoned for residential use only. Adam can be granted a variance if

    a. Adam would realize a higher return on the office building than on the duplex.
    b. all property owners within the zone agree that an office building is acceptable.
    c. granting a variance will not substantially alter the character of the area.
    d. none of the above.

SHORT ESSAY QUESTIONS

1.   What are the principal features of the four forms of concurrent property ownership (tenancy in common, joint tenancy, tenancy by the entirety and community property)?

2.   Describe the power of eminent domain and the process by which private property is condemned for a public purpose.

ISSUE SPOTTERS

(Answers at the Back of the Book)

1.   Gary owns a commercial building in fee simple. Gary transfers temporary possession of the building to Holding Corporation (HC). Can HC transfer possession for even less time to Investment Company?

2.   Metro City designates certain areas within its limits for industrial, commercial, residential, and mixed uses. Nick owns a small plot of land in a mixed-use area. Can Metro limit only Nick's land to residential use?

3.   Eve owns an acre of land in an area that allows houses on half-acres. She proposes to divide her property and build a house on each half-acre. To do so, Eve must obtain residential building permits from the local zoning authorities. On what grounds, unrelated to Eve, can the authorities refuse to grant the permits?

Chapter 26
Antitrust and Monopoly

WHAT THIS CHAPTER IS ABOUT

This chapter outlines the background, exemptions, and enforcement of the major antitrust statutes—the Sherman Act, the Clayton Act, and the Federal Trade Commission Act. Monopoly is covered in some detail. Keep in mind that the basis of the antitrust laws is a desire to foster competition (to result in lower prices and so on).

CHAPTER OUTLINE

I. **PUBLIC POLICY AND THE ORIGINS OF ANTITRUST LAW**

    A. MARKET POWER
    Market power is the extent to which a firm can ignore competitors in setting its prices or can in some way limit competition.

    B. RESTRAINTS OF TRADE
    Restraints of trade include agreements between suppliers in a market to limit output. Agreements between business firms that reduce competition are against public policy (except covenants-not-to-compete included in a sale of a business).

    C. FEDERAL LEGISLATION
    When monopolies increased in the late nineteenth century, Congress felt that the common law (under which an agreement to limit competition is unenforceable but cannot be challenged by one who is not a party to it) was not sufficient to protect against anticompetitive conduct.

II. **MAJOR FEDERAL ANTITRUST LAWS**
These laws seek to promote competitive business and limit the anticompetitive use of market power.

    A. SHERMAN ACT OF 1890
    This act prohibits—

        1. **Restraints of Trade [Section 1]**
        Requires two or more persons; focus is on agreements (written or oral) that are restrictive (see Chapter 27).

        2. **Monopolies [Section 2]**
        Applies to individuals and to several people; concerns the structure of a monopoly in the marketplace; focus is on the misuse of monopoly power (see below).

    B. CLAYTON ACT OF 1914
    Aimed at practices not covered by the Sherman Act. Violations are subject to civil, not criminal, penalties. Conduct is illegal if it substantially tends to lessen competition or create monopoly power—

        1. **Price Discrimination [Section 2]**
        Seller charges different prices to competitive buyers for identical goods (see Chapter 27).

        2. **Exclusionary Practices [Section 3]**
        Exclusive-dealing contracts and tying arrangements (see Chapter 27).

3. **Corporate Mergers [Section 7]**
    A person or firm cannot hold stock or assets in another firm if the effect may be to substantially lessen competition (see Chapter 27).

4. **Interlocking Directorates [Section 8]**
    No person may be a director in two or more corporations at the same time if either firm has capital, surplus, or undivided profits of more than a certain amount or if a firm's competitive sales are more than a certain amount. (The limits are updated annually.)

C. **FEDERAL TRADE COMMISSION ACT OF 1914**
    Section 5 condemns all forms of anticompetitive behavior not covered by other federal antitrust laws.

III.   ENFORCEMENT OF ANTITRUST LAWS

A. **DEPARTMENT OF JUSTICE (DOJ)**
    Prosecutes violations of the Sherman Act as criminal or civil violations. Violations of the Clayton Act are not crimes; the DOJ can enforce it only through civil proceedings. Remedies include divestiture and dissolution.

B. **FEDERAL TRADE COMMISSION (FTC)**
    Enforces the Clayton Act; has sole authority to enforce the Federal Trade Commission Act; issues administrative orders; can seek court sanctions.

C. **PRIVATE PARTIES**

1. **Damages**
    Can sue for treble damages and attorneys' fees under the Clayton Act if injured by a violation of any federal antitrust law (except the FTC Act).

2. **Injunctions**
    May seek an injunction to prevent antitrust violations if the violation injured business activities protected by the antitrust laws.

IV.   EXEMPTIONS FROM ANTITRUST LAWS

A. **LABOR ACTIVITIES**

B. **AGRICULTURAL ASSOCIATIONS AND FISHERIES**
    These are exempt except for exclusionary practices or restraints of trade against competitors.

C. **INSURANCE COMPANIES**
    These are exempt in most cases when state regulation exists.

D. **U.S. EXPORTERS**
    These may cooperate to compete with similar foreign associations (if the cooperation does not restrain trade in the United States or injure other U.S. exporters).

E. **PROFESSIONAL BASEBALL**

F. **OIL MARKETING**
    States set quotas on oil to be marketed in interstate commerce.

G. **OTHER EXEMPTIONS**

1. Activities approved by the president in furtherance of defense.
2. Cooperative research among small business firms.
3. Research or production of a product, process, or service by joint ventures consisting of competitors.

4. State actions, when the state policy is clearly articulated and the policy is actively supervised by the state.

5. Activities of regulated industries when federal commissions, boards, or agencies have primary regulatory authority.

6. Joint efforts by businesspersons to obtain legislative, judicial, or executive action. (Exception: an action is not protected if no reasonable person could reasonably expect success on the merits and it is an attempt to make anticompetitive use of government processes.)

V. MONOPOLIES

A monopoly may violate Section 2 of the Sherman Act.

A. MONOPOLIZATION

Requires two elements: (1) the possession of monopoly power in the relevant market and (2) the willful acquisition or maintenance of that power.

1. Monopoly Power

Monopoly power is sufficient market power to control prices and exclude competition.

a. Market-Share Test

A firm has monopoly power if its share of the relevant market is 70 percent or more.

b. The Relevant Market Has Two Elements—

1) Relevant Product Market

This includes all products with identical attributes and those that are sufficient substitutes for each other.

2) Relevant Geographical Market

If competitors sell in only a limited area, the geographical market is limited to that area.

2. Intent Requirement

If a firm has market power as a result of a purposeful act to acquire or maintain that power through anticompetitive means, it is a violation. Intent may be inferred from evidence that the firm had monopoly power and engaged in anticompetitive behavior.

B. PREDATORY PRICING

Selling substantially below costs of production to drive competitors from the market (prices can then be raised to high levels) is not a violation if firm is (1) attempting to gain access to established market and (2) unlikely to obtain monopoly profits in the future.

C. ATTEMPTS TO MONOPOLIZE

An action must (1) be intended to exclude competitors and garner monopoly power and (2) have a dangerous probability of success.

TRUE-FALSE QUESTIONS

(Answers at the Back of the Book)

_____ 1. Monopoly power is market power sufficient to control prices and exclude competition.

_____ 2. A relevant product market includes products that are sufficient substitutes for each other.

_____ 3. Market power is the extent to which a firm can exclude competition.

_____ 4. Antitrust law is intended to eliminate competition in business markets.

_____ 5. A firm that can ignore its competitors in setting a price for its product has no market power.

_____ 6. A determining factor as to whether a firm is a monopoly is its size in terms of the relevant market.

_____ 7. An unsuccessful attempt to monopolize is not a violation of antitrust law.

_____ 8. No person can be a director in two or more corporations at the same time.

_____ 9. The U.S. Department of Justice can ask a court to require a firm's dissolution for an antitrust violation.

_____ 10. Even if a private party has been injured by an antitrust violation, the party cannot sue for damages.

FILL-IN QUESTIONS

(Answers at the Back of the Book)

_____ (Monopoly power/A restraint of trade) is any agreement that has the effect of reducing competition in the marketplace. _____ (Monopoly power/ Restraint of trade) is an extreme amount of market power. A firm that can raise its prices somewhat without too much concern for its competitors' response has some degree of market power. Determining whether such power is sufficient to call it _____ (monopoly power/ a restraint of trade) is one of the most difficult tasks in antitrust law.

MULTIPLE-CHOICE QUESTIONS

(Answers at the Back of the Book)

_____ 1. Omega, Inc., controls 80 percent of the market for telecommunications equipment in the southeastern United States. To show that Omega is monopolizing that market in violation of the Sherman Act requires proof of

  a. only the possession of monopoly power in the relevant market.
  b. only the willful acquisition or maintenance of monopoly power.
  c. the possession of monopoly power in the relevant market and the willful acquisition or maintenance of that power.
  d. none of the above.

_____ 2. Central Data Corporation and Digital, Inc., are competitors. They form a joint venture to research, develop, and produce new software for a particular line of computers. This joint venture is

  a. exempt from the antitrust laws.
  b. subject to the Clayton Act.
  c. subject to the Federal Trade Commission Act.
  d. subject to the Sherman Act.

_____ 3. Alpha Company, Beta Corporation, and Gamma, Inc., are the only suppliers in a certain market. They agree to limit their output so that prices will increase. This agreement is

  a. a legitimate exercise of market power.
  b. an economically efficient contract.
  c. a restraint of trade.
  d. a socially beneficial joint venture.

____ **4.** Soft Drink Company begins to sell its products at prices substantially below cost. This is *not* an antitrust violation if Soft Drink is trying to

a. drive competitors from the market.
b. gain access to the market.
c. obtain monopoly profits.
d. none of the above.

____ **5.** Office Equipment, Inc., sells its products throughout the United States. For the purpose of determining its market share, the relevant market consists of

a. the geographical market only.
b. the product market only.
c. the geographical market and the product market.
d. none of the above.

____ **6.** The Clayton Act and the Sherman Act can be enforced through civil proceedings by

a. the Federal Trade Commission only.
b. the U.S. Department of Justice only.
c. private parties only.
d. the Federal Trade Commission, U.S. Department of Justice, and private parties.

____ **7.** Delta, Inc., has a 90-percent share of its market in the United States. This is an unlawful monopoly if Delta acquired its market share through

a. anticompetitive conduct.
b. business acumen.
c. historical circumstances.
d. any of the above.

____ **8.** Fine Foods, Inc., sells produce, charging different prices to Green Grocery and Hasty Market for the same goods, with the ultimate effect of substantially reducing competition. This is

a. attempted monopolization.
b. monopolization.
c. price discrimination.
d. none of the above.

____ **9.** Micro Corporation and Network, Inc., export computer equipment. They join to compete against foreign associations of sellers of computer equipment. This is a violation of

a. the Clayton Act only.
b. the Sherman Act only.
c. the Clayton Act and the Sherman Act.
d. none of the above.

____ **10.** United Company uses its market power to impose tying arrangements on its customers. Civil sanctions may be sought against United by

a. the Federal Trade Commission only.
b. the U.S. Department of Justice only.
c. United's customers only.
d. the Federal Trade Commission, U.S. Department of Justice, and United's customers.

SHORT ESSAY QUESTIONS

1. What is price discrimination as prohibited by the Clayton Act?

2. Under what circumstances can a private party sue to enforce antitrust laws?

ISSUE SPOTTERS

(Answers at the Back of the Book)

1. Under what circumstances would Pop's Market, a small store in a small, isolated town, be considered a monopolist? If Pop's is a monopolist, is it in violation of Section 2 of the Sherman Act?

2. Games, Inc., develops a series of computer games that, for the first time, incorporate lasers. The firm earns profits that reflect the wide appeal of the games and that eclipse those of other game sellers. For a time, Games is the only seller in the computer-laser game market. Does Games have a monopoly?

3. Sweet Company sells sugar substitutes. Sweet develops methods that cut its costs, allowing it to reduce prices and attract customers away from its competitors. The firm is sued for monopolizing its market, but contends that it has no monopoly power because the relevant market includes sugar *and* sugar substitutes. What will the court say?

Chapter 27
Antitrust and Restraints of Trade

WHAT THIS CHAPTER IS ABOUT

This chapter outlines the aspect of antitrust at which most of the statutes have been directed: anticompetitive agreements between rival firms to fix prices, restrict output, divide markets, exclude other competitors, or otherwise limit competition. The focus of this chapter is on concerted behavior.

CHAPTER OUTLINE

I. OVERVIEW OF RESTRAINTS OF TRADE

A. *PER SE* VIOLATIONS
Agreements that are blatantly anticompetitive are illegal *per se*.

B. RULE OF REASON
If an agreement is not a per se violation, it is subject to the rule of reason, under which a court considers the purpose of an agreement, the power of the parties, the effect of the action on trade, and in some cases, whether there are less restrictive alternatives to achieve the same goals. If the competitive benefits outweigh the anticompetitive effects, the agreement is held lawful.

II. HORIZONTAL RESTRAINTS

These are agreements that restrain competition between rivals in the same market.

A. PRICE FIXING
Any agreement among competitors to fix prices is a *per se* violation.

B. HORIZONTAL MARKET DIVISION
An agreement between competitors to divide up territories or customers is a *per se* violation.

C. TRADE ASSOCIATIONS
These are businesses within the same industry or profession organized to pursue common interests (exchange information, set industry standards, etc.). They are subject to the rule of reason.

D. GROUP BOYCOTTS
An agreement by two or more sellers to refuse to deal with a particular person or firm is a group boycott, and a *per se* violation if it is intended to eliminate competition or prevent entry into a given market.

E. JOINT VENTURES
A joint venture is an undertaking by two or more individuals or firms for a specific purpose. If it does not involve price fixing or market divisions, the agreement will be analyzed under the rule of reason.

III. VERTICAL RESTRAINTS

A restraint of trade that results from an agreement between firms at different levels in the manufacturing and distribution process. (Backward integration moves down the chain of production toward a supplier; forward integration moves up toward the consumer market.)

A. TERRITORIAL OR CUSTOMER RESTRICTIONS
This is an agreement between a manufacturer and a distributor or retailer to restrict sales to certain area or customers. These agreements are judged under the rule of reason.

B. RESALE PRICE MAINTENANCE AGREEMENT
This is an agreement between a manufacturer and a distributor or retailer in which the manufacturer specifies the retail prices of its products. These agreements are judged under a rule of reason.

C. REFUSALS TO DEAL
A firm is free to deal, or not, unilaterally, with whomever it wishes.

D. PRICE DISCRIMINATION
This can occur when a seller charges different prices to competitive buyers for identical goods.

1. Elements
(1) The seller must be engaged in interstate commerce, (2) the effect of the price discrimination must be to substantially lessen competition or create a competitive injury, and (3) a seller's pricing policies must include a reasonable prospect of the seller's recouping its losses.

2. Exception
It is not unlawful for a seller to charge a lower price temporarily and in good faith to meet another seller's equally low price to a buyer's competitor.

E. EXCLUSIONARY PRACTICES

1. Exclusive-Dealing Contracts
This is a contract under which a seller forbids the buyer to buy products from the seller's competitors. It is prohibited if the effect is "to substantially lessen competition or tend to create a monopoly."

2. Tying Arrangements
This occurs when a seller conditions the sale of a product on the buyer's agreement to buy another product produced or distributed by the same seller. Legality depends on the agreement's purpose and its likely effect on competition in the relevant markets.

F. MERGERS
A person or firm cannot hold stock or assets in another firm if the effect may be to substantially lessen competition.

1. Horizontal Mergers
This is a merger between firms that compete with each other in the same market. If it creates an entity with more than a small percentage market share, it is presumed illegal. Factors include market concentration.

a. Market Concentration—FTC/DOJ Guidelines
The Herfindahl-Hirschman Index (HHI) is computed by adding the squares of each of the percentage market shares of firms in the relevant market.

1) Pre-merger HHI Between 1,000 and 1,800
The industry is moderately concentrated, and the merger will be challenged only if it increases the HHI by 100 points or more.

2) Pre-merger HHI Greater than 1,800
The market is highly concentrated; if a merger produces an increase in the HHI between 50 and 100 points, it raises concerns; if more than 100 points, it is likely to enhance market power.

b. **Other Factors**
The relevant market's history of tending toward concentration, ease of entry into that market, economic efficiency, financial condition of the merging firms, nature and price of the products, and so on.

2. **Vertical Mergers**
This occurs when a company at one stage of production acquires a company at a higher or lower stage of production. Legality depends on market concentration, barriers to entry into that market, and the parties' intent.

3. **Conglomerate Mergers**

a. **Market-Extension Merger**
This is when a firm seeks to sell its product in a new market by merging with a firm already established in that market.

b. **Product-Extension Merger**
This is when a firm seeks to add a closely related product to its existing line by merging with a firm already producing that product.

c. **Diversification Merger**
This is when a firm merges with another firm that offers a product or service wholly unrelated to the first firm's existing activities.

TRUE-FALSE QUESTIONS

(Answers at the Back of the Book)

____   1. A horizontal restraint results from an agreement between firms at different levels in the manufacturing and distribution process.

____   2. An agreement that restrains competition between rivals in the same market is a vertical restraint.

____   3. An exclusive dealing contract is a contract under which competitors agree to divide up customers.

____   4. Price discrimination occurs when a seller forbids a buyer to buy products from the seller's competitors.

____   5. A horizontal merger results when a company at one stage of production acquires another company at a higher or lower stage in the chain of production and distribution.

____   6. A merger between firms that compete with each other in the same market is a vertical merger.

____   7. An agreement that is inherently anticompetitive is illegal *per se*.

____   8. An agreement between competitors to fix prices is a *per se* violation.

____   9. A *per se* violation of the Sherman Act is analyzed under the rule of reason.

____   10. Any agreement among competitors to divide up customers is a *per se* violation of the Sherman Act.

FILL-IN QUESTIONS

(Answers at the Back of the Book)

1.   Prices may be controlled by an agreement among competitors to divide their market, or a _____ (horizontal/vertical) market division. A relationship between firms at the same level of operations is a

_____ (horizontal/vertical) relationship. The division _____ (may/must) be geographical _____ (and/or) by class of customer. Such market divisions are considered *per se* violations of the Sherman Act.

2.   Another set of restraints involves those imposed by a seller on a buyer, or vice versa, in what is termed a _____ (horizontal/vertical) relationship. A relationship between firms that encompasses an entire chain of production is a _____ (horizontal/vertical) relationship. A single firm that carries out two or more of the different functional phases in the chain is a _____ (horizontally/vertically) integrated firm. Marketing decisions within such a firm are not subject to attack under the Sherman Act.

MULTIPLE-CHOICE QUESTIONS

(Answers at the Back of the Book)

_____   1.   National Coal Association (NCA) is a group of independent coal mining companies. Demand for coal falls. The price drops. Coal Refiners Association, a group of coal refining companies, agrees to buy NCA's coal and sell it according to a schedule that will increase the price. This agreement is

   a.   a *per se* violation of the Sherman Act.
   b.   exempt from the antitrust laws.
   c.   subject to evaluation under the rule of reason.
   d.   none of the above.

_____   2.   International Sales, Inc. (ISI), is charged with a violation of antitrust law. ISI's conduct is a *per se* violation

   a.   if the anticompetitive harm outweighs the competitive benefits.
   b.   if the competitive benefits outweigh the anticompetitive harm.
   c.   if the conduct is blatantly anticompetitive.
   d.   only if it qualifies as an exemption.

_____   3.   Techno, Inc., sells its brand-name computer equipment directly to its franchised retailers. Depending on how existing franchisees do, Techno may limit the number of franchisees in a given area to reduce intrabrand competition. Techno's restrictions on the number of dealers is

   a.   a *per se* violation of the Sherman Act.
   b.   exempt from the antitrust laws.
   c.   subject to evaluation under the rule of reason.
   d.   none of the above.

_____   4.   Gamma Corporation is charged with a violation of antitrust law that requires evaluation under the rule of reason. The court will consider

   a.   only the effect of the conduct on trade.
   b.   only the power of the parties to accomplish what they intend.
   c.   only the purpose of the conduct.
   d.   the effect of the conduct, the power of the parties, and the purpose of the conduct.

_____   5.   Handy Tools, Inc., charges Irma's Home Store five cents per item and Jack's Hardware ten cents per item for the same product. The two stores are competitors. If this substantially lessens competition, it constitutes

   a.   a market division.
   b.   an exclusionary practice.
   c.   price discrimination.
   d.   none of the above.

____ 6. Standard Company is charged with a violation of antitrust law subject to evaluation under the rule of reason. Standard's conduct is unlawful

   a. if the anticompetitive harm outweighs the competitive benefits.
   b. if the competitive benefits outweigh the anticompetitive harm.
   c. if the conduct is blatantly anticompetitive.
   d. only if it qualifies as an exemption.

____ 7. Alpha, Inc., and Beta Corporation are competitors. They merge, and after the merger, Alpha is the surviving firm. To assess whether this is in violation of the Clayton Act requires a look at

   a. market concentration.
   b. market division.
   c. market power.
   d. none of the above.

____ 8. Cable, Inc., manufactures DVD players and sells them to ElectriCity and other retailers. ElectriCity agrees with Cable to sell the players at a certain price. This agreement is

   a. a *per se* violation of the Sherman Act.
   b. exempt from the antitrust laws.
   c. subject to evaluation under the rule of reason.
   d. none of the above.

____ 9. Rally, Inc., and Sport Corporation are competitors. They merge, after which Sport is the surviving firm. To assess whether the merger is in violation of the Clayton Act requires a determination of the percentage of the firms' market share. Determining market share requires consideration of

   a. Sport's financial condition only.
   b. the nature and prices of Rally's products only.
   c. the ease of all competitors' entry into the relevant market only.
   d. the financial condition of both firms, the nature and prices of their products, and the ease of competitors' entry into the relevant market.

____ 10. Office Systems, Inc., sells computerized business systems under contracts that prohibit Office's buyers from purchasing supplemental or separate systems from Office's competitors. These contracts are

   a. a *per se* violation of the Sherman Act.
   b. exempt from the antitrust laws.
   c. subject to evaluation under the rule of reason.
   d. none of the above.

SHORT ESSAY QUESTIONS

1. How are horizontal restraints (price fixing, horizontal market divisions, trade associations, group boycotts, joint ventures) dealt with under the Sherman Act?

2. How are exclusive dealing contracts and tying arrangements dealt with under the Clayton Act?

ISSUE SPOTTERS

(Answers at the Back of the Book)

1. Wheels Company, a bicycle manufacturer, refuses to deal with Xtreme Bikes, a retailer. In what circumstances might Wheels's refusal to deal with Xtreme violate antitrust law?

2.   Able, Inc., Baker Corporation, and Charlie Company compete against each other in Illinois, Indiana, and Ohio. To reduce marketing costs, they agree that Able will sell products only in Illinois, Baker only in Indiana, and Charlie only in Ohio. This allows each firm to raise the price of the goods in its state and increase profits. Is this a violation of antitrust law? If so, is it a *per se* violation or is it subject to evaluation under the rule of reason?

3.   Maple Corporation conditions the sale of its syrup on the buyer's agreement to buy Maple's pancake mix. What factors would a court consider to decide whether this arrangement violates the Clayton Act?

Chapter 28
Investor Protection and Online Securities Offerings

WHAT THIS CHAPTER IS ABOUT

The general purpose of securities laws is to provide sufficient, accurate information to investors to enable them to make informed buying and selling decisions about securities. This chapter provides an outline of federal securities laws.

CHAPTER OUTLINE

I. THE SECURITIES AND EXCHANGE COMMISSION (SEC)

The SEC administers the federal securities laws and regulates the sale and purchase of securities.

A. THE SEC'S BASIC FUNCTIONS

1. Require disclosure of facts concerning offerings of certain securities.

2. Regulate national securities trading.

3. Investigate securities fraud.

4. Regulate securities brokers, dealers, and investment advisers.

5. Supervise mutual funds.

6. Recommend sanctions in cases involving violations of securities laws. (The U.S. Department of Justice prosecutes violations.)

B. THE SEC'S EXPANDING REGULATORY POWERS

The SEC's powers include the power to seek sanctions against those who violate foreign securities laws; to suspend trading if prices rise and fall in short periods of time; to exempt persons, securities, and transactions from securities law requirements; and to require more corporate disclosure.

II. SARBANES-OXLEY ACT OF 2002

Imposes strict disclosure requirements and harsh penalties for violations of securities laws.

A. RESPONSIBLE PARTIES

Chief corporate executives (CEOs and CFOs) are responsible for the accuracy and completeness of financial statements and reports filed with the SEC [Sections 302 and 906]. Penalties for knowingly certifying a report or statement that does not meet statutory requirements include up to $1 million in fines and ten years imprisonment ($5 million and twenty years for "willful" certification). Altering or destroying documents is also subject to fines and imprisonment.

B. PUBLIC COMPANY ACCOUNTING OVERSIGHT BOARD

The SEC oversees this entity, which regulates and oversees public accounting firms (see Chapter 52).

C. LIMITATIONS ON PRIVATE ACTIONS

A private action for securities fraud must be brought within two years of the discovery of the violation or five years after the violation, whichever is earlier [Section 804].

III. SECURITIES ACT OF 1933

Requires that all essential information concerning the issuance (sales) of new securities be disclosed to investors.

A. WHAT IS A SECURITY?

1. Courts' Interpretation of the Securities Act

A security exists in any transaction in which a person (1) invests (2) in a common enterprise (3) reasonably expecting profits (4) derived *primarily* or *substantially* from others' managerial or entrepreneurial efforts.

2. A Security Is an Investment

Examples: stocks, bonds, investment contracts in condominiums, franchises, limited partnerships, and oil or gas or other mineral rights.

B. REGISTRATION STATEMENT

Before offering securities for sale, issuing corporations must (1) file a registration statement with the Securities and Exchange Commission (SEC) and (2) provide investors with a prospectus that describes the security being sold, the issuing corporation, and the investment or risk.

1. Contents of a Registration Statement

a. Description of the significant provisions of the security and how the registrant intends to use the proceeds of the sale.

b. Description of the registrant's properties and business.

c. Description of the management of the registrant; its security holdings; its remuneration and other benefits, including pensions and stock options; and any interests of directors or officers in any material transactions with the corporation.

d. Financial statement certified by an independent public accountant.

e. Description of pending lawsuits.

2. Twenty-Day Waiting Period after Registration

Securities cannot be sold for twenty days (oral offers can be made).

3. Advertising

During the waiting period, very limited written advertising is allowed. After the period, no written advertising unaccompanied by a prospectus is allowed, except a tombstone ad, which simply tells how to obtain a prospectus.

C. EXEMPT SECURITIES

Securities that can be sold (and resold) without being registered include—

1. Small Offerings under Regulation A

An issuer's offer of up to $5 million in securities in any twelve-month period (including up to $1.5 million in nonissuer resales) is exempt. The issuer must file with the SEC a notice of the issue and an offering circular (also provided to investors before the sale). A company can *test the waters* (determine potential interest) before preparing the circular.

2. Other Exempt Securities

a. All bank securities sold prior to July 27, 1933.

b. Commercial paper if maturity does not exceed nine months.

c. Securities of charitable organizations.

d. Securities resulting from a reorganization issued in exchange for the issuer's existing securities and certificates issued by trustees, receivers, or debtors in possession in bankruptcy (see Chapter 30).

e. Securities issued exclusively in exchange for the issuer's existing securities, provided no commission is paid (such as stock splits).

f. Securities issued to finance the acquisition of railroad equipment.

g. Any insurance, endowment, or annuity contract issued by a state-regulated insurance company.

h. Government-issued securities.

i. Securities issued by banks, savings and loan associations, farmers' cooperatives, and similar institutions.

D. EXEMPT TRANSACTIONS
Securities that can be sold without being registered include those sold in transactions that consist of—

1. **Small Offerings under Regulation D**
    Offers that involve a small amount of money or are not made publicly.

    a. **Offerings Up to $1 Million**
        Noninvestment company offerings up to $1 million in a twelve-month period [Rule 504].

    b. **Blank-Check Company Offerings Up to $500,000**
        Offerings up to $500,000 in any one year by companies with no specific business plans are exempt if (1) no general solicitation or advertising is used, (2) the SEC is notified of the sales, and (3) precaution is taken against nonexempt, unregistered resales [Rule 504a].

    c. **Offerings Up to $5 Million**
        Private, noninvestment company offerings up to $5 million in a twelve-month period if (1) no general solicitation or advertising is used; (2) the SEC is notified of the sales; (3) precaution is taken against nonexempt, unregistered resales; and (4) there are no more than thirty-five unaccredited investors. If the sale involves any unaccredited investors, all investors must be given material information about the company, its business, the securities [Rule 505].

    d. **Private Offerings in Unlimited Amounts**
        Essentially the same requirements as Rule 505, except (1) there is no limit on the amount of the offering and (2) the issuer must believe that each unaccredited investor has sufficient knowledge or experience to evaluate the investment [Rule 506].

    e. **Offerings to Qualified Purchasers**
        Offerings up to $5 million per transaction to qualified purchasers (wealthy, sophisticated investors) only [Rule 1001].

2. **Small Offerings to Accredited Investors Only**
    An offer up to $5 million is exempt if (1) no general solicitation or advertising is used; (2) the SEC is notified of the sales; (3) precaution is taken against nonexempt, unregistered resales; and (4) there are no unaccredited investors [Section 4(6)].

3. **Intrastate Issues**
    Offerings in the state in which the issuer is organized and doing business are exempt [Rule 147] if, for nine months after the sale, no resale is made to a nonresident.

4. **Resales ("Safe Harbors")**

   Most securities can be resold without registration. Resales of blank-check company offerings [Rule 504a], small offerings [Rule 505], private offerings [Rule 506], and offers to accredited investors only [Section 4(6)] are exempt from registration if—

   a. **The Securities Have Been Owned for Two Years or More**

      If seller is not an **affiliate** (in control with the issuer) [Rule 144].

   b. **The Securities Have Been Owned for at Least One Year**

      There must be adequate public information about the issuer, the securities must be sold in limited amounts in unsolicited brokers' transactions, and the SEC must be notified of the resale [Rule 144].

   c. **The Securities Are Sold Only to an Institutional Investor**

      The securities, on issue, must not have been of the same class as securities listed on a national securities exchange or a U.S. automated interdealer quotation system, and the seller on resale must take steps to tell the buyer they are exempt [Rule 144A].

E. **VIOLATIONS OF THE 1933 ACT**

   If registration statement or prospectus contains material false statements or omissions, liable parties include anyone who signed the statement.

   1. **Defenses**

      Statement or omission was not material; plaintiff knew of misrepresentation and bought stock anyway; *due diligence* (Chapter 52).

   2. **Penalties**

      Fines up to $10,000; imprisonment up to five years; injunction against selling securities; order to refund profits; damages in civil suits.

IV. SECURITIES EXCHANGE ACT OF 1934

Regulates the markets in which securities are traded by requiring disclosure by Section 12 companies (corporations with securities on the exchanges and firms with assets in excess of $10 million and five hundred or more shareholders).

A. **INSIDER TRADING—SECTION 10(b) AND SEC RULE 10b-5**

   Section 10(b) proscribes the use of "any manipulative or deceptive device or contrivance in contravention of such rules and regulations as the [SEC] may prescribe." Rule 10b-5 prohibits the commission of fraud in connection with the purchase or sale of any security (registered or unregistered).

   1. **What Triggers Liability**

      Any material omission or misrepresentation of material facts in connection with the purchase or sale of any security can trigger liability.

   2. **What Does Not Trigger Liability**

      Under the Private Securities Litigation Reform Act of 1995, financial forecasts and other forward-looking statements do not trigger liability if they include "meaningful cautionary statements identifying factors that could cause actual results to differ materially."

   3. **Who Can Be Liable**

      Those who take advantage of inside information when they know that it is unavailable to the person with whom they are dealing can be liable.

      a. **Insiders**

         These include officers, directors, majority shareholders, and persons having access to or receiving information of a nonpublic nature on which trading is based (accountants, attorneys).

b. Outsiders

1) Tipper/Tippee Theory
One who acquires inside information as a result of an insider's breach of fiduciary duty to the firm whose shares are traded can be liable, if he or she knows or should know of the breach.

2) Misappropriation Theory
One who wrongfully obtains inside information and trades on it to his or her gain can be liable, if a duty to the lawful possessor of information was violated and harm to another results.

B. INSIDER REPORTING AND TRADING—SECTION 16(b)
Officers, directors, and shareholders owning 10 percent of the securities registered under Section 12 are required to file reports with the SEC concerning their ownership and trading of the securities.

1. Corporation Is Entitled to All Profits
A firm can recapture *all* profits realized by an insider on *any* purchase and sale or sale and purchase of its stock in any six-month period.

2. Applicability of Section 16(b)
Section 16(b) applies to stock, warrants, options, and securities convertible into stock.

C. PROXY STATEMENTS—SECTION 14(A)
Section 14(a) regulates the solicitation of proxies from shareholders of Section 12 companies. Whoever solicits a proxy must disclose, in the proxy statement, all of the pertinent facts.

D. VIOLATIONS OF THE 1934 ACT

1. Criminal Penalties
Maximum jail term is twenty-five years; fines up to $5 million for individuals and $2.5 million for partnerships and corporations.

2. Civil Sanctions

a. Insider Trading Sanctions Act of 1984
SEC can bring suit in federal court against anyone violating or aiding in a violation of the 1934 act or SEC rules. Penalties include triple the profits gained or the loss avoided by the guilty party.

b. Insider Trading and Securities Fraud Enforcement Act of 1988
Enlarged the class of persons subject to civil liability for insider-trading violations, increased criminal penalties, and gave the SEC authority to (1) reward persons providing information and (2) make rules to prevent insider trading.

V. REGULATION OF INVESTMENT COMPANIES
The SEC regulates investment companies and mutual funds under the Investment Company Act of 1940, the Investment Company Act Amendments of 1970, the Securities Act Amendments of 1975, and later amendments.

A. WHAT AN INVESTMENT COMPANY IS
Any entity that (1) is engaged primarily "in the business of investing, reinvesting, or trading in securities" or (2) is engaged in such business and has more than 40 percent of the company's assets in investment securities. (Does not include banks, finance companies, and others).

B. WHAT AN INVESTMENT COMPANY MUST DO
Register with the SEC by filing a notification of registration and, each year, file reports with the SEC. All securities must be in the custody of a bank or stock exchange member.

C. WHAT AN INVESTMENT COMPANY CANNOT DO

No dividends may be paid from any source other than accumulated, undistributed net income. There are restrictions on investment activities.

VI. STATE SECURITIES LAWS

All states regulate the offer and sale of securities within individual state borders. Exemptions from federal law are not exemptions from state laws, which have their own exemptions. Under the National Market Securities Improvement Act of 1996, the SEC regulates most national securities activities.

VII. ONLINE SECURITIES OFFERINGS AND DISCLOSURES

Federal and state laws set out the requirements for online initial public offerings. Under SEC interpretations, there is no difference in the disclosure requirements, only in the medium of disclosure, for which there may be new avenues of liability. Also, an online prospectus may not qualify for a Regulation D exemption.

VIII. ONLINE SECURITIES FRAUD

Issues include the use of chat rooms to affect the price of securities, fictitious press releases, and illegal offerings. The First Amendment protects the use of chat rooms. Also, there is a distinction between statements of fact and opinion.

TRUE-FALSE QUESTIONS

(Answers at the Back of the Book)

_____ 1. A security that does not qualify for an exemption must be registered before it is offered to the public.

_____ 2. Before a security can be sold to the public, prospective investors must be provided with a prospectus.

_____ 3. Stock splits are exempt from the registration requirements of the Securities Act of 1933, if no commission is paid.

_____ 4. Sales of securities may not occur until twenty days after registration.

_____ 5. Private offerings of securities in unlimited amounts that are not generally solicited or advertised must be registered before they can be sold.

_____ 6. A proxy statement must fully and accurately disclose all of the facts that are pertinent to the matter on which shareholders are being asked to vote.

_____ 7. All states have disclosure requirements and antifraud provisions that cover securities.

_____ 8. _Scienter_ is not a requirement for liability under Section 10(b) of the Securities Exchange Act of 1934.

_____ 9. No one who receives inside information as a result of another's breach of his or her fiduciary duty can be liable under SEC Rule 10b-5.

_____ 10. No security can be resold without registration.

FILL-IN QUESTIONS

(Answers at the Back of the Book)

The SEC can award "bounty" payments to persons providing information leading to the _____ (conviction/prosecution) of insider-trading violations. Civil penalties include _____ (double/triple) the profits gained or the loss avoided. Criminal penalties include maximum jail terms of _____ (ten/ twenty-five) years. Violators _____ (may/may not) also be subject to multi-million-dollar fines.

MULTIPLE-CHOICE QUESTIONS

(Answers at the Back of the Book)

___ 1. Under the Securities Exchange Act of 1934, the Securities and Exchange Commission is responsible for all of the following activities EXCEPT

a. investigating securities fraud.
b. prosecuting criminal violations of federal securities laws.
c. regulating the activities of securities brokers.
d. requiring disclosure of facts concerning offerings of securities listed on national securities exchanges.

___ 2. Beth, a director of Alpha Company, learns that an Alpha engineer has developed a new, improved product. Over the next six months, Beth buys and sells Alpha stock for a profit. Of Beth's profit, Alpha may recapture

a. all of it.
b. half of it.
c. 10 percent of it.
d. none of it.

___ 3. Central Brokerage Associates sells securities. The definition of a security does *not* include, as an element,

a. an investment.
b. a common enterprise.
c. a reasonable expectation of profits.
d. profits derived entirely from the efforts of the investor.

___ 4. Superior, Inc., is a private, noninvestment company. In one year, Superior advertises a $300,000 offering. Concerning registration, this offering is

a. exempt because of the low amount of the issue.
b. exempt because it was advertised.
c. exempt because the issuer is a private company.
d. not exempt.

___ 5. Huron, Inc., makes a $6 million private offering to twenty accredited investors and less than thirty unaccredited investors. Huron advertises the offering and believes that the unaccredited investors are sophisticated enough to evaluate the investment. Huron gives material information about itself, its business, and the securities to all investors. Concerning registration, this offering is

a. exempt because of the low amount of the issue.
b. exempt because it was advertised.
c. exempt because the issuer believed that the unaccredited investors were sophisticated enough to evaluate the investment.
d. not exempt.

___ 6. Ontario, Inc., in one year, advertises two $2.25 million offerings. Buying the stock are twelve accredited investors. Concerning registration, this offering is

a. exempt because of the low amount of the issue.
b. exempt because it was advertised.
c. exempt because only accredited investors bought stock.
d. not exempt.

___ 7. Omega Corporation's registration statement must include

a. a description of the accounting firm that audits Omega.
b. a description of the security being offered for sale.
c. a financial forecast for Omega's next five years.
d. all of the above.

___ 8. Frank, an officer of Gamma, Inc., learns that Gamma has developed a new source of energy. Frank tells Gail, an outsider. They each buy Gamma stock. When the development is announced, the stock price increases, and they each immediately sell their stock. Subject to liability for insider trading is

a. Frank only.
b. Gail only
c. Frank and Gail.
d. none of the above.

___ 9. National Sales, Inc., wants to make an offering of securities to the public. The offer is not exempt from registration. Before National sells these securities, it must provide investors with

a. a prospectus.
b. a registration statement.
c. a tombstone ad.
d. none of the above.

___ 10. Great Lakes Company is a private, noninvestment company. Last year, as part of a $250,000 advertised offering, Great Lakes sold stock to John, a private investor. John would now like to sell the shares. Concerning registration, this resale is

a. exempt because of the low amount of the original issue.
b. exempt because the offering was advertised.
c. exempt because all resales are exempt.
d. not exempt.

SHORT ESSAY QUESTIONS

1. What is the process by which a company sells securities to the public?

2. How is insider trading regulated by Section 10(b), SEC Rule 10b-5, and Section 16(b)?

ISSUE SPOTTERS

(Answers at the Back of the Book)

1. When a corporation wishes to issue certain securities, it must provide sufficient information for an unsophisticated investor to evaluate the financial risk involved. Specifically, the law imposes liability for making a false statement or omission that is "material." What sort of information would an investor consider material?

2. Lee is an officer of Macro Oil, Inc. Lee knows that a Macro geologist has just discovered a new deposit of oil. Can Lee take advantage of this information to buy and sell Macro stock?

3. The Securities Act of 1933, the Securities Exchange Act of 1934, and other securities regulation is federal law. In-State Corporation incorporated in one state, does business exclusively in that state, and offers its securities for sale only in that state. Are there securities laws to regulate this offering?

CUMULATIVE HYPOTHETICAL PROBLEM FOR UNIT SIX—INCLUDING CHAPTERS 23–28

(Answers at the Back of the Book)

Beta Chemical Corporation manufactures and sells chemical products to industrial customers and individual consumers.

____ 1. Beta advertises its products with slogans that consist of vague generalities. Because of this advertising, the Federal Trade Commission may

a. issue a cease-and-desist order only.
b. require counteradvertising only.
c. issue a cease-and-desist order or require counteradvertising.
d. none of the above.

____ 2. To determine whether Beta is violating regulations issued by the Environmental Protection Agency (EPA), the EPA may NOT

a. arbitrarily order Beta to shut its manufacturing site down.
b. conduct an on-site inspection of Beta's manufacturing site.
c. test Beta's products on its manufacturing site.
d. none of the above.

____ 3. Beta's manufacturing process generates hazardous waste that is transported to Gamma Company's disposal site by Omega Trucking, Inc. If the EPA cleans up Gamma's site, liability for the cost may be assessed against

a. Beta or Gamma only.
b. Gamma or Omega only.
c. Beta or Omega only.
d. Beta, Gamma, or Omega.

____ 4. Beta charges National Refining, Inc., less per item than Beta charges International Export Corporation for the same product. The two industrial buyers are competitors. This pricing difference violates antitrust law

a. if both buyers' customers pay the same price for the buyers' products.
b. if National and International know what each other pays.
c. if the pricing substantially lessens competition.
d. under no circumstances.

____ 5. The Beta board of directors decides to issue additional stock in the firm. The registration statement must include

a. a copy of the corporation's most recent proxy statement.
b. the names of prospective accredited investors.
c. the names of the current shareholders.
d. the principal purposes for which the proceeds from the offering will be used.

QUESTIONS ON THE FOCUS ON LEGAL REASONING FOR UNIT SIX— *IN RE MILLER*

(Answers at the Back of the Book)

____ 1. Alan, a broker, commits securities fraud. According to the majority in *In re Miller*, to impute liability for the fraud under Section 20 of the Securities Exchange Act of 1934 on Alan's supervisor Ben and their employer Carol requires a finding of

   a. agency.
   b. bankruptcy.
   c. partnership.
   d. none of the above.

____ 2. Under the facts in the previous question, according to the dissent in *In re Miller*, to impute liability for the fraud under Section 20 of the Securities Exchange Act of 1934 on Ben and Carol requires a finding of

   a. agency.
   b. bankruptcy.
   c. partnership.
   d. none of the above.

____ 3. In the previous questions, suppose that liability for Alan's act is imputed under Section 20 on Ben and Carol, both of whom file for bankruptcy. In the opinion of the majority in *In re Miller*, a discharge of the debt represented by this liability could be obtained by

   a. Ben only.
   b. Carol only.
   c. Ben and Carol.
   d. neither Ben nor Carol.

QUESTIONS ON THE FOCUS ON ETHICS FOR UNIT SIX— THE REGULATORY ENVIRONMENT

(Answers at the Back of the Book)

____ 1. The U.S. Fish and Wildlife Service (FWS) prohibits Victor from harvesting the timber on fifty acres of his land until it is clear that the timber is not a habitat for an endangered species. Victor files a suit against the FWS. The court is most likely to hold that this is

   a. a compensatory "taking."
   b. a "taking" but not compensatory.
   c. compensatory but not a "taking."
   d. not a compensatory "taking."

____ 2. Ann owes a debt to Best Products, Inc. In an attempt to collect, Best contacts Ann's spouse Carl at his workplace. Under the Fair Debt Collection Practices Act, this contact is

   a. permitted because Best is the creditor.
   b. permitted because Carl is Ann's spouse.
   c. prohibited because Best is the creditor.
   d. prohibited because Carl is Ann's spouse.

_____ **3.** Dave is a professional athlete. Not subject to the antitrust laws to the same extent as other professional sports is

a. baseball.
b. basketball.
c. football.
d. soccer.

Answers

Chapter 1

True-False Questions

1. T
2. F. Legal positivists believe that there can be no higher law that a nation's positive law (the law created by a particular society at a particular point in time). The belief that law should reflect universal moral and ethical principles that are part of human nature is part of the natural law tradition.
3. T
4. T
5. T
6. F. Each state's constitution is supreme within each state's borders, so long as it does not conflict with the U.S. Constitution.
7. F. The National Conference of Commissioners on Uniform State Laws drafted the Uniform Commercial Code (and other uniform laws and model codes) and proposed it for adoption by the states.
8. F. This is the definition of civil law. Criminal law relates to wrongs against society as a whole and for which society has established sanctions.
9. T
10. F. A citation may contain the names of the parties, the year in which the case was decided, and the volume and page numbers of a reporter in which the opinion may be found, but it does not include the name of the judge who decided the case.

Fill-in Questions

with similar facts; precedent; permits a predictable

Multiple-Choice Questions

1. D. Legal positivists believe that there can be no higher law than the written law of a given society at a particular time. They do not believe in "natural rights."
2. B. The use of precedent—the doctrine of *stare decisis*—permits a predictable, relatively quick, and fair resolution of cases. Under this doctrine, a court must adhere to principles of law established by higher courts.
3. D. The doctrine of *stare decisis* attempts to harmonize the results in cases with similar facts. When the facts are sufficiently similar, the same rule is applied. Cases with identical facts could serve as binding authority, but it is more practical to expect to find cases with facts that are not identical but similar—as similar as possible.
4. A. An order to do or refrain from a certain act is an injunction. An order to perform as promised is a decree for specific performance. These remedies, as

well as rescission, are equitable remedies. An award of damages is a remedy at law.

5. D. Equity and law provide different remedies, and at one time, most courts could grant only one type. Today, most states do not maintain separate courts of law and equity, and a judge may grant either or both forms of relief. Equitable relief is generally granted, however, only if damages (the legal remedy) is inadequate.

6. C. The U.S. Constitution is the supreme law of the land. Any state or federal law or court decision in conflict with the Constitution is unenforceable and will be struck. Similarly, provisions in a state constitution take precedence over the state's statutes, rules, and court decisions.

7. C. In establishing case law, or common law, the courts interpret and apply state and federal constitutions, rules, and statutes. Case law applies in areas that statutes or rules do not cover. Federal law applies to all states, and preempts state law in many areas.

8. A. This is a definition of civil law. As for the other answer choices, law that defines, describes, regulates, or creates rights or duties is substantive la w. Law that establishes methods for enforcing rights established by substantive law is procedural law. Criminal law governs wrongs committed against society for which society demands redress.

9. A. In reasoning by analogy, a judge compares the facts in one case to the facts in another case and to the extent that the facts are similar, applies the same legal principle. If the facts can be distinguished, different legal rules may apply. In either case, a judge will ordinarily state his or her reasons for applying a certain principle and arriving at a certain conclusion.

10. C. A concurring opinion makes or emphasizes a point different from those made or emphasized in the majority's opinion. An opinion written for the entire court is a unanimous opinion. An opinion that outlines only the majority's views is a majority opinion. A separate opinion that does not agree with the majority's decision is a dissenting opinion.

Issue Spotters

1. Case law includes courts' interpretations of statutes, as well as constitutional provisions and administrative rules. Statutes often codify common law rules. For these reasons, a judge might rely on the common law as a guide to the intent and purpose of a statute.

2. No. The U.S. Constitution is the supreme law of the land, and applies to all jurisdictions. A law in violation of the Constitution (in this question, the First Amendment to the Constitution) will be declared unconstitutional.

3. A case citation includes the names of the parties, the year in which the case was decided, and the volume and page number of at least one reporter in which the opinion may be found. A citation always indicates the court in which the case was decided, but does not include the name of the judge or judges who decided it.

Chapter 2

True-False Questions

1. T
2. T
3. F. The decisions of a state's highest court on all questions of state law are final. The United States Supreme Court can overrule only those state court decisions that involve questions of federal law.
4. T
5. T
6. F. Pleadings inform each party of the other's claims and specify the issues. Pleadings consist of a complaint and an answer, not a motion to dismiss.
7. F. In ruling on a motion for summary judgment, a court can consider evidence outside the pleadings, such as answers to interrogatories.
8. T
9. F. A losing party may appeal an adverse judgment to a higher court, but the party in whose favor the judgment was issued may also appeal if, for example, he or she is awarded less than sought in the suit.
10. T

Fill-in Questions

trial; reviewing; factual issues; the law to the facts; of law but not of fact

Multiple-Choice Questions

1. A. On a "sliding scale" test, a court's exercise of personal jurisdiction depends on the amount of business that an individual or firm transacts over the Internet. Jurisdiction is most likely proper when there is substantial business, most likely improper when a Web site is no more than an ad, and may or may not be appropriate when there is some interactivity. "Any" interactivity with "any resident" of a state would likely not be enough, however.
2. C. A corporation is subject to the jurisdiction of the courts in any state in which it is incorporated, in which it has its main office, or in which it does business. In the suit in this question, the court may exercise *in rem* jurisdiction.
3. A. As noted above, a corporation is subject to the jurisdiction of the courts in any state in which it is incorporated, in which it has its main office, or in which it does business. The court may be able to exercise personal jurisdiction or *in rem* jurisdiction, or the court

may reach a defendant corporation with a long arm statute. In the right circumstances, this firm might also be involved in a suit in a federal court, if the requirements for federal jurisdiction are met.

4. A. An appellate court examines the record of a case, looking mostly at questions of law for errors by the court below. If it determines that a retrial is necessary, the case is sent back to the lower court. For this reason, an appellant's best ground for an appeal focuses on the law that applied to the issues in the case, not questions concerning the credibility of the evidence.

5. D. The United States Supreme Court is not required to hear any case. The Court has jurisdiction over any case decided by any of the federal courts of appeals and appellate authority over cases decided by the states' highest courts if the latter involve questions of federal law. But the Court's exercise of its jurisdiction is discretionary, not mandatory.

6. A. Every state has at least one court of appeals, which may be an intermediate appellate court or the state's highest court. If a federal or constitutional issue is involved, the case may ultimately be appealed to the United States Supreme Court.

7. B. If a motion to dismiss is filed before a defendant answers a complaint and the motion is granted, the case is at an end. If the motion is denied, the defendant must file an answer, or a default judgment will be entered against him or her.

8. A. An important part of the discovery process is a deposition, which is sworn testimony. Interrogatories are a series of written questions for which written answers are prepared and signed under oath by the plaintiff or defendant. A pretrial conference involves the plaintiff, the defendant, their attorneys, and judge.

9. D. After a plaintiff calls and questions the first witness on direct examination, the defendant questions the witness on cross-examination. The plaintiff may then question the witness again (redirect examination), and the defendant may follow (recross-examination). Then the plaintiff's other witnesses are called, and the defendant presents his or her case.

10. C. After a verdict, the losing party can move for a new trial or for a judgment notwithstanding the verdict (also known as a judgment *non obstante veredicto* or a judgment *n.o.v.*). If these motions are denied, he or she can appeal.

Issue Spotters

1. Before a court will hear a case, it must be established that the court has subject matter and personal jurisdiction and that the matter at issue is justiciable. The party bringing the suit must also have standing to sue.

2. Yes. Whenever a suit involves citizens of different states, diversity of citizenship exists, and the suit can be brought in a federal court. In diversity of citizen-ship suits, Congress has set an additional requirement—the amount in controversy must be more than $75,000.

3. Yes. There is no absolute right of appeal to the United States Supreme Court. A party may ask the Supreme Court to issue a writ of *certiorari* (an order to a lower court to send the Court the record of the case for review), but the Court may deny the request.

Chapter 3

True-False Questions

1. F. Most lawsuits—as many as 95 percent—are dismissed or settled before they go to trial. Courts encourage alternative dispute resolution (ADR) and sometimes order parties to submit to ADR, particularly mediation, before allowing their suits to come to trial.

2. F. In mediation, a mediator assists the parties in reaching an agreement, but not by deciding the dispute. The mediator emphasizes points of agreement, helps the parties evaluate their positions, and proposes solutions.

3. F. If an arbitration agreement covers the subject matter of a dispute, a party to the agreement can be compelled to arbitrate the dispute. A court would order the arbitration without ruling on the basic controversy.

4. F. The jury verdict after a summary jury trial (SJT) is not binding. SJT is a form of alternative dispute resolution in which the parties' attorneys present their cases to a jury, but no witnesses are called, and the verdict is advisory only.

5. F. Negotiation typically does not involve a third party. The major difference between negotiation and mediation is that mediation does involve the presence of a third party—a mediator—who assists the parties in reaching an agreement and who often suggests solutions towards that end.

6. T

7. F. In court-annexed arbitration, either party may reject an award, and the case will go to trial, with the court reconsidering all evidence and legal questions as though no arbitration occurred.

8. F. The goal of *mediation* is to come to a resolution that benefits both sides in a dispute. This is one of the advantages of mediation and has contributed to its increasing popularity as a form of dispute resolution.

9. T

10. T

Fill-in Questions

Negotiation; Mediation; a mediator; Arbitration; an arbitrator

Multiple-Choice Questions

1. D. Negotiation is an informal means of dispute resolution. Generally, unlike mediation and arbitration, no third party is involved in resolving the dispute. In those two forms, a third party may render a binding or nonbinding decision. Arbitration is a more formal process than mediation or negotiation. Litigation involves a third party—a judge—who renders a legally binding decision.

2. B. In a summary jury trial, the jury's verdict is not binding, as it would otherwise be in a court trial. In a mini-trial, the attorneys argue a case and a third party renders an opinion, but the opinion discusses how a court would decide the dispute. Early neutral case negotiation is what its name suggests, involving a third party who evaluates the disputing parties' positions.

3. D. Online dispute resolution (ODR) is a new type of alternative dispute resolution. Most ODR forums resolve disputers informally and come to nonbonding resolutions. Any party to a dispute being considered in ODR may discontinue the process and appeal to a court at any time.

4. D. Neither the amount involved nor the parties' satisfaction is relevant. An arbitrator's award will be set aside if it violates pubic policy. Other grounds on which an award may be set aside arise from the arbitrator's conduct—for example, if his or her bad faith substantially prejudices the rights of one of the parties, or if he or she decides issues that the parties did not agree to submit to arbitration.

5. C. In mediation, no sanction can be imposed that the parties have not agreed to. Also, in mediation the neutral third party (the mediator) does not decide the controversy, and there is no deadline to resolving the dispute. The goal of mediation is to come to a resolution that benefits both parties.

6. A. A mini-trial is not a public proceeding held in a court. It is a private proceeding in which attorneys briefly argue each party's case. A third party indicates how a court would likely decide the issue.

7. A. A summary jury trial can look like a regular jury trial. The basic difference between a traditional trial and a summary jury trial is that in the latter the verdict is advisory only. It is required that after the verdict in a summary jury trial, the parties attempt to negotiate a resolution of their dispute.

8. C. There are certain disputes that, in most states, are not submitted to arbitration by the courts. In most states, court-annexed arbitration is available only when a dispute does *not* involve title to real estate and a court's equity powers are *not* involved. Also, court-annexed arbitration is usually available only if one of the parties has demanded a jury trial.

9. D. Many parties prefer arbitration over litigation. The advantages of arbitration include lower cost than traditional litigation, the speed with which a dispute can be resolved compared to litigation, and the possi-

bility of less formal rules and less rigid proceedings than court trials.

10. D. Mediation is becoming the most popular form of ADR, with participants reporting high rates of satisfaction with the results. The advantages of mediation include lower cost than either arbitration or traditional litigation, the speed with which a dispute can be resolved compared to arbitration or litigation, and resolutions that benefit both sides to a dispute.

Issue Spotters

1. Unlike litigation, negotiation involves no third parties.

2. The rules are likely to be less restrictive because the arbitrator is an expert in the subject matter involved and there is less fear that she will be swayed by improper evidence.

3. Yes. State-mandated alternative dispute resolution proceedings usually concern disputes that involve less than a specific amount of money. Submission of the dispute is mandatory, but compliance with a decision is voluntary.

Chapter 4

True-False Questions

1. T

2. T

3. T

4. F. According to utilitarianism, it is the consequences of an act that determine how ethical the act is. Applying this theory requires determining who will be affected by an act, assessing the positive and negatives effects of alternatives, and choosing the alternative that will provide the greatest benefit for the most people. Utilitarianism is premised on acting so as to do the greatest good for the greatest number of people. An act that affects a minority negatively may still be morally acceptable.

5. T

6. F. In situations involving ethical decisions, a balance must sometimes be struck between equally good or equally poor courses of action. The choice is often between equally good alternatives—benefiting shareholders versus benefiting employees, for example—and sometimes one group may be adversely affected. (The legality of a particular action may also be unclear.)

7. T

8. F. Simply obeying the law will not meet all ethical obligations. The law does not cover all ethical requirements. An act may be unethical but not illegal. In fact, compliance with the law is at best a moral minimum. Furthermore, there is an ethical aspect to almost every decision that a business firm makes.

9. T

10. F. Bribery is also a legal issue, regulated in the United States by the Foreign Corrupt Practices Act. Internationally, a treaty signed by the members of the Organization for Economic Cooperation and Development makes bribery of public officials a serious crime. Each member nation is expected to enact legislation implementing the treaty.

Fill-in Questions

Religious standards; Kantian ethics; the principle of rights

Multiple-Choice Questions

1. C. Business ethics focus on the application of moral principles in a business context. Different standards are not required. Business ethics is a subset of ethics that relates specifically to what constitutes right and wrong in situations that arise in business.

2. A. Traditionally, ethical reasoning relating to business has been characterized by two fundamental approaches—duty-based ethics and utilitarianism, or outcome-based ethics. Duty-based ethics derive from religious sources or philosophical principles. These standards may be absolute, which means that an act may not be undertaken, whatever the consequences.

3. A. Under religious ethical standards, it is the nature of an act that determines how ethical the act is, not its consequences. This is considered an *absolute* standard. But this standard is tempered by an element of compassion (the "Golden Rule").

4. D. In contrast to duty-based ethics, outcome-based ethics, or utilitarianism, involves a consideration of the consequences of an action. Utilitarianism is premised on acting so as to do the greatest good for the greatest number of people.

5. D. Utilitarianism requires determining who will be affected by an action, assessing the positive and negatives effects of alternatives, and choosing the alternative that will provide the greatest benefit for the most people. This approach has been criticized as tending to reduce the welfare of human beings to plus and minus signs on a cost-benefit worksheet.

6. A. A corporation, for example, as an employer, commonly faces ethical problems that involve conflicts among itself, its employees, its customers, its suppliers, its shareholders, its community, or other groups. Increasing wages, for instance, may benefit the employees and the community, but reduce profits and the ability of the employer to give pay increases in the future, as well as decreasing dividends to shareholders. To be considered socially responsible, when making a decision, a business firm must take into ac-count the interests of all of these groups, as well as society as a whole.

7. B. In any profession, there is a responsibility, both legal and ethical, not to misrepresent material facts, even at the expense of some profits. This is a clear ethical standard in the legal profession and in the accounting profession.

8. A. In part because it is impossible to be entirely aware of what the law requires and prohibits, the best course for a business firm is to act responsibly and in good faith. This course may provide the best defense if a transgression is discovered. Striking a balance between what is profitable and what is legal and ethical can be difficult, however. A failure to act legally or ethically can result in a reduction in profits, but a failure to act in the profitable interest of the firm can also cause profits to suffer. *Optimum* profits are the maximum profits that a firm can realize while staying within legal and ethical limits.

9. D. The principle of rights theory of ethics follows the belief that persons have fundamental rights. This belief is implied by duty-based ethical standards and Kantian ethics. The rights are implied by the duty that forms the basis for the standard (for example, the duty not to kill implies that persons have a right to live), or by the personal dignity implicit in the Kantian belief about the fundamental nature of human beings. Not to respect these rights would, under the principle of rights theory, be morally wrong.

10. C. The Foreign Corrupt Practices Act prohibits any U.S. firm from bribing foreign officials to influence official acts to provide the firm with business opportunities. Such payments are allowed, however, if they would be lawful in the foreign country. Thus, to avoid violating the law, the firm in this problem should determine whether such payments are legal in the minister's country.

Issue Spotters

1. The answer depends on which system of ethics is used. Under a duty-based ethical standard, it may not be the consequences of an act that determine how ethical the act is; it may be the nature of the act itself. Stealing would be unethical regardless of whether the fruits of the crime are given to the poor. In contrast, utilitarianism is premised on acting so as to do the greatest good for the greatest number of people. It is the consequences of an act that determine how ethical the act is.

2. Maybe. On the one hand, it is not the company's "fault" when a product is misused. Also, keeping the product on the market is not a violation of the law, and stopping sales would hurt profits. On the other hand, suspending sales could reduce suffering and could stop potential negative publicity if sales continued.

3.   When a corporation decides to respond to what it sees as a moral obligation to correct for past discrimination by adjusting pay differences among its employees, an ethical conflict is raised between the firm and its employees and between the firm and its shareholders. This dilemma arises directly out of the effect such a decision has on the firm's profits. If satisfying this obligation increases profitability, then the dilemma is easily resolved in favor of "doing the right thing."

Cumulative Hypothetical Problem for Unit One—Including Chapters 1–4

1.   A. Mediation involves the a third party, a mediator. The mediator does not decide the dispute but only assists the parties to resolve it themselves. Although the mediator does not render a legally binding decision, any agreement the parties reach may be legally binding.

2.   D. These state and federal courts would all have jurisdiction over the defendant. The customer's state could exercise jurisdiction over the firm through its long arm statute. The firm's state would have jurisdiction over it as a resident. A federal court could hear the case under its diversity jurisdiction: the parties are residents of different states and the amount in controversy is at least $75,000.

3.   A. Damages, or money damages, is a remedy at law. Remedies in equity include injunctions, specific performance, and rescission. The distinction arose because the law courts in England could not always grant suitable remedies, and so equity courts were created to grant other types of relief. The U.S. legal system derives from the English system.

4.   C. The power of judicial review is the power of any state or federal court to review a statute and declare it unconstitutional. Courts can also review the actions of the executive branch, which includes administrative agencies, to determine their constitutionality. A statute or rule that is declared unconstitutional is void. The power of judicial review is not expressly stated in the Constitution but is implied.

5.   D. Ethics is the study of what constitutes right or wrong behavior. It focuses on the application of moral principles to conduct. In a business context, ethics involves the application of moral principles to business conduct.

Questions on the Focus on Legal Reasoning for Unit One—*Pavlovich v. Superior Court*

1.   A. The majority noted that most jurisdictions have adopted a sliding scale analysis for determining whether to exercise jurisdiction based solely on Internet use. Under this test, in the court's words, "Creat

ing a site, like placing a product into the stream of commerce, may be felt nationwide—or even worldwide—but, without more, it is not an act purposefully directed toward the forum state. Otherwise, personal jurisdiction in Internet-related cases would almost always be found in any forum in the country."

2.   C. The dissent argued that the defendant in the *Pavlovich* case, by admittedly posting information on a passive Web site, specifically targeted two industries (the movie industry and the computer industry) that he knew were "centered in California or maintained a particularly substantial presence" there. This, in the dissent's opinion, "forged sufficient minimum contacts with California that he should reasonably anticipate being haled into court" in that state.

3.   C. The majority reasoned that "[i]n most, if not all, intentional tort cases, the defendant is or should be aware of the industries that may be affected by his tortious conduct." If this were enough to support an exercise of jurisdiction, the majority projected, "any plaintiff connected to industries centered in California . . . could sue an out-of-state defendant in California for intentional torts that *may* harm those industries . . . , even if the plaintiff was not a California resident." The majority declined to extend the state's jurisdiction this far.

Questions on the Focus on Ethics for Unit One—Ethics and the Legal Environment of Business

1.   D. As noted in a previous answer, ethics is the study of what constitutes right or wrong behavior. Legal liability is a separate question, and its answer may—or may not—indicate unethical behavior. Profitability is also a separate issue. *Optimum* profitability is the *maximum* profitability that a business may attain within the limits of the law *and* ethics.

2.   D. The *lack* of meaningful dissent to unethical decisions, or enthusiasm for them, could be an obstacle to more ethical choices, but the existence of dissent to unethical selections is not likely to encourage more of the same. Statutes that declare a priority for society's interests are also unlikely to foster unethical business behavior, as is holding a business firm accountable for its unethical actions. The corporate setting, however, in which dissent to unethical behavior may be stifled and in which a decision maker may be removed from the effects of his or her decisions, can be an obstacle to ethical decisions.

3.   A. If a business firm does not conduct its operations ethically, its goodwill, reputation, and future profits likely suffer. A firm that shows a commitment to ethical behavior often receives benefits greater than any advantages it may have sacrificed to do "what's right." A firm that is perceived as ethical may also attract investors.

Chapter 5

True-False Questions

1.   F. A federal form of government is one in which separate states form a union and divide sovereign power between themselves and a central authority. The United States has a federal form of government.
2.   F. The president does not have this power. Under the doctrine of judicial review, however, the courts can hold acts of Congress and of the executive branch unconstitutional.
3.   T
4.   T
5.   F. Under the supremacy clause, when there is a direct conflict between a federal law and a state law, the federal law takes precedence over the state law, and the state law is rendered invalid.
6.   T
7.   F. The protections in the Bill of Rights limit the power of the federal government. Most of these protections also apply to the states through the due process clause of the Fourteenth Amendment.
8.   F. Commercial speech (advertising) can be restricted as long as the restriction (1) seeks to implement a substantial government interest, (2) directly advances that interest, and (3) goes no further than necessary to accomplish its objective.
9.   F. Due process relates to the limits that the law places on the liberty of *everyone*. Equal protection relates to the limits that the law places on only *some people*.
10.   T

Fill-in Questions

states; states; state

Multiple-Choice Questions

1.   D. Under Articles I, II, and III of the Constitution, the legislative branch makes the law, the judicial branch interprets the law, and the executive branch enforces the law.
2.   A. Under the commerce clause, Congress has the power to regulate every commercial enterprise in the United States. Recently, the United States Supreme Court has struck down federal laws, to limit this power somewhat, in areas that have "nothing to do with commerce," including noneconomic, criminal conduct.
3.   C. State laws that impinge on interstate commerce are not always struck down, nor are they always upheld. A court will balance the state's interest in regulating a certain matter against the burden that the law places on interstate commerce. If the law does not substantially interfere, it will not be held to violate the commerce clause.

4.   B. The First Amendment provides corporations with significant protection of corporate political speech. As another example, a law that forbids a corporation from using inserts in its bills to its customers to express its views on controversial issues would also violate the First Amendment.
5.   D. Commercial speech does not have as much protection under the First Amendment as noncommercial speech. Commercial speech that is misleading may be restricted if the restriction (1) seeks to advance a substantial government interest, (2) directly advances that interest, and (3) goes no further than necessary.
6.   B. Aspects of the Fifth and Fourteenth Amendments that cover procedural due process concern the procedures used to make any government decision to take life, liberty, or property. These procedures must be fair, which generally mean that they give an opportunity to object.
7.   C. Substantive due process focuses on the content (substance) of a law under the Fifth and Fourteenth Amendments. Depending on which rights a law regulates, it must either promote a compelling or overriding government interest or be rationally related to a legitimate governmental end.
8.   A. Equal protection means that the government must treat similarly situated individuals in a similar manner. The equal protection clause of the Fourteenth Amendment applies to state and local governments, and the due process clause of the Fifth Amendment guarantees equal protection by the federal government. Generally, a law regulating an economic matter is considered valid if there is a "rational basis" on which the law relates to a legitimate government interest.
9.   C. Under the supremacy clause, if Congress chooses to act exclusively in an area in which states have concurrent power, Congress is said to preempt the area. The federal law takes precedence over a state law on the same subject.
10.   D. Dissemination of obscene materials is a crime. Speech that harms the good reputation of another, or defamatory speech, is not protected under the First Amendment. "Fighting words," which are words that are likely to incite others to respond with violence, are not constitutionally protected. Other unprotected speech includes other speech that violates criminal laws, such as threats.

Issue Spotters

1.   No. Even if commercial speech is not related to illegal activities nor misleading, it may be restricted if a state has a substantial interest that cannot be achieved by less restrictive means. In this case, the interest in energy conservation is substantial, but it could be achieved by less restrictive means. That

would be the utilities' defense against the enforcement of this state law.

2. Yes, the law would violate both types of due process. The law would be unconstitutional on substantive due process grounds, because it abridges freedom of speech. The law would be unconstitutional on procedural due process grounds, because it imposes a penalty without giving an accused a chance to defend his or her actions.

3. Yes. The tax would limit the liberty of some persons (out of state businesses), so it is subject to a review under the equal protection clause. Protecting local businesses from out-of-state competition is not a legitimate government objective. Thus, such a tax would violate the equal protection clause.

Chapter 6

True-False Questions

1. T

2. T

3. T

4. F. Agencies formulate and issue their rules under the authority of Congress. These rules are as legally binding as the laws enacted by Congress. It is for this reason, in part, that rulemaking procedures generally include opportunities for public comment, that the rules are subject to review by the courts, and that agencies are subject to other controls by the three branches of government.

5. F. Appeal is not mandatory, and if there is no appeal, the initial order becomes final. Either side may appeal the determination in an agency adjudication, however, to the commission that oversees the agency or ultimately to a federal court.

6. F. Congress can influence agency policy in several ways. These include that Congress can create or abolish an agency, or influence policy by the appropriation of funds for certain purposes. Congress can also revise the functions of an agency.

7. T

8. T

9. F. State and federal agency actions often parallel each other. (State and federal court review of state and federal agency decisions, respectively, is also similar.) When there is a conflict between state and federal agencies, the supremacy clause of the Constitution requires that the federal agency's operation prevail over an inconsistent state agency's action.

10. F. In most circumstances, a warrant is required for a search or the agency will be held to have violated the Fourth Amendment. Warrants are not required, however, to conduct searches in businesses in highly regulated industries, in certain hazardous operations, and in emergencies.

Fill-in Questions

Federal Register; anyone; must; *Federal Register*

Multiple-Choice Questions

1. D. Agency powers include functions associated with the legislature (rulemaking), executive branch (investigation), and courts (adjudication). Under Article I of the U.S. Constitution and the delegation doctrine, Congress has the power to establish administrative agencies and delegate any or all of these powers to those agencies.

2. C. Agencies may obtain information through subpoenas or searches. A subpoena may compel the appearance of a witness (a subpoena *ad testificandum*) or the provision of certain documents and records (a subpoena *duces tecum*). In some cases, particularly searches of businesses involved in highly regulated industries, searches may be conducted without warrants.

3. C. Procedures vary widely among agencies, even within agencies, but under the Administrative Procedure Act, rulemaking typically includes these steps: notice, opportunity for comment, and publication in the *Federal Register* of a final draft of the rule.

4. C. An agency has the authority to issue subpoenas. There are limits on agency demands for information, however. An investigation must have a legitimate purpose. The information that is sought must be relevant. The party from whom the information is sought must not be unduly burdened by the request. And the demand must be specific.

5. D. The president's veto is a method by which the authority of an agency can be checked or curtailed. The limits listed in the other responses in this question are choices available to Congress to limit the authority of administrative agencies.

6. B. The Government-in-the-Sunshine Act requires "every portion of every meeting of an agency" that is headed by a "collegial body" to be open to "public observation." The Freedom of Information Act requires the federal government to disclose certain records to persons on request, with some exceptions. The Regulatory Flexibility Act requires, among other things, analyses of new regulations in certain circumstances. The Small Business Regulatory Enforcement Fairness Act covers several matters important to businesses, including the federal courts' authority to enforce the Regulatory Flexibility Act, but it does not cover the opening of agency meetings to the public.

7. C. The Administrative Procedure Act provides for court review of most agency actions, but first a party must exhaust all other means of resolving a controversy with an agency. Also, under the ripeness doctrine, the agency action must be ripe for review: the action must be reviewable (which agency actions presumably are), the party must have standing, and an actual controversy must be at issue.

8. A. This is the "arbitrary and capricious" test under which acts committed willfully, unreasonable, and without considering the facts can be overturned. (The other choices are not legitimate grounds for judicial review.) A court may also consider whether the agency has exceeded its authority or violated any constitutional provisions. Depending on the circumstances, when a court reviews an act of an administrative agency, the court may also determine whether the agency has properly interpreted laws applicable to the action under review, acted in accord with procedural requirements, or reached conclusions that are not supported by substantial evidence.

9. B. After an agency publishes notice of a proposed rule, any interested parties can express their views in writing, or orally if a hearing is held. The agency must respond to all significant comments by modifying the final rule or explaining, in the statement accompanying the final rule, why it did not modify the rule in response to the comments.

10. B. An administrative law judge (ALJ) presides over hearings when cases are brought to the agency. Like other judges, an ALJ has the power to administer oaths, take testimony, rule on questions of evidence, and make determinations of fact. It is important to note that an ALJ works for the agency but must not be biased in the agency's favor. There are provisions in the Administrative Procedure Act to prevent the bias, and to otherwise promote the fairness, of the ALJs, for example by prohibiting *ex parte* comments to the ALJ from any party to the proceeding.

Issue Spotters

1. Checks against the arbitrary use of agency power include the courts' power to review agency actions. Congress also has considerable power over agencies. Among other things, Congress can create, restrict, or abolish an agency. Congress can also limit the funds that it appropriates to an agency. The president can exercise control over a federal agency through the appointment of its officers.

2. Under the Administrative Procedure Act (APA), the ALJ must be separate from the agency's investigative and prosecutorial staff. *Ex parte* communications between the ALJ and a party to a proceeding are prohibited. Under the APA, an ALJ is exempt from agency discipline except on a showing of good cause.

3. A formal adjudicatory hearing resembles a trial in that, in both types of proceedings, the parties can undertake extensive discovery (involving depositions, interrogatories, and so on), and during the hearing they may give testimony, present other evidence, and cross-examine witnesses. An administrative proceeding differs from a trial in that in the former, more information, including hearsay, can be introduced as evidence.

Chapter 7

True-False Questions

1. T
2. F. Felonies are crimes punishable by imprisonment of a year or more (in a state or federal prison). Crimes punishable by imprisonment for lesser periods (in a local facility) are classified as misdemeanors.
3. F. These are elements of the crime of robbery. (Robbery also involves the use of force or fear.) Burglary requires breaking and entering a building with the intent to commit a crime. (At one time, burglary was defined to cover only breaking and entering the dwelling of another at night to commit a crime.)
4. F. This is an element of larceny. The crime of embezzlement occurs when a person entrusted with another's property fraudulently appropriates it. Also, unlike robbery, embezzlement does not require the use of force or fear.
5. T.
6. F. The crime of bribery occurs when a bribe is offered. Accepting a bribe is a separate crime. In either case, the recipient does not need to perform the act for which the bribe is offered for the crime to exist. Note, too, that a bribe can consist of something other then money.
7. F. The recipient of the goods only needs to know that the goods are stolen. The recipient does not need to know the identity of the thief or of the true owner to commit this crime. Thus, not knowing these individuals' identities is not a defense.
8. T
9. T
10. T

Fill-in Questions

unreasonable; probable; due process of law; jeopardy; trial; trial by; witnesses; bail and fines

Multiple-Choice Questions

1. D. A person who wrongfully or fraudulently takes and carries away another's personal property commits larceny. Unlike burglary, larceny does not involve breaking and entering. Unlike embezzlement, larceny requires that property be taken and carried away from the owner's possession. Unlike forgery, larceny does not require the making or altering of a writing. Unlike robbery, larceny does not involve force or fear.
2. C. The elements of most crimes include the performance of a prohibited act and a specified state of mind or intent on the part of the actor.
3. C. Fraudulently making or altering a writing in a way that changes another's legal rights is forgery.

Forgery also includes changing trademarks, counterfeiting, falsifying public documents, and altering other legal documents.

4. B. Embezzlement involves the fraudulent appropriation of another's property, including money, by a person entrusted with it. Unlike larceny, embezzlement does not require that property be taken from its owner.

5. D. The standard to find a criminal defendant guilty is beyond a reasonable doubt. This means that each juror must be convinced, beyond a reasonable doubt, of the defendant's guilt. The standard in most civil cases is a preponderance of the evidence.

6. C. The federal crime of mail fraud has two elements: a scheme to defraud by false pretenses, and mailing, or causing someone else to mail, a writing for the purpose of executing the scheme. It would also be a crime to execute the scheme by wire, radio, or television transmissions.

7. B. In considering the defense of entrapment, the important question is whether a person who committed a crime was pressured by the police to do so. Entrapment occurs when a government agent suggests that a crime be committed and pressure an individual, who is not predisposed to its commitment, to do it.

8. C. A person in police custody who is to be interrogated must be informed that he or she has the right to remain silent; anything said can and will be used against him or her in court; and he or she has the right to consult with an attorney. The person also must be told that if he or she is indigent, a lawyer will be appointed. These rights may be waived if the waiver is knowing and voluntary.

9. C. If, for example, a confession is obtained after an illegal arrest, the confession is normally excluded. Under the exclusionary rule, all evidence obtained in violation of the constitutional rights spelled out in the Fourth, Fifth, and Sixth Amendments normally is excluded, as well as all evidence derived from the illegally obtained evidence. The purpose of the rule is to deter police misconduct.

10. B. A formal charge issued by a grand jury is an indictment. A charge issued by a magistrate is called an information. In either case, there must be sufficient evidence to justify bringing a suspect to trial. The arraignment occurs when the suspect is brought before the trial court, informed of the charges, and asked to enter a plea.

Issue Spotters

1. No. A mistake of fact, as opposed to a mistake of law, will constitute a defense if it negates the mental state required for the crime. The mental state required for theft involves the knowledge that the property is another's and the intent to deprive the owner of it.

2. Yes. With respect to the gas station, she has obtained goods by false pretenses. She might also be charged with forgery, and most states have special statutes covering illegal use of credit cards.

3. Yes. The National Information Infrastructure Protection Act of 1996 amended the Counterfeit Access Device and Computer Fraud and Abuse Act of 1984. The statute provides that a person who accesses a computer online, without permission, to obtain classified data (such as consumer credit files in a credit agency's database) is subject to criminal prosecution. The crime has two elements: accessing the computer without permission and taking data. It is a felony if done for private financial gain. Penalties include fines and imprisonment for up to twenty years. The victim of the theft can also bring a civil suit against the criminal to obtain damages and other relief.

Chapter 8

True-False Questions

1. F. According to the principle of comity, however, a nation will give effect to the laws of another nation if those laws are consistent with the law and public policy of the accommodating nation.

2. F. The act of state doctrine tends to immunize foreign nations from the jurisdiction of U.S. courts—that is, foreign nations are often exempt from U.S. jurisdiction under this doctrine.

3. F. As with the act of state doctrine, the doctrine of sovereign immunity tends to immunize foreign nations from the jurisdiction of U.S. courts

4. F. The Foreign Sovereign Immunities Act sets forth the major exceptions to the immunity of foreign nations to U.S. jurisdiction.

5. T

6. T

7. F. Legal systems in all nations can be generally divided into *common* law and civil law systems.

8. T

9. F. Some contract law has been internationalized through the CISG, but parties contracting internationally can agree to apply other law to their contract disputes.

10. T

Fill-in Questions

An expropriation; A confiscation; an expropriation; a confiscation

Multiple-Choice Questions

1. C. Under certain conditions, the doctrine of sovereign immunity prohibits U.S. courts from exercising jurisdiction over foreign nations. Under the Foreign Sovereign Immunities Act, a foreign state is not immune when the action is based on a commercial activity carried on in the United States by the foreign state.

2.　A. Under the act of state doctrine, the judicial branch of one country will not examine the validity of public acts committed by a recognized foreign government within its own territory. The awarding of a government contract under the circumstances described in the problem meets this criterion.

3.　C. U.S. courts give effect to the judicial decrees of another country under the principle of comity, if those decrees are consistent with the laws and public policies of the United States.

4.　C. The U.S. Congress cannot tax exports, but it may establish export quotas. In particular, under the Export Administration Act of 1979, restrictions can be imposed on the export of technologically advanced products.

5.　C. Unlike exports, imports can be taxed. A tax on an import is a tariff (generally set as a percent of the value). Imports can also be subject to quotas, which limit how much can be imported.

6.　B. Although increasingly influenced by codified (statutory) law and in some observers' opinions overwhelmed with administrative rules and regulations, common law legal systems are based on judicial decisions and precedent. Despite this general frame of reference, common law courts in different nations have developed different principles.

7.　C. Civil law systems are based on codified (statutory) law. Administrative rules and regulations and judicial decisions are, of course, part of the operation of a civil law system. In a civil law system, courts are permitted to interpret the statutes that make up the code and to apply the rules, but unlike a common law system, in which judicial precedent plays a significant role, the courts in a civil law system are not expected to develop their own body of law.

8.　B. In many countries, however, judges are actively involved in trials, such as by questioning witnesses. In the United States, besides a less participatory role at trial, a federal judge is less likely to be influenced by politics, in part because he or she cannot be removed by impeachment except in extreme cases.

9.　A. For example, mutual assent (offer and acceptance) is a common element for an enforceable contract. But the details of its application varies in different countries. In Germany, for instance, a written offer must be held open for a reasonable time, unless the offer states otherwise, and oral offers must be accepted immediately or they expire. In Mexico, if a time for acceptance is not stated in an offer, the offer is deemed to be held open for three days (plus whatever time is necessary for the mails).

10. C. In some countries, employers cannot discriminate against employees or job applicants, to varying degrees. The prohibited bases for discrimination differ among nations. Discrimination is not prohibited in all countries, however.

Issue Spotters

1.　Under the principle of comity, a U.S court would defer and give effect to foreign laws and judicial decrees that are consistent with U.S. law and public policy.

2.　A U.S. firm—or any domestic firm—can license its formula, product, or process to a foreign concern to avoid its theft. The foreign firm obtains the right to make and market the product according to the formula (or the right to use the process) and agrees to keep the necessary information secret and to pay royalties to the licensor.

3.　The practice described in this problem is known as dumping. Seen as an unfair international trade practice, dumping is the sale of imported goods at "less than fair value." Based on the price of those goods in the exporting country, an extra tariff can be imposed on the imports. This is known as an antidumping duty.

Cumulative Hypothetical Problem for Unit Two—Including Chapters 5–8

1.　C. A business firm may be subject to regulations issued by federal and state administrative agencies. The firm is no less subject to those regulations if they are conflicting or if the firm does not know of the regulations. Federal agencies include the Federal Trade Commission, the Environmental Protection Agency, and the U.S. Department of Justice, all of which have counterparts at the state level in most states. A business firm is also subject to local regulations at the county and city levels.

2.　B. A corporation can be compelled to produce its business records, even when those records incriminate its officers or other persons affiliated with the corporation. A partnership is subject to the same requirement. Only individuals can refuse, under the Fifth Amendment to the U.S. Constitution, to provide incriminating testimony, including business records.

3.　A. A corporation can be held liable for the crimes of its employees, officers, or directors. Imprisonment is not possible, in a practical sense, as a punishment for a corporation. A business firm can be fined or denied certain privileges, however.

4.　B. Congress cannot tax exports, but it may set quotas on exported products. Under the Export Administration Act of 1979, special restrictions can be imposed on the export of technologically advanced products, such as those is this problem.

5.　C. If a law affects only some persons (for example, when only some persons are prohibited from doing something), it may raise an equal protection issue. If all persons are affected, there may be a question of substantive due process. Under the Fifth Amendment, the federal government must treat all similarly situated persons in a similar manner.

Questions on the Focus on Legal Reasoning for Unit Two—*Kasky v. Nike, Inc.*

1. D. The majority set out a three-part test for determining whether speech is commercial. The three elements included the speaker, the intended audience, and the content of the message. The court seemed to emphasized the source of the speech as the dominant element. None of the other answer choices were mentioned.

2. B. The dissent argued that commercial speech should be distinguished by its content only, not by its content, the identity of the speaker, and the intended audience, as the majority held. The dissent asserted in part that "the inherent worth of the speech in terms of its capacity for informing the public does not depend upon the identity of its source" and that corporate and other business speakers contribute to the types of ideas that the First Amendment "seeks to foster."

3. D. The majority felt that its holding would have no chilling effect on commercial speech or public debate. Because commercial speech is based on a profit motive, it is "more hardy than noncommercial speech" and not likely to be much inhibited by this case. The dissent disagreed, arguing that this case "would have an undoubted chilling effect on speech," inhibiting businesses' ability to participate in debates over matters of public concern.

Questions on the Focus on Ethics for Unit Two—The Public and International Environment

1. D. All areas of the law at least touch on ethical considerations, even as they are based on practical necessity or commercial need. The public and international categories, however, involve issues that are sometimes almost entirely ethical (a desire to protect the freedom of speech versus a desire for social order, for example). These issues often require a balancing of conflicting rights and goals that can only be accomplished by making value judgments.

2. C. The First Amendment's free speech protections extend to corporations. That is not the issue in this case. The question is whether the state's action violates this protection. When speech is political in nature, by an almost universal consensus, the First Amendment protects it. Speech may concern a purely economic matter, and a corporate view on that matter may be relevant, but that speech does not warrant as much protection. Whether a corporation should use its marketing, management, and technology skills in the political arena is perhaps an ethical question, but it is not necessarily a legal concern.

3. D. The standards for conducting regulatory searches are different from those for ordinary police searches. Proof, or even suspicion, of a regulatory violation is not necessary. Business premises may be searched simply to determine whether a violation is occurring. An industry does not need to be subject to extensive regulation for its members' premises to be searched (though if it is, a search warrant is not required). An agency is limited in obtaining private information for regulatory purposes, however, which means that this goal is not a requirement for a regulatory inspection.

Chapter 9

True-False Questions

1. F. All contracts involve promises, but all promises do not establish contracts. (A contract is an agreement that can be enforced in court.) Contract law reflects which promises society believes should be legally enforced, and assures parties to private contracts that the agreements they make will be enforceable.

2. T

3. F. A contract right cannot be assigned if (1) a statute expressly prohibits its assignment; (2) a contract stipulates that it cannot be assigned; (3) it is under a contract that is uniquely personal; or (4) assignment would materially increase or alter the risk of the obligor.

4. F. One of the elements for a valid offer is that the terms be definite enough to be enforced by a court. This is so a court can determine if a breach had occurred and, if so, what the appropriate remedy would be. The term "a fair share" is too indefinite to constitute an enforceable term. An offer that invites, and receives, a specifically worded acceptance can create sufficiently definite terms.

5. F. Ordinarily, courts will not evaluate the adequacy of consideration, unless it is grossly inadequate or so unfair as to indicate the existences of fraud, duress, incapacity, undue influence, or a lack of bargained-for exchange.

6. T

7. T

8. T

9. F. The Statute of Frauds requires that contracts for all transfers of interests in land be in writing to be enforceable. Included are sales, mortgages, leases, and other transfers. Other contracts that must be in writing to be enforceable under the Statute of Frauds include contracts that cannot be performed within one year of formation, collateral promises, promises made in consideration of marriage, and contracts for sale of goods priced at $500 or more.

10. T

Fill-in Questions

objective; objective; did; circumstances surrounding; in a particular transaction

Multiple-Choice Questions

1. D. To constitute consideration, the value of whatever is exchanged for the promise must be legally sufficient. Its economic value (its "adequacy") is rarely the basis for a court's refusal to enforce a contract.

2. B. According to the objective theory of contracts, a party's intent to enter into a contract is judged by outward, objective facts as a reasonable person would interpret them, rather than by the party's own subjective intentions. A reasonable person in the position of a party receiving an offer can know what is in the offer only from what is offered. A court might consider the circumstances surrounding a transaction, and the statements of the parties and the way they acted when they made their contract.

3. C. In general, ads (which include catalogs, price lists, and circulars, or flyers) are treated as invitations to negotiate, not offers.

4. B. This statement makes a second offer without rejecting the first offer. An offeree may make an offer without rejecting the original offer, in which case two offers exist, each capable of acceptance.

5. A. Generally, a unilateral mistake—a mistake on the part of only one of the parties—does not give the mistaken party any right to relief. There are two exceptions. One of the exceptions is that the rule does not apply if the other party knew or should have known that a mistake was made.

6. A. Consideration must be bargained for. Performance or a promise is bargained for if, as in this problem, the promisor seeks it in exchange for his or her promise and the promisee gives it in exchange for that promise.

7. A. An obligation to pay will be imposed by law to prevent one party from being unjustly enriched at another's expense. This is the doctrine of quasi contract. The doctrine will not be applied, however, if there is a contract covering the matter in dispute. Also, there are some circumstances in which parties will not be forced to pay for benefits "thrust" on them, particularly if this is done over their protest.

8. C. To disaffirm a contract, a minor must return whatever he or she received under it. In a state in which there is also an obligation to return the other party to the position he or she was in before the contract, the minor must also pay for any damage to the goods.

9. D. Under the Statute of Frauds, a contract for the sale of an interest in land must be in writing to be enforceable. A party to an oral contract involving an interest in land cannot force the other party to buy or sell the property. There is an exception to this rule. If a buyer pays part of the price, takes possession, and makes permanent improvements, and the parties cannot be returned to their pre-contract status quo, a court may grant specific performance of an oral contract for the transfer of an interest in land.

10. C. A right cannot normally be assigned if the assignment would materially increase or alter the risk of the obligor (the different circumstances represented by different persons with different property alter the risk in this problem). A right under a personal service contract cannot normally be assigned, but this is not a personal service contract, which requires a service unique to the person rendering it (an insurance policy is unlikely to qualify).

Issue Spotters

1. Under the objective theory of contracts, if a reasonable person would have thought that the offeree accepted the offeror's offer when the offeree signed and returned the letter, a contract was made, and the offeree is bound. This depends in part on what was said in the letter (was it a valid offer?) and what was said in response (was it a valid acceptance?). Under any circumstances, the issue is not whether either party subjectively believed that they did, or did not, have a contract.

2. The acceptance is effective on dispatch (when the offeree sends the fax). Traditional rules of contract apply to new forms of communication. Under the mailbox rule, using a mode of communication impliedly authorized by the offeror makes an acceptance effective when sent. Here, the offeror did not specify a certain mode, so the mode the offeror used to make the offer was a reasonable means of acceptance.

3. Yes. Under the doctrine of detrimental reliance, or promissory estoppel, the promisee is entitled to payment of $5,000 from the promisor on graduation. There was a promise, on which the promisee relied, the reliance was substantial and definite (the promisee went to college for the full term, incurring considerable expenses, and will likely graduate), and it would only be fair to enforce the promise.

Chapter 10

True-False Questions

1. T

2. F. A material breach of contract (which occurs when performance is not at least substantial) excuses the nonbreaching party from performance of his or her contractual duties and gives the party a cause of action to sue for damages caused by the breach. A *minor* breach of contract does not excuse the nonbreaching party's duty to perform, however, although it may affect the extent of his or her performance and, like any contract breach, allows the nonbreaching party to sue for damages.

3. F. An executory contract can be rescinded. If it is executory on both sides, it can be rescinded solely by agreement. In any case, the parties must make a new agreement, and this agreement must qualify as a contract. (The parties' promises not to perform are consideration for the new contract.)

4.   T

5.   T

6.   T

7.   F. Liquidated damages are certain amounts of money estimated in advance of, and payable on, a breach of contract. *Liquidated* means determined, settled, or fixed.

8.   F. There can be no enforceable contract if the doctrine of quasi contract is to be applied. Under this doctrine, to prevent unjust enrichment, the law implies a promise to pay the reasonable value for benefits received in the absence of an enforceable contract. This recovery is useful when one party has partially performed under a contract that is unenforceable.

9.   T

10.   F. Damages is the usual on breach of contracts for sales of goods. To obtain specific performance, damages must *not* be an adequate remedy. If goods are unique, or a contract involves a sale of land, damages would not adequately compensate an innocent party for a breach of contract, so specific performance is available.

Fill-in Questions

Rescission; Novation; Substitution of a new contract; An accord; accord

Multiple-Choice Questions

1.   D. Accord and satisfaction, agreement, and operation of law are valid bases on which contracts are discharged, but most contracts are discharged by the parties' doing what they promised to do. A contract is fully discharged by performance when the contracting parties have fully performed what they agreed to do (exchange services for payment, for example).

2.   C. A breach of contract entitles the nonbreaching party to damages, but only a material breach discharges the nonbreaching party from his or her duty to perform under the contract. In this problem, the builder has a claim for the amount due on the contract, but the buyer is entitled to have set off the difference in the value of the building as constructed (that is, to subtract the expense to finish the construction).

3.   D. Contracts that have not been fully performed on either side can be rescinded. The parties must make another agreement (which must satisfy the legal requirements for a contract). The parties' promises not to perform are consideration for the new agreement. A contract that has been fully performed on one side can be rescinded only if the party who has performed receives additional consideration to call off the deal.

4.   B. This contract would thus be discharged by objective impossibility of performance. On this basis, a contract may be discharged if, for example, after it is made, performance becomes objectively impossible because of a change in the law that renders that performance illegal. This is also the result if one of the parties dies or becomes incapacitated, or the subject matter of the contract is destroyed.

5.   C. A novation substitutes a new party for an original party, by agreement of all the parties. The requirements are a previous valid obligation, an agreement of all the parties to a new contract, extinguishment of the old obligation, and a new contract (which must meet the requirements for a valid contract, including consideration).

6.   C. A breach of contract by failing to perform entitles the nonbreaching party to rescind the contract, and the parties must make restitution by returning whatever benefit they conferred on each other, particularly when the breaching party would otherwise be unjustly enriched.

7.   C. Under a contract for a sale of goods, the usual measure of compensatory damages is the difference between the contract price and the market price, plus incidental damages. On a seller's breach, the measure includes the difference between what the seller would have been owed if he or she had performed and what the buyer paid elsewhere for the goods.

8.   B. On the seller's breach of a contract, the buyer is entitled to be compensated for the loss of the bargain. Here, the buyer will receive what was contracted for, but it will be late. When, as in this problem, a seller knew that the buyer would lose business if the goods were not delivered on time, the loss of the bargain is the consequential damages (the amount lost as a foreseeable consequence of the breach).

9.   C. Specific performance is an award of the act promised in a contract. This remedy is granted when the legal remedy (damages) is inadequate. Damages are generally inadequate for a buyer on the breach of a contract for a sale of land, because every piece of land is considered unique. If specific performance is not available, however, as when the land cannot be sold by the contracting seller, damages are possible, and their measure is the benefit of the buyer's bargain (the difference between the contract price and the market price of the land at the time of the breach).

10.   B. A quasi contract may be imposed when a party has partially performed under a contract that is unenforceable. (An oral contract, the terms of which cannot be performed within one year, is unenforceable under the one-year rule of the Statute of Frauds.) To obtain quasi-contractual relief, a party must show that (1) he or she conferred a benefit on another, (2) he or she conferred the benefit with the reasonable expectation of being paid, (3) he or she did not act as a volunteer in conferring the benefit, and (4) the party receiving the benefit would be unjustly enriched by retaining the benefit without paying for it.

Issue Spotters

1. No. The builder has substantially performed its duties under the contract. Assuming this performance was in good faith, the builder could thus successfully sue for the value of the work performed. For the sake of justice and fairness, the buyer will be held to the duty to pay, less damages for the deviation from the contract deadline.

2. No. To recover damages that flow from the consequences of a breach but that are caused by circumstances beyond the contract (consequential damages), the breaching party must know, or have reason to know, that special circumstances will cause the non-breaching party to suffer the additional loss. That was not the circumstance in this problem.

3. This clause is known as an exculpatory clause. In many cases, such clauses are not enforced, but to be effective in any case, all contracting parties must have consented to it. A clause excluding liability for negligence may be enforced if the contract was made by parties in roughly equal bargaining positions, as two large corporations would be.

Chapter 11

True-False Questions

1. T

2. F. If a transaction involves only a service, the common law usually applies (one exception is the serving of food or drink, which is governed by the UCC). When goods and services are combined, courts have disagreed over whether a particular transaction involves a sale of goods or a rendering of service. Usually, a court will apply the law that applies to whichever feature is dominant. Article 2 does not cover sales of real estate, although sales of goods associated with real estate, including crops, may be covered. A contract for a sale of minerals, for example, is considered a contract for a sale of goods if the severance is to be made by the seller.

3. T

4. T

5. T

6. F. If the parties do not agree otherwise, the buyer or lessee must pay for the goods at the time and place of their receipt (subject, in most cases, to the buyer or lessee's right to inspect). When a sale is on credit, a buyer must pay according to credit terms, not when the goods are received. Credit terms may provide for payment within thirty days, for example. A credit period usually begins on the date of shipment.

7. T

8. T

9. F. Warranties are not exclusive. A contract can include an implied warranty of merchantability, an implied warranty of fitness for a particular purpose, and any number of express warranties.

10. F. Courts usually do enforce click-on agreements. The reasoning is that the click-on terms constitute an offer, proposed by a seller and accepted by a buyer after the buyer had an opportunity to review the terms by an act of active consent (unlike a situation involving browse-wrap terms, which sellers argue are binding without the buyer's active consent).

Fill-in Questions

conforming; and; buyer; receipt; unless

Multiple-Choice Questions

1. A. Under the UCC, a sales contract will not fail for indefiniteness even if one or more terms are left open, as long as the parties intended to make a contract and there is a reasonably certain basis for the court to grant an appropriate remedy. If the price term is left open, for example, and the parties cannot later agree on a price, a court will set the price according to what is reasonable at the time for delivery. If one of the parties is to set the price, it must be set in good faith. If it is not fixed, the other party can set the price or treat the contract as canceled.

2. D. In a transaction between merchants, additional terms in the acceptance of an offer become part of a contract *unless* they qualify as one of these exceptions.

3. B. Under a shipment contract, risk passes when the seller puts the goods into a carrier's possession. Under a destination contract, risk passes when the seller tenders delivery to the buyer.

4. A. Generally, the party who breaches a contract bears the risk of loss. Here, the seller breached by shipping defective goods. The risk would have passed to the buyer if the buyer accepted the goods in spite of their defects. (If the buyer had accepted the goods and then discovered the defects, the buyer could have revoked its acceptance, which would have transferred the risk back to the seller.)

5. A. If, before the time of performance, a party to a contract informs the other party that he or she will not perform, the nonbreaching party can treat the repudiation as a final breach and seek a remedy or wait, for a commercially reasonable time, hoping that the breaching party will decide to honor the contract. In either case, the nonbreaching party can suspend his or her performance.

6. C. The parties to a contract can stipulate the time, place, and manner of delivery. In the absence of specified details, however, tender of delivery must be at a reasonable hour and in a reasonable manner. The buyer must be notified, and the goods must be kept available for a reasonable time.

7. C. Depending on the circumstances, when a seller or lessor delivers nonconforming goods, the buyer or lessee can reject the part of the goods that does not conform (and rescind the contract or obtain cover). The buyer or lessee may instead revoke acceptance, or he or she may recover damages, for accepted goods.

8.   A. If a lessee (or buyer) wrongfully refuses to accept, the lessor (or seller) can recover the difference between the contract price and the market price (at the time and place of tender), plus incidental damages. If the market price is less than the contract price, the lessor (or seller) can recover lost profits.

9.   A. This phrase, or similar language, will generally disclaim most implied warranties. To specifically disclaim an implied warranty of fitness for a particular purpose, a writing must be conspicuous, but the word *fitness* does not have to be used. A specific disclaimer of the implied warranty of merchantability must mention *merchantability*. Note that warranties of title can be disclaimed only by specific language (for example, a seller states that it is transferring only such rights as it has in the goods), or by circumstances that indicate no warranties of title are made.

10.   D. To fall under the UETA, the parties to a contract must agree to conduct their transaction electronically. The UETA then applies in the absence of an agreement between the parties to the contrary, although they can waive or vary any or all of its provisions. Whether the contract involves computer information is irrelevant under the UETA. To fall under the UCITA, however, a contract must involve, in whole or in part, computer information, as defined by the act, unless the parties to the deal opt out (or opt in) of the UCITA's application.

Starbucks Coffee Co. International Sales Contract Applications

1.   B. As stated in the "Breach or Default of Contract" clause on the second page, this contract is subject to Article 2 of the UCC. If the parties to a sales contract do not express some of the terms in writing, including the price term, the contract is still enforceable. A sales contract that must be in writing is only enforceable, however, to the extent of the quantity stated in writing. If these parties did not state the amount of product ordered, the contract may not be enforced because if a quantity term were left out, a court would have no basis for determining a remedy.

2.   B. When a seller, as a party to a sales contract, states or otherwise expresses what the goods will be, then the goods must be that. The goods must at least conform to the seller's description of them, wherever that descriptions is, whether in the contract, in promotional materials, on labels, by salespersons, by comparison to a sample, etc. A seller's subjective belief is not the standard. The buyer's subjective belief may be the standard if the contract specifies that the goods must personally satisfy the buyer.

3.   C. This clause states the terms for payment under this sales contract and indicates that the buyer has two days after the day of tender in which to pay for the goods or will be considered in breach. The "BREACH OR DEFAULT OF CONTRACT" clause sets out what happens "if either party hereto fails to perform." These are all incentives for the buyer to pay on time.

4.   A. This clause allows the buyer to reject nonconforming product, although this is limited to a specific number of days. (Note that the buyer' right to reject does not need to be stated in a contract for the buyer to have that right.) This clause details the procedures that the parties may follow if the product does not meet its description. These are incentives for the seller to deliver conforming goods.

5.   D. This is a destination contract, as indicated by the "ARRIVAL," "DELIVERY," "INSURANCE," and "FREIGHT" clauses. This means that the seller bears the risk of loss until the coffee is delivered to its destination (a "Bonded Public Warehouse" in Laredo, Texas).

Issue Spotters

1.   A shipment of nonconforming goods constitutes an acceptance and a breach, unless the seller seasonably notifies the buyer that the nonconforming shipment does not constitute an acceptance and is offered only as an accommodation. Without the notification, the shipment is an acceptance and a breach. Thus, here, the shipment was both an acceptance and a breach.

2.   The buyer can recover the difference between the market price—at the time that the buyer learned of the breach, at the place for tender—and the contract price, plus incidental damages (reasonable expenses incident to the breach) and consequential damages (of which the seller knew at the time of the breach), less any expenses saved by the breach. Thus, in this problem, the buyer can recover $2,000 ($10,000 x $.20), plus incidental damages and consequential damages (for the halt to the buyer's operation), less any expenses saved by the breach.

3.   No, at least not on this ground. Merchantable food means food that is fit to eat. Food containing cholesterol is merchantable—that is, it is fit to eat—if it is similar to all other food of the kind on the market.

Chapter 12

True-False Questions

1.   T
2.   F. A reasonable apprehension or fear of *immediate* harmful or offensive contact is an assault.
3.   T
4.   F. Puffery is seller's talk—the seller's *opinion* that his or her goods are, for example, the "best." For fraud to occur, there must be a misrepresentation of a *fact*.
5.   T

6. F. To establish negligence, the courts apply a reasonable person standard to determine whether certain conduct resulted in a breach of a duty of care.

7. F. Disparagement of property is a general term for torts that can be more specifically referred to as slander of quality or slander of title.

8. F. This is not misconduct, in terms of a wrongful interference tort. Bona fide competitive behavior is permissible, whether or not it results in the breaking of a contract or other business relation.

9. T

10. F. Some states have statutes prohibiting or regulating the use of spam. Also, the sending of spam may constitute trespass to personal property, and could be curtailed by private lawsuits. What the government can do to restrict spam may be limited by the First Amendment's protection for freedom of speech, however.

Fill-in Questions

1. negligence
2. defense of assumption of risk
3. contributory
4. comparative

Multiple-Choice Questions

1. A. To satisfy the elements of a negligence cause of action, a breach of a duty of care must cause the harm. If an injury would not have occurred without the breach, there is causation in fact. Causation in fact can usually be determined by the but-for test: but for the wrongful act, the injury would not have occurred.

2. B. Joe committed a battery and may have committed an assault. For an intentional tort, what matters is the actor's intent regarding the consequences of an act or his or her knowledge with substantial certainty that certain consequences will result. Motive is irrelevant, and the other person's fear is not a factor in terms of the actor's intent.

3. A. To delay a customer suspected of shoplifting, a merchant must have probable cause (which requires more than a mere suspicion). A customer's concealing merchandise in his or her bag and leaving the store without paying for it would constitute probable cause. Even with probable cause, a merchant may delay a suspected shoplifter only for a reasonable time, however.

4. D. Advertising is bona fide competitive behavior, which is not a tort even if it results in the breaking of a contract. Obtaining more customers is one of the goals of effective advertising. Taking unethical steps to interfere with others' contracts or business relations could constitute a tort, however.

5. A. The basis of the tort of defamation is publication of a statement that holds an individual up to contempt, ridicule, or hatred. Publication means that statements are made to or within the hearing of persons other than the defamed party, or that a third party reads the statements. A secretary reading a letter, for example, meets this requirement. But the statements do not have to be read or heard by a specific third party. (Whether someone is a public figure is important only because a public figure cannot recover damages for defamation without proof of actual malice.)

6. D. Under the Communications Decency Act, an Internet service provider (ISP) may not be held liable for defamatory statements made by its customers online. Congress provided this immunity as an incentive to ISPs to "self-police" the Internet for offensive material.

7. C. To commit negligence, a breach of a duty of care must cause harm. If an injury was foreseeable, there is causation in fact. This can usually be determined by the but-for test: but for the wrongful act, the injury would not have occurred. Thus, an actor is not necessarily liable to all who are injured. Insurance coverage and business dealings are not factors.

8. B. Trespass to land occurs when a person, without permission, enters onto another's land, or remains on the land. An owner does not need to be aware of an act before it can constitute trespass, and harm to the land is not required. A trespasser may have a complete defense, however, if he or she enters onto the land to help someone in danger.

9. A. The standard of a business that invites persons onto its premises is a duty to exercise reasonable care. Whether conduct is unreasonable depends on a number of factors, including how easily the injury could have been guarded against. A landowner has a duty to discover and remove hidden dangers, but obvious dangers do not need warnings.

10. D. Trespass to personal property is intentional physical contact with another's personal property that causes damage. Sending spam through an Internet service provider (ISP) is intentional contact with the ISP's computer systems. A negative impact on the value of the ISP's equipment, by using its processing power to transmit e-mail, constitutes damage (the resources are not available for the ISP's customers). Also, service cancellations harm an ISP's business reputation and goodwill.

Issue Spotters

1. Yes. Adam is guilty of battery—an unexcused, harmful, or offensive physical contact intentionally performed. A battery may involve contact with any part of the body and anything (a blouse, in this problem) attached to it.

2. Yes. Trespass to personal property occurs when an individual unlawfully harms another's personal property or otherwise interferes with the owner's right to exclusive possession and enjoyment.

3.   No. As long as competitive behavior is bona fide, it is not tortious even if it results in the breaking of a contract. The public policy that favors free competition in advertising outweighs any instability that bona fide competitive activity causes in contractual or business relations. To constitute wrongful interference with a contractual relationship, there must be (1) a valid, enforceable contract between two parties; (2) the knowledge of a third party that this contract exists; and (3) the third party's intentionally causing the breach of the contract (and damages) to advance the third party's interest.

Chapter 13

True-False Questions

1.   T
2.   F. A defendant may be liable for the result of his or her act regardless of intent—that is part of the basis of the doctrine of strict liability. Similarly, it usually does not matter whether the defendant exercised reasonable care. Strict liability is liability without regard to fault or intent.
3.   T
4.   F. Product liability may be imposed for defects in the design or construction of products that cause injuries, but it may also be imposed for a failure to include a reasonable warning.
5.   T
6.   F. An action based on negligence does not require privity of contract. At one time, there was a requirement of privity in product liability actions based on negligence, but this requirement began to be eliminated decades ago. Privity of contract is also not a requirement to bring a suit based on strict product liability.
7.   F. In an action based on strict liability, a plaintiff does not have to prove that there was a failure to exercise due care. That distinguishes an action based on strict liability from an action based on negligence, which requires proof of a lack of due care. A plaintiff must show, however, that (1) a product was defective, (2) the defendant was in the business of distributing the product, (3) the product was unreasonably dangerous due to the defect, (4) the plaintiff suffered harm, (5) the defect was the proximate cause of the harm, and (6) the goods were not substantially changed from the time they were sold.
8.   T
9.   F. There is no duty to warn about such risks. Warnings about such risks do not add to the safety of products and could make other warnings seem less significant. In fact, a plaintiff's action in the face of such a risk can be raised as a defense in a product liability suit.
10.   T

Fill-in Questions

limitations; does not begin until; repose; repose; limitations

Multiple-Choice Questions

1.   A. Assumption of risk is a defense in an action based on product liability if the plaintiff knew and appreciated the risk created by the defect and voluntarily undertook the risk, even though it was unreasonable to do so.
2.   B. The manufacturer was clearly negligent to sell a product with a defective safety switch. As a defendant in a product liability suit on the ground of negligence, the manufacturer would be liable. The plaintiff knew about the defect, however, and used the treadmill anyway. Under the defense of comparative negligence, the amount of the defendant's liability may be reduced in proportion to the amount by which the plaintiff's injury was the result of the plaintiff's own negligence.
3.   C. The doctrine of strict liability extends to suppliers of component parts as well as the manufacturers, sellers, and distributors of the products made with those components.
4.   A. In terms of spreading the costs, manufacturers and others who might be liable typically have insurance to cover any losses. To pay for the insurance, the insured may simply raise its prices to its customers. Partly for this reason, manufacturers and sellers of products are in a better position to bear the costs associated with injuries caused by their products, which is one of the public policy reasons for imposing strict liability generally. Other reasons include that consumers should be protected against unsafe products, and that manufacturers and distributors should not escape liability for faulty products simply because they are not in privity of contract with the ultimate users of those products.
5.   B. If the plaintiff can prove these elements (material fact, misrepresentation, reliance, and injury), liability could be based on the circumstance that the manufacturer, when it sold its product, misrepresented the character of the product.
6.   A. A manufacturer may be held liable if its product is unsafe as a result of negligence in the manufacture or if the design makes it unreasonably dangerous for the use for which it is made. A manufacturer also has a duty to warn and to anticipate reasonably foreseeable misuses. An injury must not have been due to a change in the product after it was sold, but there is no requirement of privity. There is no liability, however, with respect to injuries caused by commonly known dangers, even if the manufacturer does not warn against them.
7.   D. In a product liability action based on strict liability, the plaintiff does not need to prove that anyone was at fault. Privity of contract is also not an element

of an action in strict liability. A plaintiff does have to show, however, in a suit against a seller, that the seller was a merchant engaged in the business of selling the product on which the suit is based. Note that recovery is possible against sellers who are processors, assemblers, packagers, bottlers, wholesalers, distributors, retailers, or lessors, as well as against manufacturers.

8. C. These choices concern the defective condition of a product that causes harm to a plaintiff. A product may be unreasonably dangerous due to a flaw in the manufacturing process, a design defect, or an inadequate warning.

9. C. All courts extend the doctrine of strict liability to injured bystanders. A defendant does not have to prove that the manufacturer or seller failed to use due care, nor is there a requirement of privity (or "intent" with regard to entering into privity). The defense of assumption of risk does not apply, because one cannot assume a risk that one does not know about.

10. C. If a manufacturer fails to use due care to make a product safe, the manufacturer may be liable for product liability based on negligence. This care must be used in designing the product, selecting the materials, producing the product, inspecting and testing any components, assembling the product, and placing warnings on the product.

Issue Spotters

1 Yes. The manufacturer is liable for the injuries to the user of the product. A manufacturer is liable for its failure to exercise due care to any person who sustains an injury proximately caused by a negligently made (defective) product. In this problem, the failure to inspect is a failure to use due care. Of course, the maker of the component part may also be liable.

2. Yes. Under the doctrine of strict liability, persons may be liable for the results of their acts regardless of their intentions or their exercise of reasonable care (that is, regardless of fault). There is no requirement of privity.

3. Yes. Most courts will consider a plaintiff's negligence in apportioning liability, resulting in an application of the doctrine of comparative negligence in strict liability cases.

Chapter 14

True-False Questions

1. T

2. F. A copyright is granted automatically when a qualifying work is created, although a work can be registered with the U.S. Copyright Office.

3. T

4. T

5. F. Anything that makes an individual company unique and would have value to a competitor is a

trade secret. This includes a list of customers, a formula for a chemical compound, and other confidential data.

6. F. Trade names cannot be registered with the federal government. They are protected, however, under the common law (when used as trademarks or service marks) by the same principles that protect trademarks.

7. F. A copy does not have to be the same as an original to constitute copyright infringement. A copyright is infringed if a substantial part of a work is copied without the copyright holder's permission.

8. F. A trademark may be infringed by an intentional or unintentional use of a mark in its entirety, or a copy of the mark to a substantial degree. In other words, a mark can be infringed if its use is intended or not, and whether the copy is identical or similar. Also, the owner of the mark and its unauthorized user need not be in direct competition.

9. T

10. F. Proof of a likelihood of confusion is not required in a trademark dilution action. The products involved do not even have to be similar. Proof of likely confusion is required in a suit for trademark infringement, however.

Fill-in Questions

70; 95; 120; 70

Multiple-Choice Questions

1. B. A firm that makes, uses, or sells another's patented design, product, or process without the owner's permission commits patent infringement. It is not required that an invention be copied in its entirety. Also, the object that is copied does not need to be trademarked or copyrighted, in addition to being patented.

2. A. The user of a trademark can register it with the U.S. Patent and Trademark Office, but registration is not necessary to obtain protection from trademark infringement. A trademark receives protection to the degree that it is distinctive. A fanciful symbol is the most distinctive mark.

3. B. Ten years is the period for later renewals of a trademark's registration. The life of a creator plus seventy years is a period for copyright protection. No intellectual work is protected forever, at least not without renewal. To obtain a patent, an applicant must satisfy the U.S. Patent and Trademark Office that the invention or design is genuine, novel, useful, and not obvious in light of contemporary technology. A patent is granted to the first person to create whatever is to be patented, rather than the first person to file for a patent.

4. A. Copyright protects a specific list of creative works, including literary works, musical works, sound recordings, and pictorial, graphic, and sculptural works. Although there are exceptions for "fair use," a work need not be copied in its entirety to be infringed.

Also, to make a case for infringement, proof of consumers' confusion is not required, and the owner and unauthorized user need not be direct competitors.

5. D. Business processes and information that cannot be patented, copyrighted, or trademarked are protected against appropriation as trade secrets. These processes and information include production techniques, as well as a product's idea and its expression.

6. C. Trademark law protects a distinctive symbol that its owner stamps, prints, or otherwise affixes to goods to distinguish them from the goods of others.

7. B. A collective mark is a certification mark used by members of a cooperative, association, or other organization (a union, in this problem). A certification mark certifies the region, materials, method of manufacture, quality, or accuracy of goods or services. A service mark distinguishes the services of one person or company from those of another. A trade name indicates part or all of a business's name.

8. D. This is not copyright infringement because no copyright is involved. This is not cybersquatting because no one is offering to sell a domain name to a trademark owner. (It is also unlikely that this violates the Anticybersquatting Consumer Protection Act because there is no indication of "bad faith intent.") Trademark dilution occurs when a trademark is used, without the owner's without permission, in a way that diminishes the distinctive quality of the mark. That has not happened here.

9. C. The Berne Convention provides some copyright protection, but its coverage and enforcement was not as complete or as universal as that of the TRIPS (Trade-Related Aspects of Intellectual Property Rights) Agreement. The Paris Convention allows parties in one signatory country to file for patent and trademark protection in other signatory countries.

10. A. Publishers cannot put the contents of their periodicals into online databases and other electronic resources, including CD-ROMs, without securing the permission of the writers whose contributions are included.

Issue Spotters

1. The owner of the customer list can sue its competitor for the theft of trade secrets. Trade secrets include customer lists. Liability extends to those who misappropriate trade secrets by any means, including modems.

2. This is patent infringement. A software maker in this situation might best protect its product, save litigation costs, and profit from its patent by the use of a license. In the context of this problem, a license would grant permission to sell a patented item. (A license can be limited to certain purposes and to the licensee only.)

3. Yes. This may be an instance of trademark dilution. Dilution occurs when a trademark is used, with-

out permission, in a way that diminishes the distinctive quality of the mark. Dilution does not require proof that consumers are likely to be confused by a connection between the unauthorized use and the mark. The products involved do not have to be similar. Dilution does require, however, that a mark be famous when the dilution occurs.

Chapter 15

True-False Questions

1. F. A mechanic's lien involves real property. An artisan's lien or an innkeeper's lien involves personal property.

2. F. This is prohibited under federal law. Garnishment of an employee's wages, for any one indebtedness, cannot be a ground for the dismissal of an employee.

3. T

4. T

5. F. This is the most important concept in suretyship: a surety can use any defenses available to a debtor (except personal defenses) to avoid liability on the obligation to the creditor. Note, though, that a debtor does need not to have defaulted on the underlying obligation before a surety can be required to answer for the debt. Before a *guarantor* can be required to answer for the debt of a debtor, the debtor must have defaulted on the underlying obligation, however.

6. F. Any individual can be a debtor under Chapter 7, and any debtor who is liable on a claim held by a creditor may file for bankruptcy under Chapter 7.

7. T

8. T

9. F. Under Chapter 11, the creditors and the debtor formulate a plan under which the debtor pays some of the debts, the other debts are discharged, and the debtor is then allowed to continue in business.

10. F. Some small businesses—those who do not own or manage real estate and do not have debts of more than $2 million—can choose to avoid creditors' committees under Chapter 11. Those who choose to do so, however, are subject to shorter deadlines with respect to filing a reorganization plan.

Fill-in Questions

contract of suretyship; surety; surety; guaranty contract; guarantor

Multiple-Choice Questions

1. A. The creditor in this problem can use prejudgment attachment. Attachment occurs at the time of or immediately after commencement of a suit but before entry of a final judgment. The court issues a writ of attachment, directing the sheriff or other officer to seize property belonging to the debtor. If the creditor prevails at trial, the property can be sold to satisfy the judgment. (A writ of execution can be used after all of the conditions represented by the answer choices in this problem have been met.)

2.   D. The creditor can use garnishment, a collection remedy directed at a debtor's property or rights held by a third person. A garnishment order can be served on the employer so that part of debtor's paycheck will be paid to the creditor.

3.   B. The debt is $200,000. The amount of the homestead exemption ($50,000) is subtracted from the sale price of the house ($150,000), and the remainder ($100,000) is applied against the debt. Proceeds from the sale of any nonexempt personal property could also be applied against the debt. The debtor gets the amount of the homestead exemption, of course.

4.   A. A guarantor is secondarily liable (that is, the principal must first default). Also, in this problem, if the president were, for example, the borrower's only salaried employee, the guaranty would not have to be in writing under the main-purpose exception to the Statute of Frauds. A surety is primarily liable (that is, the creditor can look to the surety for payment as soon as the debt is due, whether or not the principal debtor has defaulted). Usually, also, in the case of a guarantor, a creditor must have attempted to collect from the principal, because usually a debtor would not otherwise be declared in default.

5.   C. A guarantor has the right of subrogation when he or she pays the debt owed to the creditor. This means that any right the creditor had against the debtor becomes the right of the guarantor. A guarantor also has the right of contribution, when there are one or more other guarantors. This means that if he or she pays more than his or her proportionate share on a debtor's default, the guarantor is entitled to recover from the others the amount paid above the guarantor's obligation. This problem illustrates how these principles work.

6.   D. Under Chapter 11, creditors and debtor plan for the debtor to pay some debts, be discharged of the rest, and continue in business. Under Chapter 13, with an appropriate plan, a small business debtor can also pay some (or all) debts, be discharged of the rest, and continue in business. A petition for a discharge in bankruptcy under Chapter 11 may be filed by a sole proprietor, a partnership, or a corporation; a petition for a discharge under Chapter 13, however, may be filed only by a sole proprietor, among these business entities.

7.   D. Claims that are not dischargeable in bankruptcy include the claims listed in the other answer choices: claims for back taxes accruing within three years before the bankruptcy, claims for alimony and child support, and claims for most student loans (unless their payment would result in undue hardship to the debtor, as stated in the correct answer choice). There are many others.

8.   A. Other grounds on which a discharge may be denied include concealing property with the intent to defraud a creditor, fraudulently destroying financial records, and refusing to obey a lawful court order. Having obtained a discharge in bankruptcy six years earlier is also a ground for denial. The other choices represent individual debts that are not dischargeable in bankruptcy.

9.   C. The first unsecured debts to be paid are the administrative expenses of the bankruptcy proceeding. Among the debts listed in this problem, the order of priority is then unpaid wages, consumer deposits, and taxes. Each class of creditors is fully paid before the next class is entitled to anything.

10.   D. Most corporations can file for bankruptcy under Chapter 7 or 11. The same principles that govern liquidation cases also govern reorganizations. Corporate debtors most commonly file petitions for bankruptcy under Chapter 11. One important difference between the two chapters is that in a Chapter 11 proceeding, the debtor can continue in business.

Issue Spotters

1.   Larry and Midwest can place a mechanic's lien on Joe's property. If Joe does not pay what he owes, the property can be sold to satisfy the debt. The only requirements are that the lien be filed within a specific time from the time of the work, depending on the state statute, and notice of the foreclosure and sale must be given to Joe in advance.

2.   Yes. In this problem, the party who assured the lender of payment on behalf of the debtor is a surety. A surety has a right of reimbursement from the debtor for all outlays the surety makes, as here, on behalf of the suretyship arrangement.

3.   Yes. A debtor's payment to a creditor made for a preexisting debt, within ninety days (one year in the case of an insider or fraud) of the bankruptcy filing, can be recovered if it gives a creditor more than he or she would have received in the bankruptcy proceedings.

Cumulative Hypothetical Problem for Unit Three—Including Chapters 9–15

1.   B. Intellectual property law protects such intangible rights as copyrights, trademarks, and patents, which include the rights that an individual or business firm has in the products it produces. Protection for software comes from patent law and from copyright law. Protection for the distinguishing trademarks on the software comes from, of course, trademark law.

2.   D. An offeror can revoke an offer for a bilateral contract, which is what this offer is, any time before it is accepted. This may be after the offeree is aware of the offer.

3. C. The modification would not be considered a rejection. Under UCC 2–207, a merchant can add an additional term to a contract, with his or her acceptance, as part of the contract, unless the offeror expressly states otherwise.

4. D. Of these choices, the firm most likely violated tort law, which includes negligence and strict liability, both as distinct torts and as a part of product liability. Negligence requires proof of intent. Strict liability does not. These firms may also have breached their contracts and their warranties, topics that are categorized as contract law and sales law.

5. B. Only a debtor can file a plan under Chapter 11, but for the court to confirm it, the secured creditors must accept it. There is another condition that the plan must meet. It must provide that creditors retain their liens and the value of the property to be distributed to them is not less than the secured portion of their claims, or the debtor must surrender to the creditors the property securing those claims.

Questions on the Focus on Legal Reasoning for Unit Three—*Ford v. Trendwest, Inc.*

1. C. In the *Ford* case, the court reasoned that "[w]hen the parties contracted for at-will employment, Ford had no greater expectations than an at-will employee, and Trendwest had no fewer rights than an at-will employer. . . . Nothing in this contract changed the at-will employment relationship." The court concluded that "lost earnings cannot measure damages for the breach of an employment at-will contract because the parties to such a contract do not bargain for future earnings. By its very nature, at-will employment precludes an expectation of future earnings."

2. A. The majority in the *Ford* case stated that "[a]n employee's expectations under an employment at-will contract are no different from the employment itself." An at-will employee may be terminated at any time for any reason. Nothing in an agreement to hire an individual for employment at-will "change[s] the at-will employment relationship."

3. D. The dissent in the *Ford* case reasoned that if an employer "promises . . . specific treatment in specific situations and an employee is induced thereby to . . . not actively seek other employment, those promises are enforceable." If they are breached, "the mere fact an employer could have fired the employee without liability the next day or under some other circumstance not amounting to breach of contract does not render . . . a claim for lost wages speculative."

Questions on the Focus on Ethics for Unit Three—The Commercial Environment

1. A. If a contract is unconscionable, it is so unfair and one-sided as to "shock the conscience" of a court and be unenforceable. Unconscionability, which rep-

resents an attempt by the law to enforce ethical behavior, is a common law concept that is not precisely defined. Even UCC 2–302, which adopts the doctrine, does not define the term with specificity. Instead, it is the prerogative of the courts to determine its application in contract cases.

2. B. This problem presents a cybergriper. A cybergriper uses another's trademark to protest, or otherwise complain about, in good faith and usually without profit, the owner's product or policy. Courts have held that this use of a mark is protected by the freedom of speech. The business's mark is not infringed because the public is not likely to be confused by the cybergriper's use.

3. A. Protection under copyright law for creative products, including books, extend for at least the life of the author plus seventy years. Exploiting a protected work before that protection expires would be a violation of copyright. Privacy rights, trademarks, and the freedom of speech can be violated in other contexts.

Chapter 16

True-False Questions

1. F. A sole proprietorship is the simplest form of business organization. In a sole proprietorship, the owner and the business are the same. Anyone who creates a business without designating a specific form for its organization is doing business as a sole proprietorship.

2. T

3. F. Joint ownership of property does not alone create a partnership, nor is the sharing of gross returns and profits from joint ownership usually enough to create a partnership.

4. T

5. F. Partners are subject to personal liability for the debts and obligations of a partnership, and this is whether or not they have participated in its management. On the firm's dissolution, its creditors have the top priority in the distribution of the firm's assets. If those assets are not sufficient to pay the creditors, the partners are liable for the difference.

6. T

7. T

8. F. The parties to a franchise (the franchisor and the franchisee) determine its termination. Generally, the parties provide in the franchise contract that termination is "for cause" and notice is required. Of course, in the case of a dispute, litigation may ensue and the parties may end up in court, which may then have to determine whether or not to terminate the franchise arrangement. That is not the usual course, however.

9. F. A franchisor can exercise greater control in this area than in some other areas of the business, because the *franchisor* has a legitimate interest in maintaining the quality of the product or service to protect its name and reputation.

10. F. Partners in a partnership can bind other partners to contracts and other obligations to third parties. The members of a joint venture have limited power to bind other members.

Fill-in Questions

are; obligation; sued; cannot; releases; must

Multiple-Choice Questions

1. D. There are no limits on the liability of the owner of a sole proprietorship for the debts and obligations of the firm. A sole proprietorship has greater organizational flexibility, however, than other forms of business organization.

2. A. Under a partnership by estoppel theory, a person who is not a partner, but who represents himself or herself as a partner, is liable to a third person who acts in reasonable reliance on that representation. If one of the actual partners had consented to the misrepresentation, the firm would also be liable. That is not the situation in this problem, however.

3. C. There are many ways to cause the dissolution of a partnership. Partners may expressly agree to dissolve their partnership, or the addition of a new partner or the transfer of a partner's interest (with or without all other partners' knowledge or consent) may cause a firm's dissolution. Depending on a particular state's law, dissolution may also result from the withdrawal of a partner. Of the choices in this problem, however, the only one that would cause dissolution is a partner's bankruptcy. Dissolution is, of course, only the first step towards the termination of the firm's legal existence. The winding up of the partnership's affairs cover the other steps.

4. B. For most purposes, a partnership is regarded as an entity. A partnership can sue and collect judgments in its own name (rather than in the names of the individual partners). A partnership can own real estate in its name. For federal income tax purposes, however, a partnership is considered an aggregate: the firm files an informational return with the Internal Revenue Service, but does not pay taxes on its profits. The income is passed through to the partners, who pay taxes on it on their individual returns.

5. B. After a partner informs the other partners that he or she is withdrawing from the partnership, the withdrawing partner is not liable for contracts entered into by his or her former partners. In fact, the partnership has dissolved and is also not liable. The parties who sign the contract are, of course, liable, however,

as is any new partnership formed to carry on the business.

6. C. This definition is like the definition of a partnership. A joint venture is similar to a partnership, and is generally subject to partnership law, but unlike a partnership, a joint venture is created in contemplation of a limited activity. A joint venture may have more than two members, and a joint venture is not a corporate enterprise, although its members may be corporations.

7. A. A business trust is similar to a corporation. Like corporate shareholders, the owners hold shares in the trust and they are not personally liable for the organization's debts and obligations.

8. C. Under a contract between the franchisor and the franchisee, the latter may be required to pay a fee for the franchise license, fees for products bought from or through the franchisor, and a percentage of advertising and administrative costs.

9. C. Of the choices here, the franchisor can set all of the terms. There may be little for a franchisee to negotiate with some franchisors, but perhaps the chief advantage of a franchise is that the franchisee is obtaining the opportunity to profit from the sales of a proven product or service.

10. C. A franchisee may have some protection under the Franchise Rule of the Federal Trade Commission with respect to what the franchisor must disclose, and how and when the disclosure must be made, before the franchisee invests in a franchise. A franchisee may have additional protection under federal law, depending on the nature of the products or services being sold. State protection, while similar to federal law, may include more protection under deceptive practices acts or Article 2 of the UCC.

Issue Spotters

1. Too much control may result in the franchisor's liability for torts of a franchisee's employees. For example, if the employee performs in a manner that is attributed to the control of the franchisor, and this performance results in an injury to another, the franchisor may be held liable.

2. No. Under the partners' fiduciary duty, a partner must account to the partnership for any personal profits or benefits derived without the consent of all the partners in connection with the use of any partnership property. Here, the leasing partner may not keep the money.

3. There are differences between these forms of business organization, but all of them are treated under the law like partnerships. The differences include that the members of joint ventures have less authority than partners, and the members of a joint stock company are not agents of each other. Also, a joint stock company has many of the characteristics of a corporation: (1) ownership by shares of stock, (2) managed by directors and officers, and (3) perpetual existence.

Chapter 17

True-False Questions

1.   T
2.   F. Similarly, a limited partnership will not dissolve on the personal bankruptcy of a limited partner. These same events occurring to a general partner can dissolve the firm, however.
3.   F. State law applies. Like the formation of a corporation and other forms of limited liability organizations, the formation of a limited liability company (LLC) requires that articles of organization be filed in the state of formation. Otherwise, an LLC will not be held to exist, and its members will not enjoy the features that they wanted.
4.   T
5.   F. One of the chief advantages of a limited liability company (LLC) is that it offers the limited liability of a corporation. Because an LLC also offers the tax advantages of a partnership, many businesses are using this form of organization.
6.   F. A feature that makes a limited liability partnership attractive to professionals is that its partners can avoid liability for the malpractice of other partners. Of course, each partner is liable for his or her own wrongful acts. All of the partners may be held liable for other obligations of the partnership, however.
7.   F. The liability of the limited partners in a limited partnership is limited to the amount of their investment in the firm, but the liability of the general partners is the same as that of the partners in a general partnership (unlimited).
8.   T
9.   T
10. T

Fill-in Questions

members; limited liability company; limited partners; limited partnership

Multiple-Choice Questions

1.   D. Ordinarily, limited partners are liable for the debts of their limited partnerships only to the extent of their capital contributions to the firms. A general partner, in contrast, may be held personally liable for the full amount of the firm's obligations. Similarly, a limited partner, unlike a general partner does not have a right to control the partnership.
2.   B. A partner (general or limited) pays personal income taxes on his or her share of the firm's income, regardless of whether or not it is distributed to him. The other partners pay taxes on their shares of the firm's income. Note that each partner is liable for a pro rate share of the taxes even if they are not distributed.
3.   B. A limited liability company (LLC) can be taxed as a partnership, a sole proprietorship (if there is only one member), or a corporation, but when there is more than on member, electing to be taxed as a partnership is generally preferable. The income can be passed through to its members without being taxed at the company level. Generally, there is no particular advantage to being taxed as a corporation. In fact, avoiding the double corporate tax is one reason for forming an LLC.
4.   B. Normally, the members of a limited liability company are liable for the debts of their company only to the extent of their investment in the firm, like corporate shareholders or limited partners. Sole proprietors and general partners, in contrast, may be personally liable for the full amount of their firms' obligations.
5.   C. One of the advantages of the limited liability company (LLC) form of business organization is that its members are not personally liable for the debts of their firm regardless of the extent of their participation in management (unlike a limited partnership). In fact, unless agreed otherwise, an LLC's management will be considered to include all members. Another advantage is that there is generally no limit on the number of members that a firm can have (unlike an S corporation).
6.   D. Limited partnerships may be dissolved by many causes but not by any of these choices. Partners may expressly agree to dissolve their partnership, or dissolution may be caused by the withdrawal, death, or mental incompetence of a general partner (unless the others agree to continue the business). A *general* partner's death or bankruptcy causes the firm to dissolve, as would an event that makes it impossible to operate the partnership lawfully. Dissolution can also result from a court decree.
7.   B. Professionals who organize as a limited liability partnership avoid personal liability for the wrongdoing of other partners. They have only the same liability as a limited partner in a limited partnership. That is, their liability does not extend beyond the amount that they have invested in the firm.
8.   A. Also, the partners must sign a certificate of limited partnership, which must then be filed with the appropriate state official, usually the secretary of state.
9.   A. Limited partners essentially have fewer rights than general partners. (In return, they assume less liability for the debts of the firm.) One of the important rights of general partners that limited partners usually do not have is the right to participate in the management of the firm.
10. C. It is expected that eventually, state laws governing limited liability companies (LLCs) will be made relatively uniform. As for the other choices, the members are not subject to personal liability for the firm's

obligations. Also, unlike corporate income, LLC income can pass through the firm and be taxed only once.

Issue Spotters

1. A partner who commits a wrongful act, such as fraud, is liable for the results. The partner who supervises the party who commits the act may also be held liable. Some states limit this liability so that each partner is liable only up to the proportion of his or her responsibility for the result.
2. There is no law that expressly bars the participation of limited partners in the management of a limited partnership. Limited partners are, however, normally exempt from personal liability for partnership debts, torts, breaches of contract, and breaches of trust. This exemption rests primarily on the limited partner's not participating in the management of the partnership. Thus, it is the threat of personal liability that deters their participation.
3. The members of a limited liability company (LLC) may designate a group to run their firm, in which situation the firm would be considered a *manager*-managed LLC. The group may include only members, only nonmembers, or members and nonmembers. If instead, all members participate in management, the firm would be a *member*-managed LLC. In fact, unless the members agree otherwise, all members are considered to participate in the management of the firm.

Chapter 18

True-False Questions

1. F. A corporation formed in a country other than the United States, but that does business in the United States, is an alien corporation. A foreign corporation is a corporation formed in one state, but doing business in another state.
2. F. An S corporation has tax imposed only at the shareholder level. Other corporations are subject to double taxation, however, which was one of the reasons for the enactment of the S corporation statute. Only corporations with seventy-five or fewer shareholders can qualify for S-corporation status, although in some circumstances, a corporation can be an S-corporation shareholder.
3. T
4. T
5. F. Preemptive rights consist of preferences given to shareholders over other purchasers to buy shares of a new corporate issue in proportion to the number of shares that they already hold. This allows a shareholder to maintain his or her proportionate ownership share in the corporation. Generally, these rights are granted (or withheld) in the articles of incorporation.

6. F. Any damages recovered in a shareholder's derivative suit are normally paid to the corporation on whose behalf the shareholder or shareholders exercised the derivative right.
7. T
8. F. Officers and directors owe the same fiduciary duties to the corporations for which they work. They both owe a duty of loyalty. This duty requires them to subordinate their personal interests to the welfare of the corporation.
9. F. The business judgment rule immunizes directors (and officers) from liability for poor business decisions and other honest mistakes that cause a corporation to suffer a loss. Directors are not immunized from losses that do not fit this category, however.
10. T

Fill-in Questions

but ownership is not; can; recorded as the owner in the corporation's books

Multiple-Choice Questions

1. D. State incorporation laws vary, so looking for the state that offers the most favorable provisions for a particular firm is important. There are some principles that states commonly observe, however. For example, in all states a firm can have perpetual existence, but cannot do business under the same, or even a similar, name as an existing firm.
2. A. Corporate directors manage the business of a corporation. The directors normally employ officers, who oversee the daily operations. The directors may be initially designated by the incorporators or promoters, but are later elected by the shareholders (the owners of the corporation).
3. A. This firm has the characteristics of a close corporation. A close corporation is also generally allowed to restrict the transfer of its stock. Firms represented by the other answer choices could also be close corporations. To be a professional corporation, a firm must be a corporation formed by professionals (and the firm is designated by "P.A." for "professional association," or some other appropriate abbreviation). S corporations and nonprofits corporations have other requirements.
4. A. Dividends may be paid from a limited number of sources and once declared, a dividend becomes a debt enforceable at law like any other debt. Generally, state law allows dividends to be paid as long as a corporation can pay its other debts as they come due and the amount of the dividend is not more than the net worth of the corporation. But shareholders are not entitled to the payment of dividends. Their payment is at the discretion of the board of directors, who may choose not to order a dividend.
5. A. Officers and other executive employees are hired by a corporation's board of directors. The rights

of the officers and other high-level managers are defined by their employment contracts with the corporation.

6. D. The other choices do not represent proper purposes for which a shareholders' derivative suit may be filed. A shareholder's derivative suit is a claim filed on behalf of the corporation. Such a suit may allege, for example, that officers or directors misused corporate assets. Of course, any damages that are awarded must be paid to the corporation.

7. C. Cumulative voting can often be used in the election of directors to enhance the power of minority shareholders in electing a representative. In calculating a shareholder's votes under the cumulative voting method, in this problem, Mary's number of shares is multiplied by the number of directors to be elected.

8. B. If a state statute does not provide to the contrary, a quorum of directors must be present to conduct corporate business, such as the declaration of a dividend. A quorum is a majority of the number of directors authorized in the firm's articles or bylaws. The rule is one vote per director.

9. A. The board of directors hires the company's officers and other managerial employees, and determines their compensation. Ultimate responsibility for all policy decisions necessary to the management of corporate affairs also rests with the directors.

10 A. Other factors that a court may use to pierce the corporate veil include that a party is tricked or misled into dealing with the firm rather than the individual, that the firm is too thinly capitalized (not overcapitalized), and that the firm holds too few (not too many) shareholders' meetings.

Issue Spotters

1. Yes. A foreign corporation must have sufficient minimum contacts with a state for it to exercise jurisdiction. Doing business within a state is generally considered to constitute sufficient contact, as a firm does when it sells or advertises in a state, or otherwise places goods in the stream of commerce. Thus, a court in which a firm does business can exercise jurisdiction over it even if it was not incorporated in that state.

2. Under these circumstances, a minority shareholder can petition a court to appoint and receiver and liquidate the assets of the corporation.

3. Yes. A shareholder can bring a derivative suit on behalf of a corporation, if some wrong is done to the corporation. Normally, any damages recovered go into the corporate treasury.

Cumulative Hypothetical Problem for Unit Four—Including Chapters 16–18

1. A. A partnership is an association of two or more persons who manage a business and share profits. Here, the partnership began when the parties combined their assets and commenced business. Before

that time, there was no sharing of profits, no joint ownership of a business, and no equal right in the management of a business (because there was no business). The execution of a formal partnership agreement is not necessary, nor is the consent of creditors.

2. B. Unlike general partnerships, which can come into existence even when the parties do not intend to form a partnership, a limited partnership can only be created pursuant to the provisions of a state statute. This statute sets out exactly what partners must do to form a limited partnership, which must include at least one general partner who assumes personal liability for the debts of the firm.

3. D. The information that each state requires to be in articles of incorporation differs somewhat, but the information represented by the choices in this problem is generally required. It is not necessary to name the initial officers in the articles. Other information that might be required includes the number of authorized shares. Other information that is not required includes quorum requirements.

4. B. Directors' main right is their right to participate in board meetings. Directors also have a right to inspect corporate books and to be indemnified in defense of some lawsuits (regardless of the outcome of the suit). Rights that directors do not have include a right to compensation. That is, directors may be compensated for their efforts, but they have no inherent right to it. "Preemption" is not a right.

5. A. Dividends may be paid from any of the other of sources in the answer choices. Note that there is no right to a dividend. Its payment is subject to the discretion of the board of directors.

Questions on the Focus on Legal Reasoning for Unit Four—*Seven Springs Farm, Inc. v. Croker*

1. D. The majority held that "a merger is a corporate act, not a shareholder act, and therefore does not fall within" a restrictive stock-transfer agreement such as the one in this problem. Under the majority's reasoning, the parties to this sort of agreement could include a prohibition on corporate actions in this type of agreement, but there is no indication of that restriction when, as here, the agreement defines *shareholder* to include only individual shareholders.

2. B. The dissent argued that a corporation is bound by a shareholder agreement's transfer restrictions, in part on the reasoning that a merger is not solely a corporate act. The dissent stated, "While a corporation can propose a . . . merger, the transaction may not be consummated unless the stockholders have also acted to approve the deal."

3. C. The majority's holding "permits the shareholders to obtain cash for their shares by way of merger" or to "accomplish that same objective by selling their shares [subject to] the right of first re-

fusal." This means that absent a fundamental corporate act such as a merger, under a shareholders' stock-transfer agreement such as the one in this problem the shares of a closely held corporation cannot be sold without triggering a right of first refusal.

Questions on the Focus on Ethics for Unit Four—The Business Environment

1.   D. This duty arises from the legal principles of agency, and applies to all corporate officers, managers, and directors. When personal interests conflict with the interests of the corporation, the corporate party must not act against the interest of the corporation. If an officer usurps a corporate opportunity by, for example, setting up a competing firm to take advantage of an opportunity that might have otherwise been utilized by his or her corporation, a successful claim against the individual can result in the individual giving up an interest in the new company to the shareholders of the corporation.

2.   C. Corporate directors have a fiduciary duty to exercise care when making decisions that affect their corporations. Fiduciary duties may, in some extraordinary circumstances, be owed to other directors, officers, or the firm's creditors, particularly if a director's corporation is nearly insolvent. In normal situations, however, the duty of care extends chiefly to the corporation's shareholders, and may include a duty to implement a program to uncover and prevent wrongdoing by corporate personnel.

3.   B. When a franchisor's control over the operations of its franchisee is too extensive, the franchisor may be held liable for the torts of the franchisee's employees under agency principles. This may occur even if the franchise agreement between the parties specifies that the individuals are independent contractors, or otherwise.

Chapter 19

True-False Questions

1.   T
2.   F. When an agent breaches an agency contract, the principal can choose to avoid the contract.
3.   F. If an agent is negligent and harms a third party, the injured third party can successfully sue the principal. In some circumstances, the principal may also sue the agent. The same principles apply when an agent violates a principal's instructions.
4.   T
5.   T
6.   T
7.   T
8.   F. Criminal acts by an agent are not the responsibility of the principal, who will not thus be liable to a third party for any consequent harm.

9.   F. The parties to an agency may always have the *power* to terminate the agency at any time, but they may not always have the *right*. If a party who terminates an agency does not have the right to do so, he or she may be liable for breach of contract.
10.   F. An e-agent is a semi-autonomous computer program that is capable of executing specific tasks, including responding to "electronic messages or performances without review by an individual," according to the Uniform Computer Information Transactions Act.

Fill-in Questions

performance; notification; loyalty; obedience; accounting

Multiple-Choice Questions

1.   D. This is an agency relationship. An agency agreement does not have to be in writing, and an agent does not need to indicate that he or she is an agent. The business of the agent is not a determining factor in whether an agency relationship exists.
2.   A. An agent's duties to a principal include a duty to act solely in the principal's interest in matters concerning the principal's business. This is the duty of loyalty. The agent must act solely in the principal's interest and not in the interest of the agent, or some other party. It is also a breach of the duty of loyalty to use a principal's trade secrets or other confidential information (but not acquired skills) even after the agency has terminated.
3.   D. If a principal causes a third person to believe that another person is his or her agent, and the third person deals with the supposed agent, the principal is estopped to deny the agency relationship. The third person must reasonably believe that the relationship existed and that the agent had authority. An ordinary, prudent person familiar with business practice and custom would have been justified in making the same conclusion.
4.   B. A failure to disclose material information bearing on an agency relationship is a breach of an agent's duties. In that circumstance, the agency is voidable at the option of the principal. When the principal transfers the property that was the object of the agency, as in this problem, the agency relationship has been voided.
5.   C. When an agent acts within the scope of his or her authority to enter into a valid contract on behalf of an undisclosed principal, the principal is liable on the contract. Ratification is not necessary. The agent may also be liable on the contract.
6.   C. Under the doctrine of *respondeat superior*, an employer (or principal) is vicariously liable for the wrongful acts of his or her employee (or agent) committed within the scope of employment (or agency).

7.   C. When an agent acts without authority and a third party relies on the agency status, the agent may be liable for breach of any contract purportedly signed on behalf of a principal. The agent may not be liable, however, if the third party knew that the agent did not have authority to contract on behalf of the principal. In either case, the principal is not liable, unless he or she ratifies the contract.

8.   B. An employer is liable for harm to a third party by an employee acting within the scope of employment. Here, the question is whether the employee was acting within that scope. Factors which indicate he was not include that the act (theft) was not authorized, did not advance the employer's interest, is not commonly performed by employees for their employers, and involved a serious crime. The employer might be liable if it knew that the employee would commit a tort or allowed it. In this problem, the employee acted without the employer's knowledge.

9.   C. An agent (or employee) is liable for his or her own torts, whether or not they were committed within the scope of a principal's employment. The principal is also liable under the doctrine of *respondeat superior* when a tort is within the scope of the employment. One of the important factors in determining liability is whether the agent was on the principal's business or on a "frolic of his or her own."

10.   A. When an agent is employed to accomplish a particular objective, the agency automatically terminates when the objective is accomplished.

Issue Spotters

1.   Yes. A principal has a duty to indemnify an agent for liabilities incurred because of authorized and lawful acts and transactions and for losses suffered because of the principal's failure to perform his or her duties.

2.   No. An agent is prohibited from taking advantage of the agency relationship to obtain property that the principal wants to purchase. This is the duty of loyalty that arises with every agency relationship.

3.   A person in whose name a contract is made by one who is not an agent may be liable on the contract if he or she approves or affirms that contract. In other words, the employer-principal would be liable on the note in this problem on ratifying it.

Chapter 20

True-False Questions

1.   T

2.   F. Employment "at will" means that either party may terminate the employment at any time, with or without good cause. There are many exceptions to this doctrine, enacted by state legislatures and Congress, or created by the courts. These include exceptions based on contract or tort theories, or public policy.

3.   F. Employers are free to offer employees no benefits. Federal and state governments participate in insurance programs designed to protect employees and their families by covering some of the financial impact of retirement, disability, death, and hospitalization.

4.   T

5.   F. A "whistleblower" is one who reports wrongdoing. Whistleblower statutes protect employees who report their employers' wrongdoing from retaliation in the form of discharge, and sometimes other adverse employment conditions, on the part of those employers.

6.   F. The Electronic Communications Privacy Act prohibits the interception of telephone (and other electronic) communications. Some courts recognize an exception for employers monitoring employee business-related calls, but monitoring personal conversations is not permitted.

7.   F. These laws do not cover all employees. Although statutes vary in their coverage from state to state, they often exclude domestic workers (such as maids), agricultural workers, temporary employees, and employees of common carriers (such as trucking companies).

8.   T

9.   F. Under the Fair Labor Standards Act, minors (persons under the age of eighteen) cannot work in hazardous occupations.

10.   F. The Immigration Regulation and Control Act of 1986 prohibits employers from hiring illegal immigrants. U.S. employers who recruit workers in other countries must also comply with certain requirements, including a certification process.

Fill-in Questions

either; unless; may; Some; A few states; may not

Multiple-Choice Questions

1.   A. Child labor, minimum-wage, and maximum-hour provisions are included in the Fair Labor Standards Act (also known as the Wage-Hour Law), covering virtually all employees. The employer may also be subject to the other laws given as choices in this problem, but those laws concern other rights and duties of employees and employers.

2.   B. Investigating theft is the only circumstance in which an employer may require polygraph tests. Drug tests are prohibited by some states, and restricted by others or by collective bargaining agreements. Their use may also be subject to tort actions for invasion of privacy. An employer may monitor employees' *business* phone conversations but not their *private* ones.

3.   B. Intentionally inflicted injuries are not covered by workers' compensation. Many states cover problems arising out of preexisting conditions, but that is

not part of the test for coverage. To collect benefits, an employee must notify the employer of an injury and file a claim with the appropriate state agency.

4. C. Under the Immigration Act, employers recruiting workers from other countries must complete a certification process with the U.S. Department of Labor. Part of the process is to show that there is a shortage of qualified U.S. workers in the particular area and that hiring aliens will not have a negative impact on the labor market in the area.

5. B. The Federal Unemployment Tax Act of 1935 concerns the system that provides unemployment compensation. The Employee Retirement Income Security Act (ERISA) of 1974 concerns the regulation of private pension plans.

6. A. The Employment Retirement Income Security Act (ERISA) covers such employers. The Labor Management Services Administration of the U.S. Department of Labor enforces ERISA. The other laws mentioned in the choices in this problem regulate other areas of retirement and security income.

7. B. Under the Family and Medical Leave Act (FMLA) of 1993, employees can take up to twelve weeks of family or medical leave during any twelve-month period and are entitled to continued health insurance coverage during the leave. Employees are also guaranteed the same, or a comparable, job on returning to work.

8. C. Under the Consolidated Omnibus Budget Reconciliation Act (COBRA) of 1985, most workers' medical, optical, or dental insurance is not automatically eliminated on termination of employment. The workers can choose to continue the coverage at the employer's group rate, if they are willing to pay the premiums (and a 2 percent administrative fee).

9. C. When an employment relationship is "at will," either the employer or the employee may terminate it at any time—and for any reason. An employment relationship is at will when there is no contract and no law to otherwise restrict its duration or other conditions of its termination.

10. C. Depending on the particular state, and the rulings of the courts in the state, some state constitutions effectively prohibit private employers from testing for drugs. There are also state statutes that restrict drug testing by private employers. Other sources of limitation on the use of such tests include collective bargaining agreements and employee tort actions for invasion of privacy.

Issue Spotters

1. Probably. Some courts have held that an implied employment contract exists between employer and employee under an employee handbook that states employees will be dismissed only for good cause. An employer who fires a worker contrary to this promise can be held liable for breach of contract.

2. No. Generally, the right to recover under workers' compensation laws is determined without regard to negligence or fault. Unlike the potential for recovery in a lawsuit based on negligence or fault, however, recovery under a workers' compensation statute is limited to the specific amount designated in the statute for the employee's injury.

3. Generally, no, at least for the act discussed in this problem. Most states and the federal government protect employees who "blow the whistle" on the wrongdoing of their employers under whistleblowing statutes. In some instances, these statutes encourage whistleblowing by offering a monetary reward if the employee's charges lead to a successful government lawsuit.

Chapter 21

True-False Questions

1. T

2. F. An employer may be liable even though an employee did the harassing, if the employer knew, or should have known, and failed to take corrective action, or if the employee was in a supervisory position and took a tangible employment action against the injured employee.

3. F. Just as an employer may be liable for an employee's misconduct, the employer may be liable for harassment by a nonemployee, if the employer knew, or should have known, of the harassment and failed to take corrective action.

4. T

5. T

6. T

7. F. If the Equal Employment Opportunity Commission (EEOC) decides not pursue a claim, the victim can file a suit against alleged violator. The EEOC can pursue a claim in federal district court, however, in its own name against alleged violators (and this is true even if the employee has agreed to submit the dispute to arbitration). The EEOC can also intervene in a suit filed by a private party.

8. F. Title VII covers only employers with fifteen or more employees, labor unions with fifteen or more members, labor unions that operate hiring halls, employment agencies, and federal, state, and local agencies. In other words, small employers are generally exempted from the application of this federal statute.

9. T

10. T

Fill-in Questions

can; may sue if a settlement between the parties is not reached; reinstatement, back pay, and retroactive promotions

Multiple-Choice Questions

1. A. Before filing a lawsuit, the best step for a person who believes that he or she may be a victim of employment discrimination is to contact a state or federal agency to see whether the claim is justified. The appropriate federal agency is the Equal Employment Opportunity Commission. Most states have similar agencies that evaluate claims under state law.

2. A. Sexual harassment occurs when, in a workplace, an employee is subject to comments or contact that is perceived as sexually offensive. An employer may be liable even though an employee did the harassing. If the employee was in a supervisory position, as in this problem, for an employer to be held liable, a tangible employment action may need to be proved. Here, the employee's pay was cut.

3. A. The other choices would not subject the employer to liability under the Age Discrimination in Employment Act (ADEA). Discrimination is prohibited against persons forty years of age or older, even if the discrimination is unintentional. Mandatory retirement may be instituted, but not on account of an employee's age, and an employee may be discharged for cause at any age.

4. C. An employer who is subject to the Americans with Disabilities Act cannot exclude arbitrarily a person who, with reasonable accommodation, could do what is required of a job. A disabled individual is not required to reasonably accommodate an employer. Also, the standard is not "significant additional costs," to either the employer or the disabled individual.

5. C. Title VII prohibits employment discrimination on the basis of race. This includes discriminating against members of a minority with darker skin than other members of the same minority. Title VII also prohibits using physical characteristics that are typical of some races to distinguish applicants or employees.

6. C. Title VII prohibits showing a preference for members of one minority over members of another. Title VII also prohibits making distinctions according to the race of a person's spouse, friends, or other contacts. The other laws mentioned in the answer choices prohibit discrimination on the basis of age and disability, respectively, as suggested by their titles.

7. C. The Equal Pay Act of 1963 prohibits gender-based discrimination in wages for equal work. Different wages are acceptable because of any factor but gender, including seniority and merit.

8. C. Here, the employer would seem to have a valid business necessity defense. It appears reasonable that administrative assistants be able to type. An employer can insist that, to be hired, a job applicant possess the actual skills required for a job. Except for an applicant's willingness or unwillingness to acquire certain skills, the other answer choices might be legitimate defenses in other circumstances.

9. A. The Age Discrimination in Employment Act (ADEA) of 1967 requires, for the establishment of a *prima facie* case, that at the time of the alleged discrimination, the plaintiff was forty or older, was qualified for the job, and was discharged or otherwise rejected in circumstances that imply discrimination. The difference between a *prima facie* case under the ADEA and under Title VII is that the ADEA does not require a plaintiff to show that someone who is not a member of a protected class filled the position at the center of the claim.

10. C. The employer's best defense in this problem would be that being able to pass the tests is a business necessity—it is a necessary requirement for the job. Discrimination may be illegal even if it is not intentional, and whether or not all men pass the tests is not relevant to whether there is discrimination against women. If the employer hires some women for the job, it could not argue successfully that gender is a BFOQ for the job.

Issue Spotters

1. Yes, if he is a member of a protected class. These circumstances would then include all of the elements of a *prima facie* under Title VII of the Civil Rights Act of 1964: (1) the applicant is a member of a protected class, (2) he applied and was qualified for an open position, (3) he was rejected, and (4) the employer continued to seek applicants or filled the position with a person who is not in a protected class. The employer would then have to offer a legitimate reason for its action, and the applicant would have to show that this is a pretext, that discriminatory intent was the motivation.

2. Yes. One type of sexual harassment occurs when a request for sexual favors is a condition of employment, and the person making the request is a supervisor or acts with the authority of the employer. A tangible employment action, such as continued employment, may also lead to the employer's liability for the supervisor's conduct. That the injured employee is a male and the supervisor a female, instead of the other way around, would not affect the outcome. Same-gender harassment is also actionable.

3. Yes, if she can show that she was not hired solely because of her disability. The other elements for a discrimination suit based on a disability are that the plaintiff (1) has a disability and (2) is otherwise qualified for the job. Both of these elements appear to be satisfied in this problem.

Chapter 22

True-False Questions

1.   F. Secondary boycotts, including hot-cargo agreements, which are described in the question, are illegal.

2.   F. It is the central legal right of a *union* to serve as the bargaining representative of employees in negotiations with management, not the other way around, as set out in this question.

3.   T

4.   F. Employees' right to engage in collective bargaining through elected representatives, like their right to organize and their right to engage in concerted activities for those and other purposes, was established in the National Labor Relations Act.

5.   T

6.   T

7.   T

8.   F. A lockout is a shut down to prevent employees from working. An employer cannot use this tactic to break a union or to pressure employees into decertifying it.

9.   T

10.   T

Fill-in Questions

Norris-LaGuardia; National Labor Relations; Relations; allows; prohibits

Multiple-Choice Questions

1.   D. It is not a violation of any of these laws *not* to pay workers for time spent on union activities (going to meetings, soliciting support, canvassing co-workers, and so on). In fact, paying workers for participating in union activities is an unfair labor practice because it is considered to be giving support to the union.

2.   B. The National Labor Relations Act protects employees who engage in union activity and prohibits employers from refusing to bargain with employees' designated representative. Firing workers for supporting or joining a union is an unfair labor practice, as is refusing to recognize and bargain with the union.

3.   C. It is an unfair labor practice to ask employees to declare their views on a union without anonymity. An employer can poll its employees during a unionization campaign, or any time, only if their identities are protected.

4.   D. An employer cannot refuse to negotiate in good faith, during collective bargaining, over either of these terms and conditions of employment. They are mandatory subjects for collective bargaining. Because an employer must agree to talk about these subjects does not mean that the employer must accept the union's position on the topics, however.

5.   A. Management is not required to bargain with a union over a decision to close a facility—although an employer may bargain over this topic if it chooses to do so. (Economic consequences of the decision must be bargained over, however.) On the other hand, the procedure for employee grievances is an appropriate subject for the bargaining table.

6.   C. Denying nonunion workers access to a plant is illegal, whether or not the occasion is a strike and regardless of whether the nonunion workers are replacement workers for the strikers, regular company employees, supervisors, or managers.

7.   D. It is not an unfair labor practice to do either of the activities described in this problem. The picketers cannot keep others who wish to enter the workplace from going in, however, nor can they use violence or threats of violence. Also, striking workers cannot picket the worksite of a secondary employer.

8.   D. This question may seem difficult because it is phrased in the negative, but none of these choices represent unfair labor practices. Campaigning against a union during a union election campaign is not an unfair labor practice. Furthermore, an employer can campaign against a union without giving the union any opportunity for rebuttal. An employer can also make an election speech within twenty-four hours of an election if the employees are not required to listen but can attend voluntarily on their own time.

9.   D. It is an unfair labor practice for an employer to threaten employees with the loss of their jobs if a union wins a scheduled union election. What can be difficult is determining what constitutes a threat. Explicit statements, such as "if the union wins, you're all fired," are obvious violations. Less clear is whether such a statement as "if the union wins, we will lose business to our competitors" is a violation. The point, however, is that an employer cannot require rejection of a union as a condition of employment. The other choices are, of course, not unfair labor practices.

10.   D. An employer can hire permanent replacement workers during an economic strike. After the strike, the replacement workers do not have to be fired to make way for the strikers. Temporary replacement workers may be hired during any strike.

Issue Spotters

1.   No. A closed shop (a company that requires union membership as a condition of employment) is illegal. A union shop (a company that does not require union membership as a condition of employment but requires workers to join the union after a certain time on the job) is illegal in a state with a right-to-work law, which makes it illegal to require union membership for continued employment.

2.   Yes. If the employee complains, the employer can be required to show that it did not have an unlawful discriminatory motive. Factors to be considered in

determining motive include whether the employer applied its rules inconsistently and, in particular, more strictly against union advocates.

3. Yes. An action by a single employee is protected concerted activity if it is taken for the benefit of other employees, if the employee discussed the action with other approving workers, and if the employer is aware that it is concerted activity taken with the assent of other workers.

Cumulative Hypothetical Problem for Unit Five—Including Chapters 19–22

1. B. The requirements for recovery under state workers' compensation laws include the existence of an employment relationship and an accidental injury that occurs on the job or within the scope of employment. Accepting benefits precludes an employee from suing his or her employer, but it does not bar the employee from suing a third party for causing the injury.

2. D. The Social Security Act of 1935 provides payments for persons who are retired or disabled. The Social Security Administration is a federal agency that also administers the Medicare program. Unemployment benefits, however, are part of a state system created by the Federal Unemployment Tax Act of 1935.

3. D. One of the agent's fiduciary duties to the principal is the duty of loyalty. This means that the agent must not engage in conflicts of interest, and the agent cannot compete with the principal without informing the principal of the conflict of interest and obtaining the principal's consent.

4. A. Title VII of the Civil Rights Act of 1964 covers many forms of discrimination, including discrimination based on gender, race, religion, color, and national origin. But Title VII does not prohibit discrimination based on age, which is the subject of the Age Discrimination in Employment Act of 1967.

5. B. The Age Discrimination in Employment Act of 1967 prohibits discrimination against persons aged forty or more. This includes mandatory retirement of such individuals. In most circumstances, however, an employer can discharge an employee for cause, regardless of his or her age, without running afoul of this, or any other, federal anti-discrimination law.

Questions on the Focus on Legal Reasoning for Unit Five—*Redi-Floors, Inc. v. Sonenberg Co.*

1. D. In the *Redi-Floors* case, the majority explained out that "if an agent buys in his own name, without disclosing his principal, and the seller subsequently discovers that the purchase was, in fact, made for another, he may, at his choice, look for payment either to the agent or the principal." In the words of the court, a seller "who has once elected, can claim no right to make a second choice," however.

2. A. It would likely depend on the grounds for the verdict. In the reasoning of the majority in the *Redi-Floors* case, however, "it is the plaintiff who is entitled to elect against which of the defendants, principal or agent, to take the judgment." In this *Redi-Floors* case, "the trial court's erroneous granting of a directed verdict deprived the plaintiff of its right to elect which defendant it would proceed against."

3. D. The dissent in the *Redi-Floors* case reasoned that the seller made its decision against whom to pursue an action when the contracting party "procured a judgment order which was reduced to writing against" the principal. Obtaining that judgment "constituted an election of alternative remedies that precluded plaintiff from pursuing the excluded remedy against" the agent. "As the plaintiff may not obtain judgment against both, he must make an election *prior to judgment.*"

Questions on the Focus on Ethics for Unit Five—The Employment Environment

1. D. The conduct stated in the answer choices is permitted by legal and ethical considerations. Other actions that may be proscribed by ethics include secretly profiting from the agency relation, and failing to disclose the agent's interest in property that the principal is buying.

2. C. Agents and principals owe each other fiduciary duties. The law mandates for a principal duties of compensation, cooperation, and reimbursement of agency-related expenses. A principal is not legally bound to a duty of loyalty, however, although a sense of loyalty may be based on ethical obligations.

3. D. Under the employment-at-will doctrine, an employer may terminate an employee for any reason or no reason at any time. Without an employment contract, or anything from which an employment contract can be implied, and without the protection of a federal or state statute, there are only limited common law grounds on which an action against such a termination can be maintained. The set of facts in this problem do not state a violation of public policy that would support such an action.

Chapter 23

True-False Questions

1. T

2. T

3. F. Under certain circumstances, consumers have a right to rescind their contracts. This is particularly true when a creditor has not made all required disclosures. A contract entered into as part of a door-to-door sale may be rescinded within three days, regardless of the reason.

4. T

5.   F. A consumer can also include a note in his or her credit file to explain any misinformation in the file. Under the Fair Credit Reporting Act, consumers are entitled to have deleted from their files any misinformation that leads to a denial of credit, employment, or insurance. Consumers are also entitled to receive information about the source of the misinformation and about anyone who was given the misinformation.

6.   T

7.   F. The Fair Debt Collection Practices Act applies only to debt collectors that attempt to collect debts on another party's behalf. Typically, the collector is paid a commission—a percentage of the amount owed or collected—for a successful collection effort.

8.   F. The Federal Trade Commission (FTC), the Federal Reserve Board of Governors (Fed), and other federal agencies regulate the terms and conditions of sales. For example, the FTC issues regulations covering warranties and labels, and the Fed regulates credit provisions in sales contracts.

9.   F. One who leases consumer goods in the ordinary course of their business must disclose *all* material terms in writing—clearly and conspicuously—if the goods are priced at $25,000 or less and the lease term exceeds four months. The Consumer Leasing Act of 1988 requires this.

10.   T

Fill-in Questions

$50; before; prohibits; from billing; if

Multiple-Choice Questions

1.   D. The FTC has the power to issue a cease-and-desist order, but in some cases, such an order is not enough to stop the harm. With counteradvertising (also known as corrective advertising), an advertiser attempts to correct earlier misinformation by admitting that prior claims about a product were untrue.

2.   C. A regular-size box of laundry soap, for example, cannot be labeled "super-size" to exaggerate the amount of product in the box. Labels on consumer goods must identify the product, the manufacturer, the distributor, the net quantity of the contents, and the quantity of each serving (if the number of servings is given). Other information may also be required.

3.   B. In a door-to-door sale, a consumer generally has at least a three-day cooling-off period within which to rescind the transaction. Salespersons are required to give consumers written notice of this right. If a sales presentation is to a consumer who speaks only Spanish, the notice must be in Spanish, too.

4.   C. Under the Fair Debt Collection Practices Act, once a debtor has refused to pay a debt, a collection agency can contact the debtor *only* to advise him or

her of further action to be taken. None of the rest of these choices would be legitimate possibilities.

5.   B. This is required under Regulation Z (which was issued by the Federal Reserve Board under the Truth in Lending Act) and applies to any creditor who, in the ordinary course of business, lends money or sells goods on credit to consumers, or arranges for credit for consumers. The information that must be disclosed includes: the specific dollar amount being financed; the annual percentage rate of interest; any financing charges, premiums or points; the number, amounts, and due dates of payments; and any penalties imposed on delinquent payments or prepayment.

6.   D. When contracting parties are subject to the Truth-in-Lending Act (TILA), Regulation Z applies to any transaction involving an installment sales contract in which payment is to be made in more than four installments. Normally, such loans as those described in this problem require more than four installments to repay. In any transaction subject to Regulation Z, the lender must disclose all of the credit terms clearly and conspicuously.

7.   C. The Fair Packaging and Labeling Act requires that products include a variety of information on their labels. Besides the information specified in the answer to this problem, manufactures must identify themselves and the packager or distributor or the product, as well as nutrition details, including how much and what type of fat a product contains.

8.   B. Under the Smokeless Tobacco Health Education Act of 1986, packages of smokeless tobacco products must include warnings about the health hazards associated with the use of smokeless tobacco similar to warnings contained on cigarette packages.

9.   C. The Consumer Product Safety Commission (CPSC) has sufficiently broad authority to remove from store shelves any product that it believes is imminently hazardous and to require manufacturers to report on products already sold. Additionally, the CPSC can ban the make and sale of any product that the CPSC deems to be potentially hazardous. The CPSC also administers other product safety legislation.

10.   D. The Truth-in-Lending Act includes rules covering credit cards. There is a provision that limits the liability of a cardholder to $50 per card for unauthorized charges made before the creditor is notified, and exempts a consumer from liability if the card was not properly issued. When a card is not solicited, it is not "properly issued," however, and thus a consumer, in whose name unauthorized charges are made, is not liable for those charges in any amount.

Issue Spotters

1.   Yes. The FTC has issued rules to govern advertising techniques, including rules designed to prevent bait-and-switch advertising. Under the FTC guide-

lines, bait-and-switch advertising occurs if the seller refuses to show the advertised item, fails to have in stock a reasonable quantity of the item, fails to promise to deliver the advertised item within a reasonable time, or discourages employees from selling the item.

2. Under the Truth-in-Lending Act, a buyer who wishes to withhold payment for a faulty product purchased with a credit card must follow specific procedures to settle the dispute. The credit card issuer then must intervene and attempt to settle the dispute.

3. Under an extensive set of procedures established by the FDA, which administers the Federal, Food, Drug and Cosmetic Act, drugs must be shown to be effective as well as safe before they may be marketed to the public. In general, manufacturers are responsible for ensuring that the drugs they offer for sale are free of any substances that could injure consumers.

Chapter 24

True-False Questions

1. F. Common law doctrines that were applied against polluters centuries ago may be applicable today. These include nuisance and negligence doctrines.

2. T

3. F. There are different standards for different pollutants and for different polluters. There are even different standards for the same pollutants and polluters in different locations. The standards cover the amount of emissions, the technology to control them, the notice that must be given to the public, and the penalties that may be imposed for noncompliance.

4. F. The Toxic Substances Control Act of 1976 regulates substances that the production and labeling of substances of that potentially pose an imminent hazard or an unreasonable risk of injury to health or the environment. The Comprehensive Environmental Response, Compensation, and Liability Act (CERCLA) of 1980 regulates the clean up of leaking hazardous waste disposal sites.

5. T

6. T

7. F. To penalize those for whom a violation is cost-effective, the EPA can obtain a penalty equal to a violator's economic benefits from noncompliance. Other penalties include criminal fines. Private citizens can also sue polluters. It is generally more economically beneficial for a business to comply with the Clean Air Act.

8. T

9. F. Under CERCLA, a party who transports waste to a hazardous waste site may be held liable for any and all of the cost to clean up the site. There is a variety of "potentially responsible parties" who may also be held liable, including the party who generated the waste, and current and past owners and operators of the site. A party assessed with these costs can bring a

contribution action against the others, however, to recoup the amount of their proportion.

10. T

Fill-in Questions

federal; federal; environmental impact that an action will have; environment; an action might cause to the environment; and reasons

Multiple-Choice Questions

1. D. An environmental impact statement (EIS) must be prepared when a major federal action significantly affects the quality of the environment. An action that affects the quality of the environment is "major" if it involves a substantial commitment of resources and "federal" if a federal agency has the power to control it.

2. C. Under the 1990 amendments to the Clean Air Act, different standards apply to existing sources and major new sources. Major new sources must use the maximum achievable control technology (MACT) to reduce emissions from the combustion of fossil fuels. Other factories and businesses must reduce emissions of hazardous air pollutants with the best available technology.

3. D. Sport utility vehicles are now subject to the same standards for polluting emissions as automobiles. If new motor vehicles do not meet the emission standards of regulations issued under the Clean Air Act, the EPA can order a recall of the vehicles and a repair or replacement of pollution-control devices.

4. C. A polluter can be ordered to clean up the pollution or to pay for the clean-up costs, and other penalties may be imposed. For example, fines may be assessed and imprisonment ordered.

5. C. Under the Resource Conservation and Recovery Act of 1976, producers of hazardous waste must properly label and package waste to be transported. Under the Comprehensive Environmental Response, Compensation, and Liability Act of 1980, the party who generated the waste disposed of at a site can be held liable for clean-up costs.

6. C. Under the Resource Conservation and Recovery Act of 1976, the EPA monitors and controls the disposal of hazardous waste. Under the Comprehensive Environmental Response, Compensation, and Liability Act, the EPA regulates the clean up of hazardous waste sites when a release occurs.

7. B. An action that affects the quality of the environment is "major" if it involves a substantial commitment of resources. Minor landscaping does not qualify because it does not involve such a commitment. The landscaping in this problem is "federal," however, because a federal agency controls it, and any landscaping can affect the quality of the environment.

8. C. Under the 1990 amendments to the Clean Air Act, different standards apply to existing sources and major new sources. Major new sources must use the maximum achievable control technology to reduce emissions from the combustion of fossil fuels. Other factories and businesses must reduce emissions of hazardous air pollutants with the best available technology.

9.   B. One of the goals of the Clean Water Act is to protect fish and wildlife. In part, this goal is met by protecting their habitats, such as swamps and other wetlands. Protecting these areas can also protect navigable waters into which wetlands drain and other surrounding resources. Before dredging and filling wetlands, a permit must be obtained from the Army Corps of Engineers.

10.   C. Any potentially responsible party can be charged with the entire cost to clean up a hazardous waste disposal site. Potentially responsible parties include former owners and may, under certain circumstances, include a lender to the owner. Of course, a party held responsible for the entire cost may be able to recoup some of it in a contribution action against other potentially responsible parties.

Issue Spotters

1.   The Comprehensive Environmental Response, Compensation, and Liability Act of 1980 regulates the clean up of hazardous waste disposal sites. Any potentially responsible party can be charged with the entire cost to clean up a hazardous waste disposal site. Potentially responsible parties include the person who generated the waste (ChemCorp) the person who transported the waste to the site (Central), the person who owned or operated the site at the time of the disposal (Intrastate Disposal), and the current owner or operator of the site (ABC). A party held responsible for the entire cost may be able to recoup some of it in a lawsuit against other potentially responsible parties.

2.   Yes. On the ground that the hardships to be imposed on the polluter and on the community are greater than the hardships suffered by the residents, the court might deny an injunction—if the plant is the core of a local economy, for instance, the residents may be awarded only damages.

3.   The Environmental Protection Agency (EPA) was established to administer most federal environmental policies and statutes. Although not identified in the text, other federal agencies with authority to regulate specific environmental matters include the U.S. Departments of the Interior, Defense, and Labor, the Food and Drug Administration, and the Nuclear Regulatory Commission.

Chapter 25

True-False Questions

1.   T

2.   F. The owner of a life estate has the same rights as a fee simple owner except that the value of the property must be kept intact for the holder of the future interest.

3.   F. An easement merely allows a person to use land without taking anything from it, while a profit allows a person to take something from the land.

4.   F. Under the Fifth Amendment to the U.S. Constitution, when taking private property, the government is required to pay the owner just compensation.

5.   F. The government has the power to take private property, but the purposes for which such property may be taken must be *public*.

6.   F. This is a tenancy for years. A periodic tenancy does not specify how long it will last.

7.   F. To be entitled to a variance, a landowner must show that a granting of the variance would *not* substantially alter the essential character of the zoned area.

8.   T

9.   T

10.   T

Fill-in Questions

1.   possibility of reverter; original owner

2.   reversion; reversion

Multiple-Choice Questions

1.   C. A *profit* is the right to go onto land in possession of another and take away some part of the land itself or some product of the land. In contrast, an easement is a right to make limited use of another person's land without taking anything from the property. A license is a revocable right to come onto another person's land.

2.   C. The rights that accompany ownership in fee simple include the right to sell the land or give it away, as well as the right to use the land for whatever purpose the owner sees fit, subject, of course, to the law's limitations.

3.   A. A covenant runs with the land so that the successors to the original parties are entitled to its benefit (or burdened with its obligation) if it meets four requirements. It must be created in writing (in the problem, the deeds). The parties must intend that it run with the land (in the problem, each successive owner agreed to maintain the fence). The limits on the "burdened" land (maintaining the fence) must have a connection to the land (the fence is built on the land and marks the common boundary). The original parties must have been in privity of estate when the covenant was created. All of these requirements are met here.

4.   B. An easement is a right to make limited use of another's real property without taking anything from it. In this problem, it is an easement by necessity—the

owner needs access to his property. The right to take something from the property is a profit. A revocable right to come onto the property is a license.

5. A. A lease that does not specify how long it is to last but does specify that rent is to be paid at certain intervals creates a periodic tenancy. The tenancy is automatically renewed for each rental period unless it has been properly terminated.

6. A. The federal government can take private property for public use (a "taking"), but it cannot do so, under the Fifth Amendment to the Constitution, without paying the property owner just compensation. In some cases, to obtain title, a condemnation proceeding is brought before the property is taken. In a separate proceeding, a court determines the property's fair value (usually market value) to be paid to the owner.

7. C. A general development plan provides information about growth in a community. This plan may be supplemented by specific area plans that indicate special requirements. Zoning ordinances relate to particular land uses and include building and use restrictions and requirements. Other sources of relevant local policy and law include growth-management ordinances.

8. C. As a parcel of land is developed, it needs such public services as streets and sewers. When the land is developed for residential use, new schools and other public facilities, such as parks, must often be built. To meet these needs, subdivision development typically takes shape in a process of give and take between a developer and local authorities. Sometimes, a developer is asked to dedicate land to public use, or to otherwise contribute to the cost of public facilities.

9. A. What the local authorities have done is to have effectively confiscated the developer's property. In this developer's case, it does not matter that the surrounding undeveloped property was zoned for use as a nature preserve only. If the developer sues the county, the regulation will likely be held unconstitutional and void unless the county pays for its effective confiscation of the developer's land.

10. C. Most zoning laws provide means by which a property owner may be granted a variance from the laws. Factors for granting a variance include that the owner finds it impossible to realize a reasonable return on the land as zoned, that the adverse effect of the ordinance is particular to the person seeking the variance and not of similar effect on other owners within the zone, and that granting a variance will not substantially alter the character of the zone. The most important of these criteria is the effect of the variance on the character of the neighborhood.

Issue Spotters

1. Yes. An owner of a fee simple has the most rights possible—he or she can give the property away, sell it,

transfer it by will, use it for almost any purpose, possess it to the exclusion of all the world, or as in this case, transfer possession for any period of time. The party to whom possession is transferred can also transfer his or her interest (usually only with the owner's permission) for any lesser period of time.

2. Probably not. A zoning ordinance is considered discriminatory if it affects one parcel of land in a way unlike surrounding parcels if there is no rational basis for the difference. The facts as stated in the problem do not indicate any basis for zoning this land differently.

3. One important ground, unrelated to a specific property owner, on which the zoning authorities could limit the issuance of this, and other, permits is to prevent population growth from racing ahead of the local community's ability to provide public services (water and sewer, trash removal, streets, schools, and so on).

Chapter 26

True-False Questions

1. T

2. T

3. T

4. F. Antitrust law is intended to promote business competition: the sort of competition that is believed to benefit society. It is thought that competition in the marketplace leads to better products and lower prices, which benefit consumers, as well as business owners and their employees.

5. F. A firm that can substantially ignore its competitors in setting a price for its product, or that can otherwise limit competition in its market, has considerable market power.

6. T

7. F. Attempted monopolization *is* an antitrust violation. To constitute a violation, an action must be specifically intended to exclude competitors and garner monopoly power. It must have a "dangerous probability" of success, but it need not have actually succeeded.

8. F. Under the Clayton Act, no person can be a director in two or more corporations at the same time *if* elimination of competition between or among the corporations would violate any of the antitrust laws (which include a requirement that any of the corporations have capital, surplus, or undivided profits aggregating more than a certain limit).

9. T

10. F. Under the Clayton Act, a private party can sue for *treble* damages and attorneys' fees, and may obtain an injunction if the violation hurt business activities protected by the antitrust laws.

Fill-in Questions

A restraint of trade; Monopoly power; monopoly power

Multiple-Choice Questions

1. C. The elements of the offense of monopolization include monopoly power and its willful acquisition. Market domination that results from legitimate competitive behavior (such as foresight, innovation, skill, and good management) is not a violation.

2. A. Similar exemptions from the antitrust laws include cooperative research among small business firms, cooperation among U.S. exporters to compete with comparable foreign associations, and joint efforts by businesspersons to obtain legislative, judicial, or executive action.

3. C. Market power is the extent to which a firm can raise prices without concern for its competitors' response, or the extent to which a firm can otherwise exclude competition. Restraints of trade include agreements between suppliers in a market to limit output. Agreements between business firms that reduce competition are exercises of market power, but the agreements are not legitimate. They are generally restraints of trade that are against public policy and that violate the antitrust laws. An agreement that does not promote competition is not considered economically efficient or socially beneficial.

4. B. Selling a product or a service at a price substantially below cost is predatory pricing. Even if the result is to drive some competitors from the market, predatory pricing is not an antitrust violation if the firm that engages in the practice is attempting to gain access to an established market and the firm is unlikely to obtain monopoly profits in the future.

5. C. Determination of the relevant market is required to determine whether a firm has monopoly power. The relevant market has two parts: the relevant product market and the relevant geographical market. The product market consists of all products with identical attributes and products that are sufficient substitutes for each other. The geographical market is limited to the area in which a firm and it competitors sell those products.

6. D. The U.S. Department of Justice can prosecute violations of the Sherman Act as criminal or civil violations, but can enforce the Clayton Act only through civil proceedings. The Federal Trade Commission can also enforce the Clayton Act (and has sole authority to enforce the Federal Trade Commission Act). A private party can sue under the Clayton Act if he or she is injured by a violation of *any* antitrust law.

7. A. The elements of the offense of monopolization include monopoly power (market domination) and its willful acquisition. Conduct is considered to be anticompetitive if it is intended to obtain monopoly power and it is engaged in willfully. Market domination that results from historical circumstances, a superior product, or business acumen (which may involve foresight, innovation, skill, and good management) is not considered to have been acquired unlawfully.

8. C. A seller charging different buyers different prices for identical goods is a violation of the Clayton Act's price discrimination provision. (The effect of the price discrimination must also be to substantially lessen competition.) It is *not* a violation of the act if the different prices are due to different production and transportation costs. Of course, it is also not a violation to charge different prices for different goods, or if the situation involves no more than one buyer buying different kinds of goods, or no more than one price at a level no less than that charged by competitors. Price discrimination is discussed in more detail in Chapter 27

9. D. Exporters that cooperate to compete against similar foreign associations are exempt from the antitrust laws, as long as the activity does not restrain trade in the United States or injure other U.S. exporters. Other exemptions include cooperative research among small businesses, and research or production of a product, process, or service by joint ventures consisting of competitors.

10. D. Illegal tying arrangements violate the Clayton Act. Although violations of the Clayton Act are not criminal, the U.S. Department of Justice can enforce its provisions in civil proceedings. The Federal Trade Commission can also seek civil sanctions under the Clayton Act, and private parties (such as the customers in this problem) can seek civil remedies for their injuries.

Issue Spotters

1. Size alone does not determine whether a firm is a monopoly—size in relation to the market is what matters. A small store in a small, isolated town is a monopolist if it is the only store serving that market. Monopoly involves the power to affect prices and output. If a firm has sufficient market power to control prices and exclude competition, that firm has monopoly power. Monopoly power in itself is not a violation of Section 2 of the Sherman Act. The offense also requires an intent to acquire or maintain that power through anticompetitive means.

2. Yes. The term monopoly is used to describe a market in which there is a single seller. Having monopoly power is not a violation of the antitrust laws if its results from business ability, historical circumstances, or a superior product. A monopoly, or an attempt to monopolize, is a violation of the law only if anticompetitive conduct is involved.

3. The court could find that there is a sufficient degree of interchangeability between sugar and its substitutes to conclude that the firm in this problem does not control a share of the relevant market sufficient to constitute market power. The court's ultimate conclusion will depend in part on the size of the market and the firm's share of it. Even if the court concludes that the firm has a large share of market power, it seems unlikely that the firm would, in this case, be considered in violation of the antitrust laws, however. The power was acquired as a result of efficient business practices, not through willful, anticompetitive behavior.

Chapter 27

True-False Questions

1. F. This is a vertical restraint.
2. F. This is a horizontal restraint.
3. F. Exclusive dealing contracts are those under which a seller forbids a buyer from purchasing products from the seller's competitors.
4. F. Price discrimination occurs when sellers charge competitive buyers different prices for identical goods.
5. F. This is a *vertical* merger. A horizontal merger is a merger between firms that compete with each other in the same market.
6. F. This is a *horizontal* merger. A vertical merger occurs when a company at one stage of production acquires another company at a higher or lower stage in the chain of production and distribution.
7. T
8. T
9. F. The opposite is true. If an agreement is *not* deemed a *per se* violation of Section 1 of the Sherman Act, a court analyzes its legality under what is referred to as a rule of reason.
10. T

Fill-in Questions

A restraint of trade; Monopoly power; monopoly power

Multiple-Choice Questions

1. A. An agreement to set prices in the manner described in the problem is a price-fixing agreement, which is a restraint of trade and a *per se* violation of Section 1 of the Sherman Act.
2. C. Conduct that is blatantly anticompetitive is a *per se* violation of antitrust law. This is the most important circumstance in determining whether an action violates the antitrust laws. If an action undercuts competition, a court will not allow a party to undertake it. Such conduct typically includes price-fixing agreements, group boycotts, and horizontal market divisions. The U.S. Department of Justice can prosecute violations of the Sherman Act as criminal or civil violations, but can enforce the Clayton Act only

through civil proceedings. The Federal Trade Commission can also enforce the Clayton Act (and has sole authority to enforce the Federal Trade Commission Act). A private party can sue under the Clayton Act if he or she is injured by a violation of *any* antitrust law.
3. C. Territorial or customer restrictions, like the restriction described in the problem, are judged under a rule of reason. The rule of reason involves a weighing of competitive benefits against anticompetitive harms. Here, the manufacturer's restriction on its dealers would likely be considered lawful because, although it reduces *intra*brand competition, it promotes *inter*brand competition.
4. D. In applying the rule of reason, courts consider the purpose of the conduct, the effect of the conduct on trade, the power of the parties to accomplish what they intend, and in some cases, whether there are less restrictive alternatives to achieve the same goals.
5. C. Price discrimination occurs when a seller charges different buyers different prices for identical goods. To violate the Clayton Act, among other requirements, the effect of the price discrimination must be to substantially lessen competition or otherwise create a competitive injury.
6. A. Conduct subject to the rule of reason is unlawful if its anticompetitive harms outweigh its competitive benefits. Conduct typically subject to a rule of reason analysis includes trade association activities, joint ventures, territorial or customer restrictions, refusal to deal, price discrimination, and exclusive-dealing contracts.
7. A. An important consideration in determining whether a merger substantially lessens competition and hence violates the Clayton Act is market concentration (the market chares among the firms in the market). If a merger creates an entity with more than a small percentage market share, it is presumed illegal.
8. C. An agreement between a manufacturer and a distributor or retailer in which the manufacturer specifies the retail prices of its products is a resale price maintenance agreement. These agreements were once considered *per se* violations of the Sherman Act, but are now subject to the rule of reason.
9. D. If a merger creates an entity with more than a small percentage market share, it is presumed illegal. In determining market share, the factors include market concentration. Other factors include the relevant market's history of tending toward concentration, economic efficiency, and the factors that are part of the correct answer to this problem.
10. C. A contract under which a seller forbids a buyer from buying products from the seller's competitors is an exclusive-dealing contract. Subject to the rule of reason, under Section 3 of the Clayton Act, these agreements are prohibited if their effect is "to substantially lessen competition" or to "tend to create a monopoly."

Issue Spotters

1. A unilateral refusal to deal violates antitrust law if it involves offenses proscribed under Section 2 of the Sherman Act. This occurs if the firm refusing to deal has, or is likely to acquire, monopoly power and the refusal is likely to have an anticompetitive effect on a particular market.

2. This arrangement is a horizontal market division. It is a violation of Section 1 of the Sherman Act. The same violation would occur if the competitors agree that one of them would sell only to institutions (schools, government agencies, utilities) in all three states, another only to wholesalers, and the third only to retailers. Dividing up territories or customers among competitors is a *per se* violation.

3. This agreement is a tying arrangement. The legality of a tying arrangement depends the purpose of the agreement, the agreement's likely effect on competition in the relevant markets (the market for the tying product and the market for the tied product), and other factors. Tying arrangements for commodities are subject to Section 3 of the Clayton Act. Tying arrangements for services can be agreements in restraint of trade in violation of Section 1 of the Sherman Act.

Chapter 28

True-False Questions

1. T
2. T
3. T
4. T
5. F. Rule 506, issued under the Securities Act of 1933, provides an exemption for these offerings, if certain other requirements are met. This is an important exemption, applying to private offerings to a limited number of sophisticated investors.
6. T
7. T
8. F. *Scienter* is not a requirement for liability under Section 16(b) of the Securities Exchange Act of 1934, but it is required for liability under Section 10(b) and under Rule 10b-5.
9. F. Anyone who receives inside information as a result of an insider's breach of his or her fiduciary duty can be liable under Rule 10b-5, which applies in virtually all cases involving the trading of securities. The key to liability is whether the otherwise undisclosed information is *material*.
10. F. Most securities can be resold without registration. Also, under Rule 144 and 144A ("Safe harbor" provisions), there are specific exemptions for securities that might otherwise require registration with the SEC.

Fill-in Questions

prosecution; triple; twenty-five; may

Multiple-Choice Questions

1. B. Under the Securities Exchange Act of 1934, the Securities and Exchange Commission all of the other duties and more, including regulating national securities trading, supervising mutual funds, and recommending sanctions in cases involving violations of securities laws.

2. A. This purchase and sale is a violation of Section 16(b) of the Securities Exchange Act of 1934. When a purchase and sale is within a six-month period, as in this problem, the corporation can recover all of the profit. Proof of *scienter* is not required.

3. D. Under the Securities Act of 1933, a security exists when a person invests in a common enterprise with the reasonable expectation of profits derived primarily or substantially from the managerial or entrepreneurial efforts of others (not from the investor's own efforts).

4. A. Because of the low amount of the issue, it qualifies as an exemption from registration under Rule 504. No specific disclosure document is required, and there is no prohibition on solicitation. If the amount had been higher than $1 million but lower than $5 million, this offer might have qualified for an exemption under Regulation A, which requires notice to the SEC and an offering circular for investors.

5. D. The amount of this offering is too high to exempt it from the registration requirements except possibly under Rule 506 or Section 4(6). This issuer advertised the offering, however, and Rule 506 prohibits general solicitation. Thus, without filing a registration statement, the issuer could not legally solicit *any* investors (whatever it may have believed about the unaccredited investors). This offering does not qualify under Section 4(6), because unaccredited investors participated.

6. D. This issue might qualify under Rule 505 or Section 4(6), except that again, the issuer advertised the offering, which it cannot do and remain exempt from registration. In other words, the amount of this offering disqualified the issuer from advertising it without filing a registration statement.

7. B. A registration statement must supply enough information so that an unsophisticated investor can evaluate the financial risk involved. The statement must explain how the registrant intends to use the proceeds from the sale of the issue. Also, besides the description of management, there must be a disclosure of any of their material transactions with the firm. A certified financial statement must be included.

8. C. A corporate officer is a traditional inside trader. The outsider in this problem is a tippee who is liable because the tippee knew of the officer's misconduct. Liability here is based on the fact that the infor-

mation was not public. Liability might be avoided if those who know the information wait for a reasonable time after its public disclosure before trading their stock.

9.   A. Of course, the offering must be registered with the SEC before it can be sold, and this requires a registration statement. Investors must be given a prospectus that describes the security, the issuing corporation, and the risk of the security. A tombstone ad tells an investor how and where to obtain the prospectus.

10.   A. Most resales are exempt from registration if persons other than issuers or underwriters undertake the resales. Resales of restricted securities acquired under Rule 504a, Rule 505, Rule 506, or Section 4(6) may trigger registration requirements, but the original sale in this problem came under Rule 504.

Issue Spotters

1.   The average investor is not concerned with minor inaccuracies but with facts that if disclosed would tend to deter him or her from buying the securities. This would include facts that have an important bearing on the condition of the issuer and its business—liabilities, loans to officers and directors, customer delinquencies, and pending lawsuits.

2.   No. The Securities Exchange Act of 1934 extends liability to officers and directors in their personal transactions for taking advantage of inside information when they know it is unavailable to the persons with whom they are dealing.

3.   Yes. All states have their own corporate securities laws.

Cumulative Hypothetical Problem for Unit Six—Including Chapters 23–28

1.   D. Advertising that consists of vague generalities is not illegal. This is also true of advertising that includes obvious exaggerations. Advertising that may lead to sanctions by the Federal Trade Commission is deceptive advertising: advertising that misleads consumers.

2.   A. An administrative agency has a number of options to determine whether a manufacturer is complying with the agency's rules, but the agency may not use its powers arbitrarily or capriciously or abuse its discretion. The options that an agency may choose include those in the other answer choices, as well as obtaining a search warrant to search the premises for a specific item and return it to the agency.

3.   D. Under the Comprehensive Environmental Response, Compensation, and Liability Act of 1980, any "potentially responsible party" can be charged with the entire cost to clean up a hazardous waste disposal site. Potentially responsible parties include the party who generates the waste, the party who transports the

waste to the site, and the party who owns or operates the site.

4.   C. It is price discrimination when a seller charges different buyers different prices for identical products. Price discrimination is a violation of the Clayton Act if the effect of the pricing is to substantially lessen competition or otherwise create a competitive injury.

5.   D. Other information that must be included in a registration statement, under the Securities Act of 1933, includes a description of the issuer's business, a description of the security, the capital structure of the business, the underwriting arrangements, and the certified financial statements.

Questions on the Focus on Legal Reasoning for Unit Six—*In re Miller*

1.   A. In the reasoning of the majority in the *In re Miller* case, fraud in such cases as this problem "could be imputed only on a finding of agency." The court held, however, that "Section 20(a) extends liability well beyond traditional [agency] doctrines, providing expansive remedies in a highly regulated industry."

2.   D. The dissent in the *In re Miller* case reasoned that a finding of agency is not necessary to impose liability under Section 20. The dissent would have imputed liability in the circumstances described in these questions, and would have held that the debt represented by that liability was not dischargeable in bankruptcy.

3.   C. In the *In re Miller* case, the majority reasoned that there is "nothing in the Bankruptcy Code or the securities laws indicating that these two separate provisions of law should be combined" to impose liability on a fraudulent broker's innocent employer and declare that liability a non-dischargeable debt under the Bankruptcy Code. "Section 20(a) [of the Securities Exchange Act] extends liability well beyond traditional doctrines, providing expansive remedies in a highly regulated industry." However, "the Bankruptcy Code addresses actual, traditional fraud, and we are not persuaded that it should be read in such a way as to encompass the nontraditional liability imposed under [Section] 20(a)."

Questions on the Focus on Ethics for Unit Six—The Regulatory Environment

1.   D. Of course, this outcome is debatable, and the issue is contentious. The questions, which do not have certain answers, concern the extent to which the government goes in regulating individuals and businesses in the interest of protecting the environment. At what point are the costs of environmental regulations too much for an individual, a business, or society as a whole to bear? How much are we willing to sacrifice to ensure that future generations have a healthful world?

2.   A. This conduct would be a violation of the Fair Debt Collection Practices Act (FDCPA) if the party engaging in it is a collection agency. Under the FDCPA, collections agencies are allowed to contact only a debtor at his or her workplace and only with the permission of the employer. Some observers believe that the FDCPA does not offer consumers enough protection, because it does not cover creditors that collect their own debts.

3.   A. Professional baseball players can sue team owners for anticompetitive practices that include collusion to blacklist players, cap players' salaries, or forcing players to play for certain teams. Baseball may be otherwise exempt from the application of the antitrust laws. Although originally a holding of the United States Supreme Court, the Court has recently held that this situation can be changed only through an act of Congress.

Notes

Notes

Notes

Notes

Notes

Notes

Notes

Notes